The Forging of the Cosmic Race

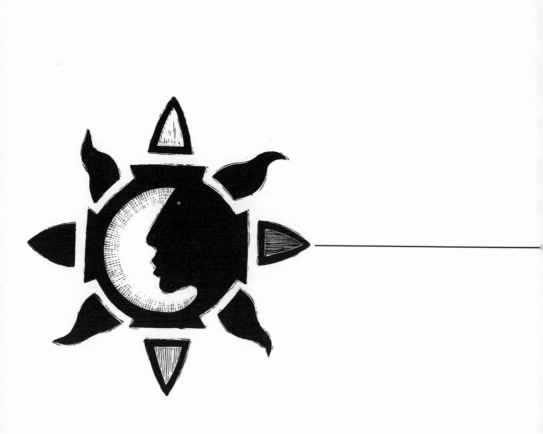

COLIN M. MacLACHLAN

JAIME E. RODRIGUEZ O.

THE FORGING OF
THE COSMIC RACE

A Reinterpretation of Colonial Mexico

UNIVERSITY OF CALIFORNIA PRESS

Berkeley / Los Angeles / London

Ornament on title page based on painting
representing the four races of Mexico,
by Manuel Hernandez Trujillo

Library of Congress Cataloging in Publication Data

MacLachlan, Colin M
    The forging of the cosmic race: A reinterpretation
      of Colonial Mexico
    Bibliography: p.
    Includes index.
    1. Mexico—History—Spanish colony, 1540–1810.
I.   Rodríguez O., Jaime E., 1940–   joint author.
II. Title.
F1231.M32   972'.02   78-68836
ISBN 0-520-03890-8

University of California Press
Berkeley and Los Angeles, California

University of California Press, Ltd.
London, England

© 1980 by
The Regents of the University of California
Printed in the United States of America

1 2 3 4 5 6 7 8 9

TO THE NATIONAL AUTONOMOUS UNIVERSITY OF MEXICO
AND ITS DISTINGUISHED FACULTY, WHOSE SCHOLARLY AND
ARTISTIC CONTRIBUTIONS HAVE ENRICHED WORLD CULTURE
FOR NEARLY FOUR AND A HALF CENTURIES

Contents

Illustrations and Maps

Illustrations follow pages 174 and 238.

1. A *gobernadoryotl* complaining to Viceroy Velasco that settlers were forcing his people to pay more in tribute than required by law.
2. An Indian complaint that an encomendero was making his tributaries work longer than legally required in his *hacienda* and in his *obraje*.
3. An Indian illustration depicting the conversion of *caciques* while Cortés and Doña Marina look on.
4. Spanish wheat farmers harvesting.
5. Spanish wheat farmers threshing.
6. An *hacienda de minas*.
7. A deep silver mine shaft, typical of the great eighteenth-century mines.
8. A small village scene in the eighteenth century.
9. Villagers on the way to market.
10. Indians going to market.
11. A typical urban market.
12. Women making tortillas for sale.
13. A local tavern.
14. Muleteers in the high country.
15. A mule train crossing the jungle.
16. An *hacendado* and his *mayordomo*.
17. *Rancheros* in Sunday dress.
18. A sheepherder.
19. Lower-class people from Puebla dressed in a popular eighteenth-century style.

Acknowledgments

We have been fortunate in receiving the aid, encouragement, and support of many scholars during the preparation of this work. Jacques Barbier, Asunción Lavrin, Murdo MacLeod, Roberto Moreno, Ignacio del Río and John TePaske kindly allowed us to use some of their unpublished research. Victoria E. Bricker, Mark Burkholder, Richard Greenleaf, Dan M. Healan, María del Refugio Gonzalez, Doris M. Ladd, Asunción Lavrin, Roberto Moreno, Francisco Xavier Noguez, Keith I. Polakoff, William F. Sater, John TePaske, and James W. Wilkie read this study in whole or in part and provided many useful comments. We are particularly grateful to Linda Alexander Rodríguez who read and criticized the entire manuscript in its several versions. We thank the Director and researchers of the Instituto de Investigaciones Históricas of the National Autonomous University of Mexico, who kindly discussed several aspects of this work with us. We have also benefitted from discussions with Nettie Lee Benson, E. Bradford Burns, Robert N. Burr, Romeo Flores Caballero, John D. Glen, Virginia Gudea, John M. Hart, María Herrera Sobek, Andrés Lira, Eric Mack, Patricia O'Brien, Bernardo Ortíz de Montellano, Alejandro Morales, Eloy Rodríguez, and Ralph Lee Woodward, Jr. We are grateful to Kendall Bailes, Samuel C. McCulloch, and especially William J. Lillyman for much-needed support and encouragement.

We are indebted to the directors and personnel of the following libraries and archives who facilitated our research: The Tulane University Latin American Library; the University of California, Irvine, Library; the University of California, Los Angeles, Research Library; the Nettie Lee Benson Latin American Collection; the Bancroft Library; the Library of Congress; the Biblioteca Nacional de México; the Biblioteca del Instituto de Antropología e Historia; and the Archivo General de la Nación.

Generous grants from the Tulane University Senate Research Committee and the University of California, Irvine, Senate Research and Travel Committee helped finance our research in this country and several summers' work in Mexico.

Colin M. MacLachlan   Jaime E. Rodríguez O.
New Orleans   *Los Angeles*

On August 13, 1521, Tlatelolco, heroically defended by Cuauhtémoc, fell into the power of Hernán Cortés.

It was neither a triumph nor a defeat, but the painful birth of the Mestizo people who are the Mexico of today.

Plaque on the Great Pyramid of Tlatelolco in the Square of the Three Cultures, Mexico City.

Introduction

In recent years politicians, economists, government planners, and revolutionaries have debated extensively the nature of Mexico's economy and society. Both critics and defenders of the status quo agree that Mexico's colonial heritage was negative and that many of the country's ills originated in that epoch. They maintain that New Spain's legacy continues to burden the nation with rigid values and inflexible institutions. Studies emphasizing the exploitive aspects of relations between Spaniards and Indians and of the institutions of empire such as the Church, the administrative system, and trade regulations have seemed to support the notion of an oppressive, semifeudal colonial heritage. However, our own archival research, as well as recent investigations of other scholars, have convinced us that there is an alternative, positive view of Mexico's colonial history.

This book reevaluates Mexico's colonial past in light of the new findings. We contend that New Spain was neither feudal nor precapitalist, as some neo-Marxist authors have argued. Instead, colonial Mexico functioned as an emerging capitalist society within the worldwide economic system that developed in the fifteenth and sixteenth centuries. Although geographically New Spain was on the periphery of the world system, we maintain that it was neither a dependent nor an underdeveloped region. Rather, colonial Mexico forged a complex, balanced, and integrated economy that transformed the area into the most important and dynamic part of the Spanish empire.

The conquest of Mexico and the subsequent incorporation of the region into the world system constituted one of the major events in modern world history. It definitively ended the relative isolation of Europe and, as Woodrow W. Borah noted, also terminated Mesoamerica's physical and cultural isolation, integrating the area into the new global culture. These events affected the Old World and the New in a variety of ways. American silver engendered a price revolution that transformed first the European and then the world economy. The Spanish silver *peso,* or "piece of eight," became the standard medium of exchange for merchants not only in Europe but throughout the world. The introduction of New World plants and foods revolutionized world diet and agriculture. Old World flora and fauna not only changed American agriculture but also wrought devastating ecological transformations. But perhaps the most significant impact was, as Edmundo O'Gorman has said, "the invention of America." For Europeans the new lands opened vistas and opportunities undreamed of in the old medieval world. These possibilities, the "invention of America," gave vitality and dynamism not only to the expansion and development of Europe, but also to the formation of a new society in America.

Cultural integration in Mexico was not accomplished primarily through violence, although the immediate cost proved high. The Spaniards unavoidably brought with them Old World epidemic diseases that decimated the native population. This demographic tragedy and the miscegenation that occurred from the beginning facilitated the formation of a hybrid, or *mestizo,* people in a biological as well as a cultural sense. The few conquerors who arrived in Mexico could not overwhelm the strong and vibrant Indian culture. No such futile undertaking was necessary, however, because significant aspects of native culture blended easily with Spanish traditions and provided the foundations for the new colonial society. The numerous and important settled Indian communities valued disciplined, sustained work habits; they had a sense of social restraint necessary for a complex society; they appreciated technological and cultural progress; and they understood the importance of an orderly political and social system. The Indian city-states had realized the advantages of economic interdependence. They did not rely solely on local resources and food supplies, but exchanged raw materials and finished products over long distances. Indeed, Mesoamerican commerce was so active that native merchants traveled on Spanish ships even before the conquest ended. Indian society also possessed features that did not correspond to accepted

European values, such as human sacrifice, which the Spaniards rejected. But these differences were minor compared to the larger and more important body of shared cultural norms that became the basis of the new Mexican society.

It is our contention that the mestizo society and culture that emerged in New Spain, while not homogeneous, was neither Indian nor European. The few isolated and rather unintegrated Indian communities remained at one end of the spectrum, while the new immigrants—white, black, and yellow—were at the other. Both groups were small and in a process of acculturation toward the hybrid mestizo culture that rapidly became dominant. This view differs from that of most accounts, in which the process of acculturation is portrayed as moving from the Indian side to the European, and the dominant society is called *Spanish*. We do not subscribe to such an interpretation. Therefore we have called the dominant society *Mexican,* to indicate its mestizo nature. Throughout this work when we speak of Mexican society, Mexican towns, etc., we are referring to the new hybrid mestizo culture that was neither Indian nor Spanish.

The creation of a new society in a populous land with an ancient and highly civilized culture required monumental adjustments. The accommodation, historically one of the major challenges of modern Western civilization, succeeded only in New Spain. There the cultural and biological intermingling of Indians, Europeans, Africans, and Asians created a new people and a new society. In part this success may be attributable to the great economic opportunities that emerged in Mexico after the conquest. Although certain aspects of a racial and caste system appeared initially, New Spain rapidly developed a class structure consonant with an emerging capitalist society. Materialism, competition, and the realization that status and social position rested on economic success engendered great stress as well as opportunity. The dynamics of a formative society produced negative reactions, including exploitation, violence, and racism. But these aspects were eclipsed by New Spain's positive characteristics, such as an expanding economy, upward social mobility, and ethnic and cultural integration. No other part of the Spanish empire attained a comparable integration of peoples and cultures. And no similar achievement can be found in other regions of the world where different races and cultures met. The blending of four races in Mexico created a new people—a "cosmic race," to use José Vasconcelos' evocative phrase.

Governing Mexico's complex society presented a great challenge to authorities. The establishment of an institutional structure sufficiently flexible, yet strong enough to permit the evolution of an orderly society, represented a major achievement. Although Mexicans still fondly recall certain astute colonial adminstrators, the political structure itself deserves credit both for producing effective officials and for surviving the incompetent. New Spain accommodated varied and often antagonistic interests, which sometimes resorted to violence, without endangering either the continuity or the legitimacy of colonial government.

This study focuses on New Spain itself rather than on the area as part of the Spanish empire. It is concerned principally with central Mexico, the most populous region of Mesoamerica. To demonstrate the area's complexity and dynamic heritage, we have examined those pre-Columbian societies which had the greatest influence on the formation of central Mexico's mestizo culture. And we have concentrated on the Kingdom of New Spain, the most important part of the larger Viceroyalty of New Spain.

PART ONE

Chapter 1

THE SETTING

M AN is a creature of geography as well as culture. This central fact becomes obvious when the physical setting is harsh, while it tends to be underestimated in more favored regions. In Mexico the connection between the land and the type of society it spawned can never be forgotten. Contrasts are too startling, and arable land too limited, to disregard the importance and the influence of geography on all Mexicans. The struggle with and for the land runs like a thread throughout the region's entire history from the pre-Columbian era to the twentieth century.

Mexico's physical setting is the result of millions of years of geologic activity which created great mountain ranges that dominate the landscape. Fray Toribio de Motolinía, a sixteenth-century observer, marveled at a land "so crowded with mountains that [when] you stand in the middle . . . and look around you, you will see one or several ranges." Similarly impressed, Fernando Cortés, the conqueror of Mexico, reputedly crumpled up a piece of paper to demonstrate the topography to a curious Emperor Carlos V.

Mountains form not only the backbone but also the major ribs dividing the country into distinct segments.

Northern and central Mexico are dominated by a cordilleran system. Both the Sierra Madre Occidental, which starts in Sonora and Chihuahua, and the Sierra Madre Oriental, beginning in the northeast, widen as they move southward, joining in central Mexico. Another range, the Sierra Madre del Sur, extends from Baja California, to somewhat beyond Oaxaca, where all three chains unite. East of the Isthmus of Tehuantepec lie the Chiapas Highlands, broken only by the Grijalva River flowing through the Chiapas valley. On the eastern side of the valley the mountains regain their 12,000-foot elevation, then rapidly subside in the limestone plain of the Yucatán peninsula.

Looking northward between the eastern and western ranges, one observes a vast, wind-eroded plateau forming an interior bowl. The Mexican Highland, connected with the Utah–Nevada basin of the Colorado Plateau, forms a tableland whose northern surface lies between 4,000 and 5,000 feet, rising as it moves south to 7,000 to 8,000 feet before dropping to a bare 600 feet above sea level at the Isthmus of Tehuantepec. The plateau is crisscrossed by canyons and eroded channels which create formidable barriers—such as Santiago Canyon, which stretches several hundred miles northwest from Guadalajara to the Pacific, and the 400-mile-long Moctezuma Gorge, which runs through the modern states of Querétaro, Hidalgo, and Veracruz. Rivers and streams cut deeply into the terrain, making access to water difficult and passage across them treacherous. Only the Lerma River, draining the Bajío country of Jalisco, Michoacán, and Guanajuato, permits easy approach to its banks. A string of snow-covered volcanoes—Orizaba (Citlaltépetl, "Mountain of the Star" in Náhuatl), Iztaccihuatl, Popocatépetl, and other notable peaks—serve as a reminder that the entire region is subject to violent and still active forces. For example, in 1943 a new volcano, Paricutín, was born near Uruapan, 150 miles west of the Valley of Mexico. It began as a little puff of smoke in a cornfield, rose 1,050 feet within ten days, and eventually reached a height of 8,248 feet. Its birth, amid fiery clouds of vapor and lava, destroyed an Indian village and its precious land, reminding Mexicans of the overwhelming power of natural forces. South of the line of volcanoes, the Balsas River and its tributaries cut a deep 50-mile-wide east-west trough into the plateau.

Mexico's coasts present interesting contrasts. On the west, the Gulf of California, a trench of relatively recent formation, separates the Baja California peninsula from the main landmass; on the east, the Yucatán peninsula marks off the Gulf of Mexico from the western Caribbean. The entire eastern shoreline is still in the process of emergence, with high sand dunes and lagoons separated from the sea by sandbars. Wind and current-driven sand block the mouths of the few significant rivers that empty into the Gulf. As a result, the few ports available depend on constant manmade improvements to keep them serviceable. But because of the barrier of the Sierra Madre Occidental, the country's natural outlet to the rest of the world is to the east rather than the west. The western coast is mostly rocky submergence, with an occasional natural harbor formed by some projection.

The physical nature of the land, with its many barriers, makes water in its various forms a major problem. As a general rule, precipitation increases as one goes south. Rain tends to be seasonal, usually falling in the summer after a dry season of up to six months. North of the Bajío, barren hills dotted with maguey and other desert plants are characteristic. In the extreme northwest, the lack of rainfall makes most of Baja California almost uninhabitable; only its southern tip, protruding into the tropical rainbelt, receives significant relief. The Sonora Desert to the east is virtually without moisture until the rising elevations of the Sierra Madre Occidental are reached, and mountain barriers effectively block rainbearing clouds from the desert between the two Sierra Madre ranges. Rainfall, when it does arrive in the region, is often driven inland by storms that drop torrential rains, destroying as much as they nourish; extremely rapid runoff and evaporation soon return the land to its parched and barren state. Modern flood control and irrigation methods have only recently modified the region's inhospitable environment.

Rainfall in the Sierra Madre Oriental is sufficiently reliable and moderate to make eastern Coahuila and Nuevo León a favored agricultural region. On the Gulf Coast plain to the east, rainfall increases southward, under the influence of moisture-laden gulf winds, until the amount of precipitation reaches a destructive level.

PHYSICAL MAP OF MEXICO
(From Lesley B. Simpson, *Many Mexicos;* Berkeley, 1960)

Excessive rain leaches out the soil's nutrients, converting the land into a series of swamps surrounded by deceptively lush jungle. Only as the rains pass over Chiapas do they moderate to a beneficial extent. The same pattern is repeated on the Pacific Coast, turning the region around Cape Corrientes, west of Guadalajara, into a dense jungle. In central Mexico, rains come in the summer, quickly and rather suddenly relieving the dusty, parched, brown terrain.

Half of Mexico suffers from a constant scarcity of water, while a third of the country must cope with a winter dry season. Summer is the most generous time, with a mere 1 percent of the land experiencing a dry season. Only 13 percent of Mexico has sufficient rainfall on a year-round basis. Understandably, the rain god (Tlaloc of the Aztecs) ranked high in the pantheon of all Indian groups. Given these climatic and physical characteristics, a scant 10 to 15 percent of Mexico's land is agriculturally usable without extensive manmade improvements.

Temperature variations, which run from the proverbial "perpetual springtime" to the stifling heat of the coast and the chilling cold of the higher elevations, are only slightly less important than rain. In the Veracruz region, heat and humidity combine to make disease a constant concern. During colonial times yellow fever regularly decimated the population despite a degree of immunity enjoyed by coastal residents. At higher elevations, frost, and even an occasional hard freeze, can cause physical suffering, kill crops, or plunge the population into famine. For example, in 1785–1786, following a serious freeze that destroyed food crops, over 300,000 people died.

Mexicans are sustained by a harsh land that alternately nourishes and destroys. The Indian concept of duality in all things seems to capture this sense of the balance between life and death in a hostile physical environment, where little can be taken for granted.

Chapter 2

ANCIENT
MEXICO

MESOAMERICA, a region that includes central and southern Mexico as well as parts of Central America, has been one of the great centers of world culture. Here a series of societies sharing many common cultural traits evolved over a period of thousands of years. Archaeologists speak of one Mesoamerican culture, even though many advanced societies formed part of it. In this chapter we are concerned with the manner in which the Mexican branches of that culture developed. The complex and varied history of most of those Mexican societies is beyond the scope of this work; instead, this section concentrates on those peoples who had the greatest impact in forging an integrated pre-Hispanic Mexico.

THE FIRST IMMIGRANTS

The Western Hemisphere has been inhabited for a long time. Human remains discovered in California, Texas, and Nevada are believed to be as much as 50,000, 37,000, and 23,000 years old respectively. Although these discoveries confirm the great antiquity of man in America, there is serious disagreement about the age of these remains, with estimates varying as much as 10,000 to 20,000 years. Excavations in the Valley of Mexico suggest that people lived there about 20,000 years ago, while female remains found at Tepexpán indicate that human beings were there at least 10,000 years ago. The results of these and other archaeological investigations have provided scholars with an incomplete but nonetheless substantial picture of man's migration into the American continent.

It is now believed that *Homo sapiens* came to the Western Hemisphere between 50,000 and 25,000 years ago, during the Wisconsin Ice Age. At that time the Pacific Ocean was about 200 feet below its present level, exposing the continental shelf between Asia and North America, which is thought to have formed a land platform about 1,000 miles wide between Siberia and Alaska. Although glaciers covered parts of North America, the western area of Alaska, Canada, and the United States was ice-free. This cold, tundra-covered region attracted big game. Camels and horses migrated from America into Asia, while elephants, deer, elk, and moose entered the New World from the Old. Over the millenia, waves of hunters followed their prey to the Western Hemisphere. In time the ice cap began to melt, raising the ocean level. By 8000 B.C. it was no longer possible to walk from Asia to America; and thereafter the American Indians, or Amerinds, developed in virtual isolation until the Spanish arrived in the sixteenth century. While a few people probably continued to come from Asia by water, their numbers and their influence were slight.

Anthropologists believe that the first immigrants traveled in small bands of perhaps 30 related individuals. Since they were hunters, who often moved in circles as they followed their prey, their progress into the American continent was very slow. It probably took 18,000 years for the Amerinds to reach the tip of South America. During that time man changed. The later immigrants were ethnically and culturally different from the first. A process of differentiation also occurred in the New World, as groups split off and lived in relative isolation. Thus, over thousands of years, an ethnically varied Amerind population developed.

The hunting and gathering stage was the longest in Mexican prehistory. During most of that period—from the time people first arrived until about 7200 B.C.—they survived by hunting animals with primitive weapons and by gathering roots, berries, seeds, and fruit. The scant archaeological remains from this era consist of projectile points, scrapers, and other simple tools. No art or sophisticated artifacts have yet been found. This does not mean, however, that these early people lived a life of material or cultural poverty. Skeletal remains indicate that the men and women of that time were tall—about six feet—well fed, and suffered few illnesses. Since their numbers were small and their resources plentiful, these hunters and gatherers apparently led lives of leisure and contentment, spending only a few hours a day obtaining food, building materials, and other necessities. Anthropologists speculate that both men and women had ample leisure time. As there were no scarcities, there was probably no need to form hierarchies, and an egalitarian society may have existed. In this idyllic situation, these early people may have developed art, religion, and philosophy; but since nothing remains, scholars can only speculate. Some anthropologists, like Marvin Harris, claim that no other people have ever lived so well. Population increase, however, changed the ecological balance and led to a declining standard of living which could only be compensated by increasing inputs of labor and technology.

Around 10,000 B.C., a major technological advance occurred with the development of the fine percussion and pressure-flaked stone points known to anthropologists as Clovis points. When attached to wooden shafts, these new points could be used to kill large animals at a distance. This was a revolutionary advance in weaponry. Although man had been an effective hunter and a dangerous predator for thousands of years, for the first time he now had the power to eliminate other animals.

The age of the early hunters came to an end around 7200 B.C. The weather changed; it became hotter and drier. While the European climate was pleasant and conducive to human development, North America became a desert. At this point in prehistory, archaeologists estimate that there were about 500,000 inhabitants in the New World, 30,000 of them in Mexico.

THE DEVELOPMENT OF AGRICULTURE

The domestication of plants, or the development of agriculture, occurred at different times in various parts of the world. Botanists believe that a semi-arid environment provides optimal conditions for plant domestication. In Mesoamerica such conditions existed in the Archaic period, from about 7200 B.C. to 2500 B.C. The investigations of Richard S. MacNeish in Tamaulipas and Puebla indicate that the development of agriculture was a lengthy process which took several thousand years.

During the Archaic period, the peoples of Mesoamerica gradually shifted from hunting and gathering to a sedentary agricultural life. While the large animals such as the camel, the giant bison, the horse, the mastodon, the mammoth, and the ground sloth perished because of the climatic change, humans successfully adapted to the new desert setting. Indian groups occupied caves and survived by hunting small game, fishing, and collecting more plant food. These small bands, whom archaeologists call the Desert Culture, were nonagricultural. The remnants of woven blankets, mattings, and sandals, however, indicate that they were developing more sedentary habits, particularly a heavy dependence on plant collection. They slowly learned to cultivate plants, but it took them a long time to rely predominantly on agriculture for their food supply. For several thousand years the Indians of Mesoamerica combined hunting and gathering with the cultivation of plants, but by 2500 B.C. many groups were becoming primarily agriculturalists. They ceased living in bands and became villagers. This was the first major step that was to lead to the formation of the great civilizations of Mesoamerica.

The investigations of the Tehuacán Archaeological-Botanical Project have recently provided the most extensive data now available on the Archaic period in Mesoamerica. Teams of botanists, geologists, geographers, ethnographers, irrigation specialists, and physical anthropologists joined archaeologists in an exhaustive study of sites in the Tehuacán Valley in the state of Puebla. These scholars have identified four early phases of development. The oldest, the Ajuereado (?–6500 B.C.), was a period in which the Indians remained nomadic hunters and gatherers. During the next three phases—El Riego (6500–4800 B.C.), Coxcatlán (4800–3500 B.C.), and Abejas (3500–2500 B.C.)—they domesticated plants and animals, and gradually shifted to a sedentary way of life.

The Ajuereado stage appears to have been a transitional period. The people continued a nomadic existence, apparently moving their camps several times a year and surviving mainly by hunting horses and antelope. As these species dwindled, the Indians began to eat smaller game: birds, gophers, rabbits, rats, and turtles. The shift to hunting smaller game seems to have required changes in social organization—the remains of large numbers of rabbit bones indicates that there was now increased cooperation, perhaps communal drives. The Ajuereado Indians also changed their tool kit as they adapted to killing smaller animals—their projectile points were now smaller, and snares and nets appeared.

During the El Riego phase, the people of Tehuacán made startling advances. Small groups, or microbands, still occupied seasonal camps, but in the spring they joined other parties, forming macrobands, the forerunners of tribes. These larger units developed a more sophisticated form of social organization. It seems likely that chieftains and shamans, or priests, assumed positions of power and leadership. Several instances of ritual burial and human sacrifice have been found. El Riego was also a time of cultural advances. Archaeologists have uncovered manufactured stone implements such as mortars, pestles, and milling stones, and the earliest indications of weaving and woodworking. The Indians also learned to domesticate plants during this period. The earliest evidence of agriculture indicates that chile peppers and avocados were probably the first plants cultivated. Toward the end of the period, the inhabitants of Tehuacán also cultivated squash, amaranth, and perhaps cotton. They still hunted animals, but domesticated plants and wild plants like corn and pumpkins formed an important part of their diet.

In the Coxcatlán and Abejas phases, advances continued along the lines already established in the El Riego period. During the Coxcatlán phase, the macrobands became semi-sedentary; they learned to cultivate corn, the common bean, and zapotes (a sweet fruit), and they developed better stone implements such as *metates* and *manos*. Later, in the Abejas period, they added other plants to their cultigens. Dogs seem to have been domesticated at this time. Perhaps the major advance of the Abejas period was the establishment of permanent settlements.

The transformation of nomadic hunters into villagers was neither rapid nor uniform. It took place in Mesoamerica around 2500 B.C. In other parts of North America the changes occurred later or not at all. Primitive hunters survived in some areas until the middle of the nineteenth century. Mesoamerica, however, pulled ahead of other regions. Social organization was becoming more complex and the centers of population were growing. The peoples of Mesoamerica had embarked on the voyage to high culture.

THE RISE OF CIVILIZATION

Explaining the rise of civilization is one of the thorniest problems in the study of prehistory. Much archaeological research remains to be done before scholars can arrive at a consensus. At the present time, we can only glimpse the process in its vague outline—new discoveries may alter our perspective completely.

In Mexican history the term *civilization* refers to settled agricultural communities and ultimately to cities where "high culture" evolved. The nomadic hunters and gatherers, in contrast, were considered barbarians; they were called *Chichimecas*—a Náhuatl term that meant either "the people of Chichiman" or, in a pejorative sense, "sons of dogs." Until the nineteenth century, the northern nomads periodically threatened the agricultural peoples of Mexico. These Chichimecas invaded the settled regions when drought or other barbarian groups threatened their food supply. The agricultural peoples to the south gave way before the invaders, but they also gradually absorbed and civilized their conquerors. This process of invasion and absorption continued until the nineteenth century, when the heirs of European culture finally conquered the steppes and plains of the North American continent.

The basis of Mesoamerican civilization was established during the Formative period (ca. 2500 B.C. to A.D. 300). During most of that time village life predominated. People still relied on hunting and fishing, but now agriculture became their main source of food. Although there were differences between the agriculture of the dry highlands and the tropical lowlands, chile peppers, corn, beans, and squash were becoming the principal sources of vitamins, starch, and protein in the diet of Mesoamericans. Depending on the region, the Indians supplemented this diet with wild game, fish, fruits, and other vegetables, as well as with domesticated dogs and turkeys.

The basic agricultural techniques used in Mesoamerica were established early. *Milpa,* or slash-and-burn agriculture, was the most common method of farming. Although scholars disagree about the effects of this type of agriculture, many believe that it was a highly productive system which could support large populations. Milpa farmers first cut the trees and brush and then cleared the area by burning it. They planted seeds with a *coa,* a digging stick with a fire-hardened point. Since this type of agriculture tended to exhaust the soil, farmers opened new lands within two or three years. Alternatively, they could leave part of the land fallow while they farmed other sections. Milpa agriculture, however, requires large areas of land. In some highland regions, a more intensive system which necessitated irrigation and terracing was also used. In marshy areas and in lakes, *chinampas* (small artificial islands, sometimes referred to as "floating gardens") provided additional food resources. But everywhere, the absence of draft animals limited agriculture.

Mesoamerican farmers lived in dispersed villages. Archaeologists have found the remains of houses constructed of wattle and daub in the highlands, and of poles in the lowlands. These villagers left evidence of various household crafts: weaving, ceramics, and woodwork. The origin of ceramics remains in dispute. Some scholars believe that the first pottery was introduced from abroad, possibly from Valdivia on the coast of Ecuador, where the oldest pottery in the New World has been found (ca. 3000 B.C.). However, recent excavations in the Tehuacán Valley have uncovered primitive ceramics from around 2300 B.C., which tends to support the view that pottery developed locally. Once acquired, the technique of ceramic manufacture spread rapidly. By 1500 B.C. pottery and small clay female figurines were common throughout Mesoamerica.

The Formative period in Mesoamerica is comparable, in many respects, to the Neolithic period of the Old World. One of the principal differences between the two is that animal husbandry did not occur in America. Another is that in the ancient Middle East, people made a rapid transition to settled village life once plants and animals were domesticated; in Mesoamerica, that process took four millenia. Scholars are unable to explain the delay. Some suggest that the absence of domesticated animals may have been the reason; others favor explanations based on the developmental effects of the types of plants cultivated, or of the cultural milieu of America. Once the transition to village life had been made, however, Mesoamerica developed at the same rate as Old World cultures.

During the Formative period, village life spread throughout Mesoamerica. Archaeologists have noted a great increase in the number of villages during this period. Apparently a greater or perhaps a more reliable food supply led to a population spiral. This in turn forced land-hungry villagers to expand the area of agriculture to the twenty-second parallel, which generally marked the limits of cultivation in pre-Hispanic Mexico. The steppes to the north were unsuited for Indian agriculture. The region under cultivation, or the civilized area, alternately advanced and retreated, depending on a variety of factors such as climatic cycles, population size, and political organization.

Village communities began to organize around ceremonial centers during the Formative period. The origin of these ritual complexes is obscure. Centers with distinctive ceremonial structures began to develop in various parts of Mexico around 1500 B.C. The appearance of elaborate and sparsely populated centers, contrasting sharply with the simpler and heavily populated villages, indicates that social differentiation was relatively advanced. These ceremonial complexes were apparently occupied by specialized elites who had the power to appropriate agricultural surpluses and labor. Only societies governed by powerful rulers and a dominant ideology could have compelled the peasantry to provide the labor necessary to build and maintain such centers, with their monumental temples and palaces, and to support nonfarming elites.

These early societies were dominated by a state religion in which the leaders were intermediaries between gods and men. Although priests must have been powerful—the art and monumental sculpture of Mesoamerica is filled with religious symbolism calculated to strike awe in the beholder—the rulers of these ancient states were warrior kings. Monuments and inscriptions depict battles and place the ruler above the priests. Some scholars believe that Mesoamerican civilization—that is, high culture—was monopolized by the elites. They built the cities, developed art and science, organized government and religion, and conducted war and commerce. The masses of peasants continued to live in a primitive fashion. This may explain the rise and sudden fall of several Mesoamerican societies: When the elites were defeated, their cultures died with them, and the rural masses continued to live as they always had.

The question of how the elites arose is a tantalizing one. Many theories have been advanced. The most popular explanation is based on the evolutionary model, which holds that people took gradual and cumulative steps toward controlling their environment. According to this view, political leaders, or a priestly class, arose from a need to impose order on a growing and increasingly complex society. This elite established the right to govern by monopolizing special knowledge necessary in an advanced agricultural society: the ability to establish land boundaries, to tell time, and to forecast the weather. Another explanation, the "hydraulic hypothesis," maintains that early civilizations were forced to accept despotic forms of government because of the exigencies of large-scale irrigation and other forms of water control. This analysis was initially advanced to explain the development of the ancient states in China, India, and the Middle East, and in recent years has been extended to the New World.

Some scholars, however, question the "hydraulic" theory. They have shown that the state existed in Mesopotamia and in America before large-scale irrigation developed. The mode of production—that is, early agriculture—does not vary, or changes very little, as society becomes more complex through the emergence of the state and urban centers of monumental scale. The validity of the evolutionary theory is also challenged by some, who point out that the difference between the earliest civilizations of the world—China under the Shangs, Early Dynastic Egypt, Sumerian Mesopotamia, the early Khmer of Cambodia, the Chavín in Peru, and the Olmec in Mexico—and the preexistent chiefdoms is not evolutionary, but sudden and sharp. To explain this rapid development, some scholars have advanced what may be called the "quantum jump" theory, of "pristine civilizations." One exponent of this explanation, Michael Coe, claims that the state was formed when an early chieftain imposed control beyond his tribal domain and established a ruling dynasty.

THE OLMECS

The oldest civilization in the New World is called *Olmec,* a name which refers to an art form and a culture, not an ethnic group. The Olmecs are important because theirs is the "mother culture" of Mesoamerica which originated the political, social, economic, and religious patterns that continued until the Spanish conquest. These remarkable people, whose culture appears around 1200 B.C., have only recently begun to be studied, and much of what is known about them remains tentative.

The word Olmec means "people of the rubber country" in Náhuatl. It refers to a mysterious group believed by Fray Bernardino de Sahagún to have inhabited the tropical area of the Gulf Coast. Sahagún, a sixteenth-century precursor of modern ethnohistory who interviewed Aztec scholars and had access to sources no longer available, recorded a Náhuatl account of Mesoamerican prehistory. It described three great empires or civilizations that had evolved, reached their apogee, and fallen: Tamoanchán, Teotihuacán, and Tula. The account ended with the founding and rise of Tenochtitlan, and the capital of the Aztec empire.

Modern scholarship has verified the importance of Teotihuacán, Tula, and Tenochtitlan, but Tamoanchán remains a mystery. Some archaeologists believe that Tamoanchán was the land of the Olmecs. The name is not Náhuatl, but Maya. It has two translations: "Land of the Bird-Snake"—the famous Feathered Serpent of Mesoamerica—and "Land of the Rainy Sky." Both meanings describe Olmec society, since the earliest cult of the serpent and the earliest manifestation of Tlaloc—the rain god—are found at Olmec sites. In addition, linguists believe that about 3,000 years ago—an epoch coinciding with the rise of Olmec culture—the people of the area spoke a Maya or related language. According to the ancient account, Tamoanchán existed

in a certain era
which no one can reckon,
which no one can remember,
[when] there was a government for a long time.

The legend probably records the legacy which the Olmecs left both to the Mayan and central Mexican branches of Mesoamerican society.

The Olmec heartland, the tropical lowland region of southern Veracruz and western Tabasco, seems an unlikely place for the rise of the first great civilization on the American continent. The weather is harsh. Violent storms scourge the coast during the winter; it is hot and dry during April and May; torrential monsoons lash it from June through November, when the winter storms begin anew. Despite the inclement weather, however, it is a rich agricultural area where game and fish abound. Apparently the region was also attractive to early man.

Little is known about the origin of the Olmecs. Their monumental stone-carving appears at their principal sites—San Lorenzo, La Venta, and Tres Zapotes—without known precedent. Tests demonstrate that the huge basalt stones came from the Tuxtla Mountains on the coast of Veracruz, which has prompted some archaeologists to speculate that Olmec culture originated there. The great fluted cone pyramid at La Venta provides yet another reason to suppose that the Olmecs migrated from the mountains: it is clearly a representation of a volcanic cone, similar to those in the Tuxtla range. Despite these tantalizing clues, other scholars maintain that the Olmecs originated in the central highlands, because some of their artifacts have been found there. They believe that future excavations will substantiate this hypothesis. Most of what is known about the Olmecs today, however, comes from sites on the Gulf Coast.

From limited excavations in the Olmec heartland, we can reconstruct the broad outlines of their history. Around 1200 B.C., outsiders with a vastly superior culture—the Olmecs—conquered the region of San Lorenzo in the Coatzacoalcos River basin. They overwhelmed pottery-using farmers who had lived in the area since 1500 B.C. The Olmecs built a great ceremonial complex at San Lorenzo which became the center of their culture until 900 B.C., when it was violently destroyed. Long before the fall of San

Lorenzo, a group of Olmecs had migrated to La Venta, an island on the Tonalá River, where they constructed the greatest Olmec ceremonial center around 1100 B.C. La Venta remained the focus of Olmec culture until it was violently destroyed between 500 and 400 B.C. Thereafter, Tres Zapotes, near the Tuxtla Mountains, continued as a center of Olmec culture. Little is known about Tres Zapotes. It may have been contemporaneous with La Venta, and it probably continued to exist until around A.D. 100.

The Olmecs were great architects. They built San Lorenzo and La Venta on a grand scale. Both of these ceremonial complexes were constructed on huge manmade platforms which required tens of thousands of tons of fill. These monuments are so massive and so clearly nonutilitarian that we assume the Olmecs erected them to demonstrate their wealth and power. Olmec architecture, with its prominent use of platforms and structures positioned along a north-south axis, became the model for later Mesoamerican cities.

The Olmec ceremonial complexes were carefully planned by a people with notable engineering and construction skills. San Lorenzo, for example, was assured a year-round water supply through the construction of stone-lined pools. The central parts of both centers contain rectangular courts surrounded by clay platforms. Each site has several pyramids, but the great fluted pyramid at La Venta, which rises 110 feet, was the most impressive structure in the Olmec heartland. San Lorenzo contains the oldest ball court in Mesoamerica—the ceremonial ball game which was an important feature of later Mesoamerican cultures may be an Olmec creation.

In order to build and maintain their ceremonial centers, the Olmecs required a huge labor force. The basalt for their gigantic monuments was quarried more than 60 miles from La Venta in the Tuxtla Mountains. Using ropes and primitive technology, thousands of workers must have labored to transport the huge stones to San Lorenzo and La Venta. Yet the centers were not highly populated. The remnants of houses suggest that about 1,000 people may have lived in San Lorenzo; La Venta probably had a smaller population. The labor force required to build and to maintain the sites lived in dispersed villages in the surrounding countryside.

The Olmecs were not only great architects, they were talented artists. Some Olmec art was realistic, portraying religious myths as well as real persons; in other instances it was abstract. Olmec artists used a variety of materials, and their works range in size from tiny figurines to massive stone sculptures. Life-size statues, huge stone altars, and stelae decorated in bas-relief portrayed gods, men, and animals. The most striking stone sculptures are the gigantic Colossal Heads, some of which are nearly 10 feet high and weigh as much as 40 tons. They wear strange headgear, somewhat like American football helmets, and their features are infantile. The Olmecs also created beautiful tiny figurines in jade depicting people, animals, and supernatural beings.

Although architectural ruins, art, monuments, and objects from elaborate tombs at La Venta provide information about Olmec life, scholars can only speculate about the nature of Olmec social organization. Some believe that a small elite exploited the peasantry, demanding exhaustive labor, great tribute, and complete obedience. Eventually the Olmec elite may have demanded too much, perhaps precipitating revolts which destroyed San Lorenzo around 900 B.C. and La Venta between 500 and 400 B.C. The savagery of the destruction at San Lorenzo, where the huge basalt monuments were mutilated—heads were smashed from the bodies of the statues, altars were shattered into pieces, and the Colossal Heads were cut—indicates tremendous anger and pent-up hatred. Once the people had vented their emotions, they may have reconsidered. The mutilated monuments were carefully buried in a ceremonial fashion, perhaps in the hope that this act of repentance would pacify the gods. The fall of La Venta was also violent; many of its monuments were deliberately destroyed.

Scholars have advanced other theories besides social revolt to explain the destruction of Olmec centers. Some archaeologists maintain that the primitive Nacaste pottery found at San Lorenzo after its fall indicates that outsiders, possibly Chichimecas, attacked the ceremonial complex and defeated the Olmecs. Facing defeat at the hands of the Nacaste invaders, the Olmecs may have decided to destroy their symbols of power and conceal them from the new conquerors. Other experts speculate that some disaster destroyed the food supply or a plague decimated the population, forcing the rulers to abandon the sites. Still others support a multicausal explanation, suggesting that a natural disaster may have created social dislocations which, in turn, precipitated a revolt, and these disruptions might have provided marauding barbarians with an opportunity to attack the Olmecs. Whatever the reason, San Lorenzo was destroyed and La Venta abandoned.

A warrior class dominated the Olmec state. Evidence of their military activities has been found in areas beyond the heartland, where Olmec art depicts warriors, conquest, and defeated prisoners in acts of submission. The Olmecs traveled widely to secure the precious jade and other materials they needed for their art; Olmec artifacts have been located as far south as western Costa Rica and as far north as the Valley of Mexico. Apparently trade and conquest went hand in hand. Like the later Aztecs, Olmec merchants may have been military representatives of their great centers. In some areas, like Tlatilco near Mexico City, the Olmecs established colonies. The end of this influence coincides with the fall of San Lorenzo, and may be an indication of a political and social crisis in Mesoamerica. Other centers were apparently under the sway of La Venta. One of the most important Olmec colonies has been located in Guerrero, and others have been found in Puebla and Morelos.

Olmec influence is also discernible in regions they did not conquer or colonize, which archaeologists call *Olmecoid*. One of the most important Olmecoid centers was Monte Albán I (ca. 700 B.C.–A.D. 200) in the Valley of Oaxaca. Although most of the structures at the site of Monte Albán date from the Classic Period (A.D. 300–900), one area, constructed along a north-south axis, corresponds to the period Monte Albán I, where archaeologists have excavated the Temple of the *Danzantes*, which is decorated with about 140 figures carved in bas-relief. These are the danzantes, or dancers, figures of nude men with Olmecoid features shown in strange poses, apparently representations of slain leaders or kings. In many of these figures the genitals are clearly shown, a sign of humiliation and captivity in Mesoamerica; in others, decapitation or sexual mutilation demonstrates the individual's defeat. Some scholars speculate that these and other pictorial representations chronicle the conquests of Olmec and Olmecoid kings.

Trade and conquest were important, but the Olmec desire to

spread their religion emerges as a significant reason for their expansion. Olmec religious tradition embraced two cults which influenced all subsequent Mesoamerican religious thought. The first, associated with the serpent cult of agricultural peoples, was later transformed into the cult of Quetzalcóatl—the Feathered Serpent—the culture hero of Mesoamerica; the other, the cult of the jaguar, was eventually associated with the rain god Tlaloc. The jaguar cult represented the merging of the hunter and warrior traditions with those of civilization. The Olmecs believed that a race of *were-jaguars* (half human and half jaguar) resulted from the union of a woman and a jaguar. Jaguar motifs, were-jaguars, and chubby were-jaguar babies appear as the most common representations of Olmec art. Were-jaguars were usually shown as feline men with infantile features, snarling mouths, and cleft heads. Even the great ceremonial center at La Venta seems to have been designed to represent a huge jaguar mask.

The Olmecs' greatest achievements were cultural. They began the development of mathematics, the calendar, and writing in Mesoamerica. Mathematics became an important tool for the construction of ceremonial centers and for recording the astronomical observations that eventually produced the calendar. The Mesoamerican numerical system—which reached its greatest development under the Mayas—utilized three symbols: a dot for one, a bar for five, and a shell-like symbol for zero. The Mesoamericans were thus far ahead of the Europeans, who did not have the zero until the Arabs introduced it in the Middle Ages. Like the Arabic system, Mesoamerican mathematics relied on positioning to give numbers their value. But it was vigesimal (operated on a base of twenty), and the symbols increased in value from the bottom to the top—in contrast to our system, which is decimal and increases from right to left. The Mesoamerican numerical system was capable of very sophisticated calculations; its principle use, however, seems to have been calendrical.

The Mesoamerican calendar was based on both the solar and the lunar year. It was calculated in calendar rounds which meshed the 365-day solar year with the 260-day lunar year. The system thus created a 52-year cycle, since a solar day would not meet the same lunar day again for 52 years. The conclusion of a 52-year cycle was an extremely significant and dangerous time for the peoples of Mesoamerica, marking the end of an era. It was a time of great fear, since tradition offered no assurance that another cycle would follow, and it was quite possible that the world would come to an end. The Olmecs may also have developed the Long Count, a system that enabled them to calculate beyond a 52-year cycle. A date corresponding to 3113 B.C. was arbitrarily selected as the starting point, just as we begin our calendar with the presumed date of the birth of Christ. Although most subsequent Mesoamerican cultures adopted the Olmec calendar, not all used the Long Count.

Many Olmec monuments and art objects bear inscriptions. The hieroglyphic writings found in the Olmec heartland are relatively primitive; the first literary texts were discovered at Monte Albán I. These glyphs have been only partially deciphered, because Mesoamerican writing is quite complex and the variety of cultures makes them difficult to interpret. Nevertheless, it is clear that the Olmecs were among the first to develop a form of writing.

The Olmecs transmitted their culture both to the Mayas in the south and to the peoples of southern and central Mexico. Archaeologists believe that Izapa, in the southernmost portion of the present state of Chiapas, on the Guatemalan border, was the point of contact between the Olmecs and the Mayas who lived in the Yucatán and Central America. Monte Albán and the Olmec colonies in central Mexico served a similar function. Olmec traditions provided a basis for the common Mesoamerican culture that evolved in the region over a period of more than two thousand years. Although many different societies, states, and empires held sway over parts of Mexico, none exerted as much influence over the region as the Olmecs until the rise of Teotihuacán.

TEOTIHUACAN

Teotihuacán was the greatest city in the New World. It became the most powerful cultural, religious, political, and perhaps economic force in Mesoamerica. The city enjoyed this unprecedented power for nearly six centuries (ca. A.D. 100–750). Its role was in many ways similar to that of Rome. At its apogee, Teotihuacán's population of between 125,000 and 250,000 people made it the most populous city on the American continent and one of the largest cities of its time in the world. Since no writings survive, all that we

know about the city comes from legends and fragmentary archaeological evidence. According to these legends, civilization
began in Tamoanchán and was later transferred to Teotihuacán, a
city said to have been constructed either by the gods or by giants.
Other legends refer to Tollán, a city where Quetzalcóatl reigned in
peace—where all the arts and sciences developed, and artisans
created works of exquisite beauty. Some scholars believe that the
legendary Tollán was Teotihuacán.

After the fall of La Venta, the peoples of the Valley of Mexico
continued to thrive in small villages that dotted the shores of the
great lake in the center. Some of these hamlets gradually became
trading and religious complexes which depended on the agricultural surpluses of the surrounding villages. Cuicuilco was the leading center around 200 B.C., but it was destroyed by a volcanic
eruption. Thereafter Teotihuacán, situated at one end of the Valley,
began to grow and compete for power, eventually becoming the
principal city in the Valley.

Teotihuacán became an important religious as well as a manufacturing and commercial center around 100 B.C. At that time it
probably contained between 5,000 and 10,000 people. A second
phase of accelerated development occurred from about A.D. 1 to
150, when the city's basic outlines were established. Two major
avenues were constructed: one, later called the "Street of the
Dead" by the Aztecs, was built along a north-south axis, and the
other great avenue ran east to west. As in most Mesoamerican
centers, these streets divided the city into four quarters, representing the four corners of the universe. At the intersection of the two
avenues, the *Teotihuacanos* erected a vast religious complex, the
Ciudadela; the imposing Temple of Quetzalcóatl dominated that
part of the city. Along the Street of the Dead they raised two
monumental pyramids which subsequently came to be known as
the Pyramids of the Sun and the Moon. The priests and the upper
classes lived along the Street of the Dead in the center of the city,
amid their temples and palaces.

Although the government was theocratic, Teotihuacán was also
a major economic complex. Across from the Ciudadela, the
Teotihuacanos built an immense marketplace, the Great Com-
pound. The city also became a major center of obsidian manufacturing, employing thousands of artisans and craftsmen who

lived in heavily populated quarters. (There are indications that Teotihuacán controlled the obsidian mines in the northern region of Hidalgo.) Other craftsmen offered a variety of items for sale. By the year 200 the city covered more than 8 square miles with more than 23 temple complexes and many palaces, markets, shops, and apartments.

Teotihuacán achieved its greatest size and power during the next two and a half centuries (A.D. 200–450). It became the largest marketplace in Mesoamerica and consolidated its position as the region's most important religious and political center. This period was characterized by enormous building activity. The older, less imposing structures were replaced by stone construction and large-scale public architecture which transformed the city into a metropolis. The great pyramids reached their final size: the Pyramid of the Sun, located on the east side of the Street of the Dead, was over 700 feet long on each side and over 200 feet high; the Pyramid of the Moon, at the north end of the Street of the Dead, was slightly smaller. These structures are testimony both to the advanced technology of Teotihuacán and to the power of the state. The Street of the Dead was extended so that it was over 100 feet wide and several miles long, and the great east-west avenue was apparently built on the same scale. The city's huge population lived in large apartment complexes. Buildings were plastered and covered with magnificent frescoes. The thousands of religious pilgrims, merchants, and political clients who visited Teotihuacán from throughout Mesoamerica must have been dazzled by the size and grandeur of the urban center.

Evidence of Teotihuacán's power and influence is found throughout Mesoamerica. The wide distribution of objects manufactured in the city indicates a complex commercial network. Teotihuacán influenced the Mayas of Central America from an outpost at the great Mayan center of Kaminaljuyú in Guatemala, where archaeologists have uncovered a complex of buildings constructed in the distinctive Teotihuacán style, indicating the presence of colonists, possibly merchants. Monte Albán II became either an ally or a dependency of the great central Mexican city: the Oaxacan center is filled with artifacts from Teotihuacán. The rulers of Monte Albán stocked their tombs with elaborate wares from

Teotihuacán. And a large neighborhood in the great metropolis was inhabited by people from Oaxaca. Thus far no other foreign colonies have been excavated in Teotihuacán, but it is possible that other peoples who flocked to the great city to trade, to worship, or merely to participate in the exciting life of the metropolis, also lived in special quarters.

The fall of Teotihuacán is one of the great mysteries of Mexican archaeology. The city probably met a violent end, since the ceremonial center was burned and destroyed. Its influence over Mesoamerica began to diminish after 650. Teotihuacán's population decreased in the seventh century, but there was no indication that this flourishing city-state would suddenly be abandoned during the eighth century. Some scholars believe that a natural disaster like an earthquake, fire, or famine destroyed the city. Other experts offer more complex explanations. Teotihuacán's destruction coincided with a climatic change which transformed the northern agricultural regions into arid wastelands. The drought forced the nomadic Chichimecas to migrate south, and they may have attacked and destroyed the city.

This explanation leaves many questions unanswered. Why was the city not rebuilt? Did social division and conflicts prevent Teotihuacán's inhabitants from cooperating to defend or reconstruct the city? Mesoamerican legends suggest the existence of sharp cleavages within the elite. Recent excavations at Teotihuacán confirm aspects of such a struggle: figures representing military orders appear with increasing frequency toward the end of the city's hegemony. Even the religious center, the Ciudadela, was fortified. It appears that a once theocratic society was being militarized. According to Rene Millon, it is possible "that Teotihuacán's Vatican was being transformed into a kind of Pentagon toward the end of the city's history."

The fall of the "city of the gods" must have had great repercussions throughout Mesoamerica. Its people dispersed. Some of them moved to a nearby area on the lake, where Azcapotzalco became a leading small state. Others traveled to Cholula, in Puebla, where they built a great pyramid to Quetzalcóatl, the largest ancient structure in America. Thereafter a series of independent cities extended their influence over limited regions. El Tajín became the most important of the coastal centers. In Oaxaca, the Zapotecs developed Classic Monte Albán Culture. In the south, the Mayas continued their independent development until 900, when they mysteriously abandoned their cities. No other city-state replaced Teotihuacán as the dominant unifying force in Mesoamerica until the rise of Tula and the Toltecs.

THE TOLTECS

The Toltecs are the first people in Mesoamerica for whom we have a history, although fact and legend are so intertwined that it is difficult to separate them. The Aztecs, who later dominated central Mexico, proudly claimed to be their descendents. Chronicles describe the Toltecs as an extraordinary people who worshiped Quetzalcóatl, the god of peace. They were supposedly taller, stronger, and more able than anyone else, excelling in the arts, sciences, and sports. They were such talented artisans that the name Toltec came to mean "craftsman" or "builder." In addition, they were accomplished agriculturalists who could grow gigantic ears of corn and cotton in different colors. Hunger and want were unknown in their society.

This ideal characterization contrasts sharply with the archaeological record. The Toltecs migrated to central Mexico from the northwest, an expanding warlike people who entered the Valley of Mexico in the ninth century. They were already acquainted with civilized behavior through earlier contacts with Teotihuacán—in this respect they were probably comparable to one of the Romanized German tribes after the fall of Rome. Although called "Tolteca-Chichimeca" in their chronicles, they considered themselves superior to other "real" Chichimecas.

There are several versions of Toltec history. According to the generally accepted interpretation, their great leader Mixcóatl conquered the Otomíes, who lived in Culhuacan, and eventually the two peoples intermarried. Mixcóatl's son Topiltzín moved the Toltec capital to Tula in the present state of Hidalgo in 968. At this point the chronicles become intertwined with myths. Topiltzín is identified with Quetzalcóatl, who had fair skin, long hair, and a beard. Tula is also described as Tollán, the legendary city which some scholars associate with Teotihuacán. In an effort to resolve the confusion, some experts hypothesize that Topiltzín became a reformer who advocated peace and the cult of Quetzalcóatl. The chronicles confuse Topiltzín with Quetzalcóatl, they say, because he became the high priest of the cult. Under his leadership the arts flourished and Tula was converted into an imposing center.

Eventually, warriors began to impose their views in Tula. The conflict between peace and war is personified in legends as the struggle between Quetzalcóatl and Tezcatlipoca ("Smoking Mirror" in Náhuatl). Supporters of the "Smoking Mirror" challenged the peaceful cult of the Feathered Serpent who only required the symbolic sacrifice of butterflies, snakes, and jades. Instead, they advocated human sacrifice and championed warfare. Tezcatlipoca triumphed through treachery: he managed to intoxicate Quetzalcóatl and cause him to neglect his religious obligations. Humiliated, the Feathered Serpent left Tula in 987 with a group of his followers, traveling to the Gulf of Mexico where, according to one source, he immolated himself. In another account, he sailed east on a raft of serpents. Before he left, Quetzalcóatl prophesied that he would return to reclaim his throne. These legends gained wide acceptance in Mesoamerica, and the prophesy of Quetzalcóatl's return would subsequently influence Moctezuma II, the last ruler of the Aztecs.

At Tula, a new group of leaders controlled the city until 1168. The Toltec capital, like Teotihuacán, extended its political influence over a large part of Mexico. Other societies, such as the Zapotecs and the Mixtecs in Oaxaca, seem to have paid them homage. In the south, Chichén Itzá became the center of their Mayan colony. The Toltecs also protected central Mexico from the northern barbarians. From their capital at Tula, they sponsored colonies along the northern frontier which served as a buffer against the Chichimecas and extended the area of cultivation. Improved climatic conditions in the tenth century favored the expansion of agriculture, but in the twelfth century droughts again ravaged north-central Mexico. Facing starvation, the Chichimecas threw themselves against the settled peoples of the south. Their savage onslaught eventually destroyed Tula. The invaders wrought such destruction on the city that archaeological reconstruction is difficult. They demolished the temples and hurled the colossal sculptures into a huge trench cut in the great pyramid.

The reign of Huémac, the last king of the Toltecs, was marred by these repeated and violent Chichimeca attacks which ultimately destroyed the city. Led by Huémac, the Toltecs abandoned Tula for Chapultepec in the Valley of Mexico, where the old king committed suicide. A few Toltecs remained at Tula for another 15 or 20 years, and then they too abandoned the city.

Although archaeologists have thus far spent little time excavating Tula, we do have some idea of the importance of Toltec culture in Mesoamerican cultural history. Built by a people who worshiped Quetzalcóatl, Tula was probably large and impressive, but it could not compare with Teotihuacán. Although images of the Feathered Serpent are prominent and no representations of Tezcatlipoca have been found, the architecture of Tula is dominated by military motifs. The Temple of the Warriors and its colossal Atlantean figures, for example, are testimony to Toltec militarism. Military orders of knights—the Coyotes, the Eagles, and the Jaguars—were prominent in Tula. The Toltecs also practiced ritual human sacrifice.

Verification of the Quetzalcóatl-Tezcatlipoca conflict comes not from Tula but from the Mayas in Yucatán. Their account, however, only tells us that a group led by the Feathered Serpent left Tula and sailed east to the Yucatán peninsula. Wall paintings and other records from Chichén Itzá ("Itzá" is the Mayan name for the Toltecs) chronicle the Toltec conquest of the Mayas. According to these accounts, the Toltecs, led by Kukulcán— "Feathered Serpent" in Maya—arrived from the west by sea in 987. The murals at the Temple of Warriors in Chichén Itzá show the Mayas in rafts going out to fight the Toltecs, who arrived in canoes. The Mayas were defeated in a bloody battle. Another fresco, in the Temple of Tigers, commemorates a great land battle in which the Mayas were once again defeated. Afterwards the Maya leaders were sacrificed, and Quetzalcóatl is shown receiving their hearts. There is little doubt that the Toltecs influenced the lowland Mayas in Yucatán; the Toltec buildings in Chichén Itzá resemble the temples of Tula.

The greatness and power of the Toltecs had a lasting influence on the peoples of central Mexico. After the fall of Tula, Toltec groups migrated south to the Valley of Mexico, where they tried to reconstruct their old society. There they mingled with other peoples, forming a complex of city-states. As they gained strength, the new city-states claimed to be the heirs of Tula. Their heritage, however, was much older; it included several thousand years of Mesoamerican culture.

Chapter 3

THE MEXICA-
AZTECS

FROM BARBARISM TO CIVILIZATION

CIVILIZATION in Mesoamerica evolved in an uneven manner—reaching impressive heights only to be leveled by barbarians, then rising again to repeat the process. The savage Chichimecas who threw themselves against advanced cultures absorbed some elements from the ruins, thereby modifying their own barbarism in the process. The general level inevitably rose as culture was repeatedly diffused by invasion. The constant intrusion of barbarians, and their incorporation into the cultural leaven, reached a historically important point with the fall of Tula in 1168. With its destruction, the Toltec civilization—itself built on the foundations of earlier advanced cultures—in turn became a font from which other cultures would draw.

The glories of Tula remained to inspire a horde of imitators. In the Valley of Mexico, self-appointed successors of the Toltecs established a number of small city-states which continued the general cultural evolution. Xaltocan, on the northern end of the central Valley's lake system, vied with Texcoco on the eastern shore. Azcapotzalco controlled the west, while Culhuacan, boasting excessively of its Toltec origins, dominated the southern area of the Valley. These small city-states ignored historical reality to claim the cultural honor of carrying on the Toltec civilization.

In 1253 the Mexica, now commonly called the Aztecs, arrived in the central Valley. Aware of their own inferiority and weakness, they gladly accepted the role of mercenaries in the service of Azcapotzalco, which allowed them to settle in the area of Chapultepec. There the Mexica began their cultural apprenticeship. Involvement in their masters' struggle for domination of the region proved costly: Culhuacan's warriors defeated the Mexica, and as a result subjected them to 25 years of tyranny and intimidation. Eventually the desperate Mexica fled to the relative safety of an isolated island in the lake. While it was not the most promising location for agriculture, the island provided a refuge from their enemies. Determined to survive and emulate their more advanced neighbors, the Mexica accepted their inferiority and, through the device of tribute, attained a measure of protection.

In 1325 they founded Tenochtitlan, a capital in name only until 1375 when the Mexica, like others before them, laid claim to the Toltec mantle as a full-fledged city-state. Another settlement, Tlatelolco, appeared on the island in 1337, established by a Mexica splinter group. The Mexica-Aztec state managed to survive, often barely, the shifting alliances that characterized city-state politics around the rim of the lake. A major step forward occurred with the appointment of Acamapichtli, grandson of Culhuacan's chief, as their leader. Acamapichtli supposedly carried the blood of the Toltecs in his veins, and by mixing it with his adopted people linked them with past high civilizations.

Azcapotzalco, however, remained the dominant power, kept at arms-length only by tribute and the rapidly building military might of the Aztecs. In 1426 Azcapotzalco reached its height of power. The Mexica-Aztecs, always cautiously ambitious and predatory, allied themselves with Texcoco's exiled leader Nezahualcóyotl, who brought his people over to Tenochtitlan's side. After four years of bitter and bloody battle, Azcapotzalco finally conceded defeat. A new Triple Alliance emerged, with Tenochtitlan and Texcoco dominating a much weaker Tlacopan (Tacuba). The

Mexica-Aztecs had thus evolved from a barbarous past to the point where they now claimed the respect due the political and cultural heirs of the Toltecs.

Significant structural and philosophical changes accompanied the rise of the Aztecs. The military became the most important institutional element dominating their supreme council. The ruler, formerly selected by tribal representatives, now received his mandate from the military. At the summit of power, two officials, the ruler and the vice-ruler, exercised executive authority. The day of tribal equality had indeed already passed, and only vestiges, largely devoid of power, remained. Not content with merely absorbing the Toltec heritage, the Aztecs now constructed their own heroic saga. Huitzilopochtli, their war god, became an important deity, competing with the older and more established gods of the central Valley. Moreover, the Mexica-Aztecs, covered with the façade of Toltec legitimacy, became his chosen people. The state myth declared that Huitzilopochtli led his people by force of arms from barbarism to civilization, incorporating the Toltec mystique along the way: under his direction, they had left their original home of Aztlán to settle where they found an eagle perched on a cactus, with a snake in its predatory grasp. Fortunately, the eagle favored an easily defended island in the lake. Recognition of the war god's patronage helped to rationalize military control of the state, as well as the subordination of all other activities to the needs of warfare.

Military hegemony in the Valley of Mexico proved insufficient to guarantee the prosperity of Tenochtitlan. By the middle of the fifteenth century the population of the city and its dependent areas had expanded to the point where the central Valley's food resources could no longer sustain the society. Natural disasters or crop failures that could previously be weathered now threatened to destroy the increasingly complex sociopolitical structure of the Aztec state. A plague of locusts attacked crops in 1446; there was a great flood three years later; and between 1450 and 1454 the Valley suffered a devastating famine, forcing thousands to flee and untold numbers to die. These disasters clearly demonstrated the Aztecs' dangerous vulnerability, and the food resources of other areas understandably attracted attention. It seemed necessary to expand and broaden the Aztecs' power beyond the Valley of Mexico. The year 1454 marked the beginning of the great campaigns which car-

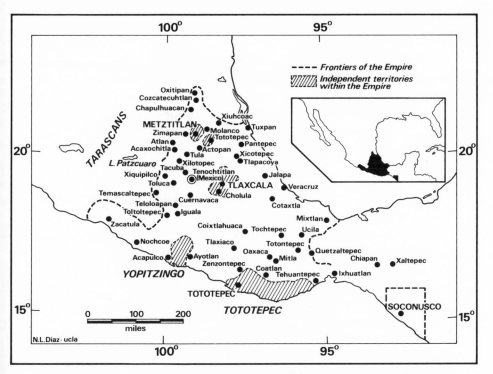

THE MEXICA-AZTEC EMPIRE, 1519.

ried Aztec authority out of the central Valley, eventually to spread across Mesoamerica.

Between 1458 and 1461, Moctezuma I directed his armies into the coastal region around Veracruz and began to overrun Mixtec towns in the west. Axayácatl (1469–1481) defeated the Matlatzinca of the Toluca Valley, and in the 1470s succeeded in isolating Tlaxcala. Tlatelolco, with a well-developed merchant and trading class which enhanced the value of its military conquests, was forcibly amalgamated with Tenochtitlan in 1473.

Ahuítzotl, Moctezuma I's third son, seized most of the territory between Zacatula, in the northwest, and Acapulco, reaching down the Pacific Coast as far as Guatusco near the present Guatemalan border. He also penetrated Oaxaca, leaving garrisons along the invasion route to facilitate further expansion and trade—among them Cuilapan, situated on a strategic hilltop that safeguarded commerce with the Isthmus of Tehuantepec. Moctezuma II, in his turn, seized some 43 towns in Oaxaca and reached Tlappan in the modern state of Guerrero. At the time of the Spanish conquest, his armies were planning a campaign to bring

the entire Isthmus of Tehuantepec under Aztec control. Even remote Mixtec and Zapotec groups found themselves under pressure
from Tenochtitlan. Nevertheless, because of certain sociopolitical
factors that caused unrest in other parts of the empire, it is evident
that under Moctezuma II the Aztec state had reached a point where
consolidation rather than expansion was necessary.

In spite of Aztec military pressure, a large part of what today
constitutes the modern Republic of Mexico remained independent.
Nomadic tribes in the north inhabiting the arid semi-desert region
hardly seemed worth conquering. Metztitlán and Tlaxcala, surrounded by Aztec dependencies, remained independent. The
Tarascans of Michoacán twice had turned back major offensives,
and Yopitzingo (Guerrero) and Tototepec still escaped total domination, as did the Maya. Nevertheless, Tenochtitlan's military
might understandably intimidated, if it did not actually conquer,
these Indian groups.

In addition to gaining access to food resources, the military
campaigns solidified warrior domination of Aztec society. War,
and the blood sacrifices that followed a successful conquest, became an important element in the continuation of the Mexica-
Aztec state. The expanding population of Indian Mexico, coupled
with religious beliefs that required blood offerings, almost inevitably led to large-scale human sacrifice. Political manipulation, the
orchestration of warfare, and blood sacrifices attained a high level
of efficiency under the direction of Tlacaélel, the power behind
several leading rulers for most of his long life.

In the absence of actual warfare, a war mentality was artificially
maintained by the use of so-called "flower wars." With the cooperation of the rulers of Tlaxcala, Huejotzingo, Cholula, and
Atlixco, the kings of the Triple Alliance arranged for military
engagements that provided sacrificial victims and permitted warriors to prove themselves in battle. The flower wars preserved the
military status system and guaranteed a high level of support for
the state, supposedly under attack by its enemies. Such adversaries,
known as "Enemies of the House," fought prearranged battles on
selected sites with the clear understanding that the participants
would not seriously attempt to destroy the power balance. Flower
wars could not be publicly announced, since this would defeat
their purpose and perhaps even push the people—many of whom

died either in battle or upon the sacrificial stone—to rebel. The well-staged battles, and the orgy of human sacrifices which followed, provided entertainment for the invited guests, who secretly observed the spectacle hidden behind a rose-covered latticework screen. The flowers which masked their faces also covered the stench of death. Dignitaries from distant and still independent regimes left intimidated and impressed with Aztec power. The authorities constantly refined the ritual sacrifices to obtain the maximum gory effect.

By warfare and intimidation, the Triple Alliance had brought most of Mesoamerica under its domination by the end of the fifteenth century.

AGRICULTURE, TRADE, AND COMMERCE

The Aztec economic base, dependent on agriculture, had evolved far beyond a simple subsistence level. Agricultural methods, however, remained somewhat primitive, apart from the technological innovation of the *chinampa* system of floating rafts to reclaim land in marshy areas and along the lakefront, and the use of irrigation.

Maize, the staple crop of the region, provided adequate nutrition and could be grown in a variety of different soils. Several different types of corn with different germination periods and uses had been developed in Mesoamerica. Crops could be planted from March through early May to provide staggered harvesting. Selected seed-corn was generally soaked in water before planting, to speed germination; the farmer then used a simple digging stick to break the ground and form the earth into hillocks arranged in rows. Squash could be planted between the corn mounds, helping to conserve moisture and itself providing food. Beans were also grown in the cornfields, providing a high degree of protein in the diet as well as adding nitrogen to the soil and stimulating crop growth. Other crops included chía, a plant of the sage group, and amaranth *(huauhtli)*. Chía seeds were used to make a gruel and its oil was used to manufacture paints; amaranth produced a massive amount of tiny seeds at the end of the rainy season, just before the major maize harvest. These two seed crops became very important in the event of the failure of other crops.

Maguey, an amazingly useful cactus, supplied fiber for cloth of a tougher quality than cotton material; syrup used in medicines as a sweetener; *octli* (pulque), a fermented alcoholic drink; dried leaves for fuel; and thatching material for the simple dwellings of the countryside. As a desert plant, maguey thrived on dry and infertile soils, yet tolerated great extremes in temperature and moisture. Peppers, tomatoes, avocados, and a number of different fruits rounded out the Aztec diet. Domesticated animals augmented to a limited extent the food obtained by hunting and fishing; domesticated bees provided honey, and ducks, turkeys, and highly prized tender dogs supplied meat. Agriculture produced an adequate surplus to free an impressive number of people from agricultural tasks. The repeated occurrence of famine, however, indicated its limitations.

Highly specialized nonagricultural functions, centered in the large urban settlement of Tenochtitlan, required the development of a complex marketing system. The immense Tlatelolco marketplace alone served 60,000 to 80,000 people daily. Items from other regions, often quite distant from the city, could be obtained by the discriminating consumer. Leather goods, finely polished stones, exquisite jewelry, fine featherwork, embroidered textiles, and many other essentially manufactured articles could be purchased. Highly regulated and orderly, each market had a staff of judges to arbitrate disputes and see to it that items on sale had an assigned place and price noted in the equivalent amount of cotton cloth. Bernal Díaz, a participant in the Spanish conquest, noted with amazement the great markets of the city, comparing them favorably to the international marketing center of Medina del Campo in Spain. While a money economy had not yet developed, the complexity of trade, as well as the multiplicity of consumer goods available, had already forced a uniform pricing system in terms of universal standard items. Small copper articles, gold dust packaged in turkey quills, and cacao beans, as well as cotton cloth, served as pricing units. In spite of such progress, barter remained the rule. But it is obvious that the Mexica were but one step removed from a monetary system.

The marketing system distributed not only local products but supplementary supplies and exotic products from distant regions also. Civilization brought a greater sophistication in tastes and demands that could not be satisfied by the products of one region alone. Trade between the high plateau of central Mexico and the tropical lowland became increasingly necessary. Regional interdependence was part of the price of civilization.

To meet the needs of trade, Tenochtitlan developed into a processing center, foreshadowing its modern role as the Mexican industrial heartland. As the capital of an empire, commodities normally flowed into the city in the form of tribute or other types of imperial taxes. Such an arrangement could not by itself maintain a high degree of economic activity, and if taken to an extreme risked impoverishment of the subject population, thereby reducing the value of the military conquest. Consumer demand and economic dependence had gone beyond the effectiveness of brute force. Military might, however, guaranteed access both to markets and to raw materials to be processed and then entered into trade by Aztec merchants. Cotton cloth had to be reworked in Tenochtitlan. Fancy featherwork, beaten copper, and semiprecious stones received the attention of craftsmen before being exported on the backs of *tamemes*, porters who plied the many trade trails. Imposed economic control, combined with an appreciation for maintaining some degree of mutual advantage, indicated the growing importance of trade.

THE ELEMENTS OF CULTURE

It would be unfair to present Aztec progress solely in military and economic terms. While the Mexicas' insistence on their Toltec origins cannot be taken seriously, they could rightfully claim to be a part of the cultural evolution of Mesoamerica. Much of what is known about Aztec society, however, applies mainly to urban culture. The rural life of the villagers remains obscure.

Dominated by imposing palaces and assorted religious buildings, including the enormous central pyramid dedicated to Huitzilopochtli, the city of Tenochtitlan presented an awe-inspiring sight. An advanced concept of engineering made it possible. Technology, much of it borrowed from Texcoco, enabled the Mexica-Aztecs to engage in irrigation, bringing in fresh water from distant sources. Great dikes spanned the lake, separating the sweet water from the brackish and regulating the water level. The dikes also served as causeways, with movable openings to permit flood control as well as to make any attack across them difficult. Fresh drinking water, historically a problem for the island, flowed into the city from distant mountain springs through a magnificent aqueduct system. Appreciation of the mathematical concepts that made such engineering projects possible was limited, however. The Aztecs readily adopted the use of the calendar and an elementary numbering system, but saw no need to develop the science beyond such pragmatic uses. The Mayan fascination with higher mathematics does not appear in Mexica culture.

While the engineering marvels of Tenochtitlan provided visual proof of Aztec progress, the finer elements of culture testified to their high degree of civilization. Náhuatl, the language of the Mexica, not only permitted dignified and pleasing expression but possessed an incredibly rich vocabulary and flexible construction that enabled its speakers to express, as well as develop, new concepts. Shades of emotion and meaning concerning the most transcendental subjects could be achieved by a cultured speaker of the language. The juxtaposition of words conveyed delicate meaning beyond the words themselves in a manner to delight the heart of a poet. Náhuatl as a language served the needs and reflected the thoughts of a civilized people.

The written language, in the process of moving toward phonetics, still remained a mixture of pictographs, ideograms, and phonetic writing at the time of the Spanish conquest. Written records outlined events, providing memory cues but in no sense capturing the richness of the spoken word. The oral, not the written, tradition dominated and provided access to accumulated knowledge. As a consequence, the Aztecs favored poetry over prose, making use of rhythmic verse that could be readily memorized. The long rhetorical orations, so esteemed by the Mexica, contained an abnormal amount of repetition, for the same reason. These orations, called *huehuetlatolli*, conveyed the social instructions, rituals, and roles necessary to function effectively in Aztec society. Salutations, congratulatory speeches, moral precepts, prayers, and social ideals, as well as important customs, were preserved through this active oral tradition of the people. In the schools students carefully committed them to memory, along with the sacred songs and poems. The ability to speak elegantly distinguished the educated individual from the masses.

Dancing and music, also closely connected with social and religious rituals, enjoyed only a limited development, with few musical instruments beyond the conch, trumpet, flute, and whistle that complemented the standard drum and two-toned gong.

Everyday life reflected a deep underlying desire to preserve dignity and form, and as a result social roles appear to have been quite rigid. This aspect of the Mexica-Aztec culture may well have been a factor in the class stratification that characterized society at the time of the Spanish conquest. Courtesy and self-restraint are evident in the innumerable orations directed at the Aztec youth, as in this instructive oration concerning an invitation to dine at the table of a respected noble:

> Take care how you enter (the house), for without your being aware you will be observed. Approach respectfully, bow, and deliver your greeting. Do not make faces when you eat; do not eat noisily and without care, like a glutton; do not swallow too quickly but little by little. . . . If you drink water, do not make noise sucking it in. You are not a small dog. Do not use all your fingers when you eat, but only the three fingers of your right hand; . . . do not cough and do not spit; and take care not to dirty the clothes of any of the other guests.

Contained within orations was the acceptance of a certain social role that enabled one to preserve dignity and respect in social interaction.

Law, and the imposition of justice, reflected a civilized understanding of the value of the judicial process. As in any society, the law reflected the degree of power as well as the interests of various social sectors. A noble and a commoner did not expect equality before the law, since each class was subject to different restrictions that defined social roles and indicated the limits of their actions. Local courts handled petty crimes, while the more serious offenses, including those involving the nobility, went to the *Tecalli* (regional courts) in provincial capitals. Cases involving nobles received a hearing from the second-highest state official. The head of state considered appeals every ten to twelve days. Court officials carefully recorded the proceedings for subsequent review by a superior tribunal that met in Tenochtitlan every eighty days. Regional representatives attended these meetings to give an account of the various cases and discuss the decisions. Obviously the Mexica accepted the existence of a philosophy of law. Nezahualcóyotl, perhaps the most famous ruler of Texcoco, drew up a legal code widely copied in the central Valley.

The Aztec state accepted the responsibility of imposing justice as part of its sovereignty. At the same time, the power of the head of state to modify the law was restricted. Once a case became notorious, public pressure apparently could not be ignored and the letter of the law had to be followed, no matter how reluctantly. The most celebrated example involved Chalchiuhnenetzin, a younger sister of Moctezuma, who had been given in marriage while still a child to the ruler of Texcoco, to strengthen the Triple Alliance. The new bride matured in a sumptuous palace, surrounded by a staff of 2,000 servants. Unfortunately, in the sybaritic court of Texcoco, Chalchiuhnenetzin participated in innumerable secret orgies which eventually came to light. Her husband, Nezahualpilli, refused for political reasons to keep the affair secret, notifying the important rulers of an impending trial that ended in the prescribed punishment—garroting and burning of all concerned, including her servants.

Punishment generally followed immediately upon conclusion of the trial. Death, rather than long imprisonment, appears to have been the rule. In cases of minor theft or personal injury, the principle of restitution was evoked. An individual might be enslaved for a set period of time in order to pay off the debt owed the victim. Nobles received harsher punishment, since their public misconduct weakened the image of the state. A commoner guilty of theft could anticipate enslavement, while a noble convicted of the same crime received death. Similarly, public drunkenness of the highborn merited death, but for the lower class the first offense called for a head-shaving and destruction of the person's dwelling, with death on the second. Preservation of public dignity constituted one of the most important objectives of the judicial system. Vices, including sexual excesses, became important only when they became notoriously public. Private pleasures had to be balanced by public restraint. An open display of weakness merited no pity, since it disgraced not only the individual, but his family and class as well.

Family life reflected the civilized desire to restrain and channel the emotions in a socially approved manner. Rhetorical orations instructed each new generation in ideal behavior as well as the individual's own role within the family. Maintaining the proper form, attention to religious ritual, and self-control guaranteed a reasonably smooth passage through an often difficult life. Fear of emotion as a destructive force pervaded all aspects of family life. It therefore became very important to understand and accept one's role as a means of avoiding emotional stress. Sex in such a repressive social environment symbolized all the dangers of losing control. The existence of an ideal standard of sexual behavior, which could not be adhered to in practice, negatively affected relations between the sexes. Women, considered morally weak, were viewed with suspicion, and the society attempted to isolate them behind rigid domestic barriers as potential threats to the family honor. The degree to which women could be protected from such imagined dangers varied among the different classes.

Male and female roles were defined ritualistically at birth. A male infant's umbilical cord became his first offering to a warrior society, being buried together with a shield and arrows. As the midwife severed the cord, she warned the newborn child that the house of his birth served only as a nest, "for you are a warrior" whose mission "is to give the sun (Huitzilopochtli) the blood of enemies and thus sustain the earth." In contrast, a female baby's first instruction emphasized a domestic role: "As the heart stays in the body, so you must stay in the house, you must never leave; . . . you must be like the embers in the hearth." Similarly, the naming ceremony symbolically defined the different social functions. A male child, surrounded by weapons of war, received his name amid the high expectation of the assembled relatives. Such expectations matured into family and then general social pressure to succeed, certainly a burden but also an incentive for male achievement. The female child's ceremony reflected the lack of aggressive social expectations. Her environment would not be one of hidden dangers in a changing and fluid world, but rather the known and relatively unchanging dimensions of domestic life. She received a name amid spindles and shuttles, passive symbols of her place and role in society.

A warrior society could easily rationalize the secondary and supportive role of women. It was harder to justify total exclusion of women from the priestly functions. In fact they could not be barred from participation in religious affairs, and in view of the large number of gods of both sexes, and the extended rites necessary to placate or gain their favor, female assistance may have been a physical necessity. Men, however, occupied the highest position in the priesthood. Even such lowly tasks as ritual sweeping of the temples reflected this. Priests swept the inner recesses with precious plumes, while the women cleaned the lower approaches to the temple.

Vows of celibacy indicated that the Aztecs considered sexual activity a bar to priestly dedication. Sexual purity was valued for both men and women priests, because society believed that sexual behavior was degrading and must be carefully repressed. Fear of sins of the flesh led priests to lower their eyes in the presence of women, and the chastity of priestesses received strict attention. To be seen with a man resulted in drastic penance, and to engage in sexual contact invited the death penalty for both parties.

Parental advice reveals the ideal behavioral model for girls. The father's instructions tended to be rather vague; however, the intent was clear—the daughter must avoid dishonoring her name and background by unseemly conduct. Carnal temptation had to be resisted while she prepared herself for domestic duties by perfecting her weaving and sewing. Once married, her father admonished her never to commit adultery and to stand by her husband no matter what his fortune or status in life. Paternal advice identified female sexual behavior as the source of potential family dishonor which could be diffused by the daughter's retreat into domesticity. It was left to the girl's mother to be more specific. Conformity and moderation in dress as well as behavior guaranteed the smooth passage of a young girl through life's dangers. Dressed modestly in order to avoid emphasis on physical beauty, she must develop a dignified walk, neither too fast nor too slow—and above all, no exaggerated movements. Her speech should be well-modulated and pleasant, without nasal overtones. When going into the public streets, her gaze should be purposeful so that her eyes did not stray and fix on strangers. Comments directed toward her by passersby must be ignored, as if she did not hear or understand the implications. Any other than a passive response raised the question of a woman's respectability. In the same vein, her mother advised her not to use makeup—since only worldly women, and those who had lost all shame, sought to advertise their charms. Above all she must never, under any cirumstance, allow herself to be seduced—a danger which required constant vigilance. A mother's fear of the sexual conquest of her daughter may well have been justified. Males, whether married or single, did not have to abide by the same standard of morality.

Marriage, that hoped-for haven for female virtue, was a male-dominated institution into which the woman entered as the subordinate partner. A household became an economic and social unit through the male. Married men received the right to farm a particular plot of land and, if they had not already inherited that right from their fathers, the *calpulli* (the tribal-kinship division) provided them with land. In keeping with male dominance, the relatives and parents of the prospective husband initiated the process of courtship. The girl's family symbolically retreated before such aggressiveness, murmuring that it must be a mistake, since she appeared rather stupid and perhaps even unworthy. Ritualistic deprecation, considered good manners, was not to be taken seriously; nevertheless, it indicated that the honor lay on the male side of a marriage, as well as reaffirming the unequal social valorization that placed women in a subordinate position. Not surprisingly, the married woman moved in with her husband's family.

For the young woman, marriage merely meant replacement of the father's authority with that of her husband. The male became the core of the new family unit, with the wife and children subordinated to his direction. While the wife could influence, and even implement, family decisions, the ultimate responsibility rested with the male head of the household. Widowhood did not change the situation substantially. A woman might attempt to remain independent if, because of age and widowhood, she was not likely to be considered sexually vulnerable or scandalous. A career as a midwife, matchmaker, or healer offered a respectable, even esteemed, means of economic livelihood for those widows protected by age. A widow of means might marry one of her deceased husband's slaves and make him her steward. Such an arrangement gave the woman a dominant voice in the disposition of her resources and facilitated her economic survival in a male-dominated environment. Society, however, definitely encouraged women to remarry, particularly those of child-bearing age. Constant wars resulted in a substantial number of broken households. The women who gathered to observe military ceremonies and publicly mourn war deaths understood the significance of high casualty rates. In these circumstances polygamy became necessary. Often a widow became a secondary wife to one of her deceased husband's brothers. This placed her in a regularly constituted household, an arrangement that offered both security and a respectable disposition of the social problem caused by widowhood.

Divorce existed for well-defined causes. Desertion, as well as proven physical abuse or failure to support the family, constituted grounds for a woman to sue for divorce. A husband could charge sterility or neglect of domestic duties. Under certain circumstances, a divorced woman retained custody of the children and half the community property, as well as the right to remarry. Divorce was probably rather infrequent, since a male ran the risk of offending his wife's family. A simpler solution to domestic unhappiness could be found by adding a secondary wife to the household. A woman, on the other hand, faced the social uncertainty and the attendant risks which divorce entailed. Except when desertion provided a clearcut case, as well as pressure to remarry, it is difficult to imagine many women seeking a divorce.

Children received loving but firm attention within the family. When a woman became pregnant, both families celebrated the impending birth. They tenderly referred to the child as a jewel, a precious quetzal feather, that graced and completed the family. The parents believed that the most important gift they could bestow on their children was to educate them to accept the harshness and unhappiness of life. Out of such resignation a measure of contentment could be achieved. As a result, a stiff formalism within the family circle covered the tenderness of the parents for their offspring. The respect taught the children for their elders rewarded the parents in their old age, when they lived out their last years as honored members of society.

SOCIAL STRUCTURE AND POWER

By the eve of the Spanish conquest, a class system, based to a large extent on political power, had emerged, with clearly demarked social roles and responsibilities for each group. The Mexica-Aztecs' tribal past, with its more egalitarian and essentially classless access to power and decision-making, remained only in theory. A far-flung military empire required centralized direction. Individual tribal members no longer influenced the course of events.

The political structure itself reflected the relatively simple, but functional, organization developed during the evolution of the Mexica from seminomadic tribesmen to their high point as the major power in the central Valley. The calpulli, an intragroup division, placed each individual within a basic institutional framework and bore primary responsibility for organizing the group's interaction within the broader society. Each calpulli had its own particular god, banners, and other elements of identification that set it apart as a separate unit. As the basic governing body, it assigned communal land rights and served as the individual's primary contact with the state bureaucracy. Headed by a *calpullec*, selected from a restricted number of families, the calpulli divided the society into from seven to fifteen sections.

The *nauhcampa*, a division of the city of Tenochtitlan into four quarters, overlay the calpulli system. Each quarter had certain social and economic responsibilities. It is evident that this division further refined access to power, with ruling elites coming from certain quarters. It may have been a means of discriminating against those of more recent Chichimeca origins. The various calpulli formed an advisory council, providing the elite with a way to gauge public support before making a sharp departure from tradition or undertaking an uncertain military campaign. Under normal conditions, the calpulli and nauhcampa served as administrative units rather than as legislative or consultive bodies.

Actual power had passed into the hands of a bureaucracy headed by a ruler and his principal assistant. The state's institutional legitimacy had already been accepted by the masses, and could rely on the twin pillars of the clergy and the military to sustain it. In theory, those who held office became nobles (*tecuhtli*) only as a consequence of their political function and not by birth. An aristocracy of merit, easy enough to satisfy in the early period of rapid expansion, came under increasing pressure with political maturity. The nobles tended to view their hold on public office, and the power that came with it, as deserved as well as earned. The slow growth of bureaucratic positions endangered the status of their offspring as well as the family itself. A hereditary nobility offered the undeniable attraction of preserving status and making their position in society independent of public office. This required a shift from privilege as a perquisite of office to the monopoly of economic resources as an inherited right, with office-holding only a part of that patrimony. Already the bureaucracy, including the standing army and the priesthood, consumed a large and ever-growing proportion of the fruits of empire. All that remained was to free the distribution of wealth from the constraints of political office.

Elements of a hereditary aristocracy had already emerged. The *pipiltin* (sons of lords) constituted a separate social group protected and favored by the tecuhtli. Nobles, according to established custom, received support as part of the head of state's household. They did not themselves engage in cultivation, but drew their support from the agriculturally based economy in several different fashions. Land in conquered areas might be assigned by the state to support the public office occupied by a noble, and the local inhabitants then supplied a labor tribute as part of their tax burden. Tenure in office, however, did not carry with it actual ownership or hereditary rights to the land. Often a son received his father's office, in which case the landed support continued, but this was not guaranteed by any legal rights.

Another means of support had evolved which vested nobles with private and hereditary ownership of land. Such titles to the land did not depend on any public function nor require confirmation by political authorities when ownership passed to the eldest son. *Mayeques*, a serf class attached to these private estates, added to their obvious economic value. Not considered part of a calpulli, they could not be sold separately from the land. Transfer of ownership of these private landholdings was possible, and the existence of transferable landed wealth offered the prospect of future concentration of resources. It is doubtful that very much alienation of property occurred, since a noble could call upon state resources in case of need. Nevertheless, the significance of this form of private land tenure for the evolution of an economically based hereditary nobility cannot be discounted.

Not all nobles lived in luxury as a result of public office. Many petty offices carried only modest support, while high officials naturally expected, as well as required, a handsome living as much for status as for comfort. Administrators above a certain rank constantly received gifts befitting their office, as well as household servants and other luxuries. On the other hand, a minor bureaucrat counted himself fortunate to acquire modest little tidbits that might soften the burden of his duties, but hardly changed his lifestyle. The opportunity to move up in the system existed, and could be speeded up by establishing a good military record.

Access to tecuhtli status was controlled, but not closed. An individual's proven merit opened the way to advancement from lower classes, as well as within the nobility itself. Distinguished military service led to advancement regardless of prior social class. Top military leaders and the officer corps enjoyed a personal status based on their military exploits, and the state recognized their influence by rewarding them politically. The common soldier who established a military reputation, thereby attaining status as well as demonstrating potential leadership qualifications, was absorbed into the nobility without regard for his low origins. Once within the tecuhtli class, his low origins might hinder his ability to function, but they did not bar his entrance to the group. Merit operated to drain leadership from the lower classes and reinvigorate the nobility.

In the struggle for upward mobility, the children of pipiltin inherited certain important advantages, while the lower class relied on abnormal individual effort. The *calmecac*, the highest level of education available in Mexica-Aztec society, did not totally exclude the lower class: however only exceptional individuals of humble origin could gain entrance. While the merchant class successfully exerted pressure to gain admittance, the calmecac's main function was to service the pipiltin. Attendance at one of the several calmecac schools attached to various temples was mandatory for entrance into political and clerical professions. It served as a barrier to the lower class and assured monopolization of the bureaucracy by the nobility, functioning not unlike the English public school system at the height of the British empire, when attendance at the "right schools" assured entrance and advancement in the imperial government. For similar reasons, the calmecac stressed mental and physical conditioning. If it could be said that "the fate of the British empire was decided on the playing fields of Eton," the same could as well be said of a calmecac education for the Aztecs. Severe and rigid, the school gave the sons of the ruling elite a shared spartan experience. While advanced knowledge and Mexica traditions received attention, self-sacrifice and discipline lay at the core of the system. Students slipped off alone at night into the mountains to offer incense to the gods, drawing blood from their legs and ears with agave thorns. Fasting and self-control learned under demeaning circumstances eliminated the weak and remade the strong. Understandably, those who survived viewed themselves as an elite bound together by a common bond.

In contrast, lower-class education did not demand a high degree of self-sacrifice and discipline, although military virtues were equally as important. Academic subjects such as history, interpretation of written records, and mathematics, that formed a part of the calmecac curriculum, could not be studied in the schools for commoners. Such schools, called *telpochcalli*, stressed vocational knowledge, not preparation for the ruling elite. One left both types of schools at the time of marriage or, in the case of the calmecac, beginning priestly religious functions.

Women's education reflected their subordinate and domestic role in a strictly pragmatic fashion, usually within the family itself or in a convent attached to a temple. Education, regardless of class or sex, reinforced the existing concepts of class and individual roles. The nobility and their offspring reserved the cultural advantages of an advanced education for themselves as much as possible. The requirement of a calmecac education for public office, coupled with family connection and a thinly disguised nepotism, gave the calmecac student all the advantages in obtaining a position as a tecuhtli through the civil or religious bureaucracy.

The merchants (*pochteca*), although legally commoners, occupied an uneasy position within the social structure. Not connected with office-holding and the wealth that accompanied state service, their social standing remained ambiguous. What power they possessed sprang from their careful use of assets to influence the political structure. While the nobility had begun the process of shifting their base of power from a political to an economic one, they were not ready to concede political power to those who already held economic power. On the other hand, the natural flow from economic control to political power could not be contained indefinitely. Already signs of the influence of merchant wealth could be identified. Access to calmecac education bestowed some of the status of the nobility on the pochteca. This important concession reflected their growing power and the attempt of the nobility to placate them. In theory, a calmecac education opened up the possibility of office-holding or entrance into the priesthood. Perhaps even more exciting to these commercial men, there was the prospect of acquiring land as an outlet for capital investment. The relatively limited amount of alienable land held by the nobility, coupled with the protection from economic pressures they enjoyed, made the transfer of land to the pochteca unlikely—yet the door had been opened.

Those restrictions which remained on the merchants indicated class competition as well as fear. The pochteca could not indulge in fine clothing, especially since the degrees of luxury dress indicated rank, nor could they construct palaces or otherwise increase their status by a public display of wealth. Spectacular feasts, to which they invited fellow merchants and members of the nobility, appear to have been one of the few legal outlets for their obvious desire for recognition. Arbitrary and artificial restrictions attempted to deny the merchants political influence. But as the empire expanded, and demand for distant as well as exotic products grew, society increasingly depended upon them. The merchants of Tlatelolco could not be swept aside, and in Texcoco they had the right to be heard on all economic matters. Taxation of merchants had to be mutually agreed upon by the state officials meeting with representatives of the pochteca. Merchant judges, totally apart from the normal judicial structure, regulated their disputes. Obviously, the nobility could not deny them indefinitely.

An interesting effort by the nobility to acquire some of the advantages of capital accumulation enjoyed by the merchants was the development of state trading. The flow of tribute from conquered territories resulted in a surplus that in theory should have been distributed to calpulli members, but in fact wealth not absorbed by the bureaucracy went into trade for the account of the state. Compelled to trade in state merchandise as well as their own, the pochteca in effect operated in direct partnership with the nobles, sometimes accepting commissioned goods for a share of the profit. In return for their valued service, the merchants claimed privileges and state protection. Garrisons protected trade routes, and any harm done a merchant resulted in swift and harsh action by Aztec armies. The ability of the pochteca to call upon the state's military force, and even direct military expansion into profitable new areas, was impressive. Caravans of merchants explored new economic and trade possibilities, often armed as well as disguised to avoid hostile acts. At their urging, Triple Alliance armies descended on rich and prosperous regions, bringing them into the Aztec economic and political network. Other Indian groups were aware of the connection between Aztec traders and military force. While an acceptable degree of mutual advantage had to be preserved, the use of force or its threat gave the pochteca the ultimate advantage.

In spite of the social progress of the pochteca, or perhaps because of it, the nobility viewed the merchant class with suspicion and removed restrictions on them only under pressure. The pochteca represented a commercial elite quite distinct from those who traded in the ordinary marketplace. With rare exceptions, they traded only with areas not under Aztec domination. As soon as a region had been conquered, tribute largely replaced commerce in the exotic items they usually dealt with, and the pochteca moved into different foreign trade channels.

Another important group apparently also undergoing significant long-range change was the craftsmen, or *amantecas*. On the surface they appeared to enjoy a secure, respected place within the class system, even if of lower status than the nobility. Their skills often received extravagant praise—yet, like the pochteca, their legal position was ambiguous. The public referred to them collectively as Toltecs, in recognition of the cultural debt of Tula, and the son of a noble might even become a craftsman without too much family disappointment. Different status levels existed within the class, based on skill or the material worked. Those involved in working fine or precious material could expect a higher degree of public appreciation. Intricate featherwork used as insignia of rank in Aztec society, or the elaboration of fine jewelry, entitled a craftsman to the respect due an artist. At the other extreme, those whose skills could not be classed as delicate, such as stonemasons, seldom rated the term "Toltec."

As a separate class, craftsmen purposely maintained a foreign and slightly exotic mystique. Lapidaries supposedly descended directly from the old culture of Xochimilco, and other craftsmen, representing the arts of Tula, remained culturally aloof from society. They worshiped separate and distinctly foreign gods. The featherworkers' divine patron, Coyotlenahual (he who masquerades as a coyote), allegedly founded Amantlan (the legendary land of the *amantecas*), and the goldsmiths' god, Xipe Totec, came from the coastal region. Actual foreign craftsmen mingled with those of Mexica-Aztec origin, adding to the exotic effect. The insistence on the alien origins of the amanteca class underscored their position of sufferance within society—certainly an appreciated group, but not an integrated part of the social structure.

Craftsmen depended almost totally on the nobility and the state for support. Many seemed to be retainers, while others worked for the state on various public projects. Society conceded them their own guild to deal collectively with higher authority; however, as a weak interest group they did not have their own judges nor access to a degree of noble status such as that acquired by the pochteca. Nevertheless, signs of a realignment of the craftsmen with the trading class had emerged. A small independent group offered their skills and products in the public market. The pochteca needed the production of these craftsmen in their trade, and increasingly pressured the nobles and the state for direct access to their skills. An alliance between craftsmen and traders, based on economic rather than political considerations, must have been a cause of concern to the nobility.

The great mass of people, the *macehualtin* (*macehualli*, singular), were organized on a lower level within the calpulli. Their role as workers carried many social responsibilities and few privileges. The term *macehualli* came from the word *macehualo*, meaning "to work to acquire merit"—obviously a lifetime struggle. Held in disdain by the more favored groups, the macehualtin expected only thinly disguised contempt in spite of their central role in the economy. The words *macehuallatoa* and *macehualtec*, derived from the terms for workers, meant to speak boorishly and to be vulgar. Contempt for the masses developed with the stratification of society, as the nobles and their offspring attempted to put as much distance between themselves and the lower classes as possible.

Dependent on the nobility, and the institutional structure

elaborated by them, the working class could be manipulated relatively easily. Over a period of time the central bureaucracy assumed many of the functions theoretically performed by the calpulli. Famine relief became a responsibility of the central authority. Judicial power, an important element of sovereignty, passed into the hands of the state bureaucracy. From the priestly wing of the nobility, the people received constant spiritual direction that influenced every aspect of their lives. Even their agricultural tasks conformed to a rhythm established and regulated by the clergy. Life and society had become so complex that such direction may have been welcomed with relief. Unquestionably, the state encouraged such reliance.

The macehualtin often faced severe economic pressure, especially in times of shortage and famine. While the state intervened to a certain extent to alleviate the impact of disaster, by distributing food or reducing tribute and tax burdens, it did not fully protect their social position in time of stress. As a result, there emerged a type of open-ended and temporary slavery that constituted a step down in status, but did not carry the same social stigma as slavery in the western European sense. The slaves *(tlacotin)* did not comprise an important group, either in numbers or economic activity. Many worked as household servants, the pochteca used some as bearers (although slaves from other regions, especially Mayan, seem to have been preferred for this task), and a limited number worked in other activities. The communal nature of agriculture, with reliance on the calpulli to assign land and labor, limited the need to use slaves in the fields. Only an estimated 5 percent of the population fell into the slave category. Lack of economic incentives, probably the most important factor, restricted development of a sizable slave class.

One became a slave in several ways. Judicial slavery for nonpayment of debts, or in order to make restitution for some injury or criminal activity, could be imposed by the state. An individual might also sell himself or his family into slavery, apparently a common enough practice in time of famine. The contract between the slave and the master could be terminated after an agreed time or by return of the original purchase price. Since the tlacotin could not be exempted from military service, they had plenty of opportunity to acquire booty and thus buy their freedom. The willingness of an individual to sell himself or his children into slavery, which so amazed the Spaniards, stemmed from the the fact that it did not have to be, nor was it likely to be, a permanent arrangement. In addition, a slave relied on well-defined rights which protected him from arbitrary and cruel treatment. The right to his labor did not imply ownership of his body. A master who stepped beyond these well-defined limits could be executed for causing harm to his slave. Children born to a slave did not automatically become the owner's property—hereditary slavery existed only in cases of high treason. A slave could own property, including other slaves, totally apart from his master's interests. Often a slave continued to live in his own house and attended his owner only during working hours.

An owner could transfer his rights to a slave's labor only for unsatisfactory performance. To be sold three times indicated bad behavior, and it made the slave liable for sacrifice by some pious individual as a personal offering to the gods. The slave still had one chance to escape such a fate. If he managed to struggle free in the marketplace while awaiting a purchaser and get to the central plaza and seat of central authority, he received his freedom on the spot. If anyone other than his owner tried to prevent him from securing supreme benevolence, it was considered a violation of the judicial process punishable by enslavement. However, slaves purchased outside Triple Alliance territory and resold served as immediate sacrificial victims and did not receive any legal protection.

If slavery had had a viable economic role in Aztec society, it would have been quite different; instead, it existed as a relatively minor institution, without pressing economic reasons to force its evolution along the lines of slavery in other regions. Its existence, along with that of the *mayeque* serf class (discussed below), did however provide the possibility of future development as the evolution toward an economic base of power advanced.

Numerically more important, and with a direct connection with the growing economic base of the nobles, were the mayeques, also referred to as *tlalmayeques*. Comprising slightly over 30 percent of the population, removed from the calpulli structure and its theoretical privileges and tribute responsibilities, they constituted a serf class. The mayeques did not have communal rights to land, but farmed the private landholdings of the nobility, with the bulk of their production going to the landholders. In land transfers they remained on the land, though they could not themselves be sold.

Once one became a member of this class, the opportunities for advancement were normally closed. Even the limited movement up to the macehualtin class, or into the open-ended slave system, could not be expected. The mayeque class apparently was expanding at the time of the Spanish conquest. Unincorporated groups displaced by war or famine might well be forced to join the serf class. An increasingly hard-pressed macehualtin may also have opted for the relative security of the mayeques. Increasing population pressures, with mounting demands on static land resources, forced part of the surplus population into their ranks.

Clearly, society was undergoing a stratification process. Upward movement by the nobility toward hereditary rights divorced from the necessity of holding public office, balanced by a downward movement of the great bulk of calpulli members, had commenced. The problem of the pochteca was in the process of being solved by its incorporation, however reluctantly, into the nobility.

THE IMPERIAL STRUCTURE

Not surprisingly, the empire, controlled by a society that had not consolidated or rationalized its own internal pressures, reflected many of the weaknesses of the dominant power. It remained an empire of conquest, united by the burden of tribute and taxation, without viable cultural and political institutions to develop common bonds. The symbol of Aztec sovereignty continued to be the *calpixque*, the resident tribute collector, who exploited his position to the maximum in occupied territory, confident that any disobedience would be punished by force of arms. Concern for the well-being of subject Indian groups appeared limited. In the case of famine or other disasters, Tenochtitlan might suspend tribute payments, but little else.

Passing Triple Alliance armies indeed seem to have constituted one such disaster, since they lived off the land, using force to extort or seize anything they desired. A feeling of being held hostage to Mexica power appears to have been the major element in the imperial relationship. Fear, rather than shared interest or cultural bonds, made for an uneasy and potentially rebellious empire. As a result, military and political authorities not only worried about unconquered hostile groups, but had to divert considerable energy to police those already subjugated. The fact that the Aztecs controlled a major portion of Mesoamerica testified only to their military might; continued domination depended on maintaining that strength. Institutions built on a degree of mutual advantage, which might have transferred a good deal of the burden from the military to less costly forms of control, did not develop. Nevertheless, the necessity of imperial integration was recognized, and at least superficially addressed.

Leaders of conquered groups clearly understood that their continuation in power depended upon the favor of Tenochtitlan. Established ruling families were often forced to intermarry with the Mexica nobility. Unfortunately, the motive appeared to be more to place a spy in their midst than to coordinate mutually advantageous interests. In an act symbolic of their approach to empire, the Aztecs imprisoned images of the gods of conquered groups in a special temple designed for that purpose in Tenochtitlan. Law, an important instrument of sovereignty in an integrated empire, was not extended to include others under Triple Alliance domination. Aztec rulers refused to compromise their power to act arbitrarily within the empire, thereby making it impossible to establish cooperation based on considerations other than force. Only in the area of trade is some limited respect for the principle of mutual advantage discernible. The extension of benefits as part of their rule, in the form of useful institutions, peace, or other manifestations of concern for the general well-being and prosperity of their imperial subjects, appears to have been almost totally absent. Military power remained virtually the only guarantor of empire.

PSYCHO-RELIGIOUS FOUNDATIONS

The acceptance of adversity exhibited by many Indian groups, and so admired by Western man, is both a virtue and a vice. When a people begins to anticipate hardship and disaster, fear, not acceptance, is the underlying emotion. The Mexica-Aztecs failed to balance pessimism with a more constructive view of life. An unhealthy foreboding, to the point of destructiveness, pervaded their thought. Religion, one of the most important expressions of Mexica culture, served more to indicate potential castastrophes than to reassure the people. Even the priests, who perhaps had a vested interest in doom since only they could ward it off with ritual sacrifices, seemed as much victims of cultural pessimism as any other group.

One of the most frightening events faced by each generation arrived every 52 years, at the end of an era, the equivalent of our century. Fearfully, all fires were extinguished, and crowds gathered on high slopes while priests, stationed on the mountaintops, anxiously awaited the first ray of light that signified the beginning of a new era. Once in the sky, the sun had to pass its zenith before one could be reasonably sure the rhythm of time would continue. Priests offered human sacrifices to the new sun (considered to be Huitzilopochtli in another form), opening the victim's chest cavity to spin the fire stick to relight the fires. Runners carried the new fire to all parts of the valley. Initial relief soon gave way to the normal uncertainty of survival.

Understandably, astrology played a vital role in Mexica society. The excessively high level of foreboding and uncertainty had to be pierced by an attempt to venture into the unknown world of the future. Unfavorable signs could paralyze rulers, delay battles, and perhaps even become self-fulfilling prophecies. On a lower level, individuals born under unfavorable signs believed themselves helplessly drawn into the expected fate. Unfortunately astrologers, like priests, could only foretell, not avert, the inevitable disaster. The scales of life could be tipped in one direction or the other, but eventually must move back.

Even their gods remained only marginally committed to the Mexica, and had to be constantly bribed by appropriate rites and offerings. Huitzilopochtli, the god of war and the sun, warmed and sustained the land only because his people supplied the required blood sacrifices. In his case, blood assured the strength necessary to battle the moon each night for survival, before rising at dawn to begin a new day in the dwindling timespan of the Aztecs. As the sun, Huitzilopochtli also required energy to attain his zenith. The superhuman efforts of the gods required a continual flow of the divine beverage—blood. Human sacrifice, believed only fitting since the gods themselves had sacrificed so much to establish the earth, did not however fully assure survival. It bought time, but not exemption from the inevitable collapse and disaster that would surely destroy the Mexica, and perhaps the world itself. Dread of the inevitable end resulted in a feverish and ever-growing volume of human sacrifices, as Aztec success and prosperity reached its zenith. The feeling that it was almost too good to last seems to have driven them to desperation. Blood sacrifices placed excessive pressure on the empire to supply human tribute, as well as on the military to take prisoners, and even on Mexica society itself. Sacrifices, as an important state service, placed an additional negative strain on the system.

The destructive nature of their religion is exemplified by the inclusion of Quetzalcóatl in the Aztec pantheon. Quetzalcóatl, the famed Feathered Serpent, had a vengeful role in direct opposition to the Mexica-Aztec state. According to Mexica beliefs, Quetzalcóatl, tricked and disgraced by Tezcatlipoca, another major deity, retired to the east (the male side of the world), vowing to return and destroy those in league with his enemies. Tezcatlipoca meanwhile destroyed Quetzalcóatl's followers, although evidently not totally, since the cult remained alive. By accepting one god in at least a temporarily dominant position, the Mexica seriously compromised themselves and risked the inevitable revenge of the Feathered Serpent. Quetzalcóatl represented the philosophical opposition to Huitzilopochtli, since he did not believe in human sacrifices and in fact supported many beliefs close to those of Christianity. Aztec efforts to appease and soften his revenge could only be minimal, because one dared not anger Huitzilopochtli. Yet priests called themselves followers of Quetzalcóatl even as they ripped open the chests of their victims. The center of culture, the calmecac, supposedly received Quetzalcóatl's protection, in spite of teaching beliefs in opposition to him. At the same time that he was venerated in Tenochtitlan, the Aztecs conceded that he would return from the east to destroy it. In effect the Mexica worshiped the instrument of their own destruction. In the end, the approach of the Spaniards from the east justified their fear of mortal danger from that direction.

Aztec religion did not develop as a binding force for the people or their empire, but rather as a rationalization for failure. Moreover, the Mexica-Aztecs of the Triple Alliance lacked a sense of mission. Perhaps because they were culturally insecure, knowing full well their debt to the Toltecs, it was impossible for them to believe that they had a civilizing mission that justified conquest and expansion. This lack of mission, coupled with the expectation of disaster, constituted one of the most important weaknesses of the Aztecs.

THE RISE OF MOCTEZUMA II

As success mounted, contemplation of the inevitable disaster became increasingly more painful. The Mexica could accept, in abstract, the notion that a marginal tribe, such as they had been when they arrived in the central Valley, might be annihilated, but the thought that their impressive empire would be destroyed seemed too much to bear. The general foreboding evident in Aztec society, coupled with unrest and gloom over the increased demand for sacrificial victims from the Mexica themselves, posed a threat to the state's continued existence. Deification of the chief of state, calculated to breach the gap between helpless mortality and the all-powerful divine state, would appreciably lower the degree of tension. Obviously useful for purposes of control, since one does not revolt against a god, this represented an attempt to bridge the uncertainty and mounting sense of doom inherent in the culture. When Ahuítzotl became chief in 1486, he proclaimed himself Huitzilopochtli's high priest; it now remained for his successor, Moctezuma II, to unite both god and priest in his own person.

Moctezuma II had a well-established reputation as a holy man, even maintaining his own private quarters in the central pyramid of Huitzilopochtli. His selection by the small ruling elite as chief seemed quite natural. As tradition demanded, Moctezuma II took to the field of battle, attacking the cities of Nopallin and Icpatepec, and returned with thousands of captives. These sacrificial victims provided more than enough blood for the gods, as well as for the ritual washing of his feet that constituted part of the ceremony of assuming power. Moctezuma's coronation was the most elaborate in Mexica history. Enemies of the house mingled with ruling groups from distant regions and watched as over 5,000 prisoners mounted the sacrificial stairs. The ceremony clearly moved Moctezuma II beyond mortal status. No longer could one look into his face, and as he passed through the streets his subjects prostrated themselves, pressing their faces into the earth. Any breach of etiquette became a spiritual failing to be punished by death. The year was 1503, eleven years after Christopher Columbus had broken the cultural isolation of the New World.

Such changes, although they appear evolutionary in retrospect, occasioned some political resistance. As a result, Moctezuma purged his army and the bureaucracy. To solidify support among the nobility, he ended the aristocracy of merit. No longer would it be possible for the exceptional individual of humble origins to rise to the top. Moreover, those of macehualtin background were removed from office and replaced with those of noble birth. In return for such favors, the nobility had to recognize the distance between themselves and the head of state. A demeaning code of conduct, befitting the relationship between men and a god, was imposed on the nobility. Such purges, power struggles, and innovations caused unrest as society attempted to adjust to them. As a consequence, captive groups seized the opportunity to revolt, requiring the army to be constantly on the move. The Enemies of the House, in a similar if more restrained fashion, challenged Moctezuma's power. Indeed, the military forces of the Triple Alliance found themselves overextended.

The macehualtin thus came under even more pressure at a time when the benefits of empire had been largely taken from their hands. The nobility seemed insatiable, demanding land, labor, sacrificial victims, and increased military service, offering in return only further sacrifices and misery. The institutional structure and intimidation, not loyalty, served to keep them under control. And to add to the considerable burden of the lower class, crop failures occurred in 1505 and 1507.

Moctezuma's attempts to strengthen his political position and overcome psychological weaknesses by becoming a personification of Huitzilopochtli caused great social strain. The state was in the process of a shuddering adjustment to centralized power in the hands of a god-chief, served by a closed nobility of inherited virtues, supported on the backs of a population being pushed downward. Such momentous changes caused repercussions throughout Mesoamerica.

While it is obvious that Moctezuma II faced a great deal of opposition, it is not equally certain that he would have failed. He temporarily weakened the state to restructure Mexica society. The excesses and the high level of intimidation would sooner or later have had to be modified to reestablish an acceptable balance between the classes. Moctezuma, however, could hardly have selected a less propitious moment. Already rumors of strange visitors approaching from the east had reached his ears. From 1507 on, news of these mysterious strangers became a constant source of concern.

Chapter 4

THE BIRTH OF
NEW SPAIN,
1519-1530

CONSOLIDATION of Spanish power in the Antilles, following Columbus' discovery of the New World, proceeded
at a rapid if erratic pace. The West Indian islands served not
only as a base, but also as an important field for experimentation.
There had been no direct preparation for the monumental task
of cultural adjustment that had to occur if the region was to
be brought into some reasonable relationship with the Western
world—both the Europeans and the Indians were surprised by
their mutual discovery. Unlike European penetration of Africa,
which occurred after long periods of familiarity on both sides,
the discovery of America broke over the European world with a
suddenness that left no time for leisurely adjustment. Important
questions that influenced the nature of Spanish rule in the entire
hemisphere were first faced in the islands. Whether or not the
Indians possessed souls, what rights the discoverers had to their
labor, the political and interpersonal relations between them—all
had to be resolved.

The Spaniards learned some valuable lessons at the expense of the inhabitants of the islands. From an imperial standpoint, the Antilles experience indicated the limits of Crown political and moral authority in the face of distant Spanish frontier settlements and the demands of highly self-centered adventurers. The Crown soon became aware that its planning and financial abilities were not equal to the task. Those Europeans who went to the Indies on voyages of discovery must do so without royal support. Only a thin façade of Crown authority covered the personal efforts of individual *conquistadores*. They went for adventure as well as profit. The booty capitalism of the *reconquista* (the Christian reconquest of the Iberian peninsula from the Moors) carried on through the discovery of America.

THE CONQUEST OF TENOCHTITLAN

The conquest of Mexico occurred in a different framework from that of the islands. A degree of familiarity with Indian cultures, and the comforting knowledge that one could fall back on permanent island settlements, made probing of the Mexican mainland less a rush into the unknown. Spanish activity along the coast of Mexico proceeded at a cautious, but ever more frequent, rate after 1507. Information on the extent of the landmass and the nature of the population, much of it vague but nevertheless useful, began to accumulate. Two major expeditions that preceded that of Fernando Cortés added significantly to the store of information available to potential discoverers. Hernández de Córdoba, blown onto the Yucatán coast by a hurricane in 1517, discovered impressive evidence of a high civilization. He also found that the Mayas were less than friendly, and after a severe defeat in Campeche returned to the islands. The following year, Cuban Governor Diego Velásquez decided to verify Córdoba's reports by sending out another expedition, commanded by Juan de Grijalva, which explored the coastline as far north as Tabasco. Grijalva and his men, short of food and travel-weary, returned to Cuba taking with them some exquisite gold jewelry, Indian artifacts, and several captives, as well as news of a powerful and rich city somewhere in the interior. Governor Velásquez, now quite excited, immediately set about organizing another expedition, to be commanded by Fernando Cortés.

Cortés seemed a good choice at the time. The governor knew him to be a resourceful and energetic individual who had at one time fallen out with him, but had subsequently proved his loyalty. Moreover, Cortés had experience in various island raids and campaigns, and was familiar with the island's indigenous population. In short, he was about as experienced an American hand as one could find in the Indies. As was usual in the early voyages of discovery, Velásquez and Cortés agreed to finance the expedition between them.

While preparations for the impending expedition went forward in Cuba, the Spanish presence along the coast had been noted in Tenochtitlan. Moctezuma II and his immediate advisors wrestled with the problem of whether or not the strangers, approaching from the east in what seemed to be floating temples, were the advanced contingent of Quezalcóatl's avenging army. The correct response to these intrusions could not be decided upon until the nature of the strangers was known. Moctezuma had received sketchy and inconclusive reports, through Mayan channels, on the Córdoba expedition. The following year, the four ships of Juan de Grijalva's expedition provided the first direct observation of the Spaniards by the Mexica-Aztecs. The resident *calpixque* in Cuetlaxtlan and his retinue, disguised as traders, had questioned the Spaniards as to their intent. After receiving some beads as a gift, they rushed to Tenochtitlan with the news. Reporting directly to Moctezuma II, they relayed the Europeans' promise to return within a year, as well as their own general impressions. Before more information could be gathered, the Spaniards returned to Cuba, leaving Moctezuma in a state of anxious uncertainty, still unsure of the proper stance to adopt.

The expected return of the mysterious strangers, this time under Fernando Cortés, occurred on April 21, 1519. Not a very impressive expedition in military terms, with only 400 men, twelve cannons, and a few horses, it nevertheless caused great apprehension in the Aztec capital. Cortés had been forced to launch his expedition prematurely because of a squabble with Governor Velásquez—departing, as a result, without proper supplies. Cortés, however, had a number of important advantages, including the advice of Pedro de Alvarado, who had accompanied the 1518 Grijalva expedition. Proceeding cautiously, Cortés stopped to ransom a Spanish captive held by the Mayas, who provided information—and most important, language skills.

Fernando Cortés believed his expedition to be a Christian crusade—hence discovery became, in essence, a spiritual revelation, with God directing, as well as protecting, the Spaniards. Already familiar with elements of the Indian religion, Cortés had no doubt that an important part of his task was to introduce the natives to Christianity, by force if necessary. The fruits of conquest could be expected to follow in full measure, because God rewarded His servants in a material as well as spiritual sense. With little rationalization, the Europeans envisioned themselves as the forces of salvation come to do battle for the souls of the deluded inhabitants of the region. Cortés' strong sense of mission complemented a desire for the fruits of conquest. Ironically, the fatal weakness that crippled Moctezuma, and stayed the hand of his army, was also psychological.

From a purely military standpoint, the Mexica-Aztecs could easily have repelled the Cortés expedition in its early stages. Well organized, in contrast to the loosely ordered and highly individualist adventurers who accompanied Cortés, the Mexica divided their soldiers into 20-man squads combined into larger units of 400 under the command of a *tiachcauh*, often a member of the prestigious Eagle or Jaguar knights. Their weapons, mainly hand ones like those of the Spaniards, included the paddle-shaped *macana*, with sharp pieces of obsidian set in rows like shark's teeth. A macana could decapitate a horse with one blow. A variety of spears, complemented by the *atlatl* or spear-thrower, lances, bows and arrows, and blowguns completed their arsenal. Cotton-padded armour, subsequently adopted by the Europeans, protected the warriors.

The invaders had the arquebus and cannon, deadly weapons but cumbersome and requiring reloading, which proved inconvenient and often fatal in the rush of battle. Horses offered some tactical advantage; however, the Indians soon learned to deal with them. Militarily, Cortés' small force, even with their more advanced weaponry, should not have proved much of a problem. Once the Spaniards allied themselves with other Indian groups, however, the military advantages of the Mexica-Aztecs were cancelled. It was imperative that the Spaniards be destroyed on the coast. Tragically, the Aztec army stood by while Moctezuma II struggled with the issue of whether these were gods or invaders.

While Moctezuma sought to acquire information that could resolve the terrible uncertainty, Cortés readily gathered intelligence on the nature of the Aztec empire as well as its religious beliefs, including the destructive myth of the return of Quetzalcóatl. The gifts offered the Spaniards, the ritual presentation by nobles squatting before Cortés, after symbolically degrading themselves by touching a finger to the earth and placing it upon their lips, all confirmed the confusion of the Indians. By shrewdly exploiting Moctezuma's uncertainty, Fernando Cortés bought the time necessary to ally himself with the Indian enemies of Tenochtitlan and convert his small force into an impressive army of Indians and Spaniards.

The Spaniards had two interpreters—Jerónimo de Aguilar, the Mayan-speaking Spaniard picked up earlier, and Malinche, one of the 20 maidens given to Cortés by the Indians of Potonchán in Tabasco. Malinche, called by the Spaniards Doña Marina, proved to be a valuable member of the invading force. Since she spoke both Náhuatl and Maya, she communicated with Cortés through Aguilar. In time she became the conqueror's mistress and trusted advisor.

In spite of Moctezuma's entreaties to stay away from Tenochtitlan, Cortés and his army relentlessly proceeded toward the seat of the empire. A victory over Tlaxcala resulted in an important alliance that in the end proved decisive. The Tlaxcalan alliance now forced Moctezuma II to take action, even though the question of the invader's divine status had not been settled. The growing military and political isolation of Tenochtitlan posed too serious a threat to be ignored. Calling upon Huitzilopochtli and Tezcatlipoca for support, Moctezuma prepared to take on the gods. Mexica guides now directed Cortés and his men to approach the capital by way of Cholula. If all went according to plan, Cortés would be taken by surprise and delivered as a prisoner.

Warned by his allies to expect treachery, Cortés carefully noted the hostile preparations underway in Cholula. Malinche managed to ferret out details of the plan, enabling Cortés to move first by butchering over 3,000 men in little more than two hours of slaughter. The Tlaxcalan allies joined in the melee and sacked the city.

Huitzilopochtli's temple, in ruins, served as a makeshift shrine for the Virgin Mary.

The psychological shock to the Aztecs was devastating. Foreigners who violated all the established rules of conduct and warfare had gained a startling and bloody triumph. Stunned and frightened, Moctezuma saw no way of avoiding contact with Cortés, and refused to listen to those who continued to plead for an all-out effort to destroy the Spaniards before it became too late. To the Aztec leader the Europeans appeared invincible, and he fearfully resigned himself to the loss of his empire.

Moctezuma's enemies multiplied as his powers waned. Indian groups rushed to ally themselves with the new conquerors and surrendered their sovereignty to Cortés. On November 8, 1519, the Spaniards finally set foot on one of the causeways leading into Tenochtitlan. Moctezuma II, carried on a richly adorned litter, came out the meet Cortés—one of the most fateful meetings in human history. The Spaniards, conducted into the city along with their Tlaxcalan friends, were lodged on the west side of the temple enclosure in the palace of Axayácatl. Cortés, well aware that his success depended upon psychological factors that could soon change, was determined to seize Moctezuma II as a hostage. Using the pretext of a clash between Spaniards and Aztecs at Veracruz, he took Moctezuma prisoner in his own palace, transferring him to his headquarters, and proceeded to govern Tenochtitlan through the emotionally exhausted ruler.

The vast empire, and the military power of the Mexica-Aztecs, had been immobilized by a classic coup d'état. At the same time, the seizure of Moctezuma weakened his authority. When he ordered his nobles to meet with him in his new quarters, many of them refused. Opponents of appeasement now felt free to press for action against the invaders. Many nobles did not accept the idea of Spanish divinity, and the behavior of the Europeans in the capital made it even more certain that they were men, not gods. The greed, the destruction of beautiful objects by melting them down into bullion, and the wanton conduct of some of the intruders shocked the Mexica. Moctezuma's decree ending human sacrifices, at the insistence of Cortés, alienated the priests. It was only a question of time before Moctezuma's legitimacy would be undermined by his puppet status. It only remained for the nobles to pull themselves together to fill the power vacuum and end the authority of their imprisoned ruler. Unfortunately, this could not be accomplished very rapidly; a consensus of opinion to support such a move had to develop. Moctezuma II rather pitifully sensed his declining power and the growing contempt of the nobles.

At the end of April 1520 news reached the capital of the arrival of more Spaniards, commanded by Pánfilo de Narváez, with a warrant for Cortés' arrest issued by the governor of Cuba. Unlike his captive, Cortés wasted little time; rushing down to the coast, he met the challenge head on, convincing Narváez's men to desert their commander and join him. The Tenochtitlan garrison meanwhile had been entrusted to Pedro de Alvarado. Cortés' absence, and the evident split between the Europeans, offered an excellent opportunity to revolt. An emissary from Narváez secretly informed Moctezuma that Cortés did not exercise legitimate authority, and in fact should be considered an outlaw—but the demoralized Moctezuma could not make the attempt to regain control.

The idea that the Spaniards represented the avenging Quetzalcóatl no longer weakened the resolve of the Indians. The nobles began the process of restructuring politically, in order to undertake decisive action against the invaders. This required a reaffirmation of the rhythm of life, to demonstrate that the institutional structure continued to function. Therefore, they celebrated the festival of the month of Toxcatl as scheduled. The extended ceremony, involving most of the nobility, represented a cultural rallying to meet the grave threat posed by the twin misfortunes of a political vacuum and the Spanish presence. The masses of unarmed men taking part in the ceremony alarmed Pedro de Alvarado, who correctly identified the threat, but incorrectly judged it to be an immediate danger to the small band of Spaniards garrisoned in Tenochtitlan. As a result, Alvarado forced the issue by falling upon the Indian nobles within the temple enclosure on the evening of May 21, 1520. The massacre cut down the flower of Mexica leadership and weakened the subsequent attempt to reestablish Mexica-Aztec power, but at the time it precipitated an immediate siege of the garrison. The Europeans became prisoners in the heart of the city. Control of the now thoroughly discredited chief of state proved useless to guarantee their safety: Moctezuma II, forced to plead for calm on the roof of the palace, received jeers and stones from the people. He deserved little else.

Cortés hurried back from the coast and entered the city, only to become part of the besieged garrison. Food, supplies, and the well dug by the trapped men could not sustain them for any extended period. Escape presented the only alternative to starvation. Cortés demanded that Moctezuma arrange for resupplying the garrison, to which the Aztec ruler responded that only a high-ranking noble could accomplish it and asked that his brother Cuitláhuac be released. In desperation Cortés agreed, only to watch in dismay as Cuitláhuac, asserting his claims of legitimacy, rallied the Mexica for the final destruction of the Spaniards.

Immediate flight now became essential, and on the evening of June 30, covered by darkness, the desperate attempt was made. The confusion and panic among the Spanish soldiers can be imagined, as they hurried toward the Tlacopan causeway in a light rain that mercifully muffled the sound of their retreat. The alarm, however, was soon given, and the Europeans and their Tlaxcalan allies became open targets, pursued from the rear and attacked from all sides of the causeway by warriors in canoes. The last few breaks in the causeway were bridged by the survivors on the trampled bodies of their comrades. Several hundred Spaniards in the rear guard found themselves pressed back to the steps of the temple pyramid and taken prisoner. According to Juan Cano, one of the conquistadores, these were some of Narváez' men whom Cortés deliberately sacrificed by misleading them as to the rendezvous, thus forcing them to serve as a diversionary force while the main body of Europeans escaped. Subsequently they served as sacrificial victims, adding their blood to help strengthen Huitzilopochtli's last supreme effort.

While the remaining Spaniards referred to their flight as the *noche triste* (sad night), it represented only a partial victory for the Mexica. An attempt to destroy the remnants of Cortés' group failed at Otumpan, as they slipped through to Tlaxcala and safety. The fact that Cortés retained the support of his Indian allies made the *noche triste* only a serious setback, rather than a total disaster, for the Spaniards. Now Tenochtitlan itself became a besieged city under attack by foreign forces. Inside the island fortress, the Europeans left a fifth column in the form of epidemic disease—smallpox, new to the region, swept through a population totally without immunity. Within two months it had carried away thousands, including Cuitláhuac himself.

Cuauhtémoc succeeded Cuitláhuac and attempted to rally the empire to the defense of Tenochtitlan. As the ring closed around the city, former allies dropped away. Texcoco, a major city in the old Triple Alliance, became Cortés' siege headquarters. Important maize sources, vital to the sustenance of the city, were sealed off by the Spaniards. In the end, the only allies Cuauhtémoc rallied were refugee warriors and their leaders—undoubtedly useful in the face of an impending siege, but not sufficient to prevent the isolation of the capital. The siege of Tenochtitlan represented the final act in the drama that began in 1519. In actual fact the battle had already been lost in the crumbling ruins of the Mexica empire. The cutting of the Chapultepec aqueduct on May 31, 1521, signaled the beginning of the struggle for the city. Spanish artillery now proved decisive in the fixed siege warfare. Reduction of the Xoloco fortress opened the southern causeway into the city, enabling Cortés to enter the central temple area. Tlatelolco now became the only viable defense perimeter. Demoralized Mexica warriors began to desert, disguised as other Indian groups, and those who remained conceded that they had been beaten.

The bitter struggle now fell on the Tlatelolcans. Spanish control of the lake with their brigantines, constructed in segments and brought up to Texcoco for assembly, gave them the necessary naval power to pound the remaining defenses and intercept supply canoes. Starvation, dysentery, and lack of war materials made Indian resistance, in the face of the impossible odds, an impressive display of courage. Tlatelolco, like Tenochtitlan, had to be reduced stone by stone. The tragic end came with the capture of Cuauhtémoc by Spanish ships. Dressed in pitiful rags, Cuauhtémoc rose in his war canoe ready to do battle. As Spanish crossbows took aim, the sheer hopelessness, the vast amount of death and destruction, overcame him, and the last of the Mexica warrior chiefs laid down his weapons. Over 40,000 bodies stacked like wood in the ruined buildings, decomposed and mutilated corpses floating in the canals and lake, provided mute evidence of the magnitude of the struggle. Death and its stench moved from Huitzilopochtli's temple to cover the entire land—Quetzalcóatl had exacted his revenge.

The consequences of defeat were extremely harsh. The pitiful remains of the Mexica-Aztecs streamed out of the ruins to be met by bands of Spanish and Indian allies who seized their remaining possessions. All were subject to a violent search for booty. The old, sick, wounded, and women received no compassion in the flush of victory. Slavery, on the grounds that they had revolted against the authority of the king of Spain, was imposed on thousands. Cuauhtémoc was tortured in an effort to make him reveal the location of treasure. Well might an unknown poet write:

> We know it is true
> that we must perish,
> for we are mortal men.
> You, the Giver of life,
> You have ordained it.
>
> . . . . . .
>
> We wander here and there
> in our desolate poverty.
> We are mortal men.
> We have seen bloodshed and pain
> where once we saw beauty and valor.

Suddenly, and incredibly, the natural evolution of Mesoamerican civilization ceased. In the future, Western civilization, as interpreted by Spain, would merge with Indian culture to form a new hybrid mestizo society.

SOCIAL ORGANIZATION AFTER THE CONQUEST

Collapse of the Mexica-Aztec empire in August of 1521 marked a high point in the military strength of the Europeans and the Indian allies operating under their direction. While the conquest was an impressive feat, the pacification and organization of the region, now aptly called New Spain, constituted an even more difficult task. Military force alone was insufficient. If the conquest was to remain permanent, Cortés must move rapidly to consolidate his victory politically.

Indian society in general, including the defeated Mexica, underwent a trauma of unimagined magnitude. The natives had to be reassured and incorporated into an acceptable institutional structure that guaranteed a reasonable degree of order and predictability. In his letters to Emperor Carlos V, Cortés stressed repeatedly that he hoped to establish Spanish sovereignty in the region. It now remained for the conqueror to make good his promise. The destruction of the city of Tenochtitlan–Tlatelolco did not endanger the established lines of authority of other Indian groups which remained functional. Many had already indicated their willingness to accept Spanish control in place of that of the Mexica-Aztecs. Cortés emphasized the political continuity of the central Valley's domination of Mesoamerica by deciding to build the Spanish city of Mexico on the ruins of Tenochtitlan.

Ironically, the presence of the conquistadores, and the other Spaniards who flocked in to feast upon the corpse of the Aztec empire, complicated the task of creating a governing structure. Bold adventurers did not easily become settlers or bureaucrats. Their goals were often immediate and limited: plunder and a hoped-for return to Spain as rich men had driven them to face the dangers of conquest. They had to be diverted from such fantasies to more long-term and stable aspirations. The Indian population also required adjustments. The lower class could not be expected to live in insecurity without endangering food production as well as the economic potential of the region. Very quickly the Europeans had to make a transition from plundering the natives in an irregular fashion to a regulated tribute or tax system which would not disrupt Indian society, but would still provide spoils for the conquerors. The native ruling class also had to be brought into a governing partnership that could guarantee order and cooperation. Christianity and Spanish law, major elements of sovereignty as well as powerful instruments of social control, had to be introduced. Obviously the establishment of Spanish rule required a keen sense of the needs of both the Indians and Spaniards, as well as an impressive degree of administrative talent. Cortés possessed both, accounting to a great extent for the relatively smooth transition of sovereignty from Indian to European hands.

Traditional Spanish organizational models provided a basic framework. Many of these had originally developed to incorporate the Moslems into Spanish society. Historically, the municipality had functioned as a primary political and administrative unit; in times of disorder it was capable of becoming a self-contained regional governing body. Faced with a frontier situation, Cortés automatically turned to a municipal structure. He had already utilized it when he established the first Spanish municipality at Veracruz, complete with the necessary officers, in order to resign his commission from the governor of Cuba and accept the mandate conferred by his own creation. Cortés' transparent manipulation of municipal authority nevertheless enabled him to claim the legitimate right to conquer the Mexica-Aztecs. The municipal structure contained all the elements of the state: *regidores* (councilmen) and *alcaldes* (judges), supported by administrative and enforcement officers, formed legislative and judicial bodies; as the legitimate representative of Castilian sovereignty, Cortés exercised executive authority.

A hierarchy of urban centers extended the basic administrative network to other areas, to hold the nascent Spanish state together. A designated city served as the head *(cabecera)* of a district which included secondary centers *(villas)*, which in turn controlled *pueblos* (villages) surrounded by small dependencies *(lugares)*. In theory, an order issued by the executive filtered down through this basically municipal structure to every last little place in New Spain. In fact, however, the many control layers enabled local interests to modify central directives to fit their own particular circumstances; nevertheless, an executive authority was recognized. Indian rulers became part of the system. Indigenous settlements of recognized and customary importance continued to operate, with their chiefs now recognized as hereditary rulers and invested by the Spaniards with governing power as *gobernadores*. Reinforced by status and position conferred by the post-conquest Spanish state, the *caciques* (a Caribbean term meaning "chief" which the Europeans introduced in Mexico) bore a major responsibility for order. Thanks to the Indian nobility and their recognized legitimacy, Cortés was able to minimize political disruption in the immediate post-conquest period.

The integration of Indian lines of authority with those of the conquerors resolved only part of the adjustment problem. An interconnected and most pressing question involved the redistribution of wealth to include—in some acceptable fashion—the Europeans. The tribute system, well understood by both the Spaniards and the Indians, appeared to offer the best solution to provide formal Spanish access to New Spain's wealth. The Indians accepted tribute as a reasonable form of taxation. Once again Spanish experience provided the model. The *encomienda*, developed during the Spanish reconquest, placed tribute-paying groups under the authority of an *encomendero*, who in return provided protection for his tributaries. The Crown restricted the institution, because its feudal aspects undermined the power of the monarchy and permitted private authority to stand between the king and his subjects. As a result the *encomienda* declined in the Old World, only to take on a new life in the islands and now on the mainland of America. Cortés, well aware of the Crown's attitude and of the sad deterioration of the island's Indians under the encomienda system, justified its introduction on the grounds of absolute necessity. As early as March of 1522, Cortés granted encomiendas to his followers. Characteristically, but perhaps deservedly, he reserved numerous encomienda towns for himself.

Tribute under the encomienda system could be in the form of labor, goods, or a mixture of the two; the amount of tribute remained open until later Crown regulations resolved the question. In practice, an individual encomendero negotiated directly with an Indian cacique for all that he could get, without concerning himself with how it was assessed or collected. A skillful cacique could minimize the amount of tribute extracted, or perhaps even become the encomendero's partner in exploitation. The fact that the individual Spaniard did not live in the midst of his tributaries, preferring the safety and comfort of the towns, made the caciques' cooperation vital. Spaniards often complained of being robbed by chiefs, probably with some justification.

Theoretically, in return for tribute, an encomendero provided his tributaries with guidance and protection. In actual fact his most important obligation was to the state, in the form of military assistance. An encomendero maintained an armed and horsed group of retainers able, and presumably willing, to defend European authority in case of Indian rebellion. The encomienda system permitted Cortés to reward his followers, and at the same time to counter Crown demands to end it with the rhetorical question of who else could be expected to defend Spanish sovereignty, if not the suitably rewarded conquistadores. Unable to answer such a challenge immediately, Crown officials grudgingly accepted the encomienda, at least as an interim measure. In operation the system varied from region to region, depending on the nature of the population and economic factors.

The encomienda system by itself was not an acceptable redistribution of wealth. Land and labor represented the true economic riches of the country—therefore Spanish access to both had to be directly facilitated. In 1523 the Crown authorized Cortés to grant land to deserving Spaniards based on their social position, prior services, or the usefulness of their current function. The Crown specified that such grants should not be made at the expense of already existing Indian holdings, whether communal or private. Cortés had already moved in that direction, acquiring for himself extensive territories formerly owned by Moctezuma II. Complementary encomienda grants supplied labor and materials. By 1529 his holdings produced maize, wheat, cotton, beans, grapes, and sugar cane, in addition to cattle, horses, and sheep. One of Cortés' first acts following the fall of Tenochtitlan was to request seeds, cuttings, and breeding stock. By doing so, the conqueror indicated his desire to settle, as well as his realization that the true wealth of the country lay in its land and labor. Cortés set the agricultural model for others to follow. His sugar mill at Tuxtla (now in the state of Veracruz) turned a profit by 1524, just three years after the collapse of the Mexica-Aztecs. While most Spaniards lacked the political advantages of the conqueror, all coveted a solid landed economic base, hopefully complemented by an encomienda grant that would provide labor tribute and a handy financial subsidy.

Land owned by the Mexica-Aztec nobility could be reallocated on the legal grounds of rebellion against the Spanish monarchy, and the holdings once used to support a particular office now belonged to the successor state. In addition, Cortés did not hesitate to reduce the landholdings of the Indian nobility or to reassign rights to more convenient areas. In Cuauhtitlán, for example, he stripped the cacique of inherited property in Chalco and other distant regions, assigning him local land as compensation. Many caciques found themselves shuffled into poverty and reduced to arguing over the relative merits of each piece of land. Agricultural holdings devoted to the support of the Aztec state religion also became available. As a result, seizure of large amounts of Indian communal property did not appear necessary in the early period. Usurpation of Indian land occurred gradually, and to varying degrees in different regions, assisted by the population decline that became a major factor later in the century.

Significant legal and cultural obstacles to land transfer were overcome during the initial organization of New Spain. The concept of inalienable land rights could not be accepted by the Spanish settlers. The use of force alone to bring about a redistribution of wealth, however, could not be accepted by either Indians or the Spaniards. Land titles required legal defenses to protect future tenure, and as a result European settlers insisted on legal façades to cover their acquisition of land, and were willing to pay dearly for confirmation of titles. The Indians themselves soon learned the value of *títulos* and notarial documents in the struggle to preserve their hold on the land.

Municipal councils assigned land, subject to royal confirmation. This gave them a powerful form of political patronage which undoubtedly strengthened their hand in the fight to impose order in the newly pacified territories of New Spain. Legally, communal land could not be granted to Europeans by the municipal councils, but once obtained it might be recognized by local authorities. The mechanism for transferring communal land to private holdings developed from the tribute feature of the encomienda. Tribute in effect constituted a legal debt owed by a particular group. In order to raise the required payment, the Indian town government or the gobernadores legally disposed of communal assets, including the theoretically inalienable land. Rental of land on a perpetual basis also constituted its effective alienation. Limitless possibilities for fraud and collusion between caciques and Europeans existed, especially in the organizational stage.

Municipal councils also granted *estancias*—grazing rights— that conveyed land-use rights over a wide area after the crops had been harvested. Cortés initially encouraged the establishment of estancias, in order to break New Spain's dependence on the islands, whose cattle monopoly allowed them to charge outrageous prices. Estancia rights enabled European settlers to acquire the use of Indian land, and subsequently attempt to drive the natives out. As early as the 1540s Indians complained of extensive crop damage caused by uncontrolled estancia stock. Complicating regulation of the estancia was the fact that some land was held in full property rights, usually enough for corrals and necessary structures, creating a nucleus which a shrewd individual could add to piece by piece, hoping at a future date to confirm de-facto titles. Viceroy Mendoza, after his arrival in 1535, attempted to gain control of the estancia situation by issuing grants covering already existing operations, then moving to make the Europeans abide by legal restrictions. Spanish pressure on Indian land, while beginning almost immediately, did not become a serious problem until after the Cortés period. Nevertheless, the essential pattern had been set.

The landed estate, as it developed during the early years of Spanish rule, reflected the goals of the European settlers. Although primarily a profit-making enterprise, it also encompassed the intangibles of status. Those Spaniards who played a part in the conquest itself, and those who soon followed, hoped to establish themselves and their families in both an economic and social sense. Cortés himself was destined to become one of the *grandes* (highest-ranking nobles) of the Spanish American empire, and others, while not able to aspire to such heights, desired to become *hidalgos* (gentry). One might arrive as a *peón* (foot-soldier), but soon claimed the honor of a *caballero* (horseman). Surrounded by a discredited Indian culture, served by tribute-paying natives, and fully conscious of their superiority, the early Spanish settlers could overlook their own humble backgrounds and attempt to become lords of the land. The encomendero's obligation to maintain an armed retinue, although often ignored, endowed the emerging European elite with some of the mystique of Spain's reconquest. The landed estate became a Spanish castle on the "new Moorish frontier." This image, mostly fantasy, has remained to color our own views of the estate as something innately grand. In actual fact many landowners were marginal, and the struggle to survive took much of the luster out of everyday life.

The problem of labor confronted Cortés simultaneously with that of reallocation of land. Labor tribute, under the conditions set forth in the encomienda, provided only temporary workers. Access to a permanent workforce was necessary if agriculture was to prosper. A floating labor supply available for wage hire did not exist. The sizable serf class attached to pre-conquest private estates could only meet some of the demand for workers. Spanish labor requirements proved beyond the normal capacity of Indian society to satisfy. The new elite demanded not only agricultural workers but porters, household servants, and mistresses in profusion. The concept of labor detached from the land proved a major cultural obstacle. Indian society thought of land and labor as indivisible. The Spaniards, however, considered land and labor as separate economic units. The question of the agricultural skill of the Indians was not an issue. They adapted to European methods, including wheat-growing, with relative ease. In contrast, the struggle to detach the Indian psychologically from the land, begun soon after the fall of Tenochtitlan, is still going on in modern Mexico.

In view of the difficulties of acquiring a permanent labor force, it is not surprising that slavery appeared as an attractive alternative to the labor-hungry Europeans. Slavery as an institution existed in both cultures, with certain superficial similarities that enabled the Spaniards to distort Indian slavery to fit their own needs. In the early period, slaves might be acquired as part of the booty of war or rebellion. With the fall of Tenochtitlan, Cortés enslaved thousands, including women and children. The conquerors fell back on the accepted theory that the victor had the right to kill his prisoners, or to spare their lives in exchange for a life of servitude. In Spain, thousands of captive Moors had become slaves during the reconquest, while warfare between Christians prohibited enslavement, but permitted ransom. As pagans, the Indians appeared to be fitting candidates for slavery. Only later were the obvious differences between the Moors and the Indians used to dispute that convenient idea. The concept of a just war, when supposedly all the proper procedures prior to actual warfare were observed, enabled the Europeans to acquire slaves. The *requerimiento,* a statement outlining the Pope's consignment of the New World to Spain in the interests of the true faith, supposedly was read to newly contacted Indian groups. The document required them to submit to Spanish authority under penalty of being declared rebels and reduced by force to slavery. The many abuses of the requerimiento caused great amusement among the Spaniards, but the legal fiction that it preserved was appreciated fully. Slaves accepted as tribute by an encomendero, or purchased directly from their Indian owners, provided another source of labor. Demand for such slaves easily exhausted the available supply, causing caciques to create more in violation of both Indian custom and Spanish law.

Initially, the Spaniards relied on Indian slavery to make their land and cattle holdings economically viable. Slaves as a small permanent core, supplemented by tribute labor at harvest time, appeared to be a reasonable solution to labor needs. The Europeans justified Indian slavery on the grounds that it brought pagans into a close relationship with Christians, thereby facilitating their conversion. Over the long term, tribute labor under the encomienda accustomed Indians to working for Spaniards, and eventually detached a number from their land to enter the free-floating labor market in urban centers. The process of creating a labor pool, however, lagged behind demand. The use of African slaves required large capital investments and was therefore not an immediately viable alternative or supplement to Indian labor. Moreover, Spain did not control slaving ports on the coast of Africa; thus the importation of black slaves would depend on foreigners, causing a drain of wealth into non-Spanish hands. Nevertheless, Father Bartolomé de las Casas proposed, as early as 1516, that African slaves replace Indians, and limited encouragement was given in 1518, when the Crown issued the first import license to introduce a number of African slaves into the Antilles. But the expense, and the availability of Indian workers, retarded the use of blacks. Nascent Mexican colonial society depended principally upon forced labor, either in the form of tribute or of Indian slaves. Nevertheless, there were a significant number of black slaves present in New Spain by the late 1530s.

RELIGION AS AN INSTRUMENT OF EMPIRE

To the Spanish mind, religion constituted an important part of sovereignty. The idea of non-Christian subjects of the Castilian monarchy seemed a contradiction in terms. During the height of the conquest, Cortés insisted on at least the superficial acceptance of Christianity. Catholic shrines replaced pagan idols in temples newly cleaned of the blood and gore of human sacrifice. The Virgin Mary reigned uneasily, and usually temporarily, amid the lingering smell of death. On occasion Cortés almost endangered alliances by insistence on replacing Indian idols, and had to be restrained by Father Bartolomé de Olmedo from precipitous and superficial conversion. With the fall of Tenochtitlan, and the subsequent establishment of Spanish authority, the replacement of the native religion went forward automatically. The Indians themselves pleaded with the Spaniards, much to their gratification, for immediate conversion.

Indian religious philosophy permitted the acceptance of useful deities without dislocation of their entire belief structure. A victorious god, powerful enough to topple the Mexica-Aztec empire, obviously could not, and should not, be ignored. Moreover, the indigenous population rightfully perceived Christianity as a social instrument offering protection as well as access to an important element of European culture. The idea that all were equal in the sight of God offered a weapon to resist the social subordination of the Indian in the temporal world. After all, the King of Spain and a minor cacique shared the same spiritual fate. In general, European settlers opposed full acceptance of the Indians within the bosom of the Church. They understood the implications of Christianity, and the danger it posed to their monopoly of that important cultural instrument. Even the lowest Indian sensed the degree of social protection offered by the European religion. Indeed, in his fourth letter to Emperor Carlos V (dated October 15, 1524), Cortés stressed the great attraction of Christianity, and consequently requested more missionaries to effect conversion. He suggested that the Franciscan and Dominican friars be given the task.

Even before Cortés' letter, the first missionary group had arrived in May of 1524, clad in the humble garb of St. Francis, to begin the methodical attempt to bring the Indians into Christian universality. When the Dominicans arrived on July 2, 1526, they also numbered twelve, the exact number of Christ's disciples. The task awed, as well as delighted, the first missionaries. Mass baptisms of hordes of Indians, seemingly anxious for Christian salvation, must have been a heady experience for European priests accustomed to Spanish practices, fervent on occasion, but often reduced to rote through familiarity. Fresh eager converts by the thousands made the hardships of missionary life meaningful and often exhilarating. At the same time, many priests unwittingly gave renewed substance to the old gods. The Dominican friar Pedro de Córdoba, who played an important role in the establishment of the Church in the islands, wrote a *Christian Doctrine* to serve as a guide for instructing the Indians that appeared to recognize the old gods. Córdoba noted that their gods were devils who had deceived them, and "therefore you should put aside and denounce Huitzilopochtli and Tezcatlipoca, and Quetzalcóatl." To the Indians the idea of a struggle for religious dominance, with one god pitted against another, required man to maintain a degree of neutrality, rendering of course all necessary obeisance and respect.

Father Córdoba's *Christian Doctrine,* published in Mexico in 1544, circulated in innumerable manuscripts for some twenty years. His guide covered the seven articles of faith, the ten commandments, seven sacraments, deeds of mercy, instructions on making the sign of the cross, a sermon for those recently baptized, a brief history of the world from creation to ascension, and two blessings to be offered before and after the meal—all in a mere 60 pages. Under the circumstances, errors of oversimplification could hardly be avoided.

Ironically, while offering spiritual salvation the early missionaries unintentionally reinforced the basic pattern of Indian inferiority. A tactical decision to proceed with baptism without full and complete religious instruction guaranteed the creation of a lower class of inferior and superficially converted Christians. To delay the rite of baptism until the Indians could be instructed in the faith, however, would condemn millions to the fate of pagans, simply because death would overtake them before the missionaries could reach them. Those introduced to Christianity in such a cursory fashion could not be expected to face a world of temptation without guidance. It was necessary to organize supplementary instruction on a long-term continuing basis in order to complete the process begun with baptism. Catechism class every Sunday and on feast days became mandatory in Indian villages. At the appropriate time, monitors or alcaldes assembled the people, called the roll, and duly noted absentees. Required religious instruction brought with it temporal penalties for tardiness and absenteeism. The possibilities of abuse prompted Bishop Juan de Zumárraga in 1539 to prohibit overzealous enforcement by lay or clerical officials. The use of rods, imprisonment, holding in irons—in effect attempts to beat Christianity into the natives—was proscribed. The idea that the Indians were children in the faith, who must be disciplined as such, condemned them to perpetual spiritual inferiority. In spite of this general tendency, several notable clerics avoided paternalism and defended the Indians' ability to accept Western culture, including religion. Pedro de Gante, a Flemish Franciscan who established a school in 1523, and others of a like mind, subsequently took up the battle for Indian cultural equality.

Conversion of the Indians involved more than the attempted destruction of religious beliefs. Physical elimination of the evidence of their pre-Christian past—idols, artifacts, and written records—was deemed necessary to bring about complete conversion. Viewed as tools of the devil, such things had to be destroyed in the interests of saving the Indian soul. To the zealous missionary, the order of priority seemed clear; to modern man, the loss of Indian records and other evidence is a cultural tragedy. Many pyramids served as building material for the new churches that began to be erected at an impressive rate. Since pyramids also served as fortresses, their destruction, and replacement by a fortified self-contained Christian church, appeared fitting as well as prudent. Paradoxically, our knowledge of pre-Cortesian society depends to a large extent on the extensive investigations carried out by Franciscan friars like Toribio de Motolinía and Bernardino de Sahagún. The early missionaries balanced their physical destruction with an impressive amount of cultural preservation. One of the most positive actions of the friars was their protective attitude toward the Indians in their dealings with the conquistadores and Spanish settlers. Collectively they exerted significant pressure to regularize life, ending the rapine associated with conquest.

THE CONQUISTADORES AND THE CROWN

As the Spanish conquistadores proudly, if somewhat regretfully, surveyed the ruins of Tenochtitlan in 1521, they had no doubt who had subdued the Mexica-Aztecs and brought a rich and populous region under the Castilian banner. After having risked everything, including their lives, they meant to profit from the investment. However, allocation of resources in the form of land, Indians, tribute, or political office, based on alleged privileges won by the sword, conflicted with the full exercise of sovereignty by the Spanish Crown, now theoretically extended to New Spain. A state must bestow favors rather than recognize claims acquired apart from any action or control of the sovereign authority. In New Spain the conquistadores, and subsequently their sons, accepted the principle of Spanish sovereignty, but on their own restrictive terms which left them lords of the land that they had conquered. The Spanish monarchy, already in the process of developing into a complex bureaucracy along the lines of a modern state, had succeeded in bringing privilege under control in Spain. Now the feudal past, which had almost destroyed central authority, appeared on the verge of a renaissance in the New World. Understandably, the monarchy viewed the conquistadores with suspicion, at the same time that it applauded their deeds. The Indians proved less a problem to the Crown than its own nominal subjects. Conquest of the Indians had to be followed as rapidly as possible by the conquest of the Spaniards in the New World.

Implantation of full royal authority, on terms acceptable to the Crown bureaucracy, could be justified on the ground that the conquistadores were incapable of imposing order upon themselves. Events in New Spain proved that even Cortés' strong personality could not effectively control his fellow adventurers, who felt that they were operating outside of any institutional structure. When Cortés dispatched Cristobal de Olid to Honduras, in order to forestall rival Spanish probes from the region of Panama, he discovered that Olid had his own ambitions and threw off the conqueror's authority. Cortés could not allow such a direct challenge to his power to go unanswered without endangering his position. Consequently he sent Francisco de las Casas to suppress the revolt, which he did violently—Olid died of stab wounds. Cortés, anxiously awaiting news from Honduras, decided to go himself. Taking Cuauhtémoc for security reasons, and a large force of Spaniards and Indians, he set off to end a rebellion that in effect had already been crushed. During the two-year journey Cuauhtémoc died at the end of a rope, accused of plotting a revolt, and Cortés constantly faced the prospect of a mutiny among his own men. The expedition failed to find another Tenochtitlan, while it left New Spain at the mercy of other ambitious conquistadores. Cortés placed the government in the weak hands of Rodrigo de Albornoz and Alonso de Estrada. News soon reached him of anarchy and rebellion; consequently he entrusted two cunning individuals, Peralmíndez Chirinos and Gonzalo de Salazar, with authority. They promptly altered Cortés' letter of appointment to give themselves absolute power, and subsequently purged the loyal faction. Rumors of Cortés' death in the jungle were circulated, in an attempt to legitimize succession. The whole episode offered proof that the unbridled ambitions of the conquistadores endangered the very existence of the new colony.

Even if a man like Cortés could successfully hold the Mexican empire, it would be in a semifeudal grip and not under Crown authority. Consequently the king decided to remove actual control from Cortés' hands, turning almost instinctively to a judicial weapon to force the incorporation of New Spain on the Crown's terms. In 1526, Emperor Carlos V dispatched a judge to investigate Cortés' conduct as governor. Unfortunately, the judge died before he could influence events. A more serious effort to implant royal control occurred in 1528, with the appointment of an *Audiencia*, a royal court, under the presidency of Beltrán Nuño de Guzmán, whose most important qualification appeared to be his hatred for Cortés. Guzmán ruthlessly reduced the power of the Cortés group, reassigning encomiendas and depriving them of wealth and property. His reputation as a decisive as well as cruel individual had already been well established during his governorship of Pánuco (1527–1528), where he unrestrainedly plundered the population, enslaving Indians, carrying off women, and otherwise exploiting the hapless inhabitants. His selection as a weapon against Cortés indicated the degree of fear of the conqueror's power in Spain. News of Guzmán's excesses eventually filtered back to Europe, through a letter which Bishop Zumárraga managed to smuggle past Guzmán's censorship, detailing his abuse of authority. But for all its faults, the first Audiencia accomplished its task of reducing Cortés' influence.

Its replacement, in 1530, by well-trained and upright *oidores* (judges) of the second Audiencia, indicated the Crown's confidence that a bureaucracy could establish royal authority in New Spain. Significantly, the second Audiencia received secret instructions to continue to reduce the power of the conquistadores and place as many encomiendas under Crown control as politically possible. A royal official, the *corregidor*, assumed authority over the Indians recovered from private encomiendas, beginning the process of returning tribute-paying subjects to Crown control and eliminating the semifeudal role played by the conquerors. The struggle of the monarchy with its Spanish subjects in the New World continued in some form or another over the entire colonial period.

While the battle to displace Cortés proceeded in New Spain, the conqueror himself had already returned to Spain. Aware of his political problems, he departed for the Iberian peninsula at the end of 1527, convinced that he could personally convince the Crown of his right to govern. He found the monarchy grateful, but reluctant to recognize political privilege as part of the booty. On July 6, 1529, Emperor Carlos V conferred the title of the Marqués del Valle de Oaxaca on Cortés, along with formal confirmation of 23,000 tributary Indians and the right to entail his estate *(mayorazgo)*. While the crown restored a good part of Cortés' economic power, and even permitted him some feudal rights inside the *marquesado*, it did not seriously consider his request for the governorship of New Spain. In the spring of 1530 the new marqués journeyed back to Mexico, well aware of royal suspicions and the bureaucracy's intent to limit his personal authority. Before his departure from Spain, officials ordered him not to enter the City of Mexico until the new Audiencia arrived and had assumed authority. It must have been a humiliating experience for the conqueror of Tenochtitlan to be denied entrance to the city he had seized in 1521.

While the second Audiencia paved the way for the installation of royal government, the other arm of the state, the Church, also received attention. The activities of the regular orders, operating as self-contained missionary units, represented only an interim step in the organization of the Church. It was necessary to introduce all the normal apparatus of the Church to bolster its power and prestige as a functioning branch of the state. Such a decision was at once a political, as well as a religious, act. Juan de Zumárraga, a Franciscan, received Emperor Carlos' nomination as the first bishop of the Diocese of Mexico in December of 1527. He proved an excellent selection and a much-needed counterbalance to Nuño de Guzmán—Bishop Zumárraga's denunciation of Guzmán may well have been partially responsible for the high quality of individuals appointed to the second Audiencia.

As the task of organizing a government in New Spain made headway, the social system itself began to get considerably more complex. The early and relatively simple division between the conquerors and the conquered could not withstand the influx of Spaniards from the islands as well as the mother country. The descent from Quezalcóatl's emissaries, to human beings, to parasitic exploiters, and ultimately to vagabonds was perhaps as inevitable as it was rapid. Moreover, a new element complicated the development of colonial society. The *mestizo*, a mixture of European and Indian who did not fit into either group, constituted a new and, in the initial period, a culturally illegitimate element. By 1530 bands of abandoned mestizo children plagued the cities. The growing complexity of the new society, and all the attendant political and social problems it posed, challenged Spain's organizational abilities. It was a challenge that to a remarkable extent would be met.

PART TWO

Chapter 5

THE INSTITUTIONAL
PROCESS

THE Castilian monarchy's approach to governing the New World reflected the often difficult evolution of the state in the Iberian peninsula. Its establishment had been neither simple nor easy. The Moorish conquest (A.D. 711) shattered earlier attempts to establish the monarch's right to rule. Waves of Moslem invaders threw the Christians back into the inhospitable northern mountains, where they desperately pieced together small and insignificant states. Politically weak monarchs, at the mercy of powerful nobles and other interest groups, barely managed to hold on to their theoretically superior positions. Only by presiding over the dissipation and dispersal of their powers could they avoid an outright collapse. As a result monarchs found it difficult to arbitrate, and came close to sinking into the social morass of feudalism. The long road back to political power required playing one group off against another and slowly insisting on royal prerogatives. Only with Queen Isabel and her consort, Fernando of Aragón, on the very eve of the discovery of the New World, did the Castilian monarchy emerge as the dominant force.

The historical evolution of the monarchy produced a very cautious and suspicious state, anxious to demonstrate its authority, whether in Spain or the New World. Carlos I of Spain (1516–1556)—the first monarch of the new Habsburg dynasty, who also became Carlos V of the Holy Roman Empire—soon acknowledged the limitations of the Crown. The Spanish state accepted the role of social arbitrator, dealing with organized and recognized interest groups, each with its own powers and privileges. The monarchy did not attempt to absorb the power of such groups; rather, it sought acceptance of royal jurisdiction over them.

THE PHILOSOPHICAL FRAMEWORK

The institutional structure implanted by Spain in the New World rested on a number of important theoretical premises. In theory, the Castilian monarchy's proprietary rights permitted the Crown to govern without reference to ancient rights and customs, as in Spain itself. The Crown's willingness to issue laws for its American holdings, many of them experimental in nature, was an obvious result of the proprietary nature of its possessions. Each part of the Crown's holdings, including the American empire, was theoretically separate, joined only in the person of the monarch himself. New Spain thus existed apart, not as a colony of Castile. While in practice Spain derived many essentially colonial benefits from its American possessions, the monarch had direct moral responsibility for the well-being of his Mexican vassals. This sense of responsibility transcended a strictly colonial relationship. As a result, New Spain developed as a distinct region with the institutional structure of a virtually independent state.

The development of a colonial society and culture different from that in Spain was thus philosophically acceptable, even without considering the totally different nature of the population. The roots of Mexican nationalism were easily nourished by the Crown's philosophical approach to empire. The monarchy's sense of responsibility for New Spain's well-being had many positive manifestations, including the early introduction of the printing press and the development of a full-scale university within the first half-century of Spanish rule. While economic realities often led Spain to exploit the wealth of New Spain, sometimes to the detriment of its inhabitants, the Crown also invested in the well-being of its American vassals. The paternalistic nature of Spanish rule was an important factor in the survival of the empire.

Spain's desire to establish a legitimate basis for its sovereignty in the New World arose from the strong sense that the monarchy must be a beneficial force—power alone could not suffice. The existence of well-organized civilized Indian groups, in New Spain and elsewhere, thus raised questions of Spain's right to impose its authority. In Hispaniola, Dominican friar Antonio de Montesinos, examining Spain's uncertain claims, challenged the monarchy in an impassioned sermon in 1511, well before the Europeans encountered the advanced Indians of the Mexican mainland. Confronting his Spanish parishioners, Montesinos demanded "By what right or justice do you keep these Indians in such cruel and horrible servitude?" The Crown, unwilling to see itself as a mere usurper of barbarous states, sought to establish an acceptable basis for Spanish rule. Christianity, and the obligation of Christian states to spread the faith to pagans, provided that basis. Pope Alexander VI, in his bull of 1493, had already provided the outlines of a religious justification of conquest, by dividing the unexplored regions of the world between Spain and Portugal.

The mandate to extend Christianity's frontiers drew upon established precedent and philosophical sources. Pope Adrian IV, for example, delivered Ireland to English King Henry II and his successors in 1155, charging him to introduce the faith. In the thirteenth century the doctrine of Henry of Susa, Cardinal Bishop of Ostia, established a legal formula justifying papal authority to assign sovereignty over pagan states. Susa's doctrine declared that while natural law supported the right of heathen peoples to their own possessions and political organizations before Christ's arrival on earth, these rights passed to him as Lord of the Earth in both the spiritual and temporal sense. Jesus subsequently delegated authority to his successors, first St. Peter and then the popes. Consequently, the pontiff could supposedly amend the rights of pagans. Spain's spiritual mission in the New World obviously required temporal intervention in the social and political life of the Indians. Thus the state's proselytizing burden provided Spain with an acceptable legal and religious justification with which to build its empire in New Spain.

THE ORGANIZATIONAL PERIOD

The philosophical underpinnings of the Castilian monarchy determined the structure as well as the functions of the state in New Spain. As the supreme and personal arbitrator, the king had to be physically present in its various dependencies. Viceroys, who supposedly represented the monarch's very person, thus served as the chiefs of state. The entrance of a new viceroy, accompanied by an impressive amount of pomp and ceremony, emphasized the royal presence. Antonio de Mendoza, the first viceroy of New Spain, represented the ideal: loyal and highborn, Viceroy Mendoza used his social status, as well as authority, in much the same fashion as the monarch himself, to assure that the Crown's jurisdiction and sovereignty were respected in the new kingdom. When Mendoza arrived in 1535, royal authority—while established, thanks to the efforts of the Audiencia—was weak; when he left to assume the post of viceroy of Peru (1551), the ability of the viceregal system to govern had been proven.

Mendoza weathered two extremely dangerous situations that ironically both liberated and restricted the Crown's freedom of action in dealing with the newly-established colonial society in Mexico. The first major crisis involved an Indian rebellion in 1541. Known as the Mixton War, it represented the long-delayed Indian challenge to Spanish sovereignty. Rebellious Indians, provoked into violence by abuses inflicted upon them by marauding Europeans—including the legacy of hate and rapine left by Nuño de Guzmán in the early "pacification" of the region—forcefully contested the Spanish presence. The uprising, in a large and vaguely defined area in the west called Nueva Galicia, threatened to spread to other regions. If other Indian groups had joined the rebellion, Spain would have found itself in almost the identical position as the isolated Aztecs immediately before the fatal siege of Tenochtitlan, and the end result would have been disaster for the Spaniards. Guadalajara, then only a poorly established provincial center, almost fell to the besieging Indians. The old conquistador Pedro de Alvarado, conqueror of Guatemala, attempted to duplicate the daring of earlier days, only to learn—at the expense of his own life—that a small band of fearless Spaniards could not overwhelm Indian warriors without the aid of Indian allies.

Viceroy Mendoza soon realized that encomenderos, in spite of their obligation to help defend the Crown, could not be relied upon. Clearly they accepted the privilege, but not the responsibility. By refusing to take their military obligations seriously, however, the encomenderos missed the opportunity to become a privileged military caste. They enjoyed the status and military trappings, but lacked professional dedication or interest in engaging in distant and costly campaigns. In desperation Antonio de Mendoza turned to the Crown's Indian allies. Taking to the field himself, along with an army of 300 Spanish horsemen and thousands of Indian warriors led by newly armed and horsed chiefs, Mendoza suppressed the rebellion. Arming Indian allies indicated the seriousness of the situation and represented a calculated risk that they would remain loyal. Once again Indian allies saved the Spaniards from disaster.

The importance of the Mixton War is underscored by the Mexican historian José López Portillo y Weber, who asserts that had the revolt succeeded, Spain would have lost not only Mexico but also Peru and the areas between these two poles of Spanish power. Besides insuring survival, victory also brought an end to the Crown's psychological dependence on the encomenderos, and to a certain extent on all European settlers. The monarch's authority indeed could be based on the loyalty of the indigenous population, which could be manipulated to balance the power of the Spanish settlers and their descendants.

Another crisis, however, demonstrated the limits of royal power vis-à-vis the European settlers in New Spain. In 1542 the monarchy issued the so-called "New Laws," directly attacking the encomienda system. Many privileges long considered well-established were abolished. Moreover, article 35 prohibited the distribution of new grants, and even more alarming, required the reincorporation of existing encomiendas on the death of the incumbent. Considering the tenuous strength of royal authority in New Spain, such drastic action proved premature. Viceroy Mendoza prudently joined with outraged encomenderos in persuading Crown officials to suspend the law pending appeal. Had he refused to do so, civil war might well have resulted. Pressure forced a reversal of article 35, although the other restrictions remained in force. A more cautious monarchy ultimately succeeded in transforming the encomiendas into a form of royal pension, devoid of political power and dependent on Crown indulgence.

The most important struggle over the Crown's right to impose its jurisdiction occurred almost half a century after the fall of Tenochtitlan. Royal policy, implemented by the viceregal administration, progressively limited the power of the Spanish settlers. As the political arbitrator, the monarchy increasingly inserted itself between the settlers and the Indians, impinging on what the Europeans claimed as their birthright. Limitations placed on the encomienda, and other attempts to achieve some sort of balance that would insure the royal jurisdiction, created a resentful, bitter, and economically insecure group of settlers. Frustration led to treason and a conspiracy to create an independent semifeudal kingdom. The arrival in 1563 of Martín Cortés, the conqueror's son and legitimate heir, provided the opportunity. As the second Marqués del Valle de Oaxaca, he became a symbolic hero of the frustrated sons of the conquistadores. Even more unsettling, perhaps, the Indians responded with tremendous enthusiasm to the young Cortés. The inherited mantle of the conqueror of Mexico, however, could not transform an immature, pretentious aristocrat into a leader. The potential for treason was heightened by internal squabbles and an open split within the viceregal government after the death of Viceroy Luis de Velasco the elder. To add to the confusion, a royal visitador, sent to investigate, merely aggravated factionalism. In the midst of political tension, treason flourished.

The conspiracy, guided by Alonso and Gil González de Avila, heirs of a conquistador—encomendero, called for a quick coup d'etat followed by the proclamation of Martín Cortés as king, to be legitimatized by a parliament of notables. Cortés himself wavered, but the conspirators felt confident that he could be dragged along by events. At the last minute the sickness of one of the conspirators disrupted the plan. The Audiencia, unsure of its power, remained paralyzed until Cortés' indecision became evident. Gathering courage, the judges lured the young marqués into their chambers and placed him under arrest. Subsequently the two major conspirators were arrested, tried for high treason, and beheaded, causing panic among those associated with the scheme. Cortés himself was returned to Spain by the newly arrived viceroy.

Felipe II, who received only the Audiencia's version of events, as well as its allegation that the new viceroy sympathized with the rebels, dispatched Alonso de Muñoz to stamp out all traces of treason. Armed with extreme power, Muñoz engaged in a reign of terror, arresting and executing those suspected of complicity. Muñoz's cruel zeal, later condemned by the monarch, succeeded in crushing feudal political ambitions in New Spain.

The ability of the viceregal system to weather the turmoil and dangers of the first half-century of Spanish rule, especially the Cortés conspiracy, established its viability as well as its legitimate right to govern. Until the independence period, the monarchy would not be seriously challenged by elements outside the system. Opposition, and various degrees of resistance to the wishes of the Castilian monarchy, continued, often reaching violent levels; however, the jurisdiction of the Crown itself was accepted. Interest groups vying for control of the political structure worked within that framework. They constantly affirmed that their actions, although often disastrous, were in the best interests of the king's subjects and motivated by a sense of loyalty to the monarch and his true wishes. The phrase that captures this thin but important distinction was that often used by protesting mobs, both in Spain and the New World: *Muera el mal gobierno, viva El Rey* ("Death to the bad government, long live the king").

INSTITUTIONAL STRUCTURE

The Church, the Audiencia, and the viceroy represented the top level of authority. Under the terms and conditions of the *patronato real* (a series of privileges granted by various popes to Spanish monarchs which gave the Crown comprehensive control of Church administration), the Church responded to the political head of state—the king. The Audiencia, entrusted with administration of the law, represented the royal jurisdiction in action, while the viceroy personified the royal presence. Although they were bound together through the monarchy, they did not necessarily interact smoothly, nor indeed did the institutional structure foster machine-like cooperation. Conflict among them often reached disruptive proportions, with each drawing upon its constituencies to bolster its position. Violent political confrontations, however, occurred within the structure and not against it.

The viceroy possessed immense powers, and a strong personality could politically dominate the viceroyalty. Yet, at the same time, the Crown balanced executive power with that of other institutions. While the balance-of-power concept was not formalized to the same extent as in a modern state, the intent was similar. Overlapping jurisdictions and vaguely defined responsibilities encouraged intrabureaucratic rivalry and discouraged any radical departures from customary procedure. As chief of state, the viceroy did not exercise uncontested or arbitrary powers.

Territorially, the Viceroyalty of New Spain included a number of separate kingdoms and provinces. The Philippine Islands, Central America, the islands of the Antilles, California, New Mexico, Nueva Galicia, and a vast expanse of uncharted territory including part of the Gulf Coast and Florida, along with the central Kingdom of New Spain, all in theory belonged to the viceroyalty. Only the Kingdom of New Spain, however, functioned directly under the authority of the viceroy. The existence of separate Audiencias (in Guadalajara, Manila, Santo Domingo, and Guatemala), governors, and captains-general, as well as sheer distance, at a time of extremely poor communications, made viceregal authority almost a technicality. Fiscal, rather than political, responsibility tied these diverse regions together. The Kingdom of New Spain subsidized marginal areas, while actual political supervision lay with Crown bureaucrats dealing directly with regional officials. For example, in the seventeenth century at least two-thirds of royal revenue sent from New Spain went to the Philippines.

As Spanish power moved northward, new provinces were organized within the viceregal structure: Nueva Vizcaya (1562), Nuevo León (1579), New Mexico (1598), Coahuila (1687), Texas (1718), Sinaloa (1734), Nuevo Santander (1746), and California (1767). In 1776 a reorganization resulted in the establishment of a military commandancy-general that encompassed northern Mexico, California, New Mexico, and Texas. Frequent divisions and changes in the territorial composition of the commandancy-general of the Provincias Internas, as well as in the political subordination of the region, continued into the nineteenth century. The Viceroyalty of New Spain served as an umbrella organization upholding—often only in a legal fashion—territorial sovereignty, pending the establishment of a viable Spanish presence in the outlying regions. In reality the viceroy's full powers applied only within the Kingdom of New Spain, the central core of the Viceroyalty of New Spain.

The viceroy performed a number of different functions under various titles, some symbolically important and others operationally significant. Long-established authority and status invested in such titles reinforced an individual's powers. The Crown combined separate jurisdictions in one individual, yet carefully maintained them under separate titles. A viceroy carried an impressive number of such titles, each with distinct responsibilities. The monarch in effect tailored the authority of an official to fit a particular situation. The combination of titles could be increased or diminished without destroying the overall office. The administration of justice—symbolically the most important function of the monarchy, as well as the theoretical basis for its right to arbitrate between the classes—was reaffirmed in the person of the viceroy.

In keeping with royal paternalism, the viceroy made himself available to individual petitioners. The Crown constantly reminded viceroys to permit Indians to present their grievances directly. Such a process reaffirmed the king's power to grant immediate redress. Around 1573, the monarchy created a special tribunal, the *Juzgado de Indios,* to provide Indians with some relief from arbitrary actions. The juzgado heard appeals by Indians against lower-ranking officials such as *alcaldes mayores* (district governors). Studies indicate that the natives consistently *won* their lawsuits because the courts recognized Indian laws and customs as precedents.

As head of the judicial system, the viceroy had overall supervision, but could not interfere in the actual judicial process. Serving as president of the Audiencia, he monitored its judicial functions: if he had legal training, he could take part in the discussions, but still could not vote; lacking legal training, he served as an outside observer. His relationship with the *oidores* (judges of the Audiencia) was that of a superior with overall responsibilities, but without power over the judicial process. Astute judges easily manipulated a weak viceroy and served as a negative balance to a strong one. A politically sensitive viceroy handled the Audiencia judges very carefully. If an impasse developed, only the Crown could break the deadlock.

The viceroy had the important power to decide whether an issue was actually administrative or a matter for the courts. In such cases he served as his own attorney general, with the ability to hand down an indictment or merely take administrative action. Such power had to be used sparingly, or the oidores would complain directly to the monarch. Nevertheless, it indicated a high degree of political sophistication. The line between political and judicial matters, especially in a time of crisis, could not be drawn too rigidly. At such times state survival might well depend on political expediency, even if the judicial process and the spirit of the law were violated. In normal times it served as just another administrative link between the viceregal authority and the court. The power of a viceroy to pardon individuals served the same political ends. In addition, a pardon publicly demonstrated the power of the monarch, exercised by his representative the viceroy, to alter criminal status. Viceregal pardons, however, were subject to review and final approval by the Crown.

As chief executive, the viceroy had his own administrative staff—yet officials in Spain often selected and appointed them. The viceroy might use his authority to reward them, or make their life difficult in order to guarantee a degree of administrative cooperation, but he could not remove them without royal approval. Any important decision or departure from standard bureaucratic procedure required the approval of the Audiencia, acting as a council of state. Similarly, financial matters required the concurrence of the Audiencia and the various members of the viceregal exchequer, meeting as the *Junta de Hacienda*.

Clearly a viceroy needed an impressive amount of political skill to chart his way through this complex bureaucracy. While it was difficult for a viceroy to depart from custom, the system did not lack flexibility. Suspension of royal decrees pending clarification obviously made sense both to bureaucrats back in Spain and the viceroys on the scene. The legal formula *obedezco pero no cumplo* ("I obey but do not execute") permitted the viceroy to affirm the royal jurisdiction, while issuing a temporary injunction until the ramifications could be made clear to distant royal authorities. Once again, moderate use of such power was prudent.

One of the viceroy's important titles was captain-general—the military head of New Spain. In this capacity he had the power to respond quickly and decisively. Yet it would be a mistake to picture him as the head of a large military establishment. In fact, until the latter half of the eighteenth century the viceroyalty did not have anything close to a strong standing army. Only the viceregal guard provided a modicum of coercive force; its main task, however, was the security of the viceregal palace as well as appropriate ceremonial duties. Security of the northern frontier regions against marauding Indians constituted the viceroy's most important continuing military problem. In case of need, such as Indian rebellions or pirate raids, the viceroy used his political power to raise temporary and irregular forces, and called upon the informal militia units maintained by various urban groups. As we can see, New Spain was not a military state.

The importance of the next level in the civil hierarchy, the Audiencia, has already been indicated. Although, like the viceroy, the oidores enjoyed high prestige and status, they were selected as a result of their legal training and experience, not aristocratic heritage. The Council of the Indies, and subsequently a separate selection agency, nominated several individuals, from whom the monarch selected one. A well-recognized hierarchy of status existed which encouraged judges to strive for promotion, perhaps from the Audiencia of Manila to that of New Spain, and eventually one of the more prominent courts in Spain itself. Judges thus developed a degree of professionalism and commitment to their functions. Individual judges also served in other semi-judicial capacities, such as mediating disputes between merchants that had come before the merchant guild *(Consulado)*. On a rotating three-year cycle, oidores made exhaustive tours of the various regions of New Spain, recommending needed changes or calling attention to special situations.

Often the judges, because of their tours and length of service, knew their territory much better than a viceroy did. Moreover, in spite of prohibitions against intermarriage or socializing with local families, oidores developed strong local attachments. Royal permission to marry within the viceroyalty could be secured in special cases, but the intent was to avoid developing an alliance between the Audiencia and the local elite. In fact, the Audiencia served as an important point of contact between royal wishes and the desires of the king's New World subjects. This became true especially after

1687, when the Crown began to sell Audiencia positions. As a result, many *criollos* (Europeans born in the New World), obviously well-connected with powerful local families, served as judges. Beginning in 1750, however, the Crown made a determined effort to regain control by ending the sale of these offices. The continuity of the court, with its members moving up the seniority ladder under the presidency of various viceroys, provided some stability as well as an important source of experience. An inexperienced viceroy would be quickly informed if his activities strayed too far from the proven path.

The Audiencia of Mexico initially consisted of four oidores and a president. As New Spain grew in complexity, the Audiencia developed into two chambers *(salas)*, with eight civil oidores and four judges *(alcaldes de crimen)* in a separate criminal unit. Judges could call upon the assistance of two crown attorneys *(fiscales)*, one in each chamber, as well as a number of subordinate staff members. Theoretically, the oidores exercised authority as a court of first instance in the viceregal capital and the surrounding five leagues, while outside of this sphere they possessed appellate and supervisory authority. Until 1767 the Audiencia also appointed agents outside those limits. Of the two divisions, the civil enjoyed the higher status; while the judges of the criminal chamber concentrated on meting out punishment, the civil judges were much more involved in political affairs. In addition, the Sala del Crimen seldom functioned efficiently—a state of affairs that emphasized its inferiority to the civil chamber.

As a result of their judicial and administrative functions, the oidores had a very direct, if not proprietary, interest in the well-being of the viceroyalty. Their relations with the viceroy were conditioned by their sense of regional responsibility, as well as by the fact that the Audiencia automatically assumed executive authority on the death of the viceroy, in the absence of any instructions to the contrary. The Audiencia's power relationship with the Church was less direct than that with the viceroy. Both the viceroy and the judges were considered patrons of the Church, vaguely responsible for its continued development. The Audiencia had the authority, however, to hear appeals from ecclesiastical courts in cases where an abuse of authority, or illegal extension of power, appeared to be involved. These *recursos de fuerzas* constituted an important monitoring of the Church's political activities.

Below the Audiencia, royal authority depended on governors, alcaldes mayores, and an array of other territorial officials. While such officials did not enjoy the same status as the judges, they were not necessarily dependent on higher authority. All acknowledged the position and vague supervision of the viceroy, yet acted largely independently of Mexico City under rules and regulations fabricated by Crown officials. The most important secondary institution within the viceroyalty was the smaller Audiencia de Nueva Galicia, located in the provincial center of Guadalajara. Originally subordinated to Mexico City's Audiencia, it became independent in 1572 and two years later formed the core of a separate government for the area, only loosely connected with the viceregal government. A separate governor, with the necessary legal background, ruled Nueva Galicia as a *presidencia* only nominally within the viceroyalty.

Initially the Audiencia or the viceroy appointed lower-level officials; however, subsequently the Crown limited the number a viceroy could appoint and subjected them to approval by the Council of the Indies. Interim commissions provided the viceroy with some patronage, especially in view of the relatively slow process of royal appointment. It is evident, however, that the Crown preferred to name such officials directly. The Audiencia appointed over 100 *corregidores* (district governors) between 1531 and 1535 to represent Crown authority at the local level. Encomenderos managed to remain outside the jurisdiction of these officials, but by 1570 all of them had been assigned to a *corregimiento*. Alcaldes mayores, who supposedly had some legal training, soon began to replace corregidores, many of whom had been drawn from the ranks of the conquistadores and were thus politically suspect. Occasionally an alcalde mayor also carried the title of corregidor, and the terms became interchangeable. Alcaldes mayores automatically became presidents of the municipal councils *(Ayuntamientos)*, representing royal authority at the lowest level of political organization. A *gobernador* usually controlled a larger territory than an alcalde and, on occasion, might carry the title and responsibility of a captain-general. Crown officials administered justice and possessed general supervisory duties within their districts. Lower-level officials appear to have had roughly the same power, in spite of their different titles. They constituted less a hierarchy of power than a separate layer of authority. Crown appointees could report and communicate their views directly to Spain—and, as a result, pressure from the viceroy could be resisted to some extent.

The municipality, known as the *Cabildo* or *Ayuntamiento*, was the bottom layer of authority in New Spain. Primitive executive and judicial authority was contained within its structure. As already noted, the conquistadores quickly established these bodies in the newly pacified territories. During the organizational stage, cabildos distributed estancias and land grants to European settlers as well as represented Spanish authority. Subsequently, as the state became better organized, municipal power waned, to be revitalized only in the latter half of the eighteenth century. The jurisdiction of a municipality included a large expanse of territory outside of the actual urban nucleus. In well-settled areas the entire region was divided up into various municipalities. Councilmen *(regidores)*, municipal magistrates *(alcaldes ordinarios)*, and a number of lesser officials made up the Cabildo. The number of officials varied according to the size and importance of the particular municipality. In Mexico City, it consisted of twelve or more regidores and two alcaldes. Originally all councilmen were elected, but under Felipe II the offices were sold, becoming private assets that could be resold or inherited. By the seventeenth century most municipal posts had become both proprietary and hereditary. Councilmen, in turn, selected the alcaldes for a one-year term. Not surprisingly, over a period of years, criollos dominated at the municipal level.

A system of honorary regidores came into use to help offset the negative effects of hereditary office-holding. In the late eighteenth century, Mexico City had fifteen hereditary and six two-year honorary council positions evenly split between criollos and European Spaniards. In smaller towns the decline in municipal power often made it difficult to find individuals willing to serve, let alone purchase an office. As a result, local inhabitants occasionally had to be pressed into office. Municipal responsibilities included regulation of markets, arranging meat and food supplies, and supervision of artisan guild activities, as well as the expected police functions. Unfortunately, municipal revenues tended to be limited and, in less prosperous towns, services appeared almost nonexistent. In an emergency the Cabildo could raise militia forces, or take other appropriate actions. In such a situation the Cabildo might broaden its membership, by strict invitation only, becoming a Cabildo *abierto*. This "open council" aimed at developing a consensus among the important elements of the town on what steps should be taken. It was not an open town meeting in the democratic sense.

The Cabildo was a relatively weak institution dominated by more powerful political elements. In Mexico City the viceroy, the archbishop, and the oidores of the Audiencia towered above the municipality in both power and prestige. Outside the capital, the alcaldes mayores or governors attempted to manipulate them. Regidores became part of the political constituency of more powerful forces, gaining some power as dependents. While the Cabildo clearly functioned as a subordinate unit, there was vague recognition that it possessed a unique type of legitimacy. As the lowest level, it operated in constant and direct contact with the people— not in a broad sense, but with local community leaders. It thus drew its legitimacy from below, rather than from the king above, as was the case with the other political layers. The popular will gained its first institutional forum at the municipal level. Moreover, the long and important heritage of Spain's own municipal tradition passed virtually intact to New Spain. Such continuity lay behind the request of the Cabildo of the City of Mexico for the privilege of voting first in any gathering of municipalities. Emperor Carlos V duly granted the honor, which both affirmed the preeminent position of Mexico City over other regions of New Spain and held open the possibility that municipalities might meet as a group, such as the *cortes* (parliament) cities of Spain. The decree granting such a privilege to Mexico City contained a warning, however, that the monarch did not intend for them to meet as a group except under Crown direction. Nevertheless, the basic representative nature of the municipalities had been recognized.

The debate over the Union of Arms (1628–1629) provides an example of this feature in action, as well as of the monarchy's desire to limit its use. Calculated to spread defense costs throughout the entire Spanish world, the Union of Arms sought to raise funds to support a common military reserve. In Spain, as was customary in voting a new tax, the proposal went before the cortes of Aragón, Valencia, Catalonia, and Castile. In New Spain the viceroy laid the matter separately before the major municipalities. Led by the Cabildos of Mexico City and Puebla, the municipalities petitioned the viceroy to convene an assembly of municipal delegates along the line of a cortes—a proposal the viceroy rejected. When the councils of Mexico and Puebla attempted to gain concessions in return for approving the tax, he had to use maximum pressure to overcome their resistance. While the episode hardly represented a triumph for the municipalities, it did indicate that the Crown accepted the basic representative nature of the Cabildos, albeit in a carefully restricted fashion.

Indian villages also selected an appropriate number of officials under the guidance of colonial authorities. Mesoamerican society had been organized into city-states. These republics usually consisted of a capital city, such as Tenochtitlan, Texcoco, Tlaxcala, etc., and their satellite towns and hinterland. The colonial government continued that organization, designating Indian provinces or districts on the basis of preconquest subdivisions. These districts *(cabeceras)*, however, were often smaller than the old Indian republics—Tlaxcala, for example, was divided into four cabeceras. Native officials recognized or appointed by the Crown administered Indian communities. A magistrate, called by the Europeans *juez gobernador* (judge-governor), elected yearly, governed each cabecera. The new functionary was acceptable to the Indians because he held a position similar to that of a local *tlatoani* (ruler) in the preconquest administrative structure. The tlatoani, however, was usually elected for life. To fill the post of juez gobernador, most Indian communities initially elected their tlatoani and began to refer to him as *gobernadoryotl*. In addition, the Crown introduced a native municipal council for each cabecera, composed of alcaldes, regidores, and other local officials. While none of these posts were hereditary, officials were generally selected from those claiming to be caciques and *principales* (nobles). The Spanish administrative innovations were not always completely accepted. Prohibitions against reelection were often flaunted, since they conflicted with the indigenous tradition of lifetime appointments. Many Indian officials served for extended periods of time, and a few for their entire lives. By the seventeenth century, a small cadre of professional Indian officials had developed which circulated from one position to another. The most famous of these principales was the seventeenth-century Indian historian Fernando de Alva Ixtilxóchitl.

The performance of officials in New Spain varied widely, governed by personality, ambition, greed, and opportunity, as well as the degree of professionalism. Office-holding still retained elements of royal beneficence to be bestowed on favored individuals. One was expected to profit, as well as demonstrate loyalty. An official ideally maintained a reasonable balance between the pursuit of his own material interests and those of the Crown. Corruption consequently cannot be defined by the act, but by the degree. At the lower levels, the Crown appeared to encourage the abuse of office by its unrealistic demands. Having purchased the post, often for a sum considerably in excess of the official salary, and paid for transportation from Spain, an individual arrived in Mexico anxious to recoup an already sizable investment. An alcalde mayor then had to be bonded, since he collected royal revenues. After 1625 the Crown also levied the *mesada,* the equivalent of one month's salary, on all officials, and subsequently on churchmen as well. Six years later (1631), secular appointments paid the *media anata,* or half of the first year's salary, and a third of other emoluments. If an official moved to a better-paying post, he then paid half of his increase to the Crown. Pope Benedict XIV in 1754 even permitted the monarchy to impose the media anata on the higher clergy.

Lower officials often received an inadequate salary, initially charged to communal funds, and after 1582 to the tribute. In order to survive, local officials lived on their wits—and more substantially, on contracts with merchant houses to control trade in their regions. Merchants covered the bond, and in return the official became a commercial agent using his position to advantageously manipulate both consumption and production through the *repartimiento de comercio* (system of commercial distribution). Through this device merchants created a series of regional monopolies, relying on their client-administrators to limit competition. In many cases an alcalde mayor left the day-to-day operation in the hands of an assistant, while he remained in a more comfortable urban location. His chief lieutenant, frequently a nominee of the merchant-patron, saw to it that commercial interests took precedence over administration. Indians might be forced to produce certain products under conditions imposed by local officials; they could also be forced to become unwilling consumers of goods. Nevertheless, the system was also beneficial to the natives and to the small farmers, because it provided a source of credit and a means of marketing local products. Attempts to limit the repartimiento de comercio failed for lack of alternatives, as well as the suspicion that the Indians must indeed be forced into the productive economy. In theory, excesses could be dealt with by the viceroy. To remove a corrupt official, however, required amassing a tremendous amount of evidence, then convincing the bureaucracy in Spain to remove the individual. Since most were royal appointees, the obstacles forced a viceroy to ignore all but the most flagrant cases.

Two major bureaucratic devices theoretically served to monitor the balance between self-interest and Crown requirements. The king might dispatch a *visitador* at any time to conduct an investigation *(visita)*, examining financial records and administrative conduct and evaluating complaints. The visitador could then make recommendations to Spain and impose immediate changes, subject to Crown approval, as well as levy fines. In addition, at the end of an official's term in office a royal investigation *(residencia)* usually occurred. A residencia judge examined an official's overall administration, sought outside testimony, evaluated complaints, and imposed fines if deemed necessary. Since the residencia judge's salary came from fines and forfeiture, he could be expected to levy a certain amount. Moderation was advisable, however, because eventually the judge could expect the same process. The Council of the Indies reviewed residencias as well as heard appeals. The imposition of moderate penalties did not necessarily brand an individual as corrupt, but merely indicated lapses in good administration. At the same time, both the visita and the residencia could end the career of an official whose conduct went beyond acceptable limits. Both must be viewed more as control and monitoring devices than as attempts to guarantee efficiency in office.

COLONIAL POLITICS

Extreme racial and cultural diversity, as well as a developing class system, made colonial politics complex. The viceregal government, the Church, and indirectly the Crown, maneuvered and manipulated intergroup, as well as intragroup, differences and interests. Subtle nuances of status played an important political role, somewhat difficult for the modern mind to appreciate or understand. But what on the surface appears to us to have been a matter of ego and pride represented an attempt to preserve a status advantage useful in the defense of political interests. The continuous process of racial transition, and the breakdown of the society of castes into one of classes, required constant social and political adjustments. Thus colonial politics evolved; yet the broad goals of economic and social advantage remained at the core of political activities.

The Indian elite constituted the base political group in New Spain. Spain might conquer native society, but it did not view itself as a usurper of the rights of the region's natural lords. Theoretically, acceptance of Spanish sovereignty implied the continuation of the Indian nobility, who became part of the *hidalguía* (gentry) of the Kingdom of New Spain, entitled to honors and privileges including that of being addressed respectfully as a *don*. Acceptance of such status by Indian nobles also implied their obligation to support the Castilian monarchy. The Spaniards, while conferring hereditary status on the Indian governing class, simplified the native structure: provincial or important city governors became collectively known as caciques, and other Indian nobles were lumped together as principales. This meant upward mobility for some and loss of status for others. Nevertheless, many members of the Indian elite perceived their incorporation into the Spanish nobility as an opportunity not only to retain status, but to improve it. As a result, many attempted to acquire European ways as rapidly as possible. Adoption of Spanish dress and manners often produced rather incongruous results, such as one cacique whose portrait shows him wearing Indian sandals, Spanish breeches, and an ocelot-skin shirt tailored in European style, topped with Indian headdress. The cacique's eclectic fashion thus identified him with symbols of both Spanish and Indian authority.

Following the conquest, caciques and principales not only requested privileges from Cortés, but also directly addressed the monarch. Indian nobles visited Spain to lay their requests before the king in person. One Indian group sent six separate delegations to Spain between 1524 and 1585. When Fernando Cortés returned to Europe he traveled with Indian nobles, including several relatives of Moctezuma II. Emperor Carlos V not only received these exotic petitioners, but granted them coats of arms and annuities and confirmed their preconquest rights and privileges. Others communicated in writing with the Crown, carefully noting their services during the conquest and outlining what they considered the appropriate reward.

In spite of such vigorous attempts, the Indian nobility failed to establish a viable political base within postconquest society. Letters directed to the Crown uniformly complained about the loss of both political and economic power. In fact, the Crown itself did not favor political power based on hereditary rights which would tend to complicate enforcement of the royal jurisdiction. Moreover, the redistribution of landed wealth inevitably enfeebled the economic basis of native power. The monarchy and the Spanish settlers could hardly have been expected to permit the formation of a powerful Indian nobility that could effectively block the social, economic, and political consolidation of the Spanish conquest. Consequently, Indian nobles were not conceded the cultural or economic tools necessary to support a politically viable native aristocracy. Pitifully, a cacique complained to the monarch in 1532 that in spite of the royal grants conferring privileges in two towns allegedly belonging to his father, no one paid any attention to or honored the claim. Another group, writing to Felipe II in 1570, noted that "the royal *cédulas* favor us, but they are not obeyed here."

The failure of the Indian nobility to consolidate its momentary opportunity immediately following the conquest is indicated by the lack of concern for their pedigrees exhibited by Spanish officials. Viceroy Mendoza recognized cacique inheritance provided the individual appeared to be of good repute and Christian habits, and the claim was uncontested. The lower rank of principales degenerated even more rapidly. In an effort to avoid labor drafts and other vexatious responsibilities, ordinary Indians claimed to be principales. By the mid-sixteenth century an alcalde mayor reported that one-third of a community had become nobles. Another observer claimed that the number of pseudo-nobles far outnumbered those rightfully entitled to the honor. Indian titles thus tended to become both suspect and devalued. *Cacicazgo* continued to survive through the colonial period, but in a weakened and ineffectual state. An Indian might become a powerful cacique, yet his power came not from the title, but from an economic base achieved within the context of the colonial society. On the surface the descendants of Moctezuma II appear to be an exception. As mestizo Condes de Moctezuma, they became wealthy *grandes* in Spain and even supplied a viceroy of Mexico in the late seventeenth century (1697–1701). The Moctezuma family, however, established an effective base outside of New Spain, unlike those caciques and principales who fought a losing battle against the economic, social, and political ambitions of the new colonial elite.

Although the Indian nobility failed to establish viable power, Crown recognition of an Indian aristocracy of caciques and principales, within a separate Indian republic, preserved the fiction of social bargaining, while in fact the state manipulated the concept of an indigenous corporate body to protect its interests against other groups. Colonial bureaucrats found the theory of an Indian republic a useful tool to balance pressure from labor-hungry property owners anxious to sweep aside the viceregal bureaucracy and control the Indian population, and its assets, directly. The usefulness, rather than actual strength, of a native corporate body accounts for the Crown's unwillingness to abandon the idea. As late as 1776, the monarchy demonstrated its theoretical concern for continued identification of an Indian nobility by including caciques in a *pragmática* that legislated against socially unequal marriages. In defiance of social reality, but in keeping with political theory and objectives, the law considered Indian caciques in the same category as distinguished Spaniards.

It perhaps is some historical consolation to the downwardly mobile Indian nobility that the early Spanish elite also suffered a decline. Restrictions on the encomienda system served as one such indication. Of 480 encomenderos in 1560, only 140 remained by 1642. Nor did the conquistadores succeed in laying the basis of many great families. By 1604 the living descendants of some 1,362 certified conquistadores numbered only 934. Cortés' heir, the fourth Marqués del Valle, Don Pedro Cortés, proved to be the last direct male descendant of the line. With his death the title and property passed to the Duchess of Terranova, and subsequently to the Duchess of Monteleone, both residents of Italy. The *criollo* nobility that survived until the end of the colonial period generally acquired their titles much later, and their importance as a ruling elite was not great.

The criollo elite that emerged in New Spain did not rest on historical membership in a well-defined and recognized nobility. With newer and different historical roots than their European counterparts, they found it difficult to insist on sharing ruling responsibilities with the monarch. Although a number possessed Spanish connections, their social standing rested upon recent events. Transformation from a group of adventuresome settlers into a new elite required them to emphasize their Mexican, as opposed to Spanish, background. As we have noted, they had only limited success in establishing their claims. Later arrivals who acquired wealth and status found it even more difficult to claim historical membership in the elite. The question of racial purity, with its implied burden of illegitimacy, further weakened the colonial upper class in its relationship with the state. *Mestizos* were absorbed into the European community in the early period, and to a lesser, but continuing, extent in later years. Many prominent families carried Indian blood in their veins. Consequently, the question of race became a sensitive issue. The notion that the geography of the New World led to behavioral and physical degeneration further separated New Spain's criollo elite from the Spanish ruling class. These factors negatively conditioned Spain's approach to the colonial upper class. While the monarchy had no intention of pushing the Mexican elite aside, it did not feel obliged to accord it the same degree of influence and status offered the Spanish aristocracy.

In spite of the differences that distinguished New Spain's elite from that of Spain, it is clear that access to corporate power based on cultural, racial, and political considerations was relatively easy for the criollos. However, while they believed that they were entitled to royal appointments within their *patria* (homeland), they conceded the Crown's prerogative to appoint men born in Spain itself to high posts. The idea that such individuals, especially the viceroy, embodied physical and personal representation of the monarch himself made acceptance of such a policy possible. The Crown for its part believed that the royal jurisdiction could best be defended by individuals familiar with the court and royal bureaucracy. While willing to concede the merits and rights of the colonial elite, the monarchy desired to hold the balance of political power. Such an imperial tendency has characterized other empires from the Roman to the British, and did not necessarily imply a direct conflict of interest.

The relative absence of institutional conflict over access to secular corporate power, however, did not rule out the individual use of cultural and racial weapons in the competitive struggle for economic and political advantage. While the Crown made no legal distinction between the European- and colonial-born, social differences existed, and were used to individual advantage. Colonial status inevitably implied the superiority of the mother country from virtually every standpoint. Such superiority was acknowledged by colonials, who patterned themselves and their activities after the perceived ideal—that of the dominant imperial power. Criollos obviously felt at a cultural disadvantage, aware of their differences, while attempting to attain a foreign ideal. Newly arrived Spanish-born immigrants (known as *peninsulares,* that is, from the Iberian peninsula), who came from an essentially different cultural milieu, considered somewhat superior, could be expected to capitalize on it as much as possible. It would be a mistake, however to overemphasize criollo–peninsular antagonism: such conflicts were inconsequential among the majority of criollos and Spaniards. The issue arose mostly with regard to access to public office, a question affecting only a small group.

Nevertheless, some friction between criollos and Europeans was present, occasionally causing bitterness and scandal. For example, in 1618 a Spanish-born Jesuit, reacting to the sale of a number of public offices to criollos, delivered a harangue in the chapel of San Hipólito Hospital, an institution closely connected with and endowed by Europeans, which specialized in treating newly arrived passengers from Spain. Criollos were incompetent to manage even a flock of hens, he said, let alone public positions. The shocked criollos in the audience reacted with hostility and drawn swords. The Society of Jesus, usually well supported by the local elite, soon dissociated itself from such an intemperate assault. While this incident is an exaggerated example of the tension be-

tween the two groups, it also demonstrates the negative possibilities of the struggle over economic and political advantage
within New Spain.

If most institutions usually avoided outright conflict between
Europeans and criollos, the same could not be said for the religious corporations. While the secular clergy, with a growing
multitude of positions and honors available, permitted reasonable
access to advancement without undue attention to place of birth,
the regular clergy adopted restrictive policies. As a result the orders allowed competition between the criollos and the peninsulares
to become a major disruptive influence. The reason such a conflict
occurred in the orders, while generally avoided elsewhere in the
institutional structure, lies in the nature of the regular clergy.

Each mendicant province elected provincials, priors, and other
minor officials, providing an opportunity for the ambitious and
politically motivated to compete. The extremely limited number of
positions within the orders that offered possible career advancement and status inevitably heightened the competition for such
honors. While ambition and envy could be somewhat contained by
religious ideals, human vices often triumphed, with disruptive
results. Moreover, the shrinking importance of the orders, following the Council of Trent's elevation of the secular over the regular
clergy, constantly narrowed their field of activity and threatened to
turn them into static and isolated organizations, in sharp contrast
to the secular clergy's dynamic expansion in New Spain. As a
result, bitter internal disputes ensued—and differences of birth
and training were utilized as political weapons in the intense competitive struggle. In these circumstances, the differences between
Mexican-born Europeans and those from Spain became an open
and major source of conflict over the limited assets of the orders.
Only the Society of Jesus avoided major clashes between the two
groups, mainly because of its centralized structure that minimized
competition over office; however, as has been noted, the Jesuits
were not immune.

Within the orders the European-born, constantly threatened
by the increasing number of criollo friars, resorted to manipulation
of the organizational structure to preserve some degree of power.
Franciscans and Augustinians elected new officials every three
years, and the Dominicans were on a four-year cycle. Rotation

between peninsulares and criollos seemed the obvious solution, and the Dominican Order instituted the *alternativa* in 1590, providing for just such a system. The Augustinians introduced the alternativa in the 1620s, as a last-ditch attempt to preserve some influence for the dwindling number of European friars—a maneuver that caused loud and bitter protest from the Mexican-born members. In the order's province of Mexico, 45 Spanish-born friars balanced 400 criollos under the alternativa.

An even more blatant attempt to hold on to power was the *ternativa* of the Franciscan Order, the largest and most influential order administering Indian parishes. The Franciscans divided their members into three groups: those who entered in Spain, Spanish-born who took their vows in New Spain, and criollos. As a result, European-born members controlled the order for six years of each nine-year period. Discrimination against Mexicans within the Franciscan order began early in the seventeenth century with an attempt to restrict the number of criollo novices, without permission from the superior-general. The European faction also imposed an age discrimination, based on an alleged delayed adolescence for criollos: while a Spaniard could enter the novitiate at 15, a criollo had to be 22 years old. In 1615, a papal decree instructed the Franciscans to institute the alternativa and divide the novice positions evenly between the two factions. Spanish-born friars nevertheless successfully insisted on the ternativa. The superior-general in Rome usually appointed a Spaniard as commissary-general to oversee and supervise Franciscan activities in New Spain, thus further strengthening European domination. The Franciscans also solicited Spanish friars passing through New Spain, on their way to the Philippines or elsewhere, hoping to associate them with the order in New Spain and thus add to the strength of the European faction.

Hostility and suspicion between the two groups did not reach the same degree of tension in society in general until the latter half of the eighteenth century. The European-born community, however, was not without internal divisions. Basque immigrants constituted a separate, close-knit, ethnic interest group. Talented, hard-working, and in general disdainful of both criollo and non-Basque Spaniards, they perceived themselves as a separate group with its own interests to defend. Basques achieved success both in commerce and in the royal bureaucracy. Basque exclusiveness reflected a tendency to react as a community in order to further their interests, and their general unpopularity forced them to view the bureaucracy as their best protection against the envy and jealousy of other groups. Criollos perceived them as archetypical Spaniards, while other Europeans resented their clannishness and overbearing sense of superiority. But although competition over land, labor, office, and status within the European community makes it difficult to speak of one unified Spanish group, they nevertheless did possess certain common interests.

The mestizos increasingly had to be recognized in the struggle for political influence, although their ambitions were restrained until the latter part of the colonial era. Since access to the upper class and to important corporate bodies proved difficult for them as mestizos, they improved their status by entering the criollo ranks. Those who were identified as mestizos managed to gain access to the lower levels of New Spain's corporate structure, particularly in the secular clergy and in the guild system. Blacks and other racial mixtures had limited access to influence and did not constitute an independent interest group, although they could be manipulated by others.

The secular clergy and the Audiencia could usually rely upon the criollos for support. The overwhelming number of secular priests, who were born in New Spain, sympathized with local desires—especially free access to Indian labor, which required an end to the regular clergy's control of the native population. The Audiencia, which was more inclined to develop regional loyalties than the viceroy, also favored local aspirations. The viceroy, on the other hand, had to placate the regular orders and the "foreign" Spanish elements as well as those born in New Spain. In the struggle for political influence, the Spanish-born could rely on their relatives and friends in Spain to apply indirect pressure on the viceroy through the imperial bureaucracy. Moreover, the viceroy continually had to deal with demands or reforms originating in Spain, which inevitably alienated one element or another. Under the circumstances there tended to be a natural identification of the peninsulares with the viceroy, more than with any other institutional figure. Politically, the viceroy had a difficult task preserving a sufficient consensus of support to be effective.

A viceroy or a churchman who overplayed his hand might be recalled to Spain. The thirteenth viceroy of New Spain, the Marqués de Gelves, for example, not only found himself outmaneuvered by Archbishop Pérez de la Serna, who opposed his reforms, but also deposed by the Audiencia. The unfortunate marqués almost lost his life in the tumult of 1624 immediately preceding his loss of power. The actions of Juan de Palafox, who arrived in New Spain in 1640 as a royal visitador and bishop of Puebla, provided an outstanding example of the degree of political disruption that could occur within the governing structure. Palafox viewed the Church as a vital guiding force, and the secular clergy as its most effective element. He believed bishops should be the guardians of society, monitoring the activities of political officials. His strong views virtually guaranteed a high degree of competition and tension. The replacement of regulars by parish priests, and collection of the tithe, provided the issues. Rather than slowly pressing the orders to relinquish control, he commanded the seizure of their parishes. The Franciscans lost 31 Indian parishes in the struggle. The most dramatic event, however, was the "taking" of Tlaxcala by a band of armed clerics and laymen who declared the "Indian" town a Spanish parish. The Indian inhabitants were told that they must come to the secular clergy for mass and the sacraments, and to break all ties with the friars under threat of punishment. Clerical strife spread to the diocese of Oaxaca, with the Dominicans bearing the brunt of such aggressive tactics.

Worried about the spreading disorder, the viceroy—the Duke of Escalona, a grande of Spain—attempted to restrain Palafox. As a result, both he and the bishop angrily appealed to imperial officials. Palafox emerged from the power struggle victorious, receiving secret instructions to assume the office of viceroy if he judged it necessary. At dawn on June 10, 1642, after revealing his written instructions to the Audiencia, the municipal council, and the Inquisition, Palafox descended on the viceregal palace, catching the viceroy in bed. A dazed viceroy, only half-dressed, retreated to the friary of Churubusco. The arrival of a new viceroy in November 1642 brought the situation back into temporary balance. By 1646, however, Bishop Palafox and the new viceroy were locked in controversy, each calling upon their local supporters for help. Violence and excommunication punctuated the struggle, which again resulted in removal of the viceroy. Only with Palafox's removal did the situation finally calm down. Such disruptive events of course affected state operations—yet significantly, the legitimacy of the political structure itself remained intact.

INDIAN PACIFICATION
AND THE REGULAR ORDERS

Spain's power in Mexico rested largely on a cultural modification of Indian society. Consolidation of European rule was a cultural as well as political task; thus the clergy appeared to be the most effective instrument of Spanish penetration. Missionary activities, intended to introduce Christianity to the Indians, inevitably modified native traditions and customs, adversely affecting the cultural cohesion of Indian groups. The missionaries perceived their society as superior, while they at best viewed the Indian's culture, after being purged, as simple and good, if often somewhat childlike and naive. While the early missionaries did not desire to destroy native practices not in conflict with European values, their vigorous attack on the native religion unavoidably enervated Indian society. Consequently the already hybrid Spanish culture, created by the unique circumstances of the reconquista, overlaid the old Indian structure.

The impact of missionary activities, and its actual influence within the various Indian communities, was not uniform throughout New Spain. Different cultural levels, and the proximity of Indian groups to areas of European penetration, combined to modify the effects of the friars from one area to another. Nevertheless, in general the regular orders helped to define the Indian's place in the emerging social structure of New Spain. By setting up villages, providing economic as well as political guidance, and deciding the important question of the degree of access to education, and hence European culture, the orders helped form the government's social and political policy toward the Indians. As political agents of pacification, they succeeded in establishing the initial balance between opposing currents of thought and interests.

To the European clergy, the discovery of the New World had definite and pressing religious implications. Influential religious beliefs interpreted world history as a series of spiritual stages moving toward the millenium. The conversion of the last Gentiles was viewed as the stage preceding the return of the Messiah. Since many Spanish clerics identified the American natives with the last Gentiles, territorial discovery was secondary to establishing contact with a vast pagan population. As a result, Fernando Cortés, the conqueror of densely populated Mexico, received much more acclaim than Christopher Columbus. Cortés, who had obviously been directed by divine inspiration, became the new Moses. Consequently the excited missionary clergy resisted the settlers' efforts to deny the humanity of the Indians, insisting that the natives possessed souls and were thus worthy of conversion. More important, they were the last Gentiles to be reached by Christianity. Understandably, the clergy approached conversion with a firm sense of mission, convinced that God's pending reign on earth could be advanced dramatically by their efforts.

Indian religion itself facilitated subordination to the more powerful European beliefs. The concept of a constant battle for dominance between spiritual forces, with some establishing their temporary ascendency, permitted the Indians to acknowledge that the new gods, bound so closely to their favored people, the Spaniards, had triumphed over the old ones. Missionaries, however, preached that—unlike the classic struggle between Tezcatlipoca and Quetzalcóatl, which surged back and forth through time—Christianity moved irreversibly toward a universal presence. The fluid religious world of the Indians in effect became static. Old beliefs did not die, but Christian deities stood on top.

The challenge and magnitude of converting the Indians inspired an amazing degree of energy and devotion which could not be supervised in the traditional fashion. Initially, secular priests, subsidized by encomenderos, established a number of Indian parishes. Individual priests, however, could not deal with such a massive task that clearly required institutional and organizational support. Pope Adrian VI thus granted the regular clergy, on whom the early burden of proselytizing fell, the privilege of acting as secular priests with parish responsibilities.

As early as 1524 the Franciscans established convents in Texcoco and Churubusco in the Valley of Mexico, and in Tlaxcala and Huejotzingo in the Valley of Puebla. Subsequently the order founded a massive convent in the heart of the rebuilt City of

Mexico. From these centers Franciscan missionary friars reached out into the northern regions by the early 1530s. The Dominicans, who arrived in 1526, expanded into the southeastern part of the present state of Mexico in a line running from Mexico City to the Mixteca region. After reaching Mexico in 1533, the Augustinians took possession of areas not controlled by the other two orders. Nueva Galicia and the north in general received less interest. Hostile and barbarous Indians, as well as the general hardships common on the frontier, deterred all but the strongest, while the provinces of Mexico and Michoacán attracted a plentiful supply of friars. The missionaries duplicated the tendency of the Spanish settlers to flock into the most populous and desirable regions, and thus helped consolidate the most valuable parts of New Spain. In the frontier region, the sparsity of the clergy matched that of the settlers.

Once a territory had been selected by a missionary order, a number of preliminaries had to be attended to before a major conversion effort could be made. Given the limited number of friars, dispersed Indian groups were congregated into villages. In some cases the friars moved entire towns situated in remote areas to more convenient locations. For example, they relocated the town of Huejotzingo, with a population numbering 40,000, from a mountainous location to its present site. Holding such artificial settlements together often proved difficult, and the orders could not always successfully counter a tendency for individuals, as well as families, to drift away. Friars frequently became urban planners on a grand and rather exciting scale. Villages, usually laid out around a central plaza with a church and municipal buildings, represented cultural centers in a broad sense. Clerics supervised civil engineering projects to bring in potable water or supply the needs of irrigation. The aqueduct stretching 45 kilometers from Zempoala to Otumba, constructed under the supervision of Franciscan friar Francisco de Tembleque, provided an outstanding example of engineering skill.

The missionary-priest became both a spiritual and de facto political leader in villages under clerical direction. The Indians often depended on the friars for decision-making at all levels. Missionaries, while making great demands on the Indians, offered a degree of protection against the demands of European settlers. Their knowledge of the Spanish system, and willingness to use that understanding in the interest of their Indian charges, encouraged dependency. As a result, the friars developed a proprietary attitude toward the Indians under their direction. They attempted to isolate them from the potentially corrupt influence of the Spanish settlers by creating an artificial environment that, in the long run, they could not sustain. They hoped that controlled and limited contact with the settlers, prohibitions against non-Indians living in the villages, and other restrictions would protect their charges against the onslaught of European vices. In return for their contribution in pacifying and controlling the natives, the friars insisted on a powerful role as intermediaries between viceregal officials and the Indians, as well as between the Indians and Spanish settlers.

The regular clergy developed an independent view of the Indians' future, based on religious values that inevitably clashed with the more immediate demands of the settlers and complicated the essentially amoral desire of the state to establish a viable economy and an acceptable balance of interests. The friars believed that God's kingdom on earth could be advanced by organizing their Indian charges in a fashion that emphasized spiritual rather than temporal values. The Bishop of Michoacán, Vasco de Quiroga, provided an example of this philosophy. Inspired by Sir Thomas More's *Utopia,* he gathered the natives into communal centers in an attempt to recreate primitive Christian communities. Attracted by what he saw as their simple virtues, Quiroga likened his charges to the Apostles. Like soft wax the Indians could be made into a type of Christian who, in a primitive fashion, combined the spiritual with the temporal to a much greater extent than the Europeans had been able to achieve.

EARLY INDIAN EDUCATION

A Franciscan lay brother, Pedro de Gante, set the initial direction of Indian education by teaching the natives all the elements of Spanish culture, including Latin, as well as vocational skills. Gante insisted that the Indians were the intellectual equals of the Europeans and that they merely required education to break old habits.

Brother Pedro viewed the conquest as a Christian mission, with the Spaniards having been dispatched by God with the sole purpose of introducing Christianity. Exploitation, creation of wealth, and other worldly considerations merely impeded the real task. He constantly reminded Emperor Carlos V of his religious role by referring to him as a "vicar of Christ." Friar Toribio de Benavente, commonly known by his Indian name of Motolinía ("poor man"), believed that God sent Cortés "to open the door" for the missionaries. Like Gante he expressed amazement at the Indian's ability to learn and adapt rapidly. Motolinía used morality plays to instruct the natives in religion and history, as well as the justness of the Spanish conquest. Equality through education, however, threatened the new society being developed by the sons of the conquistadores and subsequent European arrivals.

The greatest experiment in Indian education was the Franciscan College (secondary school) of Santa Cruz de Tlatilolco founded by Bishop Juan de Zumárraga and Viceroy Antonio de Mendoza, who shared a high opinion of the intellectual ability of the Indians. Modeled after Gante's school, the college sought to create an Indian Christian elite. Appropriately, it opened on Epiphany, January 6, 1536, symbolizing the calling of the Gentiles to the faith. The curriculum consisted of reading, writing, rhetoric, logic, sacred music, Latin, and Indian medicine, taught in a monastic environment. In spite of opposition, the College of Santa Cruz succeeded in creating an educated native elite. Unfortunately, Spanish settlers rejected the equality implied by access to higher education. They preferred a dependent Indian population less able to contest the privileged position of the Europeans. Even Bishop Zumárraga himself eventually lost faith in the Indians' ability to shake off paganism.

The initial euphoria caused by the Indians' apparent receptivity to the new culture and religion soon turned into suspicion. The authorities interpreted evidence of pagan practices as a resurgence of the old faith, rather than as inevitable lingering remnants. If the conquest represented a Christian offensive, Satan now appeared to be counterattacking. Indian constables, urged on by Zumárraga, ferreted out secret idolatry at all levels. The charges against Don Carlos, the cacique of Texcoco, who stood accused of heresy and encouraging others to revert to the old Indian religion, further bolstered the case against Indian cultural equality. Raised in Cortés' household, educated by Gante and in the College of Santa Cruz, Don Carlos threw into doubt the success of the entire process of acculturation. Predictably, the College was held accountable for his lapse and considered a hotbed of heresies.

The Dominicans, unlike the Franciscans, never championed Indian education as an immediate solution to the social problem presented by the native culture. Writing to Emperor Carlos V in 1544, Dominican provincials Fray Domingo de la Cruz and Fray Domingo de Betantos declared that Indians could not, and should not, be trained for the clergy, since the Christian spirit had barely penetrated the native mind, and to allow them to preach might result in spreading heresy. Such views, coupled with the Franciscans' disillusionment and the opposition of the settlers, combined to make higher education for the Indians impossible. The College of Santa Cruz trained Indian graduates who could not aspire to be much more than missionary assistants. They could interpret and translate, but could not enter the ultimate religious cultural level as priests. In 1539 the ecclesiastical junta decided to permit a few Indians and mestizos to take minor orders solely to serve as helpers, believing that if they proved unable to maintain celibacy they could resign, since minor vows were revokable. Very few took advantage of the limited opportunity. The Synod of 1553 further restricted access to clerical status by officially forbidding the ordination of Indians, mestizos, and Negroes. And in 1570 the Franciscans forbade minor orders on the pretext that Indians lacked even minimum qualifications. Although racial barriers to the priesthood could not be sustained, and mestizos in particular soon entered the ranks of the clergy, Indian culture was identified as a major obstacle to advancement.

The preparation of Indian women for holy orders suffered from the same opposition and disillusionment. The clergy decided to prepare them only for the roles of Christian wives and mothers. Some devoted mature women lived a secluded holy life, but, without religious status, often as servants of nuns. In a similar fashion, men devoted themselves to a religious life of their own free will without being incorporated into an organized religious fraternity.

The natives' humility and rejection of worldly vanities for the monastic life could only have been intensified by their rejection by the European religious community.

DEVELOPMENT OF THE CHURCH HIERARCHY

The quasi-political activities of the missionary orders, like that of the conquistadores, could be tolerated only during the initial organizational period. In a frontier situation, the self-contained aspects of the regular orders proved useful in the pacification of the Indians. As the state became better organized, however, it naturally emphasized hierarchy. Control and direction of the clergy soon became an objective of the central bureaucracy.

The first steps toward such a goal began almost from the moment the first groups of missionary friars started to spread the Gospel. Tlaxcala, which had been instrumental in facilitating the defeat of the Triple Alliance, received the honor of becoming the seat of the first Mexican bishopric in 1527. The Bishopric of Mexico, located in the capital itself, became the most important ecclesiastic post, however, and was subsequently elevated to an archbishopric. Emperor Carlos V chose Juan de Zumárraga, a devout Franciscan and an experienced administrator, to be the first Bishop of Mexico. Secular parish priests came under his supervision as head of the Diocese of Mexico. It would be his delicate task to reduce the power of the orders, which operated without diocesan supervision, and concentrate clerical power in the secular hierarchy. Experienced in clerical politics—in particular the bitter dispute between the conventuals and the so-called observants— and insistent on a more rigorous approach to discipline and personal sacrifice in his own order, Zumárraga appeared to be a good choice.

Carlos V dispatched Zumárraga to New Spain in 1528 under the powers authorized by the *patronato real* that granted the Castilian monarchy the right to present candidates for ecclesiastic office. Unfortunately, Zumárraga went only as bishop-elect, because the monarchy and the papacy were temporarily at odds. Such a situation indicated both the power and the limitations of the patronato real. The Crown could present, but not consecrate. Church and state cooperated under normal conditions, but in periods of conflict each could stymie the other. As a result, Zumárraga was forced to return to Spain for consecration and once again return to Mexico. Before his actual elevation to the See of Mexico, he exercised only the vaguely defined office of Protector of the Indians, a responsibility that made him acutely aware of the plight of the native population and brought him into open conflict with the first Audiencia and its ruthless president, Nuño de Guzmán. Under the circumstances, Zumárraga's tenacity, survival, and eventual victory seems even more remarkable. His long-range responsibility, to bring the religious structure into a more normal and settled order, proved equally as challenging.

Like the other bishops, Zumárraga had to find a way of subordinating the missionary friars to his authority. The regulars possessed all the powers of secular priests, yet were not subject to episcopal authority. Moreover, the friars' proprietary attitude toward the Indians made them loath to surrender any of their control. The issue became so sensitive that the orders resented the Bishop's mildest attempts to influence them, or even to visit their parishes, which they interpreted as unwarranted interference. The early prelates protested with reason that they could not direct their dioceses without more control. The missionary friars refused to surrender the extensive powers they had acquired, and rejected any criticism leveled at them by the episcopate. The bishops argued that the orders duplicated the efforts of parish priests, granted dispensation to their Indian charges without referring even the most difficult cases to the bishop, and administered the sacraments without episcopal permission.

One of the most difficult questions involved the tithe—the one-tenth that in theory all Christians owed the Church for its support. Indians initially did not pay the tithe because the missionaries believed that they should receive the faith as a free gift. Since the Indians already supported the missionaries materially, the orders believed that to further saddle them with the tithe would be counterproductive. The secular clergy, however, relied to a major extent on tithe revenues for support of the hierarchy and its priests. Understandably, the bishops believed that only formal taxation— the tithe—could regularize church administration. After considerable acrimonious debate, sprinkled with violent opposition, the issue was decided in favor of the hierarchy.

The other major issue involved the separation of Indians from the rest of the society. The proprietary attitude of the orders toward their native charges, and their desire to keep them physically and spiritually segregated, conflicted with the needs of the emerging colonial society. Labor demands, and the necessity to fit Indian production into the new economic structure, required the development of an integrated society. The regulars tended to view acculturation merely as exploitive and spiritually crippling. They characterized those Indians who left their villages to work in Mexican colonial society as lost souls beyond redemption. The missionaries believed Indian virtues could not survive contact with European vices. The secular clergy, however, drawn from criollo and, to an increasing extent, mestizo elements, believed Indian segregation harmful and unnecessary. Secular priests perceived themselves as an integrative force uniting all groups under their direction. The regulars could not rely fully on their charges in the struggle to preserve segregation. Once the uncertainty of the early years of the conquest had dissipated, many Indians appeared indifferent to the issue. The orders' reluctance to recognize New Spain's evolution toward a unified multiracial society led to physical seizure of parishes by the secular priests, as previously noted.

In charge of sufficient material resources and with the encouragement of both the Crown and colonial society, the secular clergy progressively assumed spiritual control of the Indians. A formally established ecclesiastic hierarchy, with the monarchy as its patron, strengthened the state's position in New Spain. The orders, although still involved in missionary efforts, found their activities increasingly confined to marginal frontier regions. While the regulars remained important, the balance of clerical power clearly rested with the bishops.

The Virgin of Guadalupe played an interesting role in the process of developing an integrated society, eventually becoming a symbol of a unified Mexican nationality. The origins of the cult cannot be determined with any degree of certainty. An intense religious mysticism accompanied the cult's growing popularity, making it all but impossible for us to unravel the temporal history of Our Lady of Guadalupe. Nevertheless, certain details suggest that the commonly accepted belief that the Virgin first appeared to a humble Indian a decade after the fall of Tenochtitlan is a seventeenth-century elaboration intended to identify the image as a Mexican symbol.

Shortly after the fall of Tenochtitlan, the Franciscans established a shrine dedicated to the Virgin of the Apocalypse on Tepeyac Hill close to the city, a site formerly devoted to the Aztec goddess Tonantzin. An Indian artist named Carlos painted the appropriate devotional image. The shrine soon became popular with non-Indians, as well as with the natives. European visitors noted that the Virgin's image was remarkably similar to the one exhibited in Guadalupe, Spain, and as a result the Virgin of Apocalypse began to be referred to as "Our Lady of Guadalupe." The emergence of a popular cult that included Indian elements disturbed the Franciscans, who were intent upon extirpating native religious practices. Therefore they denounced the new cult as idolatry. However the second archbishop of Mexico, Alonso de Montúfar, encouraged it as a means of weakening the power of the orders while strengthening the secular hierarchy.

A number of seventeenth-century clerics reinforced the already well-advanced process of Mexicanization of the cult. In 1648 Father Miguel Sánchez published *Imagen de La Virgen María, Madre de Dios de Guadalupe*, claiming her as a Mexican symbol. Father Sánchez traced the cult's origins to 1531, when the Virgin allegedly appeared before an Indian, Juan Diego, on the hillside at Tepeyac. Archbishop Zumárraga had supposedly confirmed the appearance. The following year (1649) Lasso de la Vega published an account written in Náhuatl that claimed that the Virgin had spoken in the Indian tongue to Juan Diego. Some scholars suggest that Lasso de la Vega actually edited an earlier Indian account. If this is true, then Indian believers played an active role in the formulation of the cult.

These and subsequent efforts firmly established the Virgin of Guadalupe as a Mexican symbol that linked all of the country's Catholics, regardless of race and class, together. In 1737 the Virgin became the Patroness of Mexico City, and in 1754 Pope Benedict XIV officially recognized the religious fervor inspired by the cult of Our Lady of Guadalupe.

THE INQUISITION

Organized in Spain by Queen Isabel in 1480, the Tribunal of the Inquisition served political, religious, and social ends. It sought to establish uniformity in thought and action in an extremely heterogeneous society beset by foreign opponents of different religions. Ironically, excesses stemmed from the very impossibility of eliminating foreign influences, not to mention reversing the cultural mixing that historically characterized the Iberian peninsula. In New Spain, however, the Inquisition operated differently.

In the initial period, Bishop Juan de Zumárraga served as an apostolic inquisitor. Assuming that duty in 1535, he appointed functionaries and established the procedure to be followed. The major consideration was to what degree the Indians of New Spain should be subject to the Inquisition. Many clerics believed that the Indians, as recent converts, could not be expected to maintain the same orthodoxy required of Spaniards, and should therefore be exempt. Bishop Zumárraga, on the other hand, maintained that idolatry and human sacrifice endangered the entire process of Christianity, and must be extirpated. Such zeal led to the controversial case against Don Carlos, cacique of Texcoco, in 1539. Don Carlos allegedly attacked the Church as well as Spanish rule— obviously a politically dangerous stance for a legitimate member of Texcoco's old ruling family. Moreover, he advocated a return to Indian traditions, including concubinage. It is difficult for us to determine to what degree he was guilty of heresy or treason, but Zumárraga, acting as inquisitor, found him guilty. Consequently Don Carlos was turned over to civil authorities for the prescribed punishment—burning at the stake.

The trial and execution of Don Carlos, although approved by Viceroy Mendoza as well as other high-ranking officials, forced the issue of Indian accountability into the open. Reaction against the execution of the cacique of Texcoco tipped the controversy toward a more paternalist approach. A royal visitor-general, Francisco Tello de Sandoval, in fact urged the formal introduction of the Inquisition to avoid the possibility of hasty arbitrary action by the bishop. In addition, the Crown suspected that diocesan inquisitors had used their powers against the regular clergy for purely partisan reasons. As a result, a permanent Tribunal of the Holy Office assumed authority in 1571. The new institution applied its inquisitorial powers in a more orderly and less controversial manner. Indians were not subject to its authority, but remained liable to less severe correction by the bishops. The exemption reflected a trend toward a diluted Christianity, fewer privileges, and inferior status for the Indians. The Tribunal often dealt with delinquent natives, however, by classifying them as mixed-bloods. An Indian offender might be forced to present positive proof of his racial background to avoid action by the Inquisition. Consequently, the Tribunal served as an inhibiting factor even among the Indians.

Dr. Pedro Moya de Contreras, an experienced inquisitor, arrived in the viceroyalty in September of 1571 as first Inquisitor-General of New Spain. Early the following month he issued a proclamation ordering the capital's entire population to attend the installation ceremony and hear the monarch's command to support the Tribunal. All high officials demonstrated their support with appropriate ceremony. Commissioners and *familiares* (associates) assumed their duties in the provinces, gathering information and enforcing the Tribunal's decisions. The Inquisition's administration became much more professional and deliberate. Detailed records listing testimony, evidence, sentences imposed, and property seized assured proper administration of its duties.

The Tribunal of the Inquisition introduced a new element into colonial politics. Charged with overall moral authority, rather than with political or economic power, the Inquisition was unlike any other institution. While one could disagree over political or economic questions, moral issues proved much more delicate, affecting both an individual's beliefs and his place within the Catholic culture of New Spain. Nevertheless, jurisdictional conflicts with other groups occurred. On occasion such disputes required the Crown's intervention. Although the Tribunal attempted to remain a neutral political force, it could be dragged into personal squabbles by those who denounced their political rivals. Often in such cases the Inquisition alienated both sides as it attempted to disengage from the partisan struggle. Watchful officials, who quickly complained about any infraction, could to a degree block the temptation of Inquisition officials to use their moral authority for political purposes. But the power of the Tribunal to require all inhabitants, including the viceroy and judges of the Audiencia, to publicly demonstrate their support and orthodoxy was a major irritant. The Inquisition required the civil authorities to participate in *autos de fé* (public acts of faith) under its direction. Such supervision, even by an institution charged with moral responsibilities, implied the inferiority of political officials, damaging their perceived prestige and status and thus weakening their ability to manipulate colonial politics.

During the first decades, the Inquisition appeared to be more concerned with suspected Protestant influence than with *judaizantes* (crypto-Jews). Consequently, it must be seen as an instrument of the Counter-Reformation as well as a preserver of acceptable beliefs and values. The survivors of the Hawkins fleet destroyed at San Juan de Ulúa in 1568 supplied unwilling Protestant victims to the Inquisition, which tried them amid tremendous public excitement and approval. Encouraged by an official who cried, "See these English Lutheran dogs, enemies of God," onlookers hounded one group as it was led through the streets. In a similar fashion, French corsairs went before the inquisitors, charged with being Huguenots. Other foreign Protestants, usually Germans and Flemings who arrived with the fleet, supplied occasional victims.

Besides warding off Protestant influence, the Tribunal hoped to weed out crypto-Jews. Suspected *judaizantes*, often of Portuguese extraction, provided many unfortunate participants in Inquisition trials and autos de fé. The process of ferreting out alleged heretics involved an investigation that could expand to include every member of a large extended family. In the end an individual might be subjected to varying penalties or, if deemed necessary, "relaxed" (turned over) to secular authorities for public burning at the stake. Other members of the same family, cleared of the charges, nevertheless remained under social suspicion. The disruptive process of separating a suspected heretic from other members of a family can be imagined. For example, García González Bergemero, a native of Portugal who came to New Spain in 1559, appeared in public as a devoted Catholic, but allegedly practiced his Jewish faith secretly. One of his sons was an Augustinian friar and other family members were undoubtedly sincere Catholics. Nevertheless, an investigation began after information arrived from Spain that a member of the family had been found guilty of being a judaizante. The unfortunate González Bergemero was found guilty, even though he refused to confess, and the authorities garroted him and burned him at the stake in the auto de fé of 1579.

Most of the work of the Tribunal, however, was less dramatic.

Tedious investigation of suspected bigamists, or of scandalous sexual misconduct by the clergy—usually, soliciting women in the course of their religious duties—consumed much of the Inquisition's efforts. Cases of blasphemy or obscenities, involving some element of the faith, might also embroil an individual in an investigation. Fortunately for most Mexicans, the inquisitors realized that swearing and blasphemy were not necessarily interchangeable. On occasion some hapless individual caught urinating against a church wall or engaged in other such misconduct was suitably punished.

One of the Inquisition's most important institutional duties was the control of printed matter. A special staff, which examined all books imported into New Spain, prevented the circulation of works published without license or on the prohibited list. In spite of their efforts, complete control proved impossible, and as a result enforcement tended to be sporadic rather than sustained. The Tribunal did not unduly hamper New Spain's flourishing book trade, and colonial scholars such as Don Carlos de Sigüenza y Góngora obtained the latest works without much difficulty.

The Inquisition operated with the support of New Spain's population. Its defense of orthodoxy appeared to Mexicans to be a laudable as well as necessary function, worthy of social esteem. The Inquisition represented a socio-religious standard of behavior in a society where religion was entwined in all aspects of life, rather than a tyrannical institution imposed on an unwilling populace. Acting as a monitor of acceptable as well as orthodox behavior, the Holy Office intervened sufficiently often to delineate the outer limits of individual behavior. The Inquisition flourished at a time when society did not consider the relative importance of or sharp distinctions among social, political, and moral offenses. Because centralized enforcement of moral standards seemed vital to New Spain's security and well-being, colonial Mexicans supported the Tribunal's activities.

EDUCATIONAL INSTITUTIONS

According to regulations, every municipality had the obligation to support at least one primary school. In practice, however, many ignored the requirement. Those interested in education sent their children to a monastery school, or to an institution operated by the secular clergy. In small villages or remote areas, the local priest might teach a few children the rudiments of knowledge. Wealthy individuals usually employed private tutors for their children. Indian villages theoretically maintained a primary school to teach the fundamentals of Spanish language and culture; often, however, the missionary or parish priest provided their only contact with European cultural traditions. Access to education depended on class. Individuals able to demand and support learning could acquire an educational background equivalent to that offered in Spain.

Young Mexican girls might attend a convent school, often living within the walls, or attend a day school operated by the nuns. Private secular schools *(escuelas de amigas)* operated by women also provided instruction. Female students learned the elements of language, reading, writing, and elementary arithmetic, as well as music and occasionally painting. Religion and the domestic arts usually completed the curriculum. In the early organizational period, Viceroy Antonio de Mendoza and Bishop Juan de Zumárraga sent a number of women teachers, under the direction of Catalina de Bustamante, to instruct Indian girls. By 1534 eight such schools operated, although subsequently they appear to have been closed. Parish priests and missionaries also provided instruction, especially in smaller villages. In 1727 the Capuchin Order established the first convent of Indian nuns, who dedicated themselves to instructing girls.

Secondary schools for females were established shortly after the conquest. In the early 1530s the Colegio de Doncellas de Nuestra Señora de Caridad, the female counterpart of the institution for mestizo boys, San Juan de Letrán, opened. Another secondary school for girls, San Miguel de Belén, enrolled over 200 students in the middle of the eighteenth century. Perhaps the most famous female institution was the Colegio de San Ignacio, commonly referred to as Las Vizcaínas. Heavily endowed by Basques, it primarily served the European community. In the latter part of the eighteenth century the teaching order of the Company of Mary was introduced into Mexico by the daughter of the Marqués de Aguayo, who traveled to Spain to enter the order. While primary and secondary education were available to women, female students could not enter the University. Those aspiring to higher education relied upon private tutors or self-discipline.

Secondary education for males depended to a large extent on the Jesuits, who arrived in 1572 and opened their first secondary school *(colegio)* shortly thereafter. The Jesuit College of San Pedro y San Pablo, subsequently incorporated with the College of San Ildefonso, became one of the most influential schools in the viceroyalty. The Society of Jesus established secondary schools in Puebla, Pátzcuaro, Valladolid, Tepotzatlán, and other centers. Their curriculum provided preparation for advanced studies in law, theology, and medicine. The close connection between the Society of Jesus and the criollo elite rested on the order's educational contributions. The colleges of other orders did not enjoy the same prestige as the Jesuit-run educational institutions. After the expulsion of the Jesuits (1767), many of their schools continued to function under the direction of the secular clergy or one of the other orders. Secondary schools established by wealthy benefactors, usually for poor students, also existed in many cities.

Instruction, even at the primary level, was limited to a relatively small number. Nevertheless, talented and determined individuals, regardless of class, could acquire an education. Race, especially for identifiable blacks and *mulatos,* might pose an insurmountable barrier to social advancement through education, but access to schooling was not rigidly exclusive. Clerics, ever on the lookout for apt seminarians, facilitated the process.

Establishment of higher education, urged on the Crown by the clergy and European settlers, became a reality a scant 32 years after the fall of Tenochtitlan. Emperor Carlos V authorized creation of a university in 1551, declaring his desire "to honor and favor our Indies, and to dissipate the clouds of ignorance." In January of 1553, the University of Mexico opened as a royal and pontifical institution, amid fanfare presided over by the viceroy. A subsidy of a thousand *pesos de oro* came directly from the viceregal treasury for its support. The faculty, drawn mainly from the bureaucracy and the Church, served on a part-time basis. University governance followed the model of Salamanca, with a rector elected for a one-year unsalaried term by the holders of advanced degrees in Mexico City. The rector, who enjoyed high status, exercised broad jurisdiction over University matters. Besides the expected administrative duties, he possessed jurisdiction in criminal offenses committed by students or other University members. In extremely serious cases the rector passed the evidence over to judicial officials for action. Theoretically the University had a degree of autonomy from political authorities, but in fact it was subject to viceregal interference and indirect influence.

Admission to the University was considered a privilege reserved for persons of pure race, such as the sons of the Indian nobility and Mexicans of proven quality. These restrictions were not always enforced—for example, mulatos could matriculate in the early years. It is doubtful, however, that many Indians or other less favored groups attempted to obtain higher education. In the eighteenth century, restrictions against the admission of racially mixed students became even more stringent. Nevertheless, this did not prevent the upwardly mobile from matriculating. Any educated racially mixed person of means entered the University by claiming white status.

Students selected their own quarters, subject to review by the University to assure that they did not live in an immoral or scandalous fashion. They were to avoid unseemly dress and conduct that tended to besmirch the University's reputation. To make sure that high standards of conduct were observed, University officials made surprise visits with unsettling frequency. Students could not marry without permission, and noncompliance automatically invalidated any hurried marriages. Constant complaints about student conduct indicate that such supervision was only marginally successful.

Reasonable fees, private and royal scholarships, and other benefits were balanced by an expensive graduation fee. The University granted bachelor's, licentiate, master's, and doctor's degrees. By 1775 the University of Mexico had conferred 29,882 bachelors and 1,162 advanced degrees. High costs and heavy course requirements apparently kept down the number of higher degrees. An elaborate ceremony capped an individual's investiture as a doctor. In addition, the degree candidate presented members of the faculty with expensive gifts as tokens of his esteem and gratitude. Fortunately, the honor and prestige of an advanced degree made it relatively easy for a student to find a patron to share the expense as well as the glory. Moreover, the state recognized that exceptional individuals born into poor circumstances deserved assistance, and in 1770 the Crown ordered the University to waive degree fees for meritorious but impoverished candidates. Although there were approximately 40 colleges and seminaries in New Spain, 19 of which prepared students for degrees, only the University could confer higher degrees.

Learning stressed rote memorization and the deductive method, following established authorities. A student generally entered the University with a knowledge of Latin grammar, rhetoric, and Aristotelian philosophy. Such a background enabled the individual to study the "seven columns" or branches of learning offered at the University—theology, scripture, canons, arts (logic, metaphysics, and physics), laws, decretals (papal decrees), and rhetoric—all taught in Latin. Not surprisingly, theology and law dominated the University. St. Thomas Aquinas and Duns Scotus provided the theological framework, while canon and Roman law were the basis of a legal education. Students regularly practiced defending a thesis with memorized knowledge at formal gatherings. Known as *pique de puntos* (picking points), the exercise required scholars to defend a thesis chosen at random by inserting a knife between the pages of a text or in some other fashion. With twenty-four hours to prepare a defense, or attack, such displays could be exciting.

It must not be assumed that reason had no place in the academic environment because of the role of memorized knowledge. Reason, held to be one of God's greatest gifts, functioned within doctrinal limits established by the scriptures and the Church. Rationalism developed within these boundaries. Mexican scholars made significant contributions to linguistics, ethnography, history, geography, botany, astronomy, and medicine. Recent studies indicate that Scholastic philosophers—once scorned by Enlightenment writers—engaged in advanced linguistic analysis of the sort carried out by twentieth-century ordinary-language philosophers. In addition, the schoolmen made discoveries in symbolic logic that are of significance today.

The famous criollo scholar, holder of the chair of mathematics and astronomy at the University, Don Carlos de Sigüenza y Gongóra, represented the possibilities of the colonial educational environment. A master of Indian languages, Sigüenza collected books, maps, manuscripts, and codices concerning New Spain's colonial and pre-Columbian history. His collection was acknowledged to be the most complete in the Spanish world. Many of his studies, including the *History of the Chichimeca Indians, Mexican Cyclography, Genealogy of the Mexican Monarchs,* and others, unfortunately have not survived. Reflecting the preoccupations of the age, his work *The Phoenix of the West* suggested a connection between Quetzalcóatl and the apostle St. Thomas. Subsequently the idea had some importance as a means of establishing a separate Mexican identity, especially in the latter half of the eighteenth century. If much of his scholarly work went unappreciated, the viceregal government recognized his ability and called upon him to describe and report various events. In addition, he received the honor and title of Royal Cosmographer of the Realm. Interestingly, Don Carlos' scientific studies of comets were challenged by a University colleague, a recently arrived Jesuit, Father Eusebio Francisco Kino. European-born, and considered well-educated, Kino published *A Cometological Discourse and Account of the New Comet* (of the year 1680) in which he explained it as the exhalations of dead bodies and human perspiration. Sigüenza immediately declared the idea preposterous, and in response published his work *Libra astronómica y philosóphica* (1690), which attacked astrology as a false science and ridiculed superstitious beliefs concerning comets. In his will he requested that his body be dissected so that the knowledge gained could alleviate the suffering of future generations. Clearly, Don Carlos possessed an admirable intellectual curiosity and a scientific outlook even though, like Isaac Newton, he believed the new knowledge would serve to confirm the accepted ideas of his age. While not all of those connected with the University of Mexico demonstrated such brilliance, it is nevertheless important to note that the intellectual atmosphere of New Spain produced, tolerated, and even recognized such intellectual talents.

Although the University's curriculum appears modest by modern standards, it was impressive for its time. It even possessed chairs of medicine and of Indian languages, to meet the needs of the missionary clergy. The quality of higher education in Mexico was roughly equivalent to that available in Spain. It reflected the vigor of the Renaissance in the sixteenth century, but in the seventeenth it sank into a rigid scholasticism. While those who chose to attend the colonial university missed the broadening experience of traveling to Europe and studying in a different society, this negative factor was counterbalanced by the stimulation of the New World itself.

The composition of the University's faculty, mainly drawn from the Church and viceregal bureaucracy, assured a direct connection between it and other institutions. A separate educational interest group did not exist. Thus the University was a relatively weak political institution within the framework of the viceroyalty. From an educational standpoint, however, the University provided New Spain with an educated elite to meet the needs of the clergy, legal, and medical professions.

IMPERIAL CONTROL

The Spanish monarchy maintained its jurisdiction in Mexico through institutions established for that purpose. Chief among these was the Council of the Indies, formed in 1524. Originally dominated by clerics, the Council soon admitted lawyers, military men, and bureaucrats with experience in the New World to its ranks. The composition of the Council grew from a few functionaries in the early days to a complex structure consisting of a president, several councillors, and other minor officials in later years. Since many members served first as Audiencia judges, either in Spain or the Indies, an appointment to the Council of the Indies represented a professional achievement second only to nomination to the Council of Castile. For example, Juan de Solórzano, a distinguished jurist and the author of *Política Indiana*—which still serves as a major interpretation of colonial law—first served as a member of the Audiencia of Lima before moving to the Council.

The Council set both long- and short-term policy as well as grappling with administrative minutiae. Since the patronato real, royal administration of the Church, fell under its jurisdiction, the Council suggested appointments and ascertained that the clergy abided by the terms of the papal concessions. Only the Inquisition, directed by the *Suprema* (Supreme Council of the Inquisition), remained outside of the Council's purview. In financial matters a separate Council of Finance authorized any project and expenditure. As a body, the Council of the Indies responded and reported directly to the king. Regulations issued in 1542 and again in 1571 governed its operation. Smaller specialized subcommittees wrestled with Indian policies, defense, and other matters. Characteristically, the Council also functioned as an administrative appeals court. An adequate secretarial structure kept records and complemented the Council's activities.

Information on a staggering amount and diversity of subjects was funneled through the Council. In an effort to keep abreast of the situation in the Indies, as well as to have an informed basis for decision-making, the Council added a *cronista mayor* in 1571 to compile a comprehensive description of the Indies—a task unfortunately never completed. Nevertheless, it became established procedure to require detailed *relaciones* (reports) on every conceivable subject. Often such reports included maps, drawings, population estimates, and economic analyses of an impressively sophisticated nature. As a result, the Council's *consultas* (recommendations or advice) to the monarch were often detailed and knowledgeable.

As befitted the legal training of many of its members, the Council of the Indies tended to be very deliberate, interested in precedent rather than innovation. Yet viceroys, oidores, bishops, and others could, and frequently did, propose necessary modifications. Once agreed on a proposal, the Council drew up royal legislation for the monarch's approval and subsequent transmittal to the Indies as a royal order. Since the slowness of the deliberative process elicited constant complaint, the Council divided into *juntas* (committees) to handle as many problems as expeditiously as possible. Yet the council found it difficult to accelerate its administrative procedures beyond a certain level because of the ambiguity of Castilian bureaucratic philosophy. The councillors perceived themselves as a body of advisors to the monarch, not as bureaucratic legislators. A separate institutional structure, resting on the well-defined constitutional responsibilities that distinguish the modern state, was only in the early stages of development.

In the last half of the seventeenth century the Council suffered from the decline affecting most of Spain's institutional structure. During the reign of Carlos II, a mentally impaired product of royal inbreeding, Spain endured economic stagnation and political decline. Not surprisingly, the Council of the Indies also degenerated because of an excessive number of appointments, some of them sold to unqualified individuals. As the bureaucracy became a haven from a stagnant economy, the council's efficiency decreased. The appointment of supernumerary salaried officials at all levels—from councillor to porter—added needless expense and confusion. Wages were usually in arrears, encouraging corruption and inattention to proper procedure. Moreover, Carlos II's government permitted the transfer of councillors' positions to heirs—at one point the Marqués de La Laguna, Conde de Paredes, then only nine years old, inherited a seat on the Council. The continuity of the Council of the Indies was seriously endangered during Carlos' reign: in the course of 35 years, only 10 councillors served more than 10 years.

The Council revived in the eighteenth century, but by then a new system of ministries had emerged, substantially improving imperial administration. Nevertheless, the Council of the Indies survived as an important administrative body into the early nineteenth century.

Chapter 6

THE ECONOMY

THE NATURE OF THE ECONOMY

AFTER the conquest, the Spaniards quickly began organizing the economy of Mexico. The few Europeans, who found themselves in the midst of millions of natives, initially sought to extract tribute and labor from the Indians. Tribute provided the conquerors with an income to maintain and consolidate their position, and the Indians supplied labor to build the new society. Against the wishes of the Crown, the conquistadores obtained encomiendas from Cortés. But the encomenderos were not feudal lords content simply to maintain exalted status. Rather, as José Miranda demonstrated in a pioneering work, the Spaniards were concerned with making money from the very beginning.

This initial acquisitive impulse was also evident in the activities of those immigrants who arrived too late to reap the benefits of the encomienda system and of settlers in sparsely populated regions. These groups also sought to engage in commercially rewarding enterprises. Generally their first impulse was to sell to Europe, where the largest and most sophisticated markets were located. But it proved extremely difficult to introduce exotic American products like cacao and tobacco, which took nearly a century to gain wide acceptance in Europe. Initially, only gold and silver found a ready market in the Old World. But while most settlers found the European markets closed to them, they quickly grasped the opportunities offered by the urban concentration in Mexico City. In particular, colonists with properties near the capital turned their energies to producing foodstuffs for the city. The urban areas were not only the focus of European settlement, they also contained large indigenous populations. Both groups had to be supplied, but the Spaniards in particular were a ready market for European staples like wheat bread and meat. Wheat and pig farms were established to meet this demand. As the size and wealth of urban markets expanded, the areas from which they drew supplies also grew. By the seventeenth century, cattle and sheep were being sent to Mexico City from as far away as Nuevo León.

Since Aztec times the Valley of Mexico has dominated the country economically as well as politically, and throughout the colonial period the viceregal capital remained the most populous and richest city in the Western Hemisphere, as well as New Spain's principal market. Smaller provincial cities, like Puebla, Guadalajara, and Zacatecas, also became centers of regional production and marketing networks.

Wherever possible, producers sought the best and largest markets for their goods. If there was no market for their products, the colonials were forced into a quasi-subsistence economy. In frontier areas, the settlers exchanged commodities through barter if necessary. Mexico City, the mining districts, and other regions of concentrated colonial population were the centers of the money economy. Other areas of Mexico tended to have dual economies, part market and part subsistence.

Money became extremely important to the settlers, because it alone provided the means to lead a "Spanish" or—as they called it—a "civilized" life. During most of the colonial period, Mexico lacked specie. Although a mint, the *Casa de Moneda,* began to function in 1535, local currency needs could not compete with export requirements. Colonists sought to conserve their scarce coin by bartering whenever possible, while they attempted to sell their own products for money. European cloth and manufactured goods, for example, could only be purchased with currency, and the best-quality local manufactures from Mexico City, Puebla, and other large centers also tended to be exchanged only for money. Settlers without coin had to wear homespun clothes and live in a manner considered primitive.

The problem of regional money shortages was exacerbated by the colonists' desire to seek the highest rate of return for their investments. Entrepreneurs put their money into silver mines regardless of location, but investors in agriculture, commerce, and manufacturing were more selective. Investment in these sectors was generally concentrated in regions with large Mexican populations. Peripheral areas remained poor and backward until the acculturated population increased sufficiently to bring the locale into the orbit of colonial Mexico, or until a valuable product was discovered. In some regions, like Oaxaca, the more measured pace of penetration was beneficial to the indigenous population. As long as there was no product valuable enough to justify large-scale Mexican settlement, the dense agricultural Indian community was not threatened. The situation changed in the eighteenth century, however, when cochineal used for dyes became an important export product. Then Mexicans moved to Oaxaca in sizable numbers, and the province became more fully integrated into the Mexican economy. But the Indians still retained substantial ownership of the agricultural lands.

THE FAMILY ENTERPRISE

The family functioned as the principal social and economic unit both in Spain and in Mexico. The conquistadores won the land as individuals, but to keep and develop the newly-conquered region they turned to the extended family. As soon as the fighting ended, many Spaniards sent for their wives and relatives. The Crown encouraged them, since it hoped to benefit from the formation of an orderly, permanent society in the new land. In this respect it facilitated the establishment of the *family enterprise,* an institution that became the standard form of economic organization throughout the colonial period. The family enterprise was a network through which extended families participated in a number of ventures in various sectors of the economy. The size and complexity of a family enterprise determined the wealth and influence of the family that controlled it: rich families participated in large ventures that often extended through all sectors of the economy; less affluent families also engaged in a variety of ventures, but on a smaller scale. The principal difference between the wealthy and the modest family was the size or scale of their activities, not the mixed form of their enterprises.

Families sought to participate in a wide range of ventures; this gave them some protection against adverse conditions in some particular segment of the economy. Families with investments in mining and agriculture were more likely to survive several crop failures than those whose investment was solely in agriculture. The existence of a family enterprise, however, did not guarantee success. Heavy losses in a risky venture such as mining might also wipe out a family's agricultural holdings. Success or failure resulted in a great deal of social mobility in colonial Mexico. Families that prospered often enhanced their social status and political influence at the expense of those whose economic interests declined. A similar process occurred within the extended family, as formerly minor branches became dominant, while others were reduced to dependent status.

The establishment of family enterprises required the incorporation of not only wives and children, but other relatives as well. Uncles, nephews, and cousins were necessary allies in family ventures. The head of the family, the patriarch, became the most important individual. Among elite families, he might be an encomendero. Having acquired land either through a grant or through purchase, he would appoint a relative as *mayordomo* to oversee his property. Another relative might be engaged in trade, and thus provide the family with access to credit, merchandise, and the means of marketing the family's products. Still another relative might be a miner or the owner of an *obraje*—a textile factory. In some cases the head of the family owned or controlled all or most of the enterprises, and put his relatives in charge of running them. Influential families often included priests, bureaucrats, and other professionals who contributed to family well-being and defended the family's economic interests. Marriage alliances were crucial to the prosperity of the family: landowners or miners would marry their daughters to merchants or important bureaucrats, thus strengthening the family's wealth, power, and influence.

The family enterprise was not limited to those related by bonds of consanguinity. Rich men—and even those of lesser means—had dependents *(allegados)* who sometimes lived in their houses. Allegados usually served the patriarch in some aspect of the family enterprise; often they provided key ties with the government. Another group known as *paniaguados,* or hangers-on, consisted of poor immigrants who depended on the largess of the family head. They lived in his house and ate his food—literally his bread and water *(pan i agua),* hence the name *pan-i-aguados.* Such persons remained hangers-on until they could obtain a small farm, begin a tiny obraje, or get started as a petty tradesman or artisan. Their ties with the patriarch gave them a minor role in the family enterprise. Through the quasi-religious institution of "godparenthood" *(compadrazgo),* families also established links with retainers and clients who further contributed to the well-being of the unit. Of course such dependents expected and received protection and support from the patriarch.

CREDIT

The mixed ventures of the family enterprise had an advantage over individual initiative in part because of the monetary and credit situation in New Spain. Throughout the colonial period, Mexico suffered from an acute shortage of specie. The country was a major silver producer, but as already noted much of the bullion went abroad. The Viceroyalty of New Spain paid its taxes to the Crown and paid for its imports from Europe in silver. It also exchanged precious metal for Far Eastern and South American products. The Church consumed a substantial amount of silver, both as decoration and to pay for ornaments and construction, and throughout the colonial period New Spain subsidized the administration and defense of Cuba, Florida, and the Philippines.

The shortage of liquid capital forced Mexicans to rely on credit. Credit was particularly important for expansion in areas like agriculture, mining, commerce, and textile manufacturing which required long-term investments. Since Spain had failed to develop sophisticated financial and commercial institutions such as banks and commercial houses, Mexicans turned to other sources of credit—personal loans and the Church.

Rich miners and merchants provided some personal credit in Mexico during the colonial period. Since their ventures were risky, successful miners and merchants tended to invest some of their profits in other enterprises. Land offered a means of diversifying their investments. A well-located estate might lose money some years, but in the long run it returned a profit. Thus it was natural for merchants and miners to lend to agriculturalists, who mortgaged their land for security. To obtain credit, however, one had to have influence and connections. Here family ties became crucial. Entrepreneurs tended to lend primarily to their relatives and to their *compadres*. Small operators relied on the patriarch to provide them with a stake. In this respect, the family enterprise operated effectively at several social levels.

The Church functioned as a major source of credit in Mexico. Convents, nunneries, schools, orphanages, and hospitals often received dowries, endowments, and bequests that had to be invested to earn a regular income. Generally Church bodies loaned these funds to property owners, who paid an annuity. Each diocese in New Spain also had a *Juzgado de Testamentos, Capellanías, y Obras Pías* (Court of Testaments, Chantries, and Pious Works) which administered the endowments entrusted to the tribunal by the faithful. (A *capellanía* was a benefice for a chaplain to say masses for the soul of the benefactor, and a pious work could be any sort of charity.) The juzgados invested the sums entrusted to them by lending primarily to landowners. As with credit extended by other Church bodies, the juzgado's primary concern was receiving an annuity of 5 to 6½ percent on the capital, so that the chaplain or philanthropy would have a regular income. Over the years Church bodies invested vast sums of money in the economy of New Spain. They generally required land or urban property as collateral, but on occasion accepted guarantees of prominent borrowers. Although the loans normally ran for a period of between five and nine years, the debtors generally renegotiated their contracts rather than paying off the debt. In many instances these debts were passed on from one generation to another.

The Church institutions willingly accepted such arrangements, because they were mainly concerned with obtaining a regular income for their endowments and not with collecting the capital. Thus the Church functioned as an investment bank which held mortgages on a sizable amount of urban and rural property in Mexico. Most real estate in New Spain was heavily encumbered and this, in a way, facilitated its transfer. Buyers often accepted the encumbrance, but in turn paid only for the portion of the property that remained free. This meant that land with mortgages could be purchased for less money than similar holdings without mortgages.

THE MEXICAN ESTATES

The Spanish Crown, which had barely managed to control the nobility in the Iberian peninsula, wanted to prevent the formation of a powerful landowning class in Mexico. Although encomiendas had been distributed against the monarch's will, these awards did not include the rights to land. The Crown favored distributing land in small parcels to all Spaniards, provided these grants did not encroach on Indian properties. In this way the monarch hoped to create a class of yeoman farmers who would oppose the pretensions of the conquistadores. In 1523 Carlos V instructed Fernando Cortés to issue *peonías* and *caballerías* to Spaniards according to their rank and degree of service: peonías were to go to foot soldiers *(peones)*, while caballerías were granted to horsemen *(caballeros)*. However, this distinction was inapplicable in Mexico, since all Spaniards in the New World claimed to be *hidalgos* (noblemen): the notion that someone would consider them commoners or of inferior status offended them. As a result, the caballería—about forty hectares—tended to become the unit of land distribution.

The pattern was established in central Mexico in 1532 with the founding of Puebla de los Angeles. The new settlers received either one or two caballerías, as well as lots in the town. They thus became the first European farmers in Mexico. Many lived on their farms part of the year and directed the work of encomienda Indians or free workers called *gañanes* or *naboríos*. The Spanish farmers grew wheat on their properties and raised pigs, sheep, and cattle on the *ejidos*, or common lands. Other towns established in the central highlands adopted a similar pattern.

Medium-sized holdings gradually gave way to larger estates as the Spaniards moved north, out of central Mexico. There were three principal reasons for this: the areas to the north were not as fertile as the central highlands; rainfall decreased as one moved northward, requiring progressively more and more land to cultivate food and raise animals; and the absence of a sedentary indigenous population acted as a constraint to agricultural development.

Land was distributed in several ways in New Spain. When towns were established, the municipal councils were empowered to grant lots within their jurisdiction. The Crown also gave the viceroy the right to grant land. After 1523, all deeds required Crown approval. In theory, therefore, the monarch had the power to dominate Mexico's new landed proprietors, but in practice royal authority was not effective. Neither the grants issued by the cities, nor those distributed by the viceroy, were ever confirmed by the Crown. Yet this did not alter their legality. The viceroy distributed gifts of land called *mercedes* in reward for services to the Crown. Initially these grants included the proviso that the holder plant fruit trees or grapevines, or grow needed products such as cereals. This was intended to prevent the settlers from simply becoming stockmen, a pursuit considered more honorable than agriculture in Spain. Economic and social pressures also worked to encourage Spaniards to become agriculturalists. After a very brief period, the settlers tired of Indian foods, such as maize, and insisted on familiar European staples like wheat. This created a demand for European agricultural products which some colonists rushed to fill.

European agriculture expanded rapidly. Spanish farmers planted cereals—wheat, oats, and barley—grapevines, olives, and a variety of fruit trees. By the mid-sixteenth century they had a secure supply of European foodstuffs. Wheat, however, was the principal European agricultural product of Mexico. At first the settlers allowed their Indian workers to plant wheat with a *coa*, the traditional tool for growing corn, but this resulted in low yields; European cereals required deeper furrows and more irrigation than native maize. The colonists thus began importing European farm implements in increasing numbers as the population grew; by 1597, 12,000 plowshares a year were being imported from Spain.

Puebla and its surrounding valleys became the major centers of European agriculture. Several thousand farmers made the Puebla, Atlixco, and San Pablo valleys the most productive in New Spain. By the end of the sixteenth century they grew between 250,000 and 300,000 *fanegas* (a fanega was about 1.5 bushels) of wheat a year. Their grain sold in the Mexico City market, supplied the Atlantic

SKETCH-MAP of MEXICO

Towards the Middle of the XVIIth Century

- ● LEÓN   Spanish, Creole, or Mixed Communities
- ● RAMOS   Mining Towns   △ PATOS   Great Estates
- ■ INDÉ   "Reales" or Mining Centers   ▲ TOLUCA   Principal Localities of the Marquesado del Valle

    Principal Agricultural Centers (wheat)

    Principal Centers of Sugar Cane Cultivation

    Principal Centers of Cattle Raising

    Principal Centers of Sheep Raising

——— Chichimec Frontier (c.1560)

——▲—— Boundary between New Spain and the "New Realms" of the north

Kilometers   50 25 0 50 100 200 300 400

Miles   50 25 0 25 50 100 200 300

Spanish Leagues   10 5 0 5 10 25 50 75 100

AGRICULTURE, LIVESTOCK, AND MINING IN SEVENTEENTH-CENTURY MEXICO
(From Francois Chevalier, *Land and Society in Colonial Mexico;* Berkeley, 1963)

fleet—about 40,000 fanegas a year—and was exported to Cuba and the rest of the Caribbean. The greater Puebla region became such an important agricultural producer that cattle were restricted. Sheep and pigs, which could be more easily controlled, were allowed, however, and sheep-raising became important as Puebla established itself as the major center of wool textile manufacture.

Wheat prices fluctuated wildly during the sixteenth century. They were very high at first, because demand far exceeded supply. But production expanded rapidly, and within a decade of the conquest prices began to fall in Mexico City markets. They dropped steadily from 1531 to 1542, leveled off for a few years, and began to climb again after 1555, when silver was discovered in the north, creating new markets. Prices in Mexico City eventually stabilized, but in frontier areas they skyrocketed. In 1560, wheat cost sixty times as much in Zacatecas as in Guadalajara, where it was higher than in Mexico City. Within a decade wheat prices at the mines began to fall, as the Bajío and other regions went into production.

By the seventeenth century, prices had stabilized as a result of the dramatic expansion of production. Wheat prices remained relatively stable during the first half of the century; transportation costs became the principal fixed variable in Spanish-Mexican agriculture after 1600. The main wheat-producing areas of New Spain were greater Puebla, the Bajío, northern Michoacán, the Valley of Mexico, the region around Guadalajara, and various small areas near the mines. By the middle of the century, wheat production had outstripped the ability of Mexico to absorb it. Since transportation costs limited the export market to the Caribbean, prices began to fall. It became common for Mexican wheat farmers to complain of poverty. In 1640 Fray Diego Basalenque reported that "If Our Lord does not quickly cause the number of consumers to multiply, farmers will of necessity, given the present rate of production, become even poorer than they are now."

Although European agriculture was firmly established in Mexico, periodic crises threatened the food supply. In New Spain even a short drought could be disastrous. Without water, fields had to be abandoned, and cattle and sheep soon overran them. To prevent such calamities, administrators joined the colonists in building extensive irrigation systems, constructing huge aqueducts to assure the water supply in major food-producing areas. Officials also tried to minimize fluctuations in the availability and prices of grain by building municipal granaries *(alhóndigas)*. Poor harvests seldom hurt the Spaniards in Mexico as they did their counterparts in Europe—for even when grain was scarce, beef and mutton abounded.

The Crown never realized its hopes for creating a land of small farmers. Although small holdings continued to exist throughout the colonial period, the tendency toward land concentration developed in the first decades after the conquest. Many small farmers sold their properties and moved to urban areas in search of greater opportunities. Rich men bought their land, as well as that of widows and Indians. Although such purchases were theoretically forbidden unless authorized by the Crown, land transfers continued, with or without official approval. Eventually in the seventeenth century the viceroy sanctioned those acquisitions in return for the payment of a *composición*, a fee to legalize titles. For large estates this could mean the legalization of deeds to dozens of parcels of land. The large estates consolidated slowly, however. Landowners seldom obtained adjoining parcels of land. Until the late seventeenth century, proprietors often owned widely scattered parcels that made centralized administration difficult. Large-scale concentration did not occur until the eighteenth and nineteenth centuries.

Although the process of land concentration occurred in most parts of Mexico, holdings varied greatly in both size and value. Large estates ranged from the northern *latifundia,* with their hundreds of thousands of hectares, to holdings in the central highlands that encompassed but a few hundred hectares. While all scholars agree that *size* was the distinguishing characteristic of an hacienda, recent studies have modified our view of what "large" meant. Early estimates by experts ranged from 2,500 to 22,000 acres as the minimum size for an hacienda. But these figures have proved to be meaningless. Studies in Yucatán, Oaxaca, central Mexico, Querétaro, Guadalajara, San Luis Potosí, and Nuevo León demonstrate that estates designated as haciendas in the colonial documents varied greatly in size. Thus an hacienda may be defined as "an estate, engaged in mixed ranching and agricultural enterprises, which was *considered large by local standards.*"

Geographic, climatic, and demographic factors primarily determined the size of haciendas. The northern latifundia, for example, often could not sustain one animal per hectare. In that region several thousand hectares might be worthless if there was little or no water. Conditions changed dramatically as one moved into the central highlands, where the most valuable property was located. In the valleys of Mexico and Puebla, fertile land, a plentiful water supply, and readily available labor combined with proximity to large markets to make medium-sized estates of several hundred hectares very valuable. Thus the worth of property cannot be judged merely in terms of size. Land prices varied from a few pesos to several thousand per caballería. The quality of the soil and the availability of water were the most important variables affecting price—but location was also important. Land distant from large population concentrations was worth much less than properties in heavily populated central Mexico. Sixteenth-century documents refer to some haciendas worth only 600 pesos, but by the seventeenth century properties had to be worth between 2,000 and 3,000 pesos before they could be designated as haciendas. Although the word *hacienda,* in its generic sense, meant *property* and was used to refer to a variety of institutions from the landed estate to government finance offices, the term acquired a special meaning late in the sixteenth century when it was used to denote a new enterprise, a large estate producing both grain and livestock for the market.

Just as recent scholarship has changed our concept of the size of the hacienda, it has also modified our image of its social and economic function. Early studies portrayed the hacienda as a grand estate dominated by a manor house called the *casco* or *casa grande,* from which the often absentee landowner ruled the land and its people in a quasi-feudal manner. In his classic work on the formation of the great estate, François Chevalier argued that in the seventeenth century the hacienda slowly retreated from the market economy into self-sufficiency, in response to the drastic decline of the Indian population and the depression in the mines. In his view, the hacienda kept the rural population in a serf-like condition through debt peonage, and thus contributed to the backwardness of the countryside. These generalizations are being challenged as detailed studies of haciendas are completed. We now know that the casa grande was often a structure of very modest proportions.

Only on a few estates, such as the Hacienda de Santa Lucía in the Valley of Mexico, could the casco be described as splendid. The suggested seventeenth-century withdrawal from the market into self-sufficiency also appears unfounded. On the contrary, the new studies indicate that trade expanded at that time. The notion that debt peonage restrained rural labor must also be modified in the light of new evidence.

Our current image of a typical estate includes a respectable main house, granaries, quarters for workers, and often a church. Larger properties had better dwellings and a more complex plant including mills, dams, obrajes, and distilleries, as well as other structures. The Hacienda Guadalupe, one of the largest in Oaxaca, had a main house, a chapel, a stable, and a granary. Built of brick and timber, the house included a vestibule, a large hall, four bedrooms, a kitchen, and several other smaller rooms, as well as a patio and a carriage house. In 1799, Guadalupe was valued at 24,385 pesos. But although a great hacienda by the standards of Oaxaca, it had relatively little invested in farm equipment: tools, draft animals, and supplies were valued at only 1,435 pesos.

Haciendas in other parts of Mexico varied in size but were similar. An extreme example was the estates of the Marqueses de Aguayo in Nuevo León, which in 1760 encompassed 14,688,634 acres and included a series of haciendas with imposing manor houses. The casco at San Francisco de los Patos, the administrative center of the entailed *marquesado,* was magnificent. Nestled in the foothills of the Sierra de la Hediondilla near two streams, the casa grande was situated among verdant pastures, irrigated fields of grain, and stands of tall trees. The casco was built like a fortress; the main house was large enough to accommodate most peones and their families in case of Indian attacks. (By the seventeenth century the word *peón*—"man on foot"—had come to mean "rural worker" or "peasant.") In 1761 the entailed estates of the Marqueses de Aguayo were worth 1,100,776 pesos. The lands were valued at 674,283 pesos; the houses, buildings, wells, irrigation works, vines, gardens, mills, farm implements, grain, and between 200,000 and 300,000 head of sheep accounted for the rest.

Despite its large size, the Aguayo family's marquesado resembled other estates in its organization. Part of it was rented or leased to individuals, and other sections were run by mayordomos. The

Aguayos visited their estates periodically, but their principal residence was in Mexico City; from there they directed their affairs. Other *hacendados* operated in a similar manner, but only the richest lived in the capital. Most resided in the largest town or city near their properties. Because of the scarcity of labor in the north and the danger of Indian raids, the Aguayo marquesado maintained a large resident population: San Francisco de los Patos had a work force of more than a thousand people. But most haciendas kept only a small permanent group of laborers. These might include a few black slaves, skilled artisans, and other trained ranching and agricultural personnel.

Although they were often in debt to the hacendados, most peones were not retained forcefully on the land through debt peonage. On the contrary, they were the best-paid and most acculturated segment of the rural work force. In some instances, the landowners were in debt to the workers for back wages. The permanent labor force remained on the estate partly because there were limited opportunities in the most rural areas. Nevertheless, there was a great deal of mobility among workers. Some hacendados even paid peones' debts and advanced wages to entice workers to their estates. Inventories show that wages were the largest single cost borne by the landowners. In comparison, investment in farm implements was modest, as has been noted. Temporary workers were hired at peak periods of the year such as planting and harvest, and the owners resided on their estates to oversee operations at these times. During the rest of the year, mayordomos ran the haciendas.

Estates developed a glamorous mystique, even though they were usually part of larger diversified enterprises. The hacendado, like the encomendero before him, represented an urban elite which dominated the countryside through intermediaries. His retainers were *vaqueros* (cowboys), and the landowner identified himself as an elite stockman, the Mexican *charro*. This patriarch ruled the countryside through informal relationships and socioeconomic ties. As a rancher he prided himself on retaining quasi-military ties to a semifeudal past. In this respect, the landed estate was important as a source of status. Yet crucial as position and distinction were, they never overshadowed the profit motive. A poor landowner could not aspire to be a patriarch—that role was reserved for the wealthy and powerful.

Hacendados tended to diversify production. Typically an hacienda raised a variety of grains—corn, wheat, barley—as well as beans, maguey, sugar, and fruits like apples, peaches, pomegranates, figs, oranges, and bananas, depending on the climate and the soil. If there were large Mexican settlements nearby, the main crop was wheat, the staple of the European diet. Otherwise corn was the principal crop. Hacendados also raised a variety of animals such as cattle, sheep, horses, mules, burros, goats, and hogs. According to the demands of local markets, they raised more of one type of animal—sheep for the wool markets; horses, mules, burros, and oxen for the mines; cattle, pigs, and lambs for the slaughterhouses of the towns. Cheese, soap, liquor, coarse textiles, hides, tequila, cigars, bread, and refined sugar were often manufactured on the haciendas. Since the proprietor was interested in making money, he produced what was most in demand and most profitable. But he seldom risked his entire wealth by committing all his resources to a single crop or type of animal. Agriculture was a risky venture—drought, disease, changes in demand, and capital shortages were constant threats. Hacendados large and small protected themselves against these dangers by diversifying output.

Although the general tendency was for landowners to diversify production, a few estates in special locations or climatic conditions did specialize in one crop. The sugar plantations are the best example of this phenomenon. The most famous and best-studied plantations are the Cortés estates in Morelos. These properties were part of the entailed marquesado of the conqueror's heirs that remained intact until the national period. Other smaller sugar estates were located in Morelos, Veracruz, and Michoacán.

Sugar plantations differed from other estates in two ways: they were specialized enterprises that required both a heavy capital investment and a highly skilled labor force. The cane was grown and processed by a small resident labor force augmented by temporary workers during peak periods. Initially, black slaves were used, but within a few decades the majority of workers were mestizos, mulatos, and gañanes. The resident workers were well-paid. Although direct comparisons are not possible at this time, it appears that they received higher wages than comparable hacienda workers. In part this was because a much higher percentage of the plantation labor force consisted of skilled artisans needed to keep the processing plant in good running order. Temporary workers also seem to have received relatively high wages.

The major investment on sugar plantations was in the mills. During the sixteenth and seventeenth centuries, the refining process was carried out in several buildings. Toward the end of the eighteenth century, it was consolidated in a single complex structure. Mills to crush the cane were either water-powered or mule-driven. Since Morelos required extensive irrigation in the fields, mule-driven *trapiches* (mills) were common there. In the early years the cane was crushed by large wooden rollers with copper sleeves; later, more complex crushing equipment with three vertical rollers was used. Parts wore out rapidly—cogs were always breaking, thus making repairs a major expense. After the cane had been crushed, it was put into a press to extract the remaining juice; by the eighteenth century, improvements abolished this step. The juice was then taken to a boiling house, where it was cooked and distilled through a series of kettles. When it reached the *punto de azúcar* (the striking point), it was placed in a copper cooler. Once cooled, the mass was transferred into containers and taken to the purging house, where the molasses dripped into canals leading to storage tanks. The dry sugar was then taken to be clayed.

The quality of processed sugar varied widely, depending on the market being served. Plantation products ranged from molasses, sold principally to distillers, to the most refined sugar, destined for the urban market. Mexican sugar was sold only in the markets of New Spain. The Canary Islands and the Caribbean supplied the mother country. There was a small European market for Mexican sugar in the early years of the sixteenth century, but Brazilian sugar, with its lower transportation costs, soon drove the Mexican product from Europe. As a result, the Mexican sugar industry did not become as important or as modern as its competitors abroad. Nevertheless, it became a significant domestic enterprise.

There were other estates in rural Mexico which were smaller than the hacienda or the sugar plantation. They were given a variety of names locally, but by the seventeenth century the terms *estancias, ranchos, labores,* and *chacras* were in common usage.

Initially the term *estancia* had referred merely to grazing rights—but as Spaniards appropriated the land, the word came to mean an estate devoted to ranching. Stock-raising was viewed as an honorable enterprise in Spain, where cattle and sheepmen considered themselves caballeros, and where indeed many noblemen engaged in stock-raising. In their view it was a calling befitting a military caste, unlike the lowly enterprise of the farmer, contemptuously called a peasant. In Spain the stockmen's guild, the *Mesta,* was very powerful. It obtained a privileged position at the expense of the agriculturalists, who were forced by law to permit flocks to pass through their fields on their way to pastures.

Initially it appeared that ranching would be as important in Mexico as it was in Spain. The Indians tilled the soil and the settlers found it easier to raise stock. The animals prospered in the New World and multiplied rapidly. In order to regulate ranching and to control damage to agriculture, the royal government authorized the formation of a Mexican Mesta. The municipal councils elected the judges *(alcaldes)* of the Mesta to hear complaints by and against stockmen, adjust disputes, make tours of inspection, and make recommendations to further stimulate the industry. Early regulations required owners of flocks of 300 or more to be members. But livestock-raising expanded so rapidly, and so many small operators considered themselves stockmen, that the rules had to be changed. By 1574 membership required at least 3,000 sheep, goats, or hogs (*ganado menor*), or 1,000 cattle, horses, burros, mules, or oxen (*ganado mayor*), as well as an estancia—which by this time meant grazing lands, not merely grazing rights.

The Mesta served as a corporate interest group: it had its own *fuero* (privileges) and court, and regulated itself. It registered brands, settled complaints, and tried to prevent abuse while protecting the privileges of its members. Like its Spanish counterpart, the Mexican Mesta had the right to sheep-walks. But in New Spain, Crown officials tried to protect the Indian communities by limiting the times when animals could be moved. In practice these limitations were ignored, and communal lands were constantly trampled by flocks traveling from winter to summer pastures and vice-versa. Lawsuits by Indian communities and small farmers fill the judicial archives of colonial Mexico. As the native population fell dramatically—from 25 million in 1500 to 1 million in 1620—

livestock multiplied, overrunning abandoned Indian lands. By 1600 there may have been as many as 10 million animals in New Spain. It was said of this phenomenon that the sheep and cattle had "eaten" the men.

Estancias tended to be located in regions of poorer soils where grazing was the most profitable enterprise. In fertile valleys, estancias were located at higher elevations, away from agricultural lands. In the north a much greater proportion of land was devoted to ranching because of climatic and geographic conditions. Stock-raising land was issued in *sitios* (parcels) of differing sizes: sitios for ganado mayor were to be 5,000 *varas*, or approximately 4,400 acres, while sitios for ganado menor were only 2,333⅓ varas, or about 1,920 acres. Stockmen often owned various sitios, but these were seldom contiguous. Sheep ranches were the most common. Even small estancias could raise large numbers of sheep, because the animals required less grazing land and could survive on shorter grasses. It was not at all unusual for a medium-sized estanciero to own several thousand animals; large landowners, like the Marqueses de Aguayo, counted their sheep in the hundreds of thousands. Goats and hogs were also raised in large numbers. Wool and mutton were in great demand in New Spain's markets. Cattle, although less numerous, were also plentiful, as were horses, mules, burros, and oxen.

Ranchos, labores, and *chacras* were small agricultural estates. Ranchos were medium-sized mixed agricultural and livestock enterprises. It is often difficult to differentiate between a large rancho and a small hacienda; an hacienda was usually managed by an overseer, whereas a rancho was run by its owner. Successful rancheros tended to become hacendados by hiring mayordomos to oversee their property and by marrying into a wealthy family. Typically this would happen when a well-to-do ranchero's daughter married a rich merchant or miner.

Labores were small agricultural estates, usually two to six caballerías large, intensely cultivated by resident owners. When irrigated, labores might produce two crops a year. The owners of labores tended to grow a variety of products. Depending on the location, they raised corn, wheat, beans, maguey, cactus, fruits, and vegetables. The larger labores also contained corrals for the few animals that grazed on unplowed land.

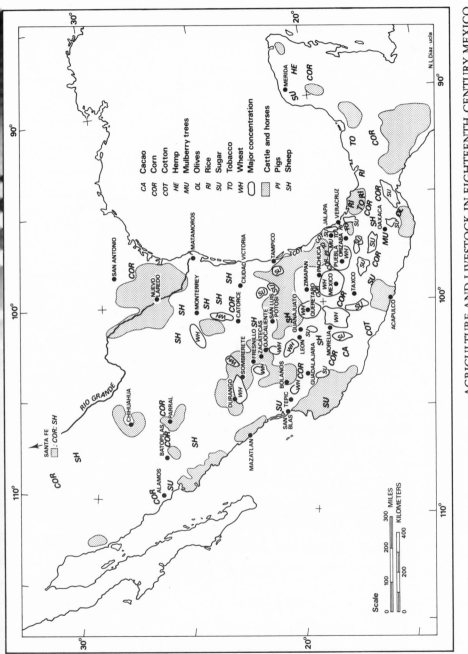

AGRICULTURE AND LIVESTOCK IN EIGHTEENTH-CENTURY MEXICO

CA   Cacao
COR   Corn
COT   Cotton
HE   Hemp
MU   Mulberry trees
OL   Olives
RI   Rice
SU   Sugar
TO   Tobacco
WH   Wheat
      Major concentration
      Cattle and horses
PI   Pigs
SH   Sheep

N. L. Díaz ucla

Scale
0   100   200   300 MILES
0   200   400 KILOMETERS

The smallest of the Mexican holdings were called chacras. They were no larger than one caballería; in many cases, they were *pedazos* (parts) of a caballería. Small pedazos might be worth as little as ten pesos or as much as several hundred pesos. Chacras were usually cultivated by poor immigrants, mestizos, or mulatos just starting out. These small agriculturalists often raised pigs, which were in much demand in Mexican towns. As a result, they were contemptuously referred to as "pig farmers."

Mexican estates belonged not only to individuals and families but also to Church corporations. The regular orders, which had initially done so much to convert and to protect the Indians, also acquired land. To accomplish their work, the friars needed not only the labor of the natives but also great economic resources. This could come only from commercial exploitation of the land. In time the orders became wealthy. Their convents, schools, hospitals, and other institutions were supported by income from a variety of sources; one of the most important was the income generated by the Church estates. The Dominicans, the Augustinians, the Carmelites, and the Jesuits owned large and prosperous haciendas.

The orders acquired their estates in a variety of ways. Initially the Crown granted them some land for their work, but they obtained much more in other ways. Clerical institutions purchased land, like any other entrepreneurs. Land was donated to the Church for a philanthropy or pious work; other bequests were made to sustain religious ceremonies, honor some particular shrine or saint, or endow a capellanía, or as a dowry for a novice entering a convent or monastery. In the early years of the colony, such donations were often made in land. But as New Spain developed, the colonials retained their properties, instead giving money or, more often, establishing a voluntary lien on their estates that rendered an annuity for the Church. Perhaps the largest contributors to the orders were the Indians. It was common for caciques and principales without heirs to bequeath their property to monasteries or other Church institutions. Often the friars persuaded or, if that was not sufficient, pressured the natives into donating land. By the seventeenth century complaints were mounting that entire Indian communities had been despoiled of their lands in such a fashion.

Like private individuals, the orders did not accumulate their properties in single holdings. Bequests often consisted of small plots, leaving Church holdings fragmented and dispersed. It was not uncommon for monasteries or convents to own haciendas, estancias, labores, ranchos, and even chacras. Although Church estates, particularly those of the Jesuits, gained a reputation for being efficient profit-making enterprises, recent studies indicate that they were administered no differently than private ventures. All Mexican estates were profit-oriented. Some were managed better than others, but as a whole they were commercial enterprises. The principal difference between church estates and private holdings seems to be that the Church lands were sold less often. The continuity of Church organization provided the Church estates with a stability that private properties could not attain.

INDIAN LANDS

The Spanish monarch, who considered the Indians his wards, felt obliged to protect them and to promote their well-being. This was all the more important since New Spain was considered one of the dynastic possessions of the king and not a colony of Castile. Thus from the outset, the Crown was determined to protect Indian property. The settlers did seize Indian lands, but this was done against the wishes of the Crown and it was a much slower process than usually imagined. Indeed, some Indian communities retained at least some of their lands well into the twentieth century.

The Crown issued a series of *cédulas reales* (royal decrees) protecting Indian lands. The cédula of 1532 stipulated that "The Indians shall continue to possess their lands, both arable tracts and grazing lands. . . ." Other decrees prohibited land distribution prejudicial to Indian communities and stipulated that if such grants had been made, they be revoked. Indian townsites *(fundos legales)* were well protected. By law a townsite required at least 500 varas (a vara was about 2,750 feet) in each of the four cardinal directions; later, in 1687, this was enlarged to 600 varas. In addition, no Mexican estate could extend to within a thousand varas of an Indian town. The requirements of the fundo legal were strictly enforced by Spanish authorities, who made periodic inspections to ensure that the laws were implemented.

The Crown intended that the Indian communities have more than merely a townsite. A later royal decree stated the Spanish intent that "Indian towns shall be given a site with sufficient water, arable lands, woodlands, and access routes so that they can cultivate their lands, plus an ejido of one league for grazing their cattle." In practice Indian pueblos varied widely in size and importance. The towns of central and southern Mexico, where sedentary Indian populations had existed before the arrival of the Spaniards, could rely upon their native rights. Such communities generally obtained validation of their titles from Spanish authorities. The resettled Indian towns in the north, however, were founded along the lines established by the Crown. While most communities possessed more than the minimum established by royal decree, they were constantly threatened by the colonists' tendency to encroach upon Indian lands. During the later sixteenth and early seventeenth centuries such conflicts diminished, in part as a result of the drastic decline in native population which permitted settlers to occupy uninhabited Indian lands. But the conflict became sharper by the mid-seventeenth century, as the Indian population recovered.

In addition to the fundos legales, native towns also owned communal lands which were divided into agricultural plots, pasture lands, and woodlands. Both pasture lands and woodlands existed for the use of the townspeople. Some Indians acquired numerous animals which they grazed on the village ejido—these were usually prosperous individuals and families who often owned private plots of land outside the community. Most villagers, however, cultivated the town lands, which were divided into plots for communal needs and tracts for individuals and families. The townspeople worked the community plots collectively to support religious activities, pay tribute, or meet other community expenses. Individuals or families, who as members of the village had the right to land and its usufruct, worked the other tracts. As a result of migration, dislocation, or special circumstances, pueblos often had landless residents and community servants who had no right to individual plots but generally enjoyed the right to cultivate communal tracts.

Many Indian lands were theoretically inalienable. Although *primitivo patrimonio* (lands dating from preconquest times) could not be sold, it proved impossible to sustain this concept in practice. The Indian nobles, who accepted the notion of private property very early, sold the conquerors lands which they claimed belonged to them and were distinct from communal holdings. Furthermore, some caciques and principales usurped communal lands, because the Spaniards often could not distinguish between the properties of the nobles and those of the communities. The authorities regarded grants made after the conquest to individual caciques or to communities as private property which could be alienated. Land transfers were not all one-sided, however. While some caciques sold land, others bought it. Indian villages soon bought and sold land according to their needs. By the end of the sixteenth century, the importance of land titles was clearly understood by most Indian towns. The mid-seventeenth-century composiciones dealt a crippling blow to the concept of primitivo patrimonio, because many of the titles thus legalized were to lands that had once belonged to Indian communities. But by that time the notion of private property had filtered down to the macehualli class.

The Indians cultivated a variety of products. Maize was their principal crop, but they also grew beans, chia, amaranth, chiles, squashes, tomatoes, cabbages, artichokes, lettuce, radishes, maguey, and *tunas* (prickly pears). While they adopted many of the European farming methods, they were unwilling to accept all European foods. The Spaniards tried to encourage the natives to grow wheat by requiring that tribute be paid in that grain. But most Indians refused to grow a crop which they did not use; instead, they bought wheat from Spanish farmers to pay the levy. Eventually the colonists had to accept other agricultural products as tribute, principally corn. The natives did adopt European animals quite readily, raising chickens, pigs, goats, and cattle.

Native agriculture had reached the limits of productivity in the years before the Spanish arrived; pressure on the land was great, and marginal soils were being cultivated for the first time. The conquest disrupted Indian agricultural patterns, and the introduction of livestock placed additional pressures on the land, in some cases leading to severe erosion and soil exhaustion. The demands of the conquerors for food and supplies as well as for labor, combined with epidemic disease, had devastating effects on the Indians, decimating the native population. Consequently there was a danger during the first few years after the conquest that the food supply might not suffice. In 1541, a sudden frost destroyed virtually the entire corn crop of the Valley of Mexico, forcing the viceregal government to import grain from other areas. Thereafter the viceroy established a system of *pósitos* (granaries) to assure a regular supply of corn. Droughts, floods, and frosts continued to damage crops during the colonial period—but although devastating, they were not catastrophic because public and private granaries assured a minimal food supply after 1541. When food shortages occurred, however, prices skyrocketed. Private landowners tended to withhold grain from the market until prices had increased substantially, causing severe hardships on the poor. Starvation never threatened the Mexican population, but some Indian communities were not so fortunate.

Although the incorporation of the native population into the money economy was gradual and remained incomplete at the end of the colonial period, they did slowly enter the colonial market system. The natives had been accustomed to surrendering part of the surplus to their rulers, a practice continued under the Spanish in the form of tribute. But in addition, Indian communities began to produce for the Mexican markets as well as for the traditional native markets. Some towns specialized in raising livestock. In the Tlaxcala, Puebla, Guadalajara, and Mixteca regions, Indian communities raised tens of thousands of sheep and hundreds of thousands of oxen, burros, mules, and horses. Indeed, by the end of the sixteenth century Indian villages became the principal suppliers of draft animals for the mule and cart trains that transported goods across Mexico. The natives also bartered or sold a variety of agricultural products and handicrafts, from chiles and tamales to firewood and sandals. In order to escape the heavy burdens of tribute and draft labor, many left their pueblos to live in towns and cities or to work on Mexican estates where the Indians became day laborers, skilled workers, and artisans. They and their children married mestizos or mulatos, eventually losing their Indian identity. In some villages, particularly those in areas of heavy Mexican concentration, the natives also adopted Mexican customs and finally ceased being Indians.

MINING

After agriculture, mining became the most important economic activity in New Spain. The development of the silver mines was the basis for the economic expansion of the sixteenth and early seventeenth centuries. Indeed, throughout the colonial period, silver mining served as the country's engine of economic growth. Although Cortés opened the first silver mines in Taxco in 1525, and other small strikes were made in subsequent years, these finds did not fulfill the Spanish dream of discovering El Dorado. Then, in 1546, Juan de Tolosa discovered the huge silver deposits in the hill of La Bufa in Zacatecas. In 1550, explorers made another great strike in Guanajuato, on the road between Mexico City and Zacatecas, and within a few years other strikes were made in San Luis Potosí, Real de Monte, Pachuca, Parral, etc. Although some mines were near the capital, the majority of the large finds were in the north, in the region called by the Spaniards the Gran Chichimeca because it was the home of nomads, or Chichimecas.

The Spaniards and their Indian retainers rushed into the area to exploit the riches. But the nomads did not give up their land willingly. Zacateco Indians harassed the intruders constantly. The main mining camps and the city of Zacatecas were secure, but the outlying areas were dominated by the nomads, who waged an incessant guerrilla war. The viceregal government tried to protect the silver trade by organizing armed convoys and by establishing towns along the road from Mexico City to the mines. These settlements served both as supply centers and as defense posts. San Miguel, founded in 1555, was the principal outpost on the way to Zacatecas; in 1562, San Felipe was established further north. Celaya, founded in 1571, and León, in 1576, protected the west. Durango and Nombre de Dios were founded north of the mines in 1563, and Saltillo in 1577. These settlements strengthened the Spanish hold in the north, but they could not prevent Indian attacks. Isolated mines and small convoys were often wiped out by marauding Chichimecas. The nomads, who adopted the horse within a few years of the arrival of the Europeans, were highly mobile and dangerous. The viceroy sent large military contingents to the north, where they built a series of forts *(presidios)* for defense. Toward the end of the sixteenth century a stalemate ensued: the Indians were unable to dislodge the Spaniards from their lands, and the colonists were unable to defeat the Chichimecas.

By the 1590s a peace of sorts settled in northern Mexico. Viceroy Luis de Velasco the younger initiated a pacification campaign. He distributed food, clothing, and agricultural goods to the nomads, and reduced the number of presidios and soldiers. This eased tension and helped end Indian hostility. Since the threat of war remained, however, Velasco established colonies of sedentary Indians from central Mexico in the Gran Chichimeca. The most famous of these civilized Indian settlers were the Tlaxcalans, who arrived in 1591. With Spanish encouragement and protection they spread to various regions in the northwest. In time the two groups of Indians intermingled, and the nomads were gradually transformed into settled agricultural peoples. But other warlike groups inhabited the far north, and the Chichimec problem continued until the late nineteenth century.

The Great Chichimec War and the silver boom consolidated the settlers' hold on the north, an area that would otherwise have remained outside the orbit of colonial Mexico. As a result of the conflict, Tarascan and Otomí Indian auxiliaries, who had fought on the side of the colonists, remained to settle the region. Other sedentary Indian groups were also attracted by jobs in the mines or by opportunities to establish agricultural communities. Silver made Zacatecas a rich city and the commercial center of the north; Nuevo León to the northeast became the principal supplier of livestock to the mines. By the turn of the century, northern settlers were strong enough to expand into New Mexico, founding Santa Fé in 1609.

Mexican silver production began to expand rapidly just as the Central European mining boom of 1451–1540 ended. Mining technology had reached its highest level in Germany and northern Italy, where drainage—the great problem of mines—had been solved by cutting adits (nearly horizontal drainage shafts) and by the use of horse-powered whims (machines used for raising or lowering heavy weights, like water or ore). The lead-smelting process was introduced in 1451, and stamp mills, driven either by water or by horses, further aided in refining. The new technology spread rapidly. Two works were extremely influential: Vannoccio Bringuccio's *De la Pirotechnia* (1540) on the latest Italian and German developments in metallurgy, and Georgius Agricola's treatise on the advances in German mining, *De re metallica* (1556). Agricola's work was significant because it included many woodcuts of mining processes and equipment. In 1557, Felipe II ordered that copies of the book be sent to miners both in Spain and in the

New World. In 1569, Bernardo Pérez de Vargas explained the best German and Italian mining techniques in his *De re metallica*. These works disseminated practical knowledge to miners in Mexico.

The Spaniards, who had had little mining experience, were ill-prepared to exploit the mineral wealth of New Spain. There were some iron mines in Asturias and the Basque provinces, but silver had not been extracted from the ground since Roman times. Ironically, silver-mining recovered in Spain only in the 1550s, after the great bonanzas had been discovered in the New World. Knowledge of advanced European metallurgy, however, did not solve the basic problem of Mexican silver-mining—a shortage of water. Since the greatest silver strikes were located in the arid north, the miners of New Spain had to develop a "dry mining" process which used limited amounts of water, in contrast to the profligately water-consuming processes of Saxony and Venice, the most advanced silver-mining areas of Europe.

Generally, silver was found in four levels in Mexico. Outcroppings contained rich ore as a result of weathering that removed the dross, leaving a high concentration of silver. Surface veins tended to mix with iron oxide, resulting in an ore of reddish color, generally called *colorados* by the miners. In the sixteenth century, the red ores were considered to be the richest as well as the most easily extracted. Below the surface lay great veins of low-grade ore known as *negros* because of their high lead-sulphide content and dark color. Deeper underground, usually below the water table at levels 400 to 600 feet below the surface, there were large deposits of native silver that had been formed through the percolation of rainwater: over the years it carried oxidized ores that were re-precipitated below the water-table level. These four levels required different forms of extraction. The surface veins were easily mined and needed little capital investment. The negros, however, required deep shafts and complex equipment. And the deep ores could only be extracted with great investments of time, labor, capital, and technology.

Although strikes were made at different times and therefore developed at different rates, the history of Mexican mining can be divided into three periods which generally coincided with the levels of the ore being extracted. In the first boom, lasting from the 1540s to the 1570s, the outcroppings were exploited. The second period, which ended in the late seventeenth century, was a time of more extensive mining, generally for the dark ores. After those veins were exhausted mining declined in the older centers, in part because of the cost and complexity of deep mining. Newly discovered mines, however, continued to produce. Then in the eighteenth century, silver-mining expanded dramatically when huge sums were invested in deep mining. A few Mexican miners sank the deepest shafts in the world in their efforts to extract silver-bearing ores.

Initially the mining of silver was a relatively simple affair. The early miners cut the outcroppings at the surface. This process was known as *de rato,* a term much later corrupted into English as the "rat-hole" method of mining. Slightly deeper ores were extracted by the *tajo abierto* process (open-cast mining). Both de rato and tajo abierto methods allowed the miners to follow the vein as it meandered haphazardly along the hillsides. The workings were generally simple, but unplanned and somewhat inefficient, and surface ores were exhausted within a few years. The most effective method would have been to dig well-designed shafts, but most miners tried to keep things as simple as possible. The laws regulating claims were partly responsible for this: a mine was defined as an area 120 yards long and 60 wide at the surface, and the discoverer could stake three claims. Companies could own four adjacent mines, while individuals were limited to one. As a result, mining sites were dotted with small workings whose owners were interested only in rapid profits. At first they tunneled into the hillsides following the veins. But as they dug deeper, they ran into the perennial obstacle of mining—water. By 1567 there were reports that some mines in Zacatecas were flooded. This meant that miners were forced to sink vertical shafts to operate the whims needed to drain underground water. Small miners who could not bear the expense either sold out or abandoned their claims. Toward the end of the sixteenth century large enterprises tended to dominate the principal mining regions, but small miners continued to be active, concentrating their activities in the new areas where outcroppings still existed.

Larger and deeper mines became common during the seventeenth century. A Zacatecan miner dug a shaft 112 feet deep. In Parral, which began its boom in the 1630s, the deepest shaft reached 130 yards, and by the end of the seventeenth century even deeper shafts became common—one in Real del Monte reached a depth of 200 yards. Deep shafts required extensive shoring and better drainage systems. Whims, generally powered by horses, were used to draw out the water in large leather bags. A few miners lined their shafts with wood to improve the draining process, but *bombas* (pumps), which had been introduced in 1609, became increasingly more common as the century progressed. While bombas were a great improvement and could be used underground, the large mines still required horse-driven whims as well as pumps to drain the water. Adits became necessary as shafts were cut deeper into the ground. Miners tried to avoid them because they were so costly, and adits were generally cooperative enterprises. In 1617 miners in San Luis Potosí constructed a drainage adit 150 yards long. The deep shafts were extremely costly: in the seventeenth century the larger ones cost hundreds of thousands of pesos; by the eighteenth century, they could cost more than a million pesos. Deep mining was also very time-consuming—excavating deep shafts and cutting adits could take years. This meant that great miners had to keep huge sums tied up for a considerable length of time. But the rewards were also immense—the great Mexican miners were among the richest plutocrats in the Spanish empire.

Some mine owners also maintained haciendas which supplied the needs of their mines. The grain- and livestock-producing estates of the largest miners not only supplied their workings with food, mules, horses, leather, lumber, charcoal, etc., but also sold supplies to smaller miners. Virtually all mine owners also possessed a refinery, known as an *hacienda de minas* or an *hacienda de beneficio,* which housed the equipment necessary to separate silver from ore.

The mines were important in developing a system of free wage labor in New Spain. It is difficult for us to tell how many persons worked in the mines. Some scholars estimate that by the sixteenth century, mine workers numbered about 10,000; in the seventeenth century, their numbers increased to no more than 45,000. Although they never constituted a large percentage of New Spain's labor force, mine workers constituted a labor elite. At first, the settlers sought forced labor for the mines, either in the form of *repartimiento* drafts or slaves. But mining required a small, skilled labor force. Draft Indian labor would not do except in the early days, and then only in areas close to Mexico City like Taxco and Pachuca. The use of slaves—blacks or Asians, usually known as *chinos*—generally proved uneconomic. Most workers were free Indians *(naboríos)*, mulatos, or mestizos who were attracted to the mines by the lure of high earnings. Mine owners, always anxious to retain workers, tried a variety of methods to keep them. At first they resorted to force: some miners locked their workers in private prisons; others tried to force them into debt peonage. But labor, particularly skilled labor, was too scarce for these methods to succeed. There were always mine owners willing to lure workers away from competition with payments in cash; in some instances they advanced as much as four to eight months' wages.

There were two kinds of belowground workers: *barreteros* (pickmen) and *tenateros* (ore-carriers). Since barreteros were skilled workers, they received higher wages. The tenateros did the heavy work of carrying 200- to 300-pound leather bags of ore to the surface. In the 1650s technical improvements, such as the introduction of whims to extract materials from the shafts, eased the lot of the carriers, but they continued to bear heavy burdens in most mines until the end of the colonial period.

Generally workers in the mines had better living and working conditions than their counterparts in other sectors of the economy. Mine owners usually maintained a mill *(hacienda de minas)* which also housed their workers. The laborers formed part of a *cuadrilla* (labor gang) who lived, ate, and worked together, perhaps giving them a sense of community which may have strengthened their ties to the mine. But it placed a substantial financial burden on the mine owners. Small operators were unable to compete with large entrepreneurs. Because of the nature of labor contracts, small mine owners were particularly vulnerable when the quality of their ore declined. Workers generally signed an agreement *(tequío)* that stipulated how much ore they were required to produce a day. Once the day's quota had been filled, each worker was allowed to gather a bagful of ore, known as a *pepena* or a *partido*. Naturally workers made certain that their share consisted of high-quality ore, which they sold to the highest bidder. This, rather than their salaries, made them the highest-paid workers in Mexico. Thus workers were attracted to mines with high-quality ores.

1. A *gobernadoryotl* complaining to Viceroy Velasco that settlers were forcing his people to pay more in tribute in wheat and animals than required by law.

2. An Indian complaint that an encomendero was making his tributaries work longer than legally required in his *hacienda* and in his *obraje*.

y-cmoquayat-eq
que tlatoque

3. An Indian illustration depicting the conversion of *caciques* while
   Cortés and Doña Marina look on.

4. Spanish wheat farmers
   harvesting.

5. Spanish wheat farmers
threshing.

6. An *hacienda de minas*.

7. A deep silver mine shaft, typical of the great eighteenth-century mines.

8. A small village scene in the eighteenth century.

13. A local tavern.

14. Muleteers in the high country.

15. A mule train crossing the jungle.

16. An *hacendado* and his *mayordomo*.

17. *Rancheros* in Sunday dress.

18. A sheepherder.

19. Lower-class people from Puebla dressed in a popular eighteenth-century style.

20. Upper-class women wearing mantillas dressed for a morning walk.

After the ore was extracted, it was carried to the hacienda de minas for refining. The silver-bearing ore was separated from the veinstone and then crushed in a *molino* (stamp mill). Molinos varied in design from very simple machines to rather complicated devices powered by teams of mules. The large refineries often had several mills which also processed the ores of small mines. The crushed ore was dropped into a sieve so that the small grains fell through, while the larger particles remained to be crushed again. Later it was ground to a powder *(harina)* in an *arrastre,* a mule-drawn device that consisted of heavy stones pulled over a stone floor. The final process of refinement consisted either of smelting or of amalgamation. In the smelting process, the crushed ore was put into a blast furnace, called a Castilian furnace, usually built of stone and equipped with bellows. Large haciendas de minas, with several furnaces, housed them in a shed *(galera)* and used mules to operate the bellows. Smelting required great quantities of wood for charcoal, which led to rapid deforestation. Furthermore, the process was not very effective with low-grade ores. By the 1560s it had become uneconomical in most areas and was abandoned in favor of the new *patio* process, although smelting continued in areas with plentiful supplies of charcoal and high-grade ores.

The patio or amalgamation process was an efficient method of extracting silver from the lower-grade ores mined during most of the Habsburg period (1519–1700). It was introduced in New Spain by Bartolomé de Medina in 1554. The process consisted of using mercury and salt to separate the silver from the rest of the ore. Workers piled the finely crushed harina into large *montones* (heaps) in a *patio* (stone-paved courtyard), where they added water until it became a muddy mixture. The *azoguero* (refiner) mixed the montón with salt and *azogue* (mercury). This was a very delicate operation requiring a highly skilled individual. Once it was mixed in the correct proportions, workers spread the montón into a thin cake *(torta)* and thoroughly stirred it. In the early days, workmen agitated the tortas with shovels; in later years, they drove teams of mules through them to speed up the mixing. The process of amalgamation could take as little as several weeks and as long as three months, depending on the weather. This was its main drawback, especially when compared to smelting, which normally took a few days. When the azoguero judged that the tortas had "cooked" enough, he ordered the mixture moved into the washing tubs *(tinas)*. In the larger operations these vats were equipped with mule-driven paddles; workers poured water into the tinas and separated the silver by agitation. Mines located near rivers or streams relied on their water to wash the blend. Finally the remaining amalgam, or *pella,* was incinerated to separate the silver from the mercury. Generally about a quarter to a third of the mercury used in the patio process was lost.

The azogue needed for the mines came principally from two sources: the Almadén mercury mine in Spain and the Huancavelica mine in Peru. During the sixteenth century, Almadén supplied New Spain, while Huancavelica met the needs of the Viceroyalty of Peru. When these sources did not suffice, the Crown purchased mercury from the Idria mine in present-day Yugoslavia, then part of the Austrian Empire. The Spanish government assumed control of the distribution of mercury in 1559, when amalgamation became important, and at first sought the greatest possible profit: azogue that cost 75 pesos to produce in Spain sold in 1560 for 215 pesos in Mexico City; by the end of the decade it had climbed to 310 pesos. Within a few years, however, the price dropped as the monarchy realized that cheap mercury encouraged greater silver production, thus yielding a higher income from taxation. Azogue prices fell to 180 pesos in 1572, to 110 pesos in 1597, and to 60 pesos in 1608. Since the 1608 price was well below production costs, it was raised to 82 pesos in 1617, and mercury remained at that price for most of the seventeenth century. Considering transportation costs, the low seventeenth-century prices were, in effect a government subsidy to the silver miners.

The Crown also sought to prevent concentration in the mines. As with agriculture, the government wanted to ensure that small producers participated. It achieved that goal by subsidizing silver miners in two ways: reducing taxes and liberalizing credit. The Spanish state owned the subsoil mineral rights and theoretically could have extracted the precious metals, but in practice it allowed its subjects to exploit that wealth in return for a payment of one-fifth of production, the *quinto.* Miners in New Spain, however, claimed that the cost of mining was so great that they could ill afford to pay a fifth, and in 1548 they obtained a reduction to a tenth, a *diezmo.* The refiners, workers, and silver merchants had to continue paying the quinto, but they gradually obtained reductions, so that by the early seventeenth century they too were paying a tenth. Eventually, in 1723, the Crown legalized the situation by requiring everyone to pay a diezmo on silver. The government also aided miners by selling mercury on credit, and did not force them to pay on schedule. The mine owners took advantage of this policy to incur large debts which they were slow to repay. By 1620, miners in Zacatecas alone owed the king 356,000 pesos for mercury.

Circumstances, however, changed in the next two decades, when reduced revenues and increasing demands for government funds forced the Crown to revise its policy. In addition, mercury production declined, making it harder to justify easy credit to Mexican miners at a time when mines in Peru were more productive. In 1643 the Crown ordered credit terminated, required that sales be for cash, and instructed the viceroy to collect the old debts. Azogue credits were abolished, but the debt proved impossible to collect. Such a drastic change in policy had profound effects on the industry. The shortage of mercury in the mines, the result both of scarcity and the terms of sale, meant that many mines were no longer profitable. Production declined sharply in the older mining centers like Zacatecas. Countless small miners were driven out of business. The later seventeenth century has generally been considered a period of decline for the mining industry in New Spain. Recent studies, however, indicate that new strikes and areas with high-grade ores, which could rely on the cheaper smelting process, continued to produce. Indeed, John TePaske and Herbert Klein argue that silver production not only did not decline but may have increased during this period.

The Crown was not the only source of credit for the miners. From the earliest days merchants entered the lucrative business of supplying the mines with food, equipment, and other necessities. Since most miners usually had their capital invested in their operation, the *aviadores* (suppliers) extended credit. Such transactions provided the first step toward making loans, and finally investing directly in the mines. Aviadores generally served as distributors at the local level. Some were independent businessmen, but quite a few were agents for large Mexico City merchants, and some doubled as both. When the Crown abolished credit for mercury, some

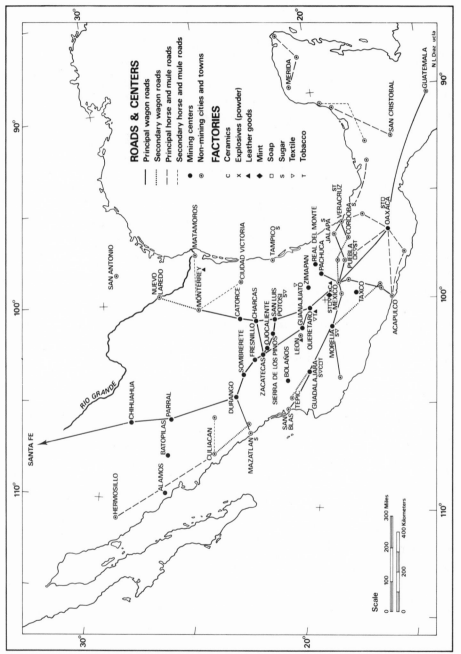

MINING AND MANUFACTURING IN EIGHTEENTH-CENTURY MEXICO

ROADS & CENTERS

Principal wagon roads
Secondary wagon roads
Principal horse and mule roads
Secondary horse and mule roads
● Mining centers
⊙ Non-mining cities and towns

FACTORIES

c Ceramics
× Explosives (powder)
▲ Leather goods
□ Mint
s Soap
s Sugar
▽ Textile
т Tobacco

Scale

0   100   200   300 Miles

0   200   400 Kilometers

SANTA FE

RIO GRANDE

CHIHUAHUA
PARRAL
BATOPILAS
ALAMOS
HERMOSILLO
CULIACAN
MAZATLAN s
SAN BLAS
TEPIC
DURANGO
SOMBRERETE
ZACATECAS
FRESNILLO
SIERRA DE LOS PINOS
CHARCAS
CATORCE
OJOCALIENTE
SAN LUIS POTOSI sv
BOLAÑOS
LEON
GUANAJUATO
QUERETARO
GUADALAJARA svccτ
MORELIA sv
TEPIC
ZIMAPAN
PACHUCA ▲
REAL DEL MONTE
MEXICO
STO DCA sv
TAXCO
ACAPULCO
JALAPA
VERACRUZ
CORDOBA s
PUEBLA DCVst
OAXACA STO
TAMPICO s
CIUDAD VICTORIA
MONTERREY ▲
NUEVO LAREDO
MATAMOROS
SAN ANTONIO
MERIDA
SAN CRISTOBAL
GUATEMALA

N L Diaz ucla

110°   100°   90°

30°   20°

merchants extended loans to miners. These entrepreneurs naturally backed successful mines, which were often large concerns. Within a few years, the major Mexico City merchants came to dominate mining. By the end of the seventeenth century, a group of powerful *mercaderes de plata* (silver merchants) composed a new plutocratic elite. Indeed, some of them became the first millionaires in the New World.

COMMERCE

Commerce in New Spain grew rapidly from the simple exchange of a few imported goods from Spain, in the early days, to a complex and extensive network of trade and credit by the end of the sixteenth century. The great commercial and financial center, Mexico City, established relations with each of the regions of New Spain, selling imported as well as locally manufactured goods and purchasing regional products. A few other cities, such as Zacatecas and Puebla, also served as regional metropolitan centers, but they could not compare or compete with the viceregal capital. Although provincial economies developed a diverse base, they did not establish interprovincial exchanges to any great extent. Each traded individually with Mexico City, which grew in size, wealth, power, and influence. During the sixteenth century, New Spain evolved its own internal market and grew increasingly less dependent on the mother country; by 1620, trade with Spain had declined drastically. But while the Atlantic commerce entered a period of depression at that time, internal trade continued to expand in Mexico as the Mexican and the acculturated populations grew, while the Indian population reached its nadir.

From the days of the conquest, the Spanish government had been concerned with controlling commerce and navigation between the Iberian peninsula and the colonies. The *Casa de Contratación* (Board of Trade), established in 1503, became one of the most important imperial institutions of the Spanish monarchy. It not only regulated commerce to meet royal needs, but also protected the interests of various groups. Members of the Casa, although subsequently subordinated to the Council of the Indies, could suggest changes to facilitate trade directly to the monarch.

As commercial activities grew more complex, the Casa extended its operations accordingly. In 1514 the office of Postmaster General was established and conferred in perpetuity on a distinguished jurist and member of the Council of Castile, Dr. Lorenzo Galíndez de Carvajal. The office remained a private concession under the overall supervision of the Casa until 1706, when the Spanish Postal Service began to function. The office of Chief Pilot, created in 1508 to chart the new seas, developed into a hydrographic bureau that was also responsible for licensing competent maritime personnel. Careful and systematic information of geographical discoveries and exploration was recorded and charted on a large master map to which all other maps and charts had to conform. Nevertheless, chronic shortages of trained pilots, as well as the rudimentary nature of navigation in the sixteenth and seventeenth century, combined to exact a tremendous toll in shipping. Ship design stressed size at the expense of maneuverability, which may have made economic sense but magnified maritime hazards. In addition, weather patterns could not be charted in the broadest sense, and consequently tropical storms often destroyed ships both at sea and in port: in 1591, for example, a storm grounded 16 ships at anchor in Veracruz harbor, and 14 ships were destroyed in a similar disaster in 1601. The Casa attempted within the limits of existing technology to deal with such problems, as well as to stimulate new breakthroughs.

The Casa de Contratación served as an administrative court with authority over civil disputes between merchants or in matters affecting royal tax revenues; it also presided over trials of crimes committed aboard ships in the transatlantic trade, although appeals might be made to the Council of the Indies. In 1583 the Crown authorized a separate judicial chamber *(sala de justicia)*, complete with a judge. The Casa also licensed passengers to the Indies, in order to assure that elements considered dangerous to the well-being of the New World, or the task of Christianization, did not reach America. Vagabonds and other socially marginal types, Jews, Protestants, Moors, and gypsies were to be screened out. In fact it proved impossible to control the flow of immigration.

In spite of the energy expended by the Casa to stimulate trade between Spain and her colonies, it failed to accomplish its goal, largely because Spanish industrial and commercial interests failed to develop sufficiently to satisfy the needs of the American empire.

Another major obstacle was the difficulty of marketing new and exotic products in Europe. Slow acceptance, in an age without organized advertising, frustrated many a hopeful entrepreneur. Cacao for making chocolate, for example, did not catch on in Europe until well into the seventeenth century. In 1620 it was in use in an Austrian monastery as an exotic elixir, prompting a Franciscan to publish an attack on cacao, allegedly because it inflamed the passions. As with any new product, a long period of experimentation was necessary before the preferred mixture or preparation could be found. Eventually the bitter chocolate brew preferred by the Aztecs gave way to a sweet mixture suited to European palates. Similarly, use of tobacco spread slowly, becoming accepted in parts of Europe in the early seventeenth century. Food crops such as potatoes and maize could be introduced and grown in the Old World, adding to its food resources but not to transatlantic trade—just as European plants and animals enriched New Spain's internal market, but did not affect export trade. Sugar, for example, introduced relatively early, soon met the needs of Mexico, with only insignificant amounts being shipped to Europe. Spain grew its own sugar in the southern regions and in the Canary Islands. It remained for the Portuguese and the Dutch in Brazil to develop a worldwide market for sugar, beginning around 1580.

There were only a few exceptions to this generally dismal trade picture. Indigo was actually cultivated for export, and hides and tallow provided some profit—but none of these products was in sufficient demand to create a healthy trading situation. The single item Mexico produced for which there was an unquenchable demand in Europe was precious metals. The transatlantic trade depended overwhelmingly on silver, although some gold was also sent from Mexico to Spain. Cargo leaving the port of Veracruz consisted of at least 80 percent bullion. In exchange for silver, Americans purchased European manufactured goods. Spain's inability to produce desirable commodities for consumption in New Spain meant that such goods had to be purchased in other countries; the products were then transshipped through peninsular ports to conform with Spanish trade regulations. As a result, foreigners profited the most from the American trade, while Spain serving as a middleman retained only a small percentage of the profits from this commerce.

Piracy, attracted by the bullion trade, soon became a serious problem, further complicating the task of the Casa de Contratación. Out of necessity a convoy system, the *flota,* developed, limiting trade contact to once a year. Illegal trade flourished outside of the flota system, and smuggling became profitable and conformed to the needs of a developing economy. By the 1630s a decline in the volume of official trade became evident, and by the 1650s fleets rarely numbered more than 40 vessels. Smuggling, and the growth of domestic manufacture in New Spain, cut deeply into regulated commerce, forcing the Crown to raise taxes on the declining legal commerce to maintain government revenues. Higher taxes merely encouraged merchants to turn to smugglers. The Casa eventually abandoned the ad valorem duties and demanded an arbitrary lump sum called the *indulto* which could be adjusted to reflect some of the value of the illegal as well as the legal trade.

Although the Casa de Contratación was charged with regulating New World trade and navigation, it did not enjoy a monopoly. The *Consulado* (merchants' guild) of Seville—a private institution—was also authorized to trade with America. Merchants from other parts of Spain and from other nations were at first excluded, but as the seventeenth century progressed other entrepreneurs entered the *Carrera de las Indias* (Indies trade) legally through partnerships with Seville merchants. Earlier, in the sixteenth century, the colonists had needed European foodstuffs, wine, and olive oil, as well as iron and iron implements, cloth, and some manufactures. But as New Spain's economy developed, the demand for these basic commodities declined. Instead, the colonists demanded manufactured goods which Spain could not provide. As a result, foreigners soon came to indirectly dominate the American trade. Of course a brisk contraband trade flourished which the Spanish Crown was unable to control.

The Consulado of Seville had its counterpart in New Spain in the Consulado of Mexico City, established in 1592. The Consulado resided in the capital rather than in Veracruz, to avoid the unhealthy climate of the port. Modeled on the Consulado of Seville, it controlled the regulated trade with the Old World. Like its Spanish counterpart, the Consulado of Mexico attempted to restrict commerce. Monopoly merchants pressured the Crown for favorable legislation to preserve advantages at the expense of the colonial consumer. To accomplish their ends, Consulado merchants retained a full-time agent in Madrid to represent their interests at court. On a more positive note, the Consulado of Mexico undertook road, warehouse, and harbor improvements to facilitate the movement of goods. It also contributed to social order by maintaining armed units for emergencies, by collecting certain taxes for the Crown, by contributing operating funds to some viceregal organizations, and by providing occasional subsidies to the king. Eventually the Consulado became a highly influential conservative interest group allied with Crown officials and Spanish merchant houses engaged in the Carrera de las Indias.

Although the Consulado was a powerful body, it did not include, nor did it represent, all the merchants of Mexico City. In 1689 there were 628 persons officially classified as merchants in the viceregal capital. Only 177, however, were engaged in large wholesale operations, and of these only 30 were elected to the merchant's guild. They in turn chose 5 deputies, 2 consuls, and a prior from their ranks, to run the institution. Thus the wealthy traders were the leaders of the Consulado as well as of the community. Merchants served in the government in various capacities, particularly as tax collectors, treasurers, and other sorts of fiscal agents. In this way the mercantile community exercised considerable influence directly as Crown officials and indirectly as members of a powerful interest group. The great merchants, naturally, profited from their posts. They could affect the distribution of mercury, ease trade regulations by the simple expedient of not enforcing them, or benefit themselves and their allies by preferential treatment. They ensured their position by extending generous credit to royal officials. The viceroy and the audiencia judges were often indebted to the great merchants, while lower officials generally borrowed from smaller local businessmen. The merchants also retained close ties with the Church, which not only provided them with credit but with influence and support as well.

The merchants of New Spain engaged in a variety of activities. The wealthiest traded on a great scale: participating in the monopoly trade with the mother country; buying cacao from Venezuela and Guayaquil; exchanging Mexican silver for Oriental luxury fabrics like silks, linens, satins, damasks, and cottons; selling Mexican leather and household goods for Peruvian silver or mercury; and financing mining in New Spain. These merchant princes consolidated their position in the seventeenth century. They lived in great townhouses in Mexico City, dominating the commerce and often the politics of New Spain. Viceroys and other Crown officials complained that merchants formed virtually an aristocracy in Mexico. Not surprisingly, the interests of the merchants often clashed with those of the Crown, particularly when the government attempted to limit trade between the viceroyalties of New Spain and Peru in 1604, and when this trade was abolished in 1631. Although the great merchants resorted to contraband and other subterfuges to continue the Peruvian trade, it declined substantially; the cacao trade continued, however. Legal intercolonial commerce was not restored until 1774. Mexico's merchants also had similar problems with regard to the trade with Manila, which served as an entrepot between America and Asia.

The Manila trade grew in importance during the seventeenth century. Since the Philippine Islands were a colony of New Spain, Mexican merchants could operate with greater freedom than when they traded with the mother country. The first Manila galleon sailed in 1565, and thereafter it made a yearly voyage between Acapulco and the Philippines. Commerce increased substantially over the years, as American silver was exchanged for a variety of Oriental wares. The Pacific trade and the subsidies New Spain sent to the Audiencia of Manila led to a substantial outflow of bullion that might otherwise have gone to Spain. The viceregal government tried to arrest this flow of silver to the East by issuing restrictions in 1593, establishing a limit of 250,000 pesos for the value of the annual trade. But merchants in New Spain regularly circumvented those restrictions through smuggling and tax evasion. By the mid-seventeenth century the Manila trade was worth about 2,500,000 pesos annually; perhaps a third of Mexico's silver flowed to Asia. Many large fortunes owed their origin to this lucrative commerce.

In a belated effort to gain control of the Manila trade, the viceroy raised the legal maximum to 300,000 pesos in 1702; to 500,000 in 1734; and finally to 750,000 in 1776, a limit which lasted until 1815, when the Manila galleon sailed for the last time. The official limits, however, were totally unrealistic and in no way restricted or diminished the illegal trade, which continued to flourish. Spanish officials were reluctant to sanction the growth of commerce with the Far East because they viewed it as a threat to national security. It not only reduced the amount of silver available to the Crown, but in their eyes also opened New Spain to Portuguese, Dutch, and English interests which were hostile to the Spanish empire. Nevertheless, the trade persisted and even expanded, because it benefitted powerful groups in Mexico who were more preoccupied with their own well-being than with that of the Crown.

Although international trade was important to New Spain's merchants, internal commerce also expanded dramatically, beginning in the late sixteenth century. The great merchants, known as *almaceneros* (warehousemen), acted as both importers and distributors. They generally purchased European as well as Oriental goods in large quantities, distributing them from their warehouses in Mexico City. Distributors—*aviadores*—sold the imported goods in provincial centers where they also traded in local products. Most aviadores were agents of the almaceneros of the capital, but a few were independent merchants. The agents, or factors, tended to reside in provincial cities for years at a time, yet they remained citizens *(vecinos)* of Mexico City. They sold a variety of textiles, both Asian and European. Initially both coarse and fine cloth had good markets, but as local textile manufacturing increased, the demand for common cloth diminished; *ropa de Castilla*—fine cloth—however remained in much demand. A similar change occurred with regard to European foods. In the early years the colonists imported cereals, but this ended by the mid-sixteenth century. Other imported foodstuffs, however, including sweetmeats, sardines, olives, and wine, remained important items in local trade. European metal utensils, particularly kitchenware and tools, were also highly desired by the settlers. Factors normally extended credit, usually not exceeding 500 pesos, to the larger provincial retail merchants.

Mexico City merchants also sold African slaves through factors. Slave traders were usually itinerant merchants who took trains of slaves to provincial centers for sale. Blacks were in great demand in prosperous areas like Mexico City, Zacatecas, and Puebla, as well as in tropical regions like Veracruz and Morelos. The slave trade was very volatile. Prices rose quickly during the sixteenth century, leveled off in the early seventeenth, and declined by the mid-seventeenth century. By that time free labor had become much more important. The slave trade was quite lucrative, however, for about a century.

Independent merchants with limited capital and commercial contacts traveled with their merchandise from place to place. Although they operated on a smaller scale than their merchant-factor competitors, these itinerant merchants were also engaged in the wholesale trade. They generally marketed their goods to local retailers. In this respect they differed from *tratantes* (itinerant peddlers), who sold directly to the public on the retail level. These smaller entrepreneurs, often new arrivals or subordinates of a new marginal enterprise attempting to enter the local market, aspired to become more important merchants.

In addition to professional merchants, numerous government officials also engaged in trade as a sideline. Some were substantial entrepreneurs, operating on a relatively large scale. They acted as agents for Mexico City merchants, and often continued in business after their appointments ended. Local officials also extended credit to small ranchers and agriculturalists. In Indian communities, they supplied seeds, tools, and credit, as well as other goods, through the system of *repartimiento de comercio*. In exchange, they marketed the village's crop in the regional market. Although merchant-bureaucrats became crucial links between the capital and local economies, they often abused the system. There were many complaints that Indian towns were being forced to buy large quantities of books, statues, and other goods they did not need simply to pacify the local bureaucrat.

Although the national merchants were important, they did not control the provincial markets, being principally concerned with the wholesale trade. Local businessmen dominated the retail trade. Local merchants relied on Mexico City, Zacatecas, and Puebla for goods and credit, but they also engaged in provincial trade. They bought and sold local products such as wool, grain, hides, animals, and silver. The major provincial businessmen developed ties with Mexico City, and some of the more successful of them married their daughters into prominent metropolitan merchant families. Nonetheless, they retained an independence from the great almaceneros. Local stores, run by poor immigrant relatives of local businessmen-landowners, generally handled a diverse merchandise including foodstuffs, household goods, tools, furniture, cloth, clothing, and weapons. A local *tienda* might also carry special goods, such as tools for the miners.

Despite its varied and complex economy, New Spain did not adopt the advanced forms of commercial organization then common in northern Europe; business ventures were either partnerships or *compañías*, formed for limited periods and objectives. The compañía was a common type of arrangement among merchants; usually it was an agreement between a wholesaler who supplied the merchandise and the agent who sold it at the local level. The compañía contract specified the contributions each was to make, listed the limitations of the agreement, and specified the benefits that were to accrue to both parties. Similar arrangements were made informally among family members. The importance of the family enterprise probably had much to do with retarding the development of modern business institutions in Mexico.

MANUFACTURING

Although the colonists initially imported finished products from Spain, by the 1570s nearly all commonly used goods were made in Mexico. Manufacturing (producing hand-made products) became an important sector of the economy employing a sizable portion of the urban population. Furniture, clothes, soap, ceramics, glass, leather goods, metal products, paper, and countless other necessities were produced in artisan shops in Mexico City, Puebla, Guadalajara and, on a smaller scale, in the other cities and towns of the colony.

Textile factories became the largest manufacturing enterprises in Mexico. When the Spaniards arrived, they found that the Indians were highly skilled in weaving textiles. Indeed, Cortés was so amazed at the quality of Aztec cottons that he declared, "Nothing in the world could match their texture, [which was] incomparably softer than silk." These fabrics were produced in large quantities. Moctezuma II collected an annual tribute of nearly three million yards of fine cotton cloth, and an overall annual production of six to seven million yards was probably needed to meet the needs of the Aztec empire. After the conquest, cotton cloth production declined. Demand fell because of the drastic reduction in the native population and because the Indians accepted the heavier woolens preferred by the Europeans. Postconquest cotton textile production did not surpass that of the Aztecs until the mid-nineteenth century, and then only by employing modern machinery. During most of the colonial period, cotton cloth manufacturing continued as a minor part of the textile industry, restricted largely to rural Indian areas.

Silk was the first textile introduced by the colonists. In 1523, Cortés received mulberry trees and silkworm eggs along with the livestock, cuttings, seeds, and implements he had requested from the Spanish government. During the late 1520s and 1530s the settlers established silk production as an important enterprise in the Mexico City area. Skilled Spanish silk weavers arrived in Mexico City as early as 1535. Within a decade the capital had more than 20 operating looms, with others under construction. They produced satin, taffeta, velvet, and fine red silk cloth as well as sashes, ribbons, and laces. The capital's artisans sought to restrict competition by obtaining the exclusive right to produce silk. They also established a silk guild that excluded slaves. The Mexico City monopoly did not last long, however, for the silk industry expanded rapidly to Puebla, where some slave labor was used, and south to the Mixteca. By 1550, silk production had spread to most areas settled by Spaniards, but the center and near south remained the main area.

The Mexican silk industry prospered during the sixteenth century. Manufacturers met not only the needs of New Spain but also supplied the Viceroyalty of Peru. Toward the end of the century, however, the industry began to decline, and it ceased to exist early in the seventeenth century. Most observers blame the demise of the silk industry on competition from imported Oriental silks and on Crown restrictions, particularly the 1634 prohibition of trade with South America. But there is little evidence to support such views. The importation of Chinese silks ruined the market for Spanish silks, but not for Mexican products. The silk guilds of New Spain responded to the competition by improving the grade of their weaves and using the Asian yarn to vary their fabrics, and this innovation increased silk manufacturing in Mexico City, Puebla, and Oaxaca. A more plausible explanation for the demise of the silk industry was the decline in the production of raw silk that began in the 1580s, as a result of Mexico's demographic crisis.

Silk production was a labor-intensive enterprise which was economically viable only where there was abundant, cheap labor. Such conditions existed only during the first half of the sixteenth century, when thousands of Indian villages labored at the tedious and time-consuming task of raising silkworms. But during the next decade, epidemics decimated the native population. The great plague of 1576–1579 apparently reduced the Indian population by half. Many prosperous silk-producing communities, particularly those in the Atlixco and Mixteca areas, simply ceased to exist, or so few Indians survived that they could no longer care for the insects. After 1592 the viceregal government unsuccessfully attempted to revive the silk industry, which remained stagnant until the eighteenth century.

Woolen textile production became the largest and most important Mexican manufacturing enterprise. Woolen *obrajes*—large-scale factories employing as many as 200 to 300 workers—were common in Spain. But high transportation costs between Europe and the New World limited trade to fine cloth. Demand for cheap textiles had to be met locally, and shortly after the conquest obrajes were established in New Spain. The market for woolens grew because the Indians, as well as the colonists, preferred them to the light native cotton cloth. When Puebla was founded in 1532, some of the new settlers established obrajes to produce both coarse and fine cloth. Within a few years woolen manufacturing spread to central and southern Mexico: Puebla, Mexico City, Querétaro, Valladolid, Texcoco, and Tlaxcala became the principal woolen centers. The vast expansion of sheep-raising provided cheap and abundant raw materials; 300,000 pounds of wool was being produced yearly in New Spain by 1580. At that time Puebla had more than 40 obrajes in operation, employing about 12,000 workers; Mexico City ranked second with 35 obrajes. These two cities remained important centers of textile production throughout the colonial period, but in the seventeenth century Querétaro took the lead in woolen textile manufacturing in New Spain.

Woolen manufacturing was carried out in three settings: o-brajes, *obrajes de comunidad,* and *trapiches.* Obrajes de comunidad were Indian-run enterprises, initially established by encomenderos who required the natives to work in their obrajes. The Crown outlawed the practice in 1549 when personal services were forbidden as a form of tribute. Thereafter many encomenderos demanded tribute payment in cloth. To satisfy this tax, some Indian communities engaged in large-scale woolen manufacturing. They not only produced enough to pay their tribute and supply their needs, but also generated a surplus which they sold to other native villages and to Mexican towns.

Many colonists who were engaged in wool manufacturing operated trapiches, small enterprises of one or two looms. Individuals with little capital and few connections could begin with trapiches. These small entrepreneurs had a difficult time in the late sixteenth and seventeenth century when obrajes—the larger, better-capitalized colonial enterprises—dominated the field. But trapiches survived to prosper in the eighteenth century, when they manufactured more than one-third of the woolen cloth produced in New Spain.

Obrajes, however, dominated woolen manufacturing. Those located in Puebla, Mexico City, and Querétaro were urban factories employing thousands of workers by the seventeenth century. The *obrajeros* (manufacturers) often attempted to cut costs through vertical integration—many raised sheep in their own estancias and then processed the wool from raw material to finished product at a single site. This was true of urban factories as well as rural obrajes situated on large haciendas throughout Mexico. In a few areas, like Querétaro, however, an alternate method evolved: Indian villages received wool from the obrajeros, spun it, and delivered it to the obraje, or they spun their own wool and then sold it to the manufacturers. Thereafter, the remaining steps in cloth production took place in the factory under a single roof.

The obraje represented a substantial investment in physical plant. A typical factory was a flat-roofed building with many rooms to house the complex manufacturing operations. The roof and the basement generally served as storage areas. Looms, spinning wheels, teasels, boilers, and other elaborate machinery were required to operate the factory. The wool was carded and combed for weaving in a room called the *emborrito;* in another room, the *batán* (fulling mill), machines with large wooden hammers rotating on a water-powered axle pressed and shrank the wool after it had been cleansed. Then it was dyed in special rooms where large cauldrons were often built below ground level. Finally, the weaving was done in the largest room in the factory, the *obrador,* where the looms *(telares)* and warping frames *(urdidores)* were located. Other rooms were used to store the firewood and lard needed for manufacture. The larger obrajes included a separate area complete with sleeping quarters, kitchens, pantries, and a chapel for the workers.

Obrajes provided employment for a large segment of the labor force. Initially the settlers relied on the encomienda and the repartimiento to supply them with workers. By the end of the sixteenth century, slaves—African and Asian—as well as mulatos, mestizos, and free Indians comprised the bulk of the workers. The Crown established a complex series of regulations governing obraje workers, who included free contractual laborers, indentured servants, prisoners, and slaves. Although the regulations were not rigorously enforced, they seem to have given some protection to the workers. During the period from 1590 to 1680, average monthly obraje wages increased from 1.50 pesos to 5 pesos, a substantial wage at that time. Although obrajes acquired a reputation for wretched working conditions, principally because prisoners were often sent to work there, recent studies indicate that the lot of the workers in textile factories was no worse than in the mines, on the landed estates of Mexico, or in comparable enterprises in Europe. Notarial records indicate that many workers appeared to be content, that they were paid regularly, and that even involuntary workers—slaves, indentured servants, and prisoners—were usually treated reasonably well. Since obrajeros generally faced a shortage of labor, they did their best to attract workers to their factories. Like the mine owners and the hacendados, they paid off their workers' debts, advanced salaries to some, and even arranged for husbands and wives to work together. Parents sometimes apprenticed their sons in obrajes, where they learned some skill such as weaving during their three-year apprenticeship.

Obrajeros, like other entrepreneurs, operated within the context of the diversified family enterprise. Generally the manufacturers were also merchants and, in a few instances, landowners. They typically borrowed from the Church to finance their operations and they employed their relatives in supervisory capacities. The finished cloth was sold in bulk to local *tiendas de paños* (cloth shops), to landowners and miners for their workers, and to wholesale merchants. Most obrajeros established complex distribution networks through family connections. By the seventeenth century, obrajeros had become an important group. Some were wealthy and had established ties with the great merchant, mining, and landowning families of New Spain.

TRANSPORTATION

The wealth of the Mexican economy, the regional specialization of production, and the high level of circulation of consumer goods required an efficient transportation system. Although Mexico had extensive shorelines on both sides of the continent, coastal shipping was limited because the country had few good harbors and the major population and production centers were located in the central highlands, away from both coasts. Since the interior lacked navigable rivers, it became essential to create a system of land transportation. This was difficult in New Spain, a large colony with an extremely rugged topography. Although important regions were often separated by high mountains, great gorges, rampaging rivers, and vast distances, colonial Mexico developed an extensive and complex network of transportation.

New Spain utilized both Indian and European systems of transport. Since Mesoamerica lacked draft animals, the natives relied on professional porters, *tamemes*. These carriers, who transported goods throughout Mexico, could travel in trains over very rugged terrain. After the conquest, many Spaniards continued to use tamemes to haul goods and products, but—as with other traditional Indian practices—abuse soon became common. By 1529 Bishop Zumárraga denounced the use of human transport, declaring, "The Indians are very badly used by Spanish travelers, who take them, laden like pack animals and even without feeding, wherever they wish to go, and for this reason the Indians suffer great harm and even die along the road."

The Crown prohibited the use of human carriers on humanitarian grounds. But the colonists protested strenuously that the practice was acceptable to the natives and, in any case, necessary, owing to the topography of the country. In the face of determined opposition, the king compromised and merely sought to regulate the system. Royal decrees ordered that Indians not be forced to work as tamemes, that operators be licensed, routes fixed, distances and time worked reduced, and limits placed on the size and weight of the loads. The monarch sought to create a voluntary labor force, free to choose its work and able to command fair wages. In practice, many of the decrees were disregarded, since the Crown could not force its distant subjects to comply with the law. Eventually economic reality, rather than legislation, relegated human carriers to a secondary position. Had tamemes been the most efficient carriers, they would have remained the principal means of transport, but they could not carry heavy loads, like bullion, far enough or fast enough to suit the needs of the expanding economy. In time, porters were limited to carrying goods in peripheral areas or in places not accessible by other forms of transport.

With the expansion of agriculture and the discovery of silver in the north, the colonists turned to European methods of transport. Spain, a country with a mountainous terrain similar to Mexico's, had a highly developed transport system—mule trains and carts—which could be adapted to the new land. Extremely mountainous roads, such as the one between Veracruz and Mexico City, could only be traversed by mule trains. But the north, with its plateaus and less rugged sierras, was well suited for carts. Short-distance carting was originally handled by farmers who hauled freight when not engaged in agriculture. They met local needs by transporting regional products to market. In some parts of the country, part-time carriers provided most of the short-distance service throughout the colonial period, but professional short-haul carriers took over a significant sector of the transport business around major urban concentrations. Cross-country hauling also required full-time professional muleteers, *arrieros;* long-distance mule trains were large, with 30 to 40 animals and 10 or more arrieros. Initially, individuals owned their own mules and joined other muleteers to form a train. But within a few decades, the risks—particularly the danger of Indian raids, in the north—and the volume of shipping required a more sophisticated arrangement, and larger mule trains owned by a single individual replaced the small operators on the most lucrative routes. The large trains were often financed by entrepreneurs—such as merchants or miners—who depended on their services. Sometimes a successful arriero purchased more mules, hired helpers, and expanded his operation. As with other enterprises, successful muleteers diversified their holdings by investing in merchandise and in land.

The other major component of the European transport system, the cart, had to be modified to fit Mexico's needs. The *carreta,* an ox-driven cart used in Spain, was not large or strong enough to transport Mexico's most valuable product, silver. Besides, oxen, while reliable, were quite slow. Thus carretas became prime targets for Chichimeca attacks along the road from the Zacatecas mines to Mexico City. In the mid-sixteenth century Juan Carrasco, a professional carter, solved the problem by developing the Mexican *carro*—a large cart, pulled by as many as 16 mules in a team, which could carry 4,000 to 5,000 pounds, as compared to the 1,000-pound capacity of the carreta. Carros were often covered with heavy planking and armed with spikes and clams as protection against hostile nomads. Since mules moved much faster than oxen, the carro was ideal for the conditions of New Spain. Depending on the volume of freight and the area to be traversed, trains ranged in size from 20 to 80 carros. Such trains *(cuadrillas de carros)* represented a heavy capital investment and were owned by entrepreneurs *(señores de carros)* who operated on a large scale. This was particularly true of the cuadrillas de carros plying the lucrative northern routes.

Carting changed during the second half of the seventeenth century. The large armed carros were in less demand once the hostile nomads became peaceful villagers. Shifts in the pattern of silver production forced some large haulers to abandon the business, opening the way for the entry of new entrepreneurs who operated on a reduced scale. Trade in textiles and agricultural commodities increased, but these products did not require the massive carros, and as a result mule trains became more common.

The scale of Mexican transport operations was unmatched in the rest of the Hispanic world. By the seventeenth century, the largest freighters were wealthy entrepreneurs: their success mirrored the growth and development of the Mexican economy. Mule and cart trains moved a variety of goods. The greatest volume of traffic consisted of agricultural and pastoral products like cereals, hides, and wool. Smaller amounts of imported European goods were brought to Mexico City and from there distributed throughout the country. Regional centers exchanged agricultural products and local manufactures. Long-range hauling consisted mainly of textiles, supplies for the mines and larger population centers, and silver and a few agricultural products—sugar, indigo, hides, and tobacco—for export. Silver was not only the most glamorous but also the most lucrative commodity transported, since it involved a regular and voluminous return load: the carters hauled timber, mercury, machinery, and other supplies to the mines.

As the government was particularly interested in facilitating the transportation of silver, a series of forts *(presidios)* were constructed to protect the northern routes to the mines, and military escorts were provided for the cart trains. A road was also constructed from Veracruz to Mexico City, the major route for the export of silver. Because of the rugged terrain, this was a difficult and a costly project. After its completion, the Consulado of Mexico undertook to keep it in repair. But this proved costly, and the merchants' guild repeatedly obtained funds from the government to maintain the *camino real* (royal road). The viceroy also assisted freighters by requiring towns to provide free grazing for their animals. As the economy expanded in the sixteenth and early seventeenth century, long-haul transport trains became more numerous. A series of *posadas* (inns) were opened along the main routes, and Indian communities as well as Mexican towns supplied the muleteers and carters. Some native villages specialized in raising mules and oxen for the freighters; by the seventeenth century, they had become the main suppliers of animals for mule and cart trains.

A good system of transportation was necessary for the development of a complex and varied economy in Mexico, and the network of tamemes, mule trains, and carts served the colony well. As a result, New Spain developed the most balanced economy in the Spanish world.

Chapter 7

SOCIETY

A NEW Mexican society, formed through the intermingling of races and cultures, evolved after the conquest. The process was facilitated by one of the great demographic catastrophes in modern history: as the result of a series of epidemics, the Indian population of Mexico fell from about 25 million in 1519 to about 1 million in 1620. By the 1650s nearly half a million non-Indians resided in New Spain—about 185,000 whites, 110,000 *mestizos*, 155,000 blacks and *mulatos*, and a few thousand Asians (see table). The Europeans, Africans, and Asians who immigrated to New Spain adapted their cultures to the new situation; as a consequence, the society that developed in Mexico was not a replica of the mother country. The Spanish settlers enjoyed opportunities that did not exist in Europe. The Africans and Asians, though most of them came as slaves, also found themselves with new, if limited, opportunities. And many Indians learned ways not only to cope but also to benefit from the emerging society. Sixteenth-century Mexico forged a more open, more dynamic society than either pre-Columbian Mesoamerica or contemporary Europe, Africa, or Asia.

ESTIMATES OF NEW SPAIN'S POPULATION

	1570	1646	1742	1793
Indians	3,336,860	1,269,607	1,540,256	2,319,741
Europeans	6,644	13,780	9,814	7,904
Criollos	11,067	168,568	391,512	677,458
Mestizos	2,437	109,042	249,368	418,568
Blacks	20,569	35,089	20,131	6,100
Mulatos	2,435	116,529	266,196	369,790
Asians*	—	—	—	—
Total	3,380,012	1,712,615	2,477,277	3,799,561

SOURCE: Gonzalo Aguirre Beltrán, *La Población Negra de México* (Mexico: Fondo de Cultura Económica, 1972).
*Asians were not identified in the census reports, so it is impossible to estimate their numbers.

THE LEGAL FOUNDATIONS OF SOCIETY

As has been noted, the Crown regarded the welfare of the Indians as one of its major responsibilities. The papal bull of 1493 granted the Catholic Monarchs dominion over the American continent on the condition that they spread the gospel and convert the natives to Christianity. In the decades that followed, the Spanish Crown attempted to resolve the conflict between settler interests and the well-being of the Indians through legislation that recognized a dual society, one for the natives *(república de los indios)* and another for the colonists *(república de los españoles)*. This was accomplished by declaring the Indians to be legal minors and making them wards of the state. The settlers—white, black, and yellow—were governed by laws that established their rights and responsibilities in a hierarchical society.

The dual society was a legal expression of the monarch's desire to protect native society, and appeared desirable for several reasons. The division reflected the postconquest settlement pattern: Mexican society became predominantly urban, while the Indians became rural. In the eyes of the missionaries, segregation seemed desirable as a way of protecting innocent natives from Spanish vices. In the early days of New Spain, some friars believed that it was possible to create a millenarian society in Mexico. Finally, the Spanish *reconquista* had conditioned the Europeans to accept a dual system, one for the conquered peoples and another for the dominant society.

Although the law recognized separate Indian and Spanish republics, a precise separation was neither possible nor desirable. From the outset, Indians, Europeans, Africans, and Asians began to evolve a complex multiracial Mexican society. The orderly ideal of the two republics failed because miscegenation and acculturation broke down the artificial barriers between the two societies. From the early days, the Europeans obtained women either through war or as a result of alliances with Indian groups. The Spaniards and the small number of blacks who accompanied them took many native women as concubines, although a few Spaniards married aristocratic Indian women.

Recognizing the advantages of allying themselves with the Europeans, the Indians hastened to join them through sexual alliances. While the Spaniards tended to view native women as part of the booty, a process of absorption had in fact begun. The eventual formation of a new Mexican society represented, in a biological sense, the victory of the Indians over the invaders. The development of a hybrid culture, moreover, paralleled the emergence of a multiracial society. Europeans might persuade themselves that their culture was dominant, but conditions in Mexico forged a mestizo culture open enough to absorb Spanish values, yet equally quick to modify them to fit the environment of New Spain. At no point can colonial society be characterized accurately as a Spanish society transplanted in the New World. Miscegenation, perhaps more than any other factor, led to the acculturation of both the Indians and the Europeans to the changed conditions of life following the conquest.

At first the children of these unions became Indian or Spaniard, depending on the society in which they were raised. The arrival of more Europeans, including women, reinforced Old World values in a frontier society. There was a parallel increase in the number of children, regardless of race, who were educated as Europeans. Within a generation, a settled Mexican society had emerged in New Spain.

THE CASTE SYSTEM

Mexico developed a distinctive social structure that differed from the European society of estates. Although sixteenth-century Spain was also in a state of flux, traditional corporate hierarchies remained important there. In theory the Europeans recognized four estates—the clergy, the nobility, the townspeople, and the peasants—but in practice the most important distinction was between those of noble status *(hidalguía)* and the commoners. The nobility enjoyed special privileges—for example, exemption from personal taxes and imprisonment for debt, and immunity from judicial torture or base punishment.

However, as has been noted, in the New World all Spaniards, no matter how poor, claimed hidalgo status. This unprecedented expansion of the privileged segment of society could be tolerated by the Crown because in Mexico the indigenous population assumed the burden of personal tribute. In the New World the *sistema de castas* (system of castes) replaced the European society of estates for official purposes such as assessing tribute, restricting entry into the professions, and requiring military service. *(Casta* is a Castilian word used to designate groups of people or animals.) Under this system, society was divided into three castes: Spaniards, Indians, and blacks. Spaniards were *gente de casta limpia* (people of pure caste), a distinction which in Spain indicated the absence of Jewish or Moorish ancestry, but in New Spain came to mean freedom from the "taint" of Negro blood. Africans, considered to be physically and psychologically base, were *infames por derecho* (legally debased) because of their slave status or origins. Therefore they were legally excluded from the civil and clerical bureaucracy, prohibited from marrying Indians or whites, and forbidden to bear arms. The natives, although thought to be of good caste, were considered to be *gente sin razón* (people without reason) and legally minors.

This simple official trichotomy of Spaniards, Indians, and blacks did not reflect Mexican reality. The caste system gradually expanded in popular usage to account for the distinctions resulting from racial mixture. Although a variety of terms were used locally, four major ethnic mixtures can be identified for purposes of analysis: *mestizos* (Euro-Indians), *mulatos* (Euro-Africans), *zambos* (Afro-Indians), and *chinos* (Asians of various mixtures). These terms, however, are ideal types and could not be applied to individuals according to strict ethnic criteria, because cultural, social, and economic distinctions were as important as ethnicity in determining a person's identity. In addition, usage changed over time. For example, the official category *Spaniard* included both *European Spaniards*, born in Spain, and *American Spaniards*, born in Mexico. Later in the eighteenth century, European Spaniards were also popularly called *peninsulares* and *gachupines*, while American Spaniards came to be known as *criollos*. Yet initially the term *criollo*, a Castilian word meaning "native to" which could be used to distinguish objects made in the New World as well as people born there, referred mostly to non-Europeans born in Mexico— e.g., *negros criollos*, New World blacks.

These are not the only difficulties in analyzing race and class in colonial Mexico. The category *American Spaniard*, in fact, included Europeans born in Mexico as well as a great many biological mestizos who were regarded as *white* because of their social position. In the sixteenth century, the term *mestizo* referred to the illegitimate offspring of Europeans and natives who were not raised in their respective communities either as "Spaniards" or as "Indians." By the seventeenth century, *mestizo* was used to identify Euro-Indians and acculturated natives in the lower socioeconomic levels of Mexican society. Although authorities differentiated between mulatos and zambos, the populace generally did not, and both groups were usually perceived as *mulatos*. Together with the mestizos, they constituted the poorer elements of urban society and came to be known collectively as *castas*. When used in that sense, the word *casta* acquired a pejorative connotation and referred to people who did not possess *limpieza de sangre* (purity of blood), popularly thought to be the mark of a good race. In a society that placed a high value on lineage, castas—generally considered to be persons of illegitimate descent—labored under a serious impediment.

Miscegenation and economic growth, however, engendered flexibility. Over the years, upwardly mobile mestizos joined the ranks of American Spaniards, causing a perceptible "darkening" of the criollo strata that, in turn, facilitated the entry of other mixed peoples into the upper classes. Light-skinned mestizos and mulatos of means, if they had "European" features, easily entered the

"Spanish" category. Wealthy but distinctively mixed persons found it difficult to pass into the upper caste; but if they married someone of light skin, their children might be accepted as Spanish. Consequently the Europeans charged that the American Spaniards—the criollos—were not really white.

The number of claimants to white status increased to such proportions that in the eighteenth century the Crown established a legal procedure to accomplish it. In return for a sum of money, the king granted his American subjects a certificate of whiteness, a *Cédula de Gracias al Sacar*. Long before that time, however, the sistema de castas ceased to function as the principal determinant of status. As a result of economic development and population growth, social position became much more dependent on economic considerations. The rate of social mobility was not constant throughout the colonial period: the greatest social mobility occurred in the sixteenth and seventeenth century; by the eighteenth century, population growth and increased immigration from Spain had reduced the opportunities for social advancement. Indeed, for many Mexicans the last years of the colony were a time of social retrenchment. Most groups sought to maintain the status they had achieved rather than to improve it.

LA REPUBLICA DE LOS INDIOS

Although the Indians of Mesoamerica shared a broad common culture, they were divided by language, politics, and social customs. The Aztec empire had only superficially unified the region when the Spaniards' arrival shattered that fragile bond. Old divisions among Indian groups erupted anew. The conquest and subsequent catastrophic population decline profoundly affected the Indians. Faced with the trauma of political and cultural defeat, with their religion under attack and authority structures changed, the natives struggled to adapt to the new order.

The precipitous fall in the Indian population is one of the major calamities of modern demographic history. Scholars estimate that in 1519 the population of Mesoamerica numbered about 25,000,000, exceeding France and Spain at that time. Such a large population put acute pressure on the land's ability to support it, and it is likely that a demographic crisis would have occurred even if the Spaniards had not arrived. Although the Europeans and their livestock further aggravated the pressure on natural resources, the most devastating new factor was the introduction of diseases to a population which had no immunity against them. Measles, small-pox, and the plague swept across Mexico.

A series of pandemics struck Mesoamerica in 1520–21, 1545–48, 1576–79, 1629–31, and 1634–35. These great epidemics, called *cocoliztli* by the Indians, decimated the native population. By 1532 the number of Indians had fallen to 16,800,000. The most virulent epidemic, that of 1545–48, reduced the native population to a little more than 6 million. A generation later the great cocoliztli of 1576–79 diminished the Indian population to about 2½ million. By 1600 a mere 1½ million natives survived. The low point was reached between 1620 and 1630, when about 1 million Indians lived in Mexico.

The effects of such a demographic catastrophe were far-reaching. The character of Indian society changed from urban to rural after the conquest. Traditional native cities lost population faster than the overall rate of depopulation. Texcoco fell from around 110,000 people on the eve of the conquest to less than 8,000 in 1644. Tlatelolco, once heavily populated, numbered 6,000 souls in 1646. Cholula's population had been reduced to less than one-fifteenth its preconquest size by 1669. Other Indian cities experienced similar declines. Native society became predominantly rural with no big cities, only small towns.

The pandemics were only one factor in the decline of Indian cities. Many natives fled from their communities to escape from the burden of tribute and forced labor, and entered the new, expanding free wage-labor force in Mexico City and the newly-founded provincial towns. In 1640, Puebla had 17,000 Indians, mostly Mixtecs, Zapotecs, Tlaxcalans, and Cholulans; Valladolid had approximately 3,000 Tarascans living within its borders; Querétaro was settled by some 10,000 Aztecs, Tarascans, Otomíes, and Chichimecas; Zacatecas and Celaya had several thousand natives of mixed origin, many of them part of a large floating population attracted to the prosperous new cities.

The majority of the surviving Indians, however, continued to live in their traditional communities under native officials, responsible for the well-being of their towns, who administered communal lands, assured food and water supplies, and supervised the local market. Their most important role, however, was defending Indian interests against the settlers. Initially there was little conflict over land; expropriated lands which had belonged to Moctezuma II, the Indian clergy, and some Aztec nobles satisfied the needs of the few Europeans. In the early postconquest period, the Spaniards were more concerned with access to labor than to land. The potential for conflict between natives and colonists remained limited because, as the settlers increased in number, the Indian population decreased dramatically. By the mid-sixteenth century, large areas of central Mexico lay abandoned, thus permitting the new immigrants to obtain land in the depopulated regions of New Spain. Although Europeans dispossessed some Indians of their properties, in general such tactics were not necessary.

The situation began to change and become a point of conflict in the latter part of the seventeenth century, when the Indian population began to recover. Since this period also coincided with the general growth of colonial society, the competition for available land increased. Although the settlers managed to obtain large quantities of land in northern and central Mexico, native communities retained substantial amounts of property, and in the south the Indians retained control of most of the land. The balance between people and land deteriorated in the eighteenth century as a result of population increases. The lands retained by the Indian pueblos no longer yielded enough to support most native communities, so many Indians found temporary work outside their villages.

Tribute payment constituted one of the major burdens of the Indian communities. The Spaniards did not retain the Aztec tribute system; instead they established the encomienda, which resulted in the decentralization of tribute collection by placing the burden on the individual cabeceras. Indian officials collected tribute in money, in kind, and in personal service, first for the encomenderos and later for the Crown as well as for themselves. When the Crown abolished personal service, it attempted to establish a uniform method of tribute collection by assessing a head tax gathered by cabecera officials. To prevent abuse, the colonial government created local treasuries, *cajas de comunidad,* to hold the revenue. These measures, however, failed to create a uniform tribute system. The Indians continued to recognize distinctions in tribute obligations based on preconquest classes as well as on landholding patterns. Native officials allocated and collected the assigned levy according to custom.

Tribute obligations hastened the process of acculturation. In addition to labor, the settlers demanded tribute in the form of European crops and animals. Consequently, the Indians not only raised these new items, but also accepted many of them as part of their diet. While the natives never became accustomed to wheat, they rapidly adopted chickens, pigs, and cows. Subsequently, the requirement to pay tribute in coin forced the Indians to sell their products or their labor in the market economy. These activities brought the natives into close contact with colonial society. Efforts to avoid tribute payment hastened the acculturation of many Indians. Since the decline in the native population increased the burden of tribute on the surviving members of the community, many Indians abandoned their villages to seek refuge in Mexican cities or estates. Hard-pressed native officials found it difficult to collect tribute from these expatriates. Large entrepreneurs occasionally agreed to pay their Indian workers' tribute obligations, but smaller operators generally refused either to pay their workers' tribute or to permit community officials to collect it. In either case, the natives who left their villages came into prolonged contact with Mexican society and began the process of becoming mestizos. This phenomenon was most advanced in northern and central Mexico, where the acculturated population was concentrated and economic opportunities were greatest.

Forced labor demands were even more onerous than tribute obligation. A carefully regulated system of directed labor, considered a socially accepted contribution to the well-being of the community, had functioned in Mesoamerica. The Spaniards, however, transformed voluntary community service into forced labor. After the conquest, the Europeans forced Indians to work on projects that often had little or no value to them. Civilian and clerical officials drafted native labor to construct public buildings and other facilities, while the encomienda initially provided labor for the settlers. In 1549 the Crown outlawed these coercive practices, hoping to transform the Indians into a free wage-labor force. Royal legislation prohibited unpaid labor, limited working hours, and regulated working conditions. Settlers blamed the new rules, which coincided with one of the great epidemics, for the subsequent scarcity of labor, and never fully accepted them. Nevertheless, the royal legislation transformed the labor system and ultimately led to the introduction of the *repartimiento,* or distribution of labor.

The repartimiento attempted to reconcile the objectives of the Crown with the increasing demands of the settlers for Indian workers. The new system required native communities to supply a quota of workers, approximately 2 percent of their number of tributaries, to meet the needs of the settlers. A region, known as a repartimiento and administered by a *juez repartidor* (judge distributor), included one or more Indian towns. Early Monday morning, native officials assembled their quota of laborers at a given point, where the juez repartidor distributed the workers to the settlers. The employers paid the judge and his officials a percentage for each Indian assigned to them. The native laborers worked, often under the supervision of a black overseer, from Tuesday to the following Monday afternoon, with Sunday off; at the end of the week they received their pay and returned to the pueblos. Their places were then taken by a new group of repartimiento laborers. This system provided the settlers with a guaranteed workforce, at a time of declining native population, and assured that the Indians would not work away from their home for long periods. In practice, corrupt judges abused the system by accepting bribes to provide workers for some entrepreneurs, and forcing many Indian communities to provide more than their legally required quota of laborers. In spite of these irregularities, the repartimiento met most of the labor requirements of central and southern Mexico without the extreme exploitation common in Peru.

The *desagüe,* or flood-control work in Mexico City, however, was very exploitive. During the sixteenth and early seventeenth century, thousands of Indians worked building dikes to protect the capital from periodic floods. Then in the early seventeenth century the viceregal government began a great project to cut a tunnel through the mountains, in order to drain the flood-waters of the Valley of Mexico. The great tunnel, which required immense amounts of Indian labor, was finished in 1608—but it proved ineffective, and devastating floods continued to beset the city. Eventually the government decided to cut an open trench through the mountains, a project which took more than a century to complete. The natives often worked waist-deep in cold water for prolonged periods, and the harsh conditions took a heavy toll in human life. The desagüe was the last major enterprise which used draft labor.

Forced native labor became increasingly impractical as the economy of colonial Mexico developed. Many entrepreneurs preferred to employ *gañanes* (independent Indian laborers) who worked for longer periods of time, or slaves for more skilled work. During the late seventeenth century many Indian communities entered into direct arrangements with the owners of Mexican estates to provide seasonal labor. Since agriculture constituted the largest sector of the economy, these agreements were very important. *Capitanes* (Indian labor bosses) organized *cuadrillas* (work gangs) and sold their services to estate administrators. This system profited agriculturalists, because the capitanes assumed responsibility for supervising their cuadrillas. The natives also benefited, because they could bargain for better pay and working conditions as a group. These arrangements became more common as the Indian population increased beyond the capacity of communal lands to adequately support it. The new system of labor continued to function until the end of the colonial period.

The most important institutions in Indian Mexico were the community and the family. The strength and vitality of the community derived from both pre-Hispanic patterns and postconquest accommodations. Although they accepted some of the individualist values of the Europeans, Indians retained a strong sense of responsibility to the community. The village therefore received their first allegiance. For most villagers, the family was a secondary institution; the protection of community interests was foremost.

Indian communities generally acknowledged the authority and legitimacy of the Spanish Crown. But they also had a clear sense of what was acceptable in their relations with the authorities. If those boundaries were violated, the villagers were likely to rebel. Throughout the colonial era, violence was common and an accepted way of obtaining redress for grievances. Indeed, to some villagers rebellion was the fastest and most efficient method of settling conflicts. Unlike litigation, which might take years to decide, the causes for a revolt might be resolved in a few weeks.

Most revolts that have been studied erupted spontaneously, in response to specific grievances. They remained local and of short duration; none challenged colonial rule. Villagers usually rebelled to oppose new taxes, fees, or restrictions; to protect their lands from encroachment by entrepreneurs, municipalities, or the Church; or because of rivalries with other nearby pueblos. Rebels attacked local authorities, including priests, and damaged public buildings, particularly the jail—a hated symbol of oppression—in their outbursts. The degree of violence varied, depending on the circumstances, but local authorities were often unable to control such rebellions and had to request assistance from the viceroy. In many cases, women led the uprisings. Typical is the 1719 revolt of Santa Lucía in Oaxaca. Led by Mariana, a tall scar-faced woman, the villagers demanded that a group of royal officials, including priests and militiamen who had arrived to mark the pueblo's boundaries, leave. When the authorities proceeded to survey the land, Mariana cut the measuring rope, fought one of the officials, and was wounded. Her injuries incited the villagers. Armed with rocks, sticks, and tools, the townspeople drove the officials back to the city of Antequera.

Judicial authorities were generally lenient in the aftermath of village uprisings. They understood that there were limits to Crown authority and that Indian communities were necessary to the economic and social well-being of the viceroyalty. They generally settled the conflicts in favor of the villagers. The dignity of the king's law was maintained by singling out purported ringleaders for punishment, and the sentences were usually mild, consisting of a short jail term, exile, or a public whipping. The major exception to such realistic leniency was the sentences handed down by the Spanish visitador José de Gálvez during the rebellions that coincided with the expulsion of the Jesuits in 1767. He ordered executions, extended exiles and jail sentences, and severe whippings. His actions, however, were generally regarded as brutal and misguided and not in keeping with Mexican practices.

Although surviving documentation makes it difficult to study the evolution of Indian family life after the conquest, there is strong evidence to indicate that it continued to be a basic unit of social organization. The structure of the preconquest Indian family closely resembled its Spanish counterpart, since both were patriarchal and based on an extended kinship network. Some modifications in Indian relationships occurred after the arrival of the Europeans—for example, polygamy among the upper classes was abolished—but in general the native family adapted easily to the new society. Indian nobles, like European aristocrats, demonstrated a strong interest in lineage, and the colonial archives contain extensive genealogical records for the native aristocracy. Some of them, like Fernando de Alva Ixtlixóchitl and Fernando Alvarado Tezozómoc, wrote histories that glorified their ancestors.

Although the family and the community maintained many Indian values, European influence penetrated even isolated enclaves, shaping and transforming native culture. Fray Bernabé Nuñez de Páez described this process in 1692 when he wrote: "When an Indian takes to wearing mestizo clothes and grows his hair long, he becomes a mestizo, and in a short time he will be a Spaniard." Central and northern Mexico witnessed a rapid erosion of native culture and the emergence of cultural mestizos. Even in the south, where fewer Spaniards settled, the process of acculturation accelerated toward the end of the colonial period.

In general, acculturation occurred whenever important colonial settlements were established, and these occurred wherever there were economic reasons to attract the colonists. Undesirable or out-of-the-way areas tended to remain culturally Indian longer than economically attractive regions. In some cases, as Gonzalo Aguirre Beltrán indicated, the natives withdrew into *regiones de refugio* (zones of refuge) to escape colonial society. Other native communities failed to adapt, retaining an essentially Indian subculture. Such groups remained outside the dynamic social structure, forced to contribute to the economy but not perceiving themselves as part of that structure. Alienated, uncomprehending, and hence unable to manipulate society in their own interests, culturally blocked from participation or opportunity to acquire status and its symbols, they became passive and resigned. The Indian subculture might be reasonably positive in remote or marginal areas where the demands of colonial society were light; but when subjected to massive intervention, their leadership could not adequately respond. Such groups reinforced the negative stereotype of the Indian culture held by colonial society. The greatest active opposition to Mexican culture came from the nomads who continuously fought the settlers for control of the north; however, even these Indians adopted the horse, and used it effectively against the colonists.

The process of acculturation proceeded rapidly in cities and towns where individuals became separated from their traditional communities. Indian *barrios* (neighborhoods) existed from the beginning in the new colonial centers. There urban Indians, often from many different regions, adopted the mestizo culture. Native quarters continued to exist in most of the cities of New Spain until the end of the colonial era. In general they housed the newcomers, while those who had acculturated sufficiently joined the growing mestizo ranks. Ultimately the mestizo became the archetypical Mexican. This transformation, although not completed until the twentieth century, was well advanced by the end of the colonial period.

THE SPANIARDS

The conquistadores and European settlers came from a land in political transition. Spain did not exist as a political entity in the fifteenth century. The Catholic Monarchs, Isabel and Fernando, jointly administered the Crowns of Castile and Aragón, rather than a unified state. Castile, the larger of the two, consisted of Old and New Castile, Galicia, Estremadura, Asturias, Andalucía, Navarra, and the Basque provinces of Vizcaya, Guipúzcoa, and Alava. The Basque provinces and Navarra had special legal status, while the other Castilian provinces recognized the same laws and *cortes* (parliament). The Crown of Aragón was a confederation of kingdoms: Aragón, Valencia, the Principality of Catalonia, and the Balearic Islands, each with its own laws and cortes. These variations in legal and administrative structures reflected the strong sense of regionalism which Spain's rugged topography and linguistic diversity fostered. People identified with their *patria chica* (local region) rather than with Spain, which was only a geographic expression. Until the late seventeenth century, Spaniards thought in terms of Spanish "nations" rather than a single unified country.

The Old World divisions survived in Mexico, although linguistic differences blurred. Settlers tended to be clannish and to favor their own *paisanos,* persons from the same town, and considered those from other provinces *gringos,* or foreigners. *(Gringo* is a Castilian word meaning "someone who speaks an unintelligible tongue.") Regionalism was so pervasive that some Castilian speakers considered others with different accents gringos. Eventually Galician, Basque, Catalán, and Portuguese speakers abandoned their languages and adopted Castilian. By the seventeenth century, Castilian became the dominant language in Spain and the official language of the New World. Popularly, the tongue came to be known as Spanish.

Immigration patterns varied over the years. Initially, Mexico attracted bold adventurers; however, after the conquest of Tenochtitlan many unskilled young men came in search of fortune, although the authorities of New Spain encouraged professionals and artisans to immigrate to the colony. Emigrants from the Spanish textile manufacturing town of Guadalajara, for example, settled in Puebla, where they rapidly developed New Spain's textile industry. By the middle of the century, the number of women and children immigrants had increased substantially. Many Spaniards went to Mexico to join relatives, to work for established settlers, or as part of the retinue of important civil or church officials. Others came as members of large households, particularly as servants. Indeed, by the end of the century, one-sixth of the women and more than half of all men emigrated as servants. Some hoped to escape Spain's depressed economy, but most came because Mexico provided opportunities not available at home even under prosperous conditions. After a few years of service, servants could expect to buy a small plot of land or start a small business. Although detailed studies are lacking for later periods, the pattern established in the sixteenth century seems to have persisted. Census data indicates that poor people comprised the majority of immigrants throughout the colonial era. The eighteenth century, a period of great population growth in Spain, witnessed an expanded emigration to Mexico.

Castilians, most of them from southern Spain, were the largest group of immigrants. According to Peter Boyd-Bowman, who studied emigration patterns in the sixteenth century, 40 percent of the immigrants to Mexico came from Andalucía, and nearly a quarter came from Seville. This is understandable, since the city of

Seville was the main center for American trade and, during the period, one of the most prosperous ports in the Iberian peninsula. New Castile and Estremadura also supplied a significant number of emigrants. Asturias, Galicia, the Basque provinces, Navarra, Catalonia, and Aragón altogether contributed less than 4 percent of the immigrants to New Spain. The pattern of emigration changed in the late seventeenth and eighteenth centuries as northerners, especially from Santander and the Basque provinces, came in larger numbers. Nevertheless, the influence of Andalucíans remained dominant in the development of colonial Mexico.

Among the Spanish settlers, the Basques formed a special group, unique even in regionalist Spain. Their language was not Indo-European and their provinces had neither been invaded by the Moors nor settled by Jews. Thus in a land where limpieza de sangre remained important, the Basques claimed exclusive purity. By virtue of their unique status within the Crown of Castile, the Basques not only retained their *fueros* (ancient privileges) but claimed Crown recognition as *hidalgos* (petty nobles). Able and industrious, the Basques gained distinction in business, industry, and government.

Only a few Basques emigrated to Mexico, but they achieved great wealth and influence. They were the explorers and conquerors of northern Mexico and the Philippines, and subsequently became influential in the Church and in the civil bureaucracy. In addition, they achieved prominence in commerce and mining. In the eighteenth century, Basque entrepreneurs were among the wealthiest in the colony. Indeed, the richest silver mine in the world, La Vizcaina (the Biscayan), belonged to a Basque nobleman.

The Basques' success, as well as their sense of superiority, galled other Spaniards. In the New World they flaunted their racial purity and treated the criollos, whom they regarded as no better than mixed-bloods, with contempt. For example, the Basque Archbishop Juan de Mañosca declared that "although the creoles do not have Indian blood in them, they have been weaned on the milk of Indian women, and are therefore, like the Indians, children of fear." While the Basques were of course not contemptuous of their own criollo children, they labeled other American Spaniards inferior and unfit to hold public office.

THE JEWS

For about a century, between 1580 and 1680, Jews comprised the third-largest European group in New Spain. They were the only people to come to Mexico, albeit surreptitiously, to escape religious persecution. The Jewish community had deep roots in Spain; it had been large, wealthy, and very influential. Through centuries of coexistence, many Jewish and Christian families had intermarried, but the harmony between the two religious groups broke down during the last years of the Christian reconquest of the peninsula. Although directed primarily against Moslems, the Catholic struggle in time considered all non-Christians a threat. Finally in 1492, after the fall of the last Moorish kingdom of Granada, the Catholic Monarchs ordered all Jews who would not convert to Christianity expelled from their realms. Many converted, but the majority chose exile. Some Jews settled in Portugal and Holland beyond the reach of the Spanish Inquisition. Spain's preoccupation with Jews did not end with their expulsion. Many New Christians (converts) continued to practice their old faith, and Portuguese and Dutch Jews later defied legal restrictions by secretly emigrating to the New World. Most of this clandestine immigration took place after 1580, when Felipe II inherited Portugal. Under his direction, the previously dormant Portuguese Inqusition sprang to life. To escape it, many Jews secretly returned to Spain or went to the New World. A relatively large number settled in Mexico.

Forced to live as *judaizantes* (crypto-Jews), the community was sustained by the determined efforts of women who kept customs and ritual alive. On several occasions, devoted wives revived their husbands' faith and transformed them into leaders of the Jewish community. In times of persecution, Jewish women suffered martyrdom. Although generally acquainted with Jewish laws and customs, Mexican Jews had little knowledge of Hebrew and recited their prayers in Spanish or Portuguese. Without rabbis, the Mexican community maintained its religion only with difficulty. Messianic dreamers emerged in the repressive atmosphere; Luis Nuñez Pérez, an itinerant peddler, and Captain Antonio Váez spoke of a great armada that would come to conquer Mexico and save the Jews. But the majority of the Jewish population in Mexico remained loyal Spanish subjects. Those Jews who wanted spiritual solace, and could afford to travel, visited parts of Europe or the Dutch West Indies where they could worship openly.

Mexican Jews lived in constant danger of being exposed and seized by the Inquisition. Since they publicly professed Christianity, they were guilty of heresy if they practiced their ancient faith. Crypto-Jews brought before the Inquisition who were *reconciled* (abjured their errors) returned to society, but if they failed to recant, or were deemed guilty of a heinous crime, the Holy Office turned them over to the civil authorities for punishment. Throughout the colonial period, judaizantes continued to be discovered. Generally officials handled their cases quietly, but in some instances autos de fé, held for the edification of the faithful, publicly punished them. Some wore penitential robes and performed other acts of contrition, and others were executed.

The most celebrated case involved the politically prominent Carvajal family. The authorities found Luis Carvajal, governor of Nuevo León, and his family guilty of being judaizantes. He died in jail in 1590, but his sister, nieces, and nephew, Luis de Carvajal the younger, were reconciled. Six years later, in the greatest auto de fé of the century, the Inquisition condemned 40, including the Carvajal family, for Judaism, and 9 died at the stake, among them Doña Francisca de Carvajal, her three daughters, and Luis de Carvajal the younger, a brilliant writer. This tragedy did not end the persecution of the Carvajal family. In 1601, 3 more went before the Holy Office; the tribunal reconciled Ana and Leonor, aged 19 and 14 respectively, but condemned their aunt, Mariana Nuñez de Carvajal, to death.

No other major auto de fé was held until the political conflict between Viceroy Escalona and Archbishop Palafox led to the discovery of the so-called "great conspiracy" in 1642. Palafox accused the viceroy of pro-Jewish and pro-Portuguese sentiments as part of the campaign to oust Escalona, and then sought to consolidate his political victory by unleashing an inquisitorial investigation that led to the arrest of more than 150 crypto-Jews in the years 1642–1649. The flower of the Jewish community was destroyed, among them Antonio Váez, Luis Nuñez Pérez, and the now aged Ana Carvajal. In order to process so many prisoners, the Holy Office held small autos de fé in 1646, 1647, and 1648. The persecution culminated in 1649 with the largest auto de fé of the colonial period; 500 carriages filled with notables, together with a horde of common people, arrived for the spectacle. A total of 109 Jews were involved, including 57 who had died in jail and 8 escapees who were punished or reconciled in effigy. Of the 52 prisoners actually present at the auto de fé, 13 died at the stake and the rest were reconciled. Of those killed, 6 men and 6 women were first garroted and then burned; one man, Tomás Treviño de Sobremonte, steadfastly refused to repent, and his proud defiance condemned him to the horrible death of being burned alive.

The records of the Mexican Inquisition indicate that Jews could be found at all levels of society. The majority were peddlers, shopkeepers, craftsmen, and vagabonds; a few were soldiers, priests, and university students. The elite consisted of wealthy entrepreneurs, mostly merchants, and government officials. Merchants like Simón Váez and Matías Rodríguez de Oliveira traded on an international scale in the seventeenth century; others, like Melchor Rodríguez López, who owned a cacao estate, engaged in local commerce. Jewish public officials gained important posts: Don Luis de Carvajal the elder settled Nuevo León; Don Bernardo López de Mendizabal served as governor of New Mexico in the mid-seventeenth century; and Simón Enríquez was a member of the Mexico City Council in the 1620s. The Jewish upper class mingled with the elite of Mexico by keeping their religion secret. As a result of their isolation, and the assaults of the Inquisition, the Jews of Mexico slowly lost their identity. They had assimilated by the end of the colonial period.

OTHER EUROPEANS

The non-Spanish European community in Mexico included Portuguese, Dutch, Germans, Italians, and English. Never large, they numbered no more than perhaps 2,000 at any time. The makeup of the foreign community depended on the international politics of the Spanish monarch. During the reign of Carlos V, Dutch and German clergymen, bureaucrats, artisans, and professionals emigrated to New Spain. Many Portuguese came to Mexico in the years 1580–1640 when the Spanish monarchy controlled Portugal. Later, in the eighteenth century, French and Irish immigrants became common. Although the Laws of the Indies restricted immigration to the subjects of the Crown of Castile, such prohibition could not be enforced. Foreigners entered Mexico either with Crown permission or illegally, by bribing officials. The viceregal administration solved the problem through *composición,* a device whereby illegal aliens received residency permits and even naturalization papers by paying a fine. The 1619 composición, for example, legalized the status of 338 foreigners, half of them Portuguese, a number of Italians, and a few Flemings, Germans, French, Scots, and Greeks.

Foreigners were found at all levels of Mexican society. Pedro Gante (Peter of Ghent) was a distinguished clergyman and the emperor's relative. Ana von Rieder, a seventeenth-century Austrian, married the Marqués de Guadalcazar. Heinrich Martin, a German, and Adriaen Boot, a Fleming, were two of the leading engineers and architects employed in the desagüe in the 1620s. Other foreigners were merchants, craftsmen, servants, and vagabonds.

THE CRIOLLOS

Within a generation of the conquest, the *American Spaniards,* known as *criollos* in the eighteenth century, constituted the largest segment of the "Spanish" population in Mexico. Although theoretically composed only of descendants of Europeans born in New Spain, in practice the group included a large number of biological mestizos. The inclusion of socially and economically prominent mestizos in this category meant that the size of the group was not primarily determined by the reproductive rate of European immigrants. Thus the criollos quickly outnumbered the Europeans, who never surpassed 15,000. This same phenomenon limited the number of individuals classified as mestizo, so that throughout the colonial period criollos were the largest non-indigenous group in Mexico (see table on p. 197). Criollos considered themselves *españoles,* even though they shared in New Spain's hybrid culture. Like their fathers, the criollos functioned at all levels of Mexican society, and thus did not have a unified class or group interest. Instead they tended to react, together with their families, along caste and class lines.

European civil and clerical bureaucrats viewed criollos with only vaguely concealed disdain. The colonial relationship implied superiority, both cultural and administrative, over the subject population. This assumed superiority led officials to measure colonial social behavior against a theoretical Castilian standard. Thus they negatively compared Mexico's hybrid culture against an idealized version of Europe. Some Spaniards denigrated criollo accomplishments and maintained that European culture and achievements would always be superior to those of America. Such attitudes became prevalent in the eighteenth century, engendering a sense of inferiority among criollos. Some attempted to refute the claims by extolling the virtues of their homeland. For most criollos, however, such conflicts were either nonexistent or attenuated by family relationships, since many of their relatives were European-born Spaniards.

THE MESTIZOS

The mestizos, like the criollos, are a difficult group to identify. Although some scholars have noted the rapid growth of the biologically mestizo population, colonial Mexicans did not have the same perception. In the sixteenth century, the term *mestizo* referred to the illegitimate children of Spaniards and Indians who lived in Mexican society. Legitimate children of such unions raised as "Spaniards" in effect became criollos, while the offspring raised among the natives became Indians. A recognized and separate mestizo group did not emerge rapidly. Official reports indicate that during the sixteenth, seventeenth, and early eighteenth century the mestizo population numbered less than that of blacks and mulatos (see table on p. 197).

Since biologically mixed individuals tended to be identified as either criollos or Indians, depending on their education and station in life, the mestizo category applied only to marginal persons unacceptable to either group. Generally considered illegitimate, these mestizos labored under heavy legal and psychological burdens. As early as 1540, the Crown barred illegitimate mestizos from public office. The Church, divided on the issue, ordained some while rejecting others. The guilds also adopted an ambivalent approach: some, like the cotton dealers, glovemakers, milliners, and porcelain-makers, allowed mestizos to become craftsmen; others, like the pressers, manglers, and calenderers, restricted mestizos to journeyman status. Eventually, society considered them part of the third community—neither Spanish nor Indian.

Colonial society had great difficulty in adjusting to the growth of the mestizo population. Although they were considered gente de razón, upper-class Mexicans often perceived mestizos as base and closer to blacks than to Spaniards. In frontier areas, short of population, mestizos were viewed as sons of Spaniards. In 1621 a scholar of Nueva Galicia described the mestizos as "talented, energetic, and honorable, owing to their Spanish blood," but in central Mexico the authorities took a more jaundiced view. In the 1670s, Viceroy Mancera declared mestizos to be as arrogant as blacks—but more rational and responsible, since Spanish blood flowed in their veins.

Mestizos emerged as a distinct social group in the late seventeenth and early eighteenth centuries. Marriages among mestizos became more common as their numbers increased. Indeed, in the late eighteenth century they constituted the fastest-growing segment of the population. A separate mestizo class, however, did not emerge; mestizos, like Europeans and criollos, moved into all levels of society. Eighteenth-century Mexico still made ethnic distinctions, but relied more on socioeconomic criteria than on race to determine a family's status. Successful biological mestizos continued to be considered white. Numerically, they became the dominant group in Mexico. Some of them gradually developed the notion of a mixed culture, but they did this as criollos, not as mestizos. The notion of a cosmic race, formed by the intermingling of many peoples and cultures, was not consciously accepted in Mexico until the twentieth century, when José Vasconselos advanced the concept.

THE AFRICANS

Although a black freedman, Juan Garrido, participated in the conquest of Mexico, became the first wheat farmer in New Spain, explored Michoacán and lower California, and died a citizen of Mexico City, most Africans arrived in New Spain as slaves. Cortés began introducing black slaves shortly after the conquest. Only a few hundred a year arrived during the first decade, but their numbers increased so rapidly that by 1537 the authorities feared a black uprising. In 1553 Viceroy Luis Velasco urged the Crown to prohibit the importation of slaves, because the more than 20,000 blacks and mulatos already outnumbered the whites and mestizos and were seen as a threat to the viceroyalty. Such fears did little to stem the tide of forced African immigration, which reached its peak in the years 1580–1640 when Portugal, the chief slave-trading nation, was a possession of the king of Spain. Although precise figures are not available, scholars estimate that Mexico received more than 200,000 Africans during the colonial period. In the late sixteenth and early seventeenth centuries, New Spain employed more black slaves than any other part of the New World.

During the sixteenth century, slaves arrived chiefly from Guinea-Bissau, Senegal, Gambia, and Sierra Leone. In the seventeenth century, the Portuguese shifted their operations south, to escape the pressures of English, Dutch, and French traders, and took slaves principally in Angola, Luanda, and the Congo. Studies indicate that most seventeenth-century African slaves in Mexico had been born in the Congo and Angola. Slaves possessed a variety of backgrounds and skills. Moslems mingled with people who practiced tribal religions, while skilled artisans and agriculturalists arrived with hunters and gatherers. A few were literate. As usual, buyers preferred males; women and children accounted for less than a quarter of the Africans imported.

In New Spain, blacks were divided into three categories: *bozales, ladinos,* and *negros criollos.* The bozales, or slaves who came directly from Africa, were initially the most numerous, because there were relatively few African slaves in the Spanish empire in the sixteenth century. Ladinos, or acculturated slaves who had lived in Spain or the Caribbean before arriving in Mexico, were in great demand, since they already understood Spanish ways. The number of negros criollos born in the New World increased only slowly, because of the low ratio of black women to men. Instead, zambos and mulatos became the most rapidly-growing sector of the Afro-Mexican community, and were generally called mulatos regardless of whether they were Afro-Indians or Euro-Africans.

African slaves performed a variety of tasks in New Spain. On the coast they labored in pearl fisheries and sugar plantations, while in the central highlands and the north they worked on estates, in mines, in obrajes, and in other enterprises. Many slaves held important positions as artisans and overseers. Some entrepreneurs relied on blacks to control Indian workers, because the slaves identified with the dominant culture and looked upon the natives with contempt. Spanish officials often relied upon blacks to enforce their edicts. Corregidores, for example, sometimes employed slaves as intermediaries in forcing the natives to purchase goods. Some owners did not employ their slaves directly; rather, they hired out their blacks for a specified period of time such as a day, week, or month. Normally, the parties signed a contract specifying the wages to be paid, the working conditions, the duties of the slave, and the employer's obligations such as food, lodging, and medical care. In some instances, as in the case of Beatríz de la Loa y Alvarado of Mexico City in 1615, the income the slave earned constituted the master's only source of revenue.

Urban slaves were among the most privileged forced laborers in New Spain. While many served as artisans, the majority worked as servants who provided great social prestige for their masters. The ostentatious upper classes employed slaves to emphasize their high status. According to the seventeenth-century English traveler Thomas Gage:

> The gentlemen have their train of blackmor slaves, some a dozen, some half a dozen, waiting on them in brave and gallant liveries, heavy with gold and silver lace, with silk stockings on their black legs, and roses on their feet, and swords by their sides. The ladies also carry their train by their coach's side of such jet-like damsels. . . .

The most prestigious convents in Mexico City had more black women slaves than nuns. Despite the constant fear of uprisings, many high-ranking officials maintained armed retinues of slaves as bodyguards.

Although slaves lived in close and intimate contact with the settlers, officials considered them a potential threat to New Spain. The first black scare occurred in 1537, when Negroes and mulatos had already begun to outnumber whites and mestizos. The authorities kept close watch on the black population, which they considered vicious, cruel, defiant, and naturally turbulent. Many agreed with Gómez de Cervantes, who declared in 1599 that Negroes "are well known to be our enemies." In spite of this vigilance, slave revolts erupted in 1546 and 1570, and rumors of a black conspiracy circulated in 1607. According to reports, the Negroes of Mexico City planned to elect a king and nobles and then butcher the white population of New Spain. The authorities launched an investigation, tortured many blacks and mulatos, but discovered no plot. The "election" of a black king during a drunken revel spawned the wild rumors.

While little danger of a slave revolution existed, black revolts did pose a threat. In 1612, some 1,500 Negroes rioted in Mexico City after a black woman had been flogged to death by her master. The rioters stoned the house of the dead woman's owner and demonstrated in front of the viceregal palace. The authorities, fearing that all whites would be slaughtered, arrested the heads of the black *cofradías* and tortured them, forcing the hapless victims to confess to a conspiracy. As a result, the government declared a state of emergency, mobilized the militia, and eventually imprisoned suspected conspirators. Finally, on May 2, 1612, the viceregal government hanged 29 black men and women and ordered their heads displayed on pikes in the Plaza Mayor. Other riots occurred in 1646 at Veracruz and in 1665 at Mexico City, but these did not equal the tumult of 1612. In retrospect, it appears that the authorities allowed their fears to run away with them. Blacks, both slave and free, remained loyal to the Crown and never joined foreign invaders in an attempt to overthrow the regime.

Runaway slaves known as *cimarrones* did pose a problem for local authorities, particularly in the countryside. The most serious cimarron challenge occurred during 1607–1611 when Yanga, a runaway who claimed to be a Congolese prince, organized and sustained a revolt along the road from Veracruz to Puebla. The viceroy Luis de Velasco II sent a heavily armed force of 600 men to subdue the rebels. But Yanga and his men proved to be skillful *guerrilleros*. Although the authorities feared that the cimarrones would incite the Indians to rebellion, the black insurgents made no attempt to join forces with the natives. In the end, the government accepted a stalemate. The viceroy signed a treaty granting Yanga and his followers freedom and the right to settle in the mountains near the city of Córdova. In return, the cimarrones agreed to return all future runaway slaves to the authorities. Three other known cimarron risings that occurred in the seventeenth and early eighteenth centuries ended in a compromise similar to the one struck with Yanga. In all four cases, the free black rebels established communities complete with municipal councils. Because of a shortage of black women, the cimarrones took Indian mates and the communities eventually lost their African identities.

Blacks also obtained their freedom through manumission. Masters freed their slaves for a variety of reasons. Some allowed slaves to earn enough money to buy their liberty. Others freed their concubines, especially if they had borne children. Some pious persons left instructions in their wills freeing their slaves. A few manumitted their slaves when they were too old to be capable of working. As a consequence, a population of free blacks emerged in New Spain almost from the conquest.

The black community developed kinship networks of surprising strength. Although slaves were legally entitled to marry, their masters did not always comply with the law. Even when marriages occurred, there was no guarantee that a family would remain united. Never very secure, the slave family could be broken by the sale of one of the spouses or the children. Nevertheless, black slaves sought to establish households whenever possible. A few married in the Church, but most slaves formed consensual unions, and if a husband and wife separated, they attempted to visit each other to keep the marriage alive. When this was not possible, one or the other established a bigamous household. Normally this only happened when the mates had been separated for a long time and lacked information about one another, so that it was reasonable to assume that the other partner had died. The uncertainty in nuclear family relations made the larger kinship network very important. Brothers, sisters, aunts, uncles, and cousins kept in close contact with one another and made certain that the children of their extended family received care. In this respect, the kinship network served as the basic family unit.

Blacks, like other groups in New Spain, could not resist the twin forces of miscegenation and social change. Since the ratio of women to men never exceeded one to four, black men generally took Indian women as mates. In some cases the Negroes kidnapped and raped the native women, but in most instances the Indian women entered such unions willingly, because blacks often possessed a higher social status than their own men. Slave men also preferred to marry Indians, because their children by native women, unlike the offspring of slave women, became legally free. In contrast, Spaniards and criollos preferred mulatas to Indian women.

Within a generation, the mulato population became the largest segment of the "black" community; their numbers increased from 2,435 in 1570 to 116,529 in 1646 and 369,790 in 1793. During most of the colonial period, mulatos were more numerous than mestizos. The overwhelming majority of mulatos were free and, like other groups, economically active and socially mobile. The most successful among them bought certificates of whiteness in an attempt to adjust their racial status to their economic success. The black and mulato population merged with the larger criollo and mestizo population. By the end of the colonial period, blacks had all but disappeared into Mexico's mestizo society, a process completed in the nineteenth and twentieth centuries.

THE ASIANS

The Asians, like the Africans, came to Mexico principally as slaves. Although their numbers are difficult to estimate with accuracy, about 600 Asians a year entered Mexico during the seventeenth century. They arrived in the Manila galleons from the Philippines, China, Japan, and Portuguese India. Most were either *ladinos* (acculturated) or mixed Spanish and Asian whom the authorities considered "Chinese Indians." Asians could live in native communities and marry Indian women, but most Oriental immigrants lived in the cities, where they worked as peddlers, artisans, barbers, and servants. Most institutions did not recognize the existence of the Asian population. There were few special rules governing their conduct unlike those which restricted mestizos, mulatos, and blacks. Most Asians adopted Spanish names and merged with the colonial population of New Spain. They generally occupied the lower levels of Mexican society, although there is some evidence that a few successful Asians entered the upper class.

The most famous Asian Mexican was Catarina de San Juan (1613–1688), renowned as *la china poblana*. Captured as a child in Cochin China, Catarina arrived in Puebla as a slave. There she was raised by a pious couple, eventually becoming famous as an ascetic, a mystic, and a saintly woman. During her life, the people of Puebla attributed miracles to her. After her death in 1688, her confessor, Father Alonso Ramos, published her biography in three volumes, thus initiating an unsuccessful campaign to have her canonized. Today *poblanos* consider Catarina de San Juan and Bishop Palafox the two most distinguished religious figures in the history of their city.

SOCIAL STRUCTURE

New Spain evolved a complex social structure. By the seventeenth century, colonials assumed that ethnic groups could be ranked in the following descending order: European Spaniards, American Spaniards, mestizos, mulatos, blacks, chinos, and Indians—or, in its simpler version, peninsulares, criollos, castas, and Indians. Although many historians have accepted this hierarchy, social categories based on ethnic distinctions are misleading. Notarial records indicate that the different socioeconomic strata were composed of more than one ethnic group. Wealth and status could not be limited to whites. Similarly, the poor strata included all racial groups. Some European immigrants remained quite poor. Indeed, mestizos of means occasionally had Spanish-born servants.

For purposes of analysis, the social structure of colonial Mexico can be broken into seven categories: (1) the royal officials, (2) the great magnates, (3) the secondary elite, (4) the *pequeña burguesía*, (5) the artisan class, (6) the workers, and (7) the *léperos*. The royal officials, although always few in number, were the governing class of New Spain. A few thousand at most, they held great power. During the seventeenth and early eighteenth century some local criollos purchased high offices, particularly in the Audiencia. This practice was curtailed in the second half of the eighteenth century, and did not fundamentally alter the relationship between royal officials and the rest of Mexican society. The viceroy, the prelates, and most of the high bureaucrats were peninsulares. Although the governing class did not control great wealth, it represented the interests of the Crown and thus formed a distinct group. While the higher officials often received a generous salary, the lower bureaucrats seldom expected more than a comfortable living wage. In the eighteenth century, salaries ranged from 1,000 pesos a year for lower officials to 40,000 for the viceroy, who also received a 20,000-peso allowance for his court. The Crown also generally provided administrators with official quarters that permitted the highest officials to live ostentatiously while the lower echelons lived more modestly in rented rooms. Throughout the colonial period, Mexicans perceived royal officials as a quasi-foreign elite representing a just but distant king.

The great magnates were the most powerful group in Mexico. Their interests were essentially tied to the colony, although some were engaged in the monopoly trade with Spain. This group consisted of the largest miners, merchants, hacendados, and obrajeros. By the end of the seventeenth century, they constituted an interlocking network of families that dominated the economy and society of New Spain. Throughout the colonial period, successful or important immigrants married into wealthy Mexican families. As a result of this process, criollos were often both the sons and the fathers-in-law of Spaniards. The interests of the great magnates transcended any criollo-peninsular rivalry. Their position derived from wealth, influence, and power, not from ethnic differences. Indeed, some titled nobles made much of their Indian ancestry—and in a form of reverse snobbism, flaunted their mestizo background. All considered themselves loyal subjects of the Crown which granted them recognition and privilege. They were important allies of the royal officials, supporting them financially in return for political considerations. When their interests conflicted, they found it advantageous to resolve their differences amicably.

Wealth distinguished the great magnates as a group. Their incomes ranged from hundreds of thousands to more than a million pesos a year in the eighteenth century. The richest elite in the Spanish empire, they maintained large households with numerous servants. Their Mexico City townhouses were renowned: at a time when most people considered 300 pesos a year a living wage, the great silver miner José de la Borda built a house at the cost of 300,000 pesos; as a wedding gift for his daughter, the Marqués de Jaral rebuilt a mansion at the cost of 100,000 pesos, while the Marqués de Prado Alegre spent 37,000 pesos merely to refurnish his palace. Although not all the magnates had titles, nearly all the Mexican nobles were magnates. Before granting a title, the Crown determined if the family possessed sufficient wealth to maintain noble status. A noble lifestyle required owning great townhouses in Mexico City; building luxurious cascos in haciendas; endowing churches, hospitals, and other charities; and displaying wealth in the form of a large retinue, jewels, plate, fine furnishings, horses, and carriages.

The eighteenth century was the period of greatest ostentation for the Mexican nobility—60 of the 80 titles bestowed during the colonial epoch were granted in that century. Wealthy families coveted titles of nobility not only for prestige, but also because titles helped plutocrats protect their fortunes through entail. But reverses did occur, and more than a dozen titles lapsed owing to family poverty. Just as with non-noble magnates, fortunes could be made and lost within three generations.

A group of families closely associated with the great magnates formed the secondary elite in colonial Mexico. Like the plutocrats, the secondary elite engaged in a variety of enterprises, although on a much smaller scale. The holdings of the secondary elite ranged from tens of thousands to more than 100,000 pesos. Secondary elite families often engaged in food-processing enterprises, cattle-raising, substantial bakeries, *pulquerías* (pulque-processing plants), and markets which could not be supplied entirely from their own estates. To assure adequate supplies, they often entered into contracts with the great landowners. Some also worked for the magnates in a professional capacity. Men of the secondary elite dominated the professions of New Spain, becoming the leading lawyers, physicians, and churchmen. Well-educated as a group, their professions only provided part of their family income. Other endeavors allowed them to emulate the lifestyle of the magnates. This kept many members of the secondary elite in debt, despite their high incomes.

Criollos and successful mestizos formed the bulk of the secondary elite, although some European immigrants also married into this group. The secondary elite tended to identify with local interests—they were particularly concerned about access to public office and Church posts. Self-interest often placed this group in conflict with the Spanish-born royal administrators, who monopolized higher office and placed the Crown's interests ahead of New Spain's. In contrast to the magnates, the secondary elite found it difficult to resolve these conflicts. In the eighteenth century, the professionals among them developed a sense of Mexican nationality which historians have called "criollo nationalism."

Considerably below the royal officials, the magnates, and the secondary elite was the *pequeña burguesía,* a group composed of families engaged in medium- to small-scale operations. In the eighteenth century their annual incomes ranged from 700 to a few thousand pesos. They owned small ranchos, trapiches, mule trains, inns, tiendas, etc. While not a middle class in the sociological sense of the term, they considered themselves *gente decente* (decent people) who strove to maintain a respectable lifestyle. In Mexico City and other large cities and towns they lived in rented rooms, often above or near their businesses. In the country they owned small estates. Pequeña burguesía families were principally composed of criollos, mestizos, and mulatos, but poor immigrants often married into these families. Upwardly mobile during the sixteenth and seventeenth century, pequeña burguesía families were much more concerned with protecting their status in the eighteenth century, when opportunities for social improvement decreased.

The artisan class, closely allied with the pequeña burgesía, tended to own very little property other than their tools. The more successful artisans produced a variety of consumer goods in their own shops. Generally they lived in small adobe houses on the outskirts of the city or in rented rooms on side streets in the central parts of town. Most artisans worked in haciendas, sugar plantations, ranchos, obrajes, and other large-scale enterprises. Their incomes ranged from 400 to 700 pesos a year. Although they made no pretense about their status, they nonetheless considered themselves honest, productive people. Dependent on the upper classes, they identified with their social superiors. A mixed ethnic group like the pequeña burguesía, artisan families were predominantly mestizo and mulato but also included a sizable number of downwardly mobile criollos and poor Spanish immigrants.

In the late sixteenth and seventeenth centuries, black slaves formed a special sector of this artisan class and aspired to a standard of living similar to that of free artisans. Colonials, however, did not place them in the same category as other artisans because of their slave status. As has been noted, guilds and other artisan organizations frequently barred slaves from membership. By the eighteenth century, slavery had declined and the descendants of slave artisans had become mulatos and therefore more acceptable.

The workers were the most numerous group in Spanish Mexico. They generally owned no property and relied entirely on their earnings. Most were members of the acculturated population and could not turn to the native community for assistance in times of adversity, although in some cases urbanized Indians returned to their villages. Families often separated if they did not find work in the same place. Many employers, however, tried to hire families, because they were a more stable and more productive labor force. Workers generally resided in their places of employment: servants in their master's houses; day workers in accommodations provided at construction sites; laborers in obrajes, estates, stores, etc.; rural workers in estates; and miners in haciendas de beneficio. Salaries ranged from about 200 to 300 pesos for most workers in the eighteenth century; salaries for mine workers were much higher, particularly if the mine was prosperous. The majority of workers were mestizos, mulatos, and chinos, but the group also included a number of criollos and peninsulares.

The destitute in Mexico were called *léperos* (lepers) because they wore filthy and tattered clothing. These unfortunates had no employment and no place to live. They begged in the streets, stole for food, and slept in the streets or found shelter in hovels, stables, and the stalls of public markets. The léperos, viewed by the more favored elements as a floating criminal class, in fact constituted a surplus and marginal labor force pushed from the countryside into the cities by miserable conditions. In the viceregal capital, officials blamed the economic attraction of the city, in particular the royal tobacco factory, for the number of *gente baja* (lower-class people) who crowded into the poorer districts and contributed to crime and disorder. Unemployment and underemployment often reduced workers to the lépero level. In the late eighteenth century, Mexico City seemed filled with scantily-clad léperos who sold their meager clothes to raise money for more urgent necessities. They formed a lumpen-proletariat that shocked and frightened visitors and residents alike. The léperos were most numerous in Mexico City because it was the largest and wealthiest city in the kingdom. There they not only threatened public order but also constituted a health menace. Many léperos, chronically ill with contagious diseases and weakened by malnutrition and alcoholism, easily fell victim to epidemics, particularly in times of severe food shortage. In the late eighteenth century, thousands died as the result of these conditions.

Although the study of colonial society is in its infancy, enough is known to indicate that the Mexican social structure was not rigid, but a flexible system that changed substantially over three centuries of colonial life. It is also clear that social change occurred at different rates in the various regions of Mexico. The principal variable was the size of the Mexican and the acculturated population—and this, in turn, depended upon the economic possibilities of the area. Prosperous centers of mining, agriculture, and manufacturing attracted a sizable Mexican population and were the foci of significant social change. Poor or outlying areas where opportunities were limited tended to be places where rigid social structures were more likely to endure. Throughout New Spain, the rate of social change and social mobility was related to the rate of economic growth. Periods of depression were times of social retrenchment.

Chapter 8

WOMEN AND
THE FAMILY

THE development of the Mexican family structure drew upon both the Indian and the European experience. Conflict between preconquest familial norms and those introduced by the Spaniards varied among different native groups. Civilized Indians, however, subscribed to similar norms and defined family roles in much the same manner as did the Spaniards. Both shared a strong sense of lineage, a belief in male supremacy, and a preference for a tight-knit family structure, surrounded by a protective web of extended family relationships. Role concepts, family honor, and the expectation that the family would serve as the major depository of cultural values coincided. Superficial differences—in particular the polygamy practiced by the Indian nobility—scandalized the early missionaries, and occasioned light comments from European settlers. Yet the acceptance of extramarital arrangements, often on a permanent basis, also characterized European society. Differences were usually more a matter of form than of substance. As with Aztec society, our knowledge of the nature of family life and the role of women derives principally from the urban experience of the new Mexican society. Life in the predominantly Indian villages is difficult for us to reconstruct.

Spanish men and their Indian women established the first households that reflected the new hybrid culture beginning to emerge after the conquest. The uncertainty and confusion of the early period tended to undermine the stability of such unions: nevertheless, the formation of family units did not depend on the introduction of Spanish women. The few European women who arrived in 1521 served only to reinforce the beginnings of settled Mexican society. They taught the new society the preferred behavior and the social forms of Spain.

Spanish men in Mexico perceived European women as the conservators of cultural values. Therefore they and their sons, many of whom were biological mestizos, preferred to marry Spanish women or mestizas raised as "Spaniards." Despite such preferences, the initial rate of immigration for European women was low, constituting no more than 6 percent in the first decade. But by the mid-sixteenth century, 16.5 percent of all immigrants to New Spain were women. The high point was reached at the turn of the century, when the figure jumped to 28 percent; thereafter the ratio of women to men immigrants remained about one to four. After the first years, however, Mexican society no longer needed Spanish women to continue to transmit European culture, as the number of American Spanish women and the daughters of mixed unions brought up in the new Mexican culture increased. By the end of the sixteenth century, there was a surplus of eligible women in Mexican society, who had difficulty finding suitable husbands.

MARRIAGE

The institution of marriage was an alliance between families intended to promote their mutual interests. Social and economic considerations, rather than love, were the principal basis for marriage. Mexican families of all castes, classes, and races were concerned with preserving or improving their social and economic status. A complex combination of racial, social, and economic criteria determined a family's position in society. The higher the family's social position, the greater their fear of a *mésalliance*. Parents were particularly concerned with finding suitable husbands for their daughters, as it was generally believed that women had more to lose from a bad marriage than men. Good birth or lineage were major considerations in choosing a mate, but high status derived from economic standing was also important. Thus European Spaniards of means were in much demand as mates. Since few high-status European women arrived in New Spain unmarried, upper-class American Spanish men tended to marry criollo heiresses. Ideally, lineage, status, and wealth were related, but in practice those of good birth did not always possess high status or wealth, and vice versa. Distinguished but impoverished families often married their daughters to lower status wealthy newcomers.

The reasons for marriage among the lower castes differed little from those of the elite, even when they formed consensual unions. Money permitted those in the lower castes to improve their positions through marriage into families with social and racial prestige. Social mobility was greatest in the sixteenth and seventeenth centuries; by the eighteenth, population growth and other changes limited the possibilities for upward mobility. As a result, the family's principal concern became preserving and protecting its status.

There was a tendency toward endogamy among wealthy and even moderately wealthy families, in order to preserve fortunes. Since few families were protected by entail *(mayorazgo)*, the death of a rich individual could result in dissipating his wealth among many heirs. In such circumstances, marriage between relatives often provided the solution. For example, men sometimes married their sisters-in-law upon the death of their wives. In many of these cases, the prospective bride was already living in her sister's house, helping to take care of the children. Their families encouraged marriage with the deceased wife's sister, because it strengthened their alliance and retained wealth within the group. Uncles tended to marry nieces for similar reasons. The most common endogamous marriages were between second cousins. European Spaniards who became prosperous businessmen in Mexico sent for their poorer nephews from Spain, put them to work in their enterprises, and, if successful, let them marry their daughters. In this way the business remained in the family.

Unlike men, women married at an early age. Most women married between the ages of 14 and 18, but girls of 12 were considered old enough to marry and, in a few instances, children of 7 or 8 were married to older men to cement important family alliances. Women between 19 and 25 were still of marriageable age, but not as desirable as their younger sisters. A female over 25 was considered past her prime; she might be acceptable if she conferred status or brought a large dowry with her. Although a few widowers chose to marry "mature older women" in their late twenties, most men preferred to marry young women, because society placed a high value on chastity. The older a woman grew, the less likely that this quality could be preserved. Even though she might remain a virgin, she could not retain her innocence of the world. Men, on the other hand, tended to marry late. Although they reached their majority at 25, men normally did not marry until they had established themselves financially. Only the sons of the wealthy could afford to marry in their twenties. While Mexicans valued youth and innocence in a woman, they prized maturity and economic success in a man.

THE FAMILY

Mexican society was patriarchical; law granted the father *patria potestad,* authority in the family. Responsible for the physical, economic, and social welfare of his wife and his direct descendants, the father retained legal authority over his children even after they married or reached the age of maturity. In practice, however, such power could be effectively exercised only if they lived in his house or depended economically upon him. The patriarch of the extended family was usually the richest and often the oldest man. But there were exceptions: sometimes the strong-willed widow of a patriarch became a matriarch if no male family member was rich or powerful enough to become family head.

A supportive institution that attempted to care for all its members, the extended family in turn expected each individual to contribute to the well-being of the group. Rich or powerful relatives provided their kinsmen with jobs, recommendations, and financial assistance. Poor relations helped in the household, worked in the family business, and served as a reserve force in the family. Widows often raised the family's orphaned children. Rich female relatives contributed to the welfare of the children, particularly by providing dowries for needy girls. Servants were also considered, and believed themselves to be, part of the family. They were expected to remain loyal and work to further the family's interests. Extended families can be described as a series of alliances. Although they varied in size, wealth, and influence, most families in Mexico tried to conform to the ideal.

Families extended their alliances through the quasi-religious bond of *compadrazgo,* godparenthood. Important families generally requested influential friends or kinsmen to become the *padrinos* (godparents) of their children. The godparents thus acquired religious as well as social obligations to their godchildren, and through them to their parents. Lower-status families generally asked their socioeconomic superiors to be godparents to their children. In this way they obtained ties with powerful families and became their clients. A less formal but nonetheless functional alliance existed among *paisanos,* people from the same hometown. This was particularly true of immigrants from Spain, who tended to form clannish groups in the New World.

Extended families did not generally share living accommodations. This, however, did not reduce the importance of the extended family network. Most couples moved into their own home after marriage; rich families often provided the couple with a dwelling. The records indicate that a typical urban Mexican household consisted of parents, children, and servants. In some instances unmarried sisters or aunts also lived in the house. Widows and widowers remarried, or continued to live in their homes, rather than moving in with married children. In the larger cities, particularly in Mexico City, nuclear families often established separate households in rented rooms, apartments, and houses. By the eighteenth century, the Church had become the largest owner of urban real estate in Mexico, and therefore the largest landlord in the colony. In general its moderate rents were conducive to family formation.

The establishment of a household could be either formal or informal, although Mexicans considered marriage—a public, religious, and legal union—the norm. This was particularly true among the middle and upper groups which had property and position at stake. Consensual unions, the mutual agreement to cohabit, occurred in frontier areas where priests were not readily available, and in settled regions because of legal and financial considerations.

Such unions were more common among the lower strata of Mexican society, but in special cases members of the upper classes entered into such arrangements temporarily. Since the Crown forbade officials to marry local women, some of them entered into consensual unions with the daughters of prominent families, with the understanding that the couple would marry when permission arrived from Spain or when the bureaucrat moved to another post. In some cases worthy but poor individuals entered into consensual unions until they could afford to marry. Modest church fees did not pose an obstacle; the expense lay in the festivities normally expected to accompany a marriage ceremony. Though theoretically unacceptable to the Church and to decent society, in practice consensual unions were generally accepted by both families and provided a workable alternative to the ideal norm. Among the lower classes these arrangements could last a lifetime and, in effect, became permanent informal marriages. This seldom occurred among the upper strata, where the woman's family usually insisted that its interests and its honor be protected.

Married men sometimes established a second household, or a *casa chica*. Normally an arrangement entered into with the approval of the woman's family, it provided security for the woman and her children. Usually in such unions the woman and her family were of lower status than the man. Since Spanish law provided for a father's legal recognition of his natural children, casa chica arrangements served as an avenue for upward social mobility. Illegitimacy, although not socially approved, did not prevent both families from acknowledging bastard children. The illegitimate children of middle and upper groups were usually well received by the father's family and suffered little social opprobrium. Children of lower-caste unions were also accepted by their families, but there was a greater tendency—especially by the upper classes—to consider them bastards tainted by bad blood, particularly if the children had black or mulato features. Nevertheless, at the level of individual family, kinship ties were more important than legal norms.

Marriages, although normally arranged to the mutual satisfaction of both families, could be forced upon them. Elopement and, in rare instances, bride rape, occurred when the girl's parents opposed the match on the grounds that the man was their social, racial, or economic inferior. The female, usually quite young—

between 12 and 15—either lost her virginity, or the public believed that she had been deflowered, thereby endangering the family's honor and status. A young girl whose chastity had been violated was unlikely to find a suitable husband. If she were from a decent but modest family, she would become the prey of other men who would consider her a public woman. To avoid such shame, the girl's father would agree to the couple's marriage. The bride's dowry and her family's connections would then enable the newlyweds to start a respectable married life.

Elopement could be initiated by either the man or the woman. While men normally "seduced" girls into eloping, in a few cases attractive young women sought out men of higher standing. The girl's family denounced their daughter's seducer to the authorities—and fearing scandal, and perhaps disturbed by their son's actions, the man's family occasionally forced him to marry. Bride rape, unlike elopement, was of course solely a male prerogative. In the very few instances recorded, young heiresses were kidnapped and sexually violated and their "dishonor" made known to their parents, who agreed to accept the rapist into the family rather than publicize their "shame." Generally aggressive and driven individuals, the men involved often amassed sizable fortunes and became important in their communities.

An elaborate ideological justification reinforced a dual standard of sexual and social mores. Colonial Mexicans considered *honor,* a sense of personal and family pride, the essense of masculinity. Manliness also implied strength, fearlessness and virility. Society considered a man who fulfilled such expectations a *macho,* a male animal. Men, assumed to be naturally inclined to sexual passion, were expected to seduce many women. This created a psychological conflict for men who thought it perfectly justifiable for them to seduce someone else's wife, sister, or daughter, but considered it a mortal insult for someone else to seduce their female relatives.

Women, unlike men, did not possess honor, but they could injure family honor. Society placed a high value on female premarital virginity and marital fidelity; any indiscretion by the "weakest" member of the family could damage its reputation and endanger its property and status. Female sexuality, although not denied, was feared. Therefore *vergüenza* (shame) became the essense of femininity, considered to be a moral quality, like innocence, which once lost could not be recovered. Vergüenza was not simply sexual

virtue, but also a regard for the moral values of society. True vergüenza made women sensitive to their reputations and caused them
to accept the sanctions of public opinion. Thus a *sinvergüenza*—a
person without shame—was someone who did not acknowledge
or who abused the values of society. Women who did not adhere to
established norms, or publicly flaunted their lack of shame, suffered severe penalties. Fornication and adultery were crimes only
when committed by women. More important, however, society
rejected such women. (Here it is important to distinguish between
fornication and consensual unions, which were considered an informal marriage. While the first violated social norms, the second
did not.) Some fathers drove errant daughters from their homes.
Wronged husbands and fathers could even kill the guilty women
with impunity. Such women became *mujeres públicas* (public
women), entitled to no respect and considered little better than
prostitutes.

Once expelled from the protective network of the family,
women had no place in decent society. Only noble or elite women
could successfully challenge the commonly accepted sexual norms.
Their family status was considered to be legally or socioeconomi-
cally so superior that an individual's actions could not diminish the
family's position.

The importance of the family and the weakness of other institutions left no place in Mexican society for the lone individual. Even
bachelors, priests, and nuns functioned as members of extended
families. The only organizations of any importance outside the
family were corporate bodies like the Consulado, the artisan
guilds, and Church-sponsored sodalities. Yet even in these institutions, family ties were crucial, and factions often formed around
members of prominent families and their supporters. Those unfortunates who had no family ties became true outcasts, living on the
fringes of society. They made up the tragic and troublesome group
of vagrants, prostitutes, alcoholics, and criminals that concerned
Mexican authorities throughout the colonial period.

WOMEN

The role of women in New Spain, like the role of other groups,
varied according to social and economic circumstances. The popular notion that Mexican women were kept in harem-like seclusion

has no basis in fact. A woman's role was principally determined by the socioeconomic status of her family: the greater the family wealth and prestige, the more opportunities opened to women in the family. The notarial records indicate, however, that the differences in the roles rich and poor women played were differences in scope, not in kind. Wealthy women had wider and more varied activities than poorer ones, but most women were active in family enterprises. In this sense, marriage was more of a partnership than is commonly understood. The man and the woman represented their respective families in a new socioeconomic alliance. Unions were based on mutual interests and advantages; women brought with them not only their family names and influence, but also their dowries, which provided them with economic independence.

The development of a permanent society in colonial Mexico depended on women. From the outset, their presence contributed to the stability of personal relationships, assured the transmission of culture, and added to the success and continuity of business enterprises. Their true social role, however, often remained hidden behind social conventions and the law.

The legal rights and duties of women varied according to their marital and social status. The legal system recognized two kinds of distinctions with respect to women: the difference between "decent" and "shameless" women and between single and married women. "Honest" women had rights and privileges, whereas "loose" women lost virtually all legal protection. There was also a pronounced disparity between the rights accorded single and married women. Most scholars have examined the laws as they pertained to married women and have concluded that all women in colonial Mexico were held in a subordinate and dependent position. In fact, single women possessed virtually all the rights and privileges enjoyed by men. They were prohibited from holding most public offices and from entering the priesthood; otherwise they were free to act as they chose.

Single women and men shared a similar legal status. Both were subject to the authority of their father until they reached legal maturity at 25. Thereafter they assumed legal responsibility for their actions. Single women could inherit, enter into contractual agreements, administer their property, litigate, serve as witnesses, guarantee bonds, etc. Indeed, single women had opportunities denied their married sisters, a factor that apparently influenced many women to remain unmarried. Scholars have generally assumed that because of social pressure women had very few alternatives to marriage. In the early days of the colony, when population was limited, Mexican society exerted great pressure for single women to marry and for widows to remarry, but as the number of acculturated women increased, social pressures relaxed and some women remained single. Indeed, the records indicate that by the eighteenth century, a substantial number of women chose not to marry.

Widows occupied a special position in Mexican society. They exercised great independence because they were considered more experienced and less vulnerable than single women. Widows had all the rights and privileges of single women, as well as the benefits and obligations derived from marriage. They were responsible for the welfare of their children and the administration of the family's property. Notarial records indicate that widows were among the most active businesswomen.

Married women were burdened with legal restrictions not applied to single women or to widows. A wife was subject to her husband's authority and generally could not act legally without his permission. If she entered into a contract without his consent and incurred losses, the arrangement was considered null and void. But if she profited from their transaction, the law recognized her actions as valid. These rules were justified on the grounds that they offered protection to married women who were not considered competent to manage their affairs. But since widows and single women were held to be legally able to protect their interests, one must conclude that these discriminatory laws existed to maintain the husband's superiority over his spouse. In practice, however, many married women obtained exemptions from these regulations. Husbands usually granted their wives permission to engage freely in business. Indeed many women, particularly those from wealthy families, entered into prenuptial agreements which preserved their ability to act autonomously.

Spanish law also afforded married women the ultimate protection against exploitation by their husbands by providing a way to terminate the marriage. The Church and the state recognized a woman's right to "divorce"—that is, legal separation. Although a "divorced" couple was no longer required to cohabit, neither

21. *Mulatos* from the hot country around Nepantla.

22. A Veracruz black in Sunday clothes.

23. A black family in a highland market.

24. A wealthy Spaniard, his Indian wife, and child.

25.
A prosperous Spaniard,
his *mestiza* wife, and
child.

26. A poor Spaniard, his
mestiza wife, and child.

27. The family of an Indian *cacique* wearing Spanish dress.

28. The family of an Indian commoner.

29. A nomadic Indian from the North—an Apache *cacique*.

30. A *lépero*.

31. A porter with a tumpline, carrying an old man.

32. A water carrier, typical of those who delivered water in cities and
towns throughout Mexico.

33.
A public scribe, writing
a document for an
illiterate
businesswoman.

34. The *plaza mayor* of Mexico City.

35. A great Mexican intellectual: Sor Juana Inéz de la Cruz.

36. A great Mexican scientist: Carlos de Sigüenza y Gongora.

37. José Alzate's design for a new machine to clean cotton.

spouse could remarry as long as the other lived. The Church attempted to maintain marriages intact, accepting "divorce" only in cases of extreme physical or spiritual danger to one of the parties. It recognized physical cruelty, threats of murder, the occurrence of an incurable contagious disease, attempts to force the spouse to commit crimes, particularly prostitution, and the attempt to lead the spouse into heresy or paganism as grounds for "divorce." "Divorce" trials were normally complex and lengthy affairs requiring lawyers. Church records indicate that the poor availed themselves of the right to "divorce" as readily as the rich. In such cases, the Church provided legal counsel at no cost to the needy. "Divorce" not only granted a married woman the right to separation, it also restored her juridical identity. If the woman were the aggrieved party, she received custody of the children and her share of community property, as well as her dowry. But if she were found guilty, she might lose everything, including her dowry. Thus, women did not enter lightly into "divorce" suits.

Although there were undoubtedly weak and passive women in the colony, the records indicate that most asserted themselves, sometimes acting well beyond the limits of the law. Wealthy and upper-class women even had the opportunity to participate in public life. They could inherit titles of nobility as well as entailed estates *(mayorazgos)*. The Crown recognized their rights to encomiendas and cacicazgos. They administered feminine institutions, like schools, *recogimientos de mugeres* (houses of correction for women), *beaterios* (religious centers for lay women), and convents. In one outstanding case, doña Beatríz de la Cueva acted as captain-general of Guatemala in the absence of her husband, Pedro de Alvarado. But while this was possible in the early days after the conquest, it would have been unthinkable once the Audiencia was established and bureaucratic rules were enforced. As Mexican society evolved, social mores and legal restrictions circumscribed women's roles.

Nevertheless, there were exceptional women even in the mature colony. One of the most famous women in colonial Mexico was Catalina de Erauzú, better known as *la Monja Alferez*, the Nun Ensign. Erauzú was born in Spain in 1592 to a pious Basque family who made her enter a convent. While still a novitiate, she fled. Thereafter she lived a life of high adventure disguised as a man. She became a celebrated soldier, swordsman, and daredevil. Erauzú's escapades took her from Spain to Peru and then to Chile. Eventually her dueling brought her into conflict with the authorities. When they discovered her identity, they returned her to Spain in 1622. Still dressed as a man, Catalina de Erauzú aroused great curiosity because of her exploits and her knowledge of the New World. When she visited Rome, the pope gave her dispensation to wear male clothing for the rest of her life. Not to be outdone, the king of Spain granted her a pension.

Catalina de Erauzú returned to the New World about 1630, establishing herself in Mexico as an *arriera*. Within a short time her mule trains were operating between Veracruz and Mexico City. Her competitors accused her of intimidation, and the authorities complained that she terrorized the king's highway. Her most scandalous act, however, occurred years later, when the husband of a close friend forbade Erauzú to enter his house to visit his wife. Outraged, Catalina de Erauzú challenged her friend's husband to mortal combat. In a bold letter she declared that his actions were an affront both to her noble lineage and to her valor, thus flaunting the traditional Spanish view that honor was a male prerogative. The authorities prevented the duel and Erauzú angrily returned to her business, which continued to prosper until her death in 1650. By that time she had become so renowned that her life was recounted in an autobiography, a play, and shortly thereafter in the first Mexican novel, *La Monja Alferez*.

Very few women, however, could challenge traditional mores with impunity. The life of Juana Inés de Asbaje y Ramírez de Santillana, better known as Sor Juana Inés de la Cruz, is indicative of the restrictions society imposed on a woman of genius. Born in 1648 in the town of San Miguel de Napantla, Juana Inés de Asbaje displayed a precocious and inquiring mind, learning to read at the age of 3. At 8 she was sent to live in Mexico City with relatives. The child prodigy wanted to prepare for the university, which she hoped to enter dressed as a man. Persuaded that her goal was impossible, she continued her studies at home. By the age of 16, Asbaje had become a well-known figure in the city. The *virreina*, the Marquesa de Mancera, took an interest in her and brought her to live in the palace as one of her ladies, and the social whirl and sophistication of the court transformed the girl into a fascinating young woman. Her wit, intellect, and beauty made Juana de Asbaje a favorite of the palace.

Although she enjoyed her role, the young woman was also torn by a desire to devote herself to the life of the mind. In New Spain, most scholarship was carried out within the confines of the Church; therefore Juana Inés de Asbaje decided to enter a convent. During her years at the Jeronymite convent, Sor Juana Inés de la Cruz wrote some of the finest lyric poetry in the Castilian language. Although a master of the Baroque style, her verse expressed both her profound inner conflicts and her search for a rational world. Sor Juana is justly considered a great poet, but she was also a rationalist constantly at odds with Mexican society. In her writings she criticized scholastic pedantry and Baroque exaggerations. She questioned Mexican mores and the restrictions placed on women. She even dared to challenge the double standard, as the following verses reveal:

> Obstinate men who blame
> Women for no reason,
> Oblivious that your acts incite
> The very faults of your censure.
>
> Which has the greater sin when burned
> By the same lawless fever:
> She who is amorously deceived,
> Or he, the sly deceiver?
>
> Or which deserves the sterner blame.
> Though each will be a sinner:
> She who sins for pay,
> Or he who pays to win her?

As a consequence of her wide-ranging interests, Sor Juana collected a library of more than 4,000 volumes. She studied contemporary science and philosophy and carried out scientific experiments in her cell. Mexico's most distinguished scholar, Carlos de Sigüenza y Gongora, became her frequent visitor. Sor Juana encouraged his poetry while he stimulated her studies in science and philosophy. When other scholars visited Mexico City, Sigüenza brought them to the convent to meet Sor Juana.

The nuns at the convent, however, were deeply opposed to her writings, and the bishop questioned her interest in profane letters. On many occasions Sister Juana defended her right to free inquiry, but at other times her resolve weakened under the attack of her obscurantist opponents. Sor Juana was ultimately forced to capitulate tragically. In 1690 the Bishop of Puebla criticized her neglect of religious literature and her love of secular philosophers. For months she brooded because of the bishop's censure. Then in March 1691, she wrote a *Reply,* a bold document which discussed her intellectual development and, like Descartes, argued that the best way to learn about God was to study His creations. Sor Juana's response, interpreted as an indication of arrogance and worldliness, caused her long-time confessor to withdraw and nuns to severely criticize her. Her friend and kindred spirit, Sigüenza y Gongora, was away on an expedition to Florida, and she bore ostracism alone for several years. Ill and nearly broken in spirit, Sor Juana finally capitulated in February 1694, when she renounced all her possessions. Thereafter she gave herself to acts of penance and self-flagellation. The death she sought did not come until the following year, when an epidemic swept Mexico City.

Few women in New Spain, or in the rest of the world, led lives of adventure like Catalina de Erauzú or of great artistic and intellectual achievement like Sor Juana. Most women had more limited spheres of action, but within those boundaries they lived varied and active lives. A woman's role was principally determined by the socioeconomic status of her family and by the dowry she received.

The dowry was a basic socioeconomic institution for the middle and upper classes. For the woman, it provided the economic leverage used to attract a suitable mate and to maintain her dignity and status after marriage. The dowry always remained the property of the wife. It normally consisted of money, but it also included property and goods—land, animals, clothing, furniture, mortgages, slaves, interests in mining, commerce, and manufacturing enterprises, and rights to hereditary offices. Dowries were considered so important that relatives were often expected to aid in providing an adequate dowry, and paisanos formed groups to raise acceptable dowries for orphaned or needy girls. Dowries appear to have been most important in the sixteenth and seventeenth century—in the eighteenth, the number of marriages without dowries increased dramatically. This phenomenon appears to have been the result of both population increase and the reduced possibilities for social advancement.

Since dowries represented important economic assets, they were sometimes subject to much dispute. The decision of who controlled the dowry was not always easily settled. Families did not always pay the dowry immediately: in one case, a mother did not turn over her daughter's dowry until ten years after the wedding. In other instances, husbands were slow to acknowledge officially that they had received the dowry, or they claimed receipt of only a portion. It is not uncommon to find wills, written after years of marriage, in which the husband originally declared that his wife's dowry had been small, with codicils indicating that the dowry had been much larger. Some wives refused to wait for years to have their economic rights confirmed. Melchora Hernández, a seventeenth-century resident of Querétaro, took her husband to court when he failed to give her a *carta de dote*, a letter of confirmation for her 10,000-peso dowry, after two years of marriage. Such cases were not frivolous. It was crucial for women to have their dowries acknowledged, because it was their principal economic safeguard in case of their husband's death. For many widows, the dowry and the income it generated provided their sole means of support.

The husband was the legal administrator of the dowry, but there were restrictions on his authority. He could not alienate any part of the dowry without his wife's permission; if he was guilty of malfeasance, she could take legal action for the right to administer her property. A widow who remarried had absolute control of her first dowry; the new husband could only manage the second dowry. In practice, the wife assumed a great deal of control over the property she brought into the marriage. In many cases wives functioned as silent partners, active behind the scenes. For instance Juana Pérez de Gama, a merchant's daughter in Tlaxcala, owned half of her husband's obraje: she often acted as joint purchaser of raw materials, supplies, and machinery, and she had considerable influence in all decisions relating to the family business. Señora Pérez de Gama's role was not unusual; women shared ownership of farms, mines, mule trains, and virtually every other economic enterprise.

Although married and single women participated in economic ventures, the most active businesswomen were widows. They engaged in all kinds of undertakings, from garden plots and small tiendas to complex agricultural, commercial, and manufacturing enterprises. Women, like men, relied on their relatives to assist them in the businesses; thus widows often employed their sons or other male relatives as overseers, particularly if their holdings included distant properties. But this did not mean that they were not independent to manage their own affairs. Doña Melchora de Puga was typical of the many shrewd widows in business. After the death of her husband, the encomendero of Querétaro, in 1606, she managed her agricultural properties without her son's help. Initially she retained the mayordomos her husband had hired, but when some of them did not meet her standards she replaced them. Apparently she had difficulty finding suitable overseers, because she changed the managers of some of her properties several times. Doña Melchora, a highly successful entrepreneur, retained close control over her estates. Of course, not all widows were so astute and, like many men, some mismanaged their properties, became involved in litigation, and ended up destitute. Other widows were divested of their properties by ruthless men. Mexicans tended to believe that women could not operate their estates as well as men; consequently, some people tried to take advantage of widows. But most women, well aware that their social and economic future rested on their own shoulders, took steps to protect themselves and their families.

Economic activity and success in business were not limited to well-to-do or upper-class women. Indeed, many successful businesswomen emerged from the mestizo lower class. A good example of such success was Mencia Pérez, an illiterate mestiza from the province of Tlaxcala. Before her marriage to José Aragón, a Basque innkeeper, in 1570, Pérez had a small farm. After the wedding the couple moved to the town of Huemantla, where they invested in real estate, a mill, and agricultural properties. Mencia Pérez de Aragón continued to expand her holdings even after her husband's death in 1578. During her second marriage—to Rodrigo Arias, a prosperous carter and merchant—she worked behind the scenes, as she had done in her first marriage; but when Rodrigo died in the late 1590's, Mencia Pérez took control of the business. She became so successful that by the turn of the century she was the wealthiest person in Huemantla, and one of the wealthiest in the province. By that time, no one dared to call the successful businesswoman a mestiza!

The majority of mestizas, mulatas, free black women, and Indian women living in towns operated on a much smaller scale than Mencia Pérez. Since their dowries had been small or nonexistent, they had little capital upon which to build. Nevertheless, they owned small garden plots, ran tiendas, sold prepared foods, and operated cafes, inns, and taverns. Many women worked in obrajes, in artisan shops, or as servants. Indian women often sold produce and other products from their native communities. Some women worked in licensed brothels as prostitutes; Mexican society accepted them as fulfilling a useful, if not respectable, social role. The authorities, however, viewed streetwalkers and other unregulated prostitutes with alarm. Although Church and government officials always lamented the increase in prostitution, in colonial Mexico it never reached the magnitude of the problem in Spain and other parts of the Mediterranean world. As population increased in the late seventeenth and eighteenth century, the number of vagrant and loose women without families grew, although not in the same proportion as unattached men.

New Spain provided wealthy single women with an alternative to spinsterhood. They could choose—or in some cases, were forced—to enter convents. Bishop Zumárraga established La Concepción, the first convent in Mexico City, in 1547. As Mexican society grew, so did the number of nuns—in part because the number of acculturated women increased to such an extent in the second half of the sixteenth century that many elite women had difficulty finding suitable husbands. Several nunneries had been established in Mexico City, Puebla, Querétaro, Guadalajara, and other centers of Mexican population by 1600. Convents could only be founded in prosperous cities, since the state did not support them. The dowries of the nuns supplied part of the income, and convents were often endowed with gifts of money and—more commonly—property. Consequently, the convents of New Spain, like other Church institutions, acquired large properties and substantial sums of money over the years. They generally invested their resources wisely—lending money, renting their properties, or hiring someone to manage them. By the end of the seventeenth century, nunneries had become an important part of the Mexican economy.

Women entered convents for a variety of reasons. Those who wished to lead a life of prayer and contemplation joined the few nunneries that maintained a rigid discipline, requiring nuns to lead a strict communal life of prayer, penance, and poverty. But such rigor was unusual, and in the seventeenth century most convents relaxed their discipline substantially. Many women believed that a religious life did not require great deprivation, while others took the veil because they or their families believed they could not find a suitable mate. The easier atmosphere reflected the role nunneries played in colonial Mexico. Convents served as retreats for the daughters of wealthy families. The dowry required to enter a nunnery in the 1600s was about 2,000 pesos; it increased to 3,000 in the next century. For prominent families with several eligible daughters, it provided a socially accepted method of maintaining a prestigious life for their children.

With the exception of a few strict orders, most convents were comfortable and some, like La Concepción, even sumptuous. Many women employed servants or slaves, lived in luxurious quarters, and spent their time playing musical instruments, sewing, or otherwise engaged in "feminine" activities. Only a few nuns led a communal life. Most lived and ate in their own cells, often furnished to their taste. Some, like Sor Juana Inés de la Cruz, spent their time writing and studying. Indeed, nuns wrote a sizable body of literary, theological, philosophical, and scientific works. Although they could never leave the walls of the convent without permission, nuns could have visitors in the *locutorio*, and there they met relatives and friends and exchanged presents, letters, and news. The life of most convents was active and complex. Factions formed around nuns from illustrious and prominent families. Like their male counterparts in the Church, nuns often became determined politicians. The election of a mother superior could be a time of great tension; on a few occasions, the losing faction left the convent to form a new one.

New Spain also experimented with an institutional alternative for poor single women, the *recogimiento de mujeres*. The first recogimiento was established in Mexico City in 1572, when "prominent gentlemen" founded a place where Spanish prostitutes, repentant of their sinful ways, could live. The archbishop ordered five nuns to administer the recogimiento and teach the public women a new way of life. The new institution proved to be a great success because of the administrative talents of Sister Ana de San Jerónimo and because it provided poor women without dowries or other means an alternative to prostitution. Reports of the time indicate that repentant women came from all parts of the colony.

Other prostitutes, however, refused to repent. To deal with them, the archbishop established another recogimiento, the Hospital de Misericordia, in 1577. Authorities rounded up streetwalkers and other prostitutes who did not work in authorized brothels and sent them forcefully to the new establishment. Later, delinquent girls and women were also sent to the corregiemiento. The Hospital de Misericordia and similar institutions became reform schools for single women judged delinquent or criminal; more than a dozen recogimientos operated in Mexico City, and another dozen in the provinces. Approximately half were created in the sixteenth and seventeenth century and the remainder were formed in the eighteenth century, a period of population growth.

The inmates generally found these institutions harsh, and many attempted to escape. Only a few women benefited from the instruction provided by the recogimientos. In time, some of these institutions were converted into regular nunneries, and several were transformed into houses for "divorced" women. Apparently it was an attempt to provide such women, many of whom were probably battered wives, with a safe place to stay with their children until a more satisfactory arrangement could be made, or until a family reconciliation took place. The woman's family often attempted to mediate between the husband and wife in such cases. Although some women managed to establish independent lives as legally separated wives, most returned to their husbands. The recogimiento de mujeres represented an institutional attempt to deal with the growing problems of delinquents, vagrants, and women without families. Although it sought to alleviate the burdens borne by such females, it was not a feminist institution. Rather, it was designed to maintain and enforce the male supremacy considered normal in Mexican society.

The wealth, dynamism, and greater openness of colonial Mexican society provided the people of New Spain, including women, with ample opportunities to lead active and varied lives. In addition, Spanish law was progressive and more cognizant of women's rights than most other legal systems. As a result, colonial Mexican women enjoyed more rewarding lives than most of their contemporaries in other parts of the world.

PART THREE

Chapter 9

RATIONALIZATION, REFORM, AND REACTION

THE era of reform associated with the Bourbon monarchs of Spain had its roots in philosophical and economic changes evident even before the eighteenth century. Spain's relationship with New Spain and other parts of the American empire did not remain static over the first two centuries of Spanish rule. As Mexico expanded and developed, the nature, as well as the extent, of dependence on the mother country changed. Growing Mexican self-sufficiency, coupled with Spain's inability to service the colonial economy, pushed the metropolis into a parasitic relationship with its empire. New Spain developed direct access to wider and needed markets through the contraband activities of the English, French, Dutch, and others. Under the circumstances, illegal trade was a natural development beyond the power of an economically weak Spain to control.

The downward trend in Spanish–colonial trade began only three years after the record tonnage exchanged in 1608. By 1611, New Spain's volume of trade had dropped dramatically, and by 1620 only 47 ships sailed for the mother country. The increasing amounts of capital that Spanish merchants preferred to invest in the New World, rather than in their own declining economy, was an ominous sign. That tendency was strengthened by a desperate and penniless Crown's frantic seizure of private capital. Reluctantly, Spain began to see itself as a victim of its own backwardness, forced to be a broker between the rising economic power of its colonies and a worldwide commercial network dominated by more dynamic European powers. The meager profits that fell to the imperial administrator made a mockery of its theoretical possession of such vast and wealthy territories.

Various structural changes appeared necessary to reverse the situation and rescue the economy. The Crown abated the economic and social misery of Spain by boldly devaluating silver coinage and by providing tax relief. After 1686 currency and prices stabilized, laying the basis for economic revival under the new Bourbon dynasty. The resolution of the other major problem, a swollen and inefficient bureaucracy that beggared the treasury and corrupted the functions of government, proved more difficult. Political realities made any sudden or drastic reduction in the number of bureaucrats impossible. Nevertheless, the Crown attempted major reforms. A 1677 decree restricted the Council of the Indies to a president, 8 councillors, a *fiscal,* 2 secretaries, and 8 minor officials. Ten years later the Crown ordered the abolition of all purchased positions, but offered to pay 5 percent interest on the amount originally invested as well as allow the discharged official to keep his title. Moreover, all supernumerary positions were to be eliminated as they fell vacant. And in 1691, all officials over the authorized limit went into temporary retirement on half pay, with the right of first consideration should an authorized position become available. Although actual implementation of these rules proved difficult, the Crown clearly indicated its desire to reduce the bureaucracy to manageable levels.

The state also attempted to rationalize the tax structure to encourage trade and economic development, rather than merely to raise revenue. In 1687 the Marqués de los Vélez prepared an exhaustive study that analyzed the negative effect of ill-conceived and confiscatory taxes. He also recommended the introduction of chartered companies modeled on English and Dutch examples, and that foreign shareholders be included. The philosophical shift was not by any means complete: in 1690 a committee charged with making recommendations to improve the American trade advocated all the methods which had already been unsuccessfully employed, including prohibitions against foreigners.

Significantly, the Crown requested the opinion of Manuel de Lira. A man of wide bureaucratic experience, Lira denounced unrealistic regulations and taxes, arguing that earlier attempts to exclude foreigners had forced them to seize outposts in the Caribbean. He urged that a distinction be made between hostile and friendly powers seeking to trade with the empire. To bring about international cooperation, Lira suggested the formation of open trading companies, so that it would be in the interest of foreign capital to eliminate illegal trade; mutual advantage, rather than unworkable regulations, would both protect and develop the commerce of the empire. While attempts to reform the bureaucracy, trade, and taxes, and to rationalize relations with European trading powers, did not advance beyond a preliminary stage, the debate laid the foundations of national revival. When the unfortunate Carlos II died, bequeathing his troubled empire to Felipe V (1700–1746), grandson of Louis XIV of France, these ideas provided a ray of hope in an otherwise grim picture. The new Bourbon king, already familiar with the attempts to centralize power in France, proved receptive to Spanish reformers who sought to modify the old Habsburg state.

IMPERIAL REFORMS:
THE DEBATE IN SPAIN

Felipe V's victory in the War of the Spanish Succession allowed the new monarch to initiate a series of changes designed to centralize the Spanish government, restore finances, and reorganize the armed forces. Reformers such as José Patiño and José Campillo revived the economy by applying mercantilist policies. The most important transformation, however, was the introduction of strong regional administrators. New provincial officials with military, financial, economic, and judicial authority reported directly to the king. The new structure reduced regionalism and strengthened the national government—and as Spain began to prosper, the forces of change gathered momentum.

During the reign of Carlos III (1759–1788), zealous officials, bent on creating a more efficient and more rational society, attacked the problems of education, administration, agriculture, industry, trade, and transportation. These men of the Enlightenment wanted a better, more equitable, rational, and effective government. They also believed in a secular community, and sought to reduce the Church's immense role in the Spanish world by espousing the cause of regalism. A symbolic high point in the struggle to create a secular state came in 1767 with the expulsion of the Society of Jesus from Spain and its empire. More important, however, was the Bourbon concept of government, which rejected the Habsburg reliance on corporations in favor of administration by civil and military bureaucrats.

The Bourbon program of regeneration was not limited to Spain. While an appreciation of the effects of unrealistic trade regulations was evident before 1700, José Campillo, Felipe V's minister of war and finance, moved the debate further in the direction of realistic—and hence viable—controls over the colonial economy. In 1743 his penetrating study, *Nuevo sistema de gobierno económico para la América* ("New system of economic governance for America"), circulated within the bureaucracy in manuscript form; Campillo proposed a radical reorganization of the colonial government and commerce to obtain for Spain the advantages other imperial powers appeared to derive from their possessions. He advocated making legal trade more lucrative than contraband by reducing taxes, liberalizing regulations, and eliminating both the Cádiz monopoly and the outmoded convoy system. One of his most innovative ideas involved a new approach to the Indians. Campillo suggested that more land could be brought into production by making tax-free land grants to Indians and providing them with the necessary technical advice. He demonstrated that Spain had failed to make adequate and rational use of its New World resources. In 1765 a royal commission recommended many of his proposals, and Campillo's influence is obvious in another reform program, Bernardo Ward's *Proyecto económico* (1762). The Bourbon reformers' almost exclusive concentration on economic objectives constituted a departure from the more balanced Habsburg approach to government.

The popularity of such ideas in influential circles in Madrid tended to overwhelm any real appreciation of the obstacles. The role of British technical and capital resources, in dominating trade in the Americas and elsewhere, was not understood fully. Consequently, planners stressed structural reforms which inevitably clashed with realities that an economically weak Spain could not totally reverse. Broad royal reforms founded on eighteenth-century rationalism went beyond pragmatic necessity and inevitably unsettled well-established interests and social patterns, ignoring already existing adjustments. Bourbon planners did not adequately consider the extent of Mexican resistance to a new and adverse colonial relationship. The wisdom of attempts to increase productivity, or of rationalizing trade regulations that forced merchants to deal in contraband, appeared to the reformers to be self-evident and beyond question.

Jurisdictional modifications, as well as territorial changes, were always under some degree of consideration. Indeed, plans to create a separate viceroyalty in northern New Spain had been reviewed in 1751—but the expense, among other factors, led to shelving the proposal. While committed to the idea of structural changes in the political system, Spanish planners tended to favor bolder and more innovative approaches that attacked what they saw as the root cause of decadence. Pragmatic tinkering alone did not seem sufficient to meet the needs of the modern era.

INTERNAL ADJUSTMENTS

New Spain, responding to its own needs, did not wait passively for imperial initiatives. Facing specific issues, and able to draw upon its own considerable resources, colonial Mexico made realistic and pragmatic adjustments as the situation warranted. Such modifications often clashed with the theoretically structured reforms demanded by Crown planners.

One of the most important pragmatic measures instituted by colonial authorities dealt with the control of criminal activity. The state's ability to guarantee a reasonable degree of security of life and property constituted a major element of its legitimacy, quite apart from more immediate concerns. As colonial society became increasingly complex, moving from domination by a small group of conquistadores and their successors to a multiracial class system, maintaining order became more difficult. Social mobility, in both the economic and the social sense, brought problems as well as opportunities. The rapid forging of a mestizo culture, necessitating replacement of the caste system by one based on class, opened a race for economic and social advantage unlike anything Europeans had experienced. Such a fluid situation created uncertainty as well as advancement. Competition for wealth and status in New Spain's materialistic society encouraged restricted group loyalties and a corresponding lack of concern for those outside the accepted circle. Extended families or corporate bodies often pitted themselves against the rest of society in an attempt to gain and to hold social advantage. In such a tense and fluid society, people perceived crime as a much greater problem than it really was. This was particularly true in the eighteenth century, a period of lessened upward social mobility.

Banditry, in particular, worried political authorities, because it undermined local control, restricted normal commerce and communication between urban centers, and ultimately damaged viceregal sovereignty. If the viceroy failed to control disruptive activities, public respect for the government would be dangerously undermined. Judicial officials, functioning within the traditional structure, appeared unable to contain criminal activity. Local alcaldes, restricted by territorial divisions, could not control bandits who moved across a number of different jurisdictions in the course of their depredations. A new approach had to be found to stem the perceived crime wave. The actions of Miguel Velázquez de Lorea suggested the solution.

In 1710, at the request of the inhabitants of Querétaro, Velázquez assumed the duties of an alcalde provincial de la hermandad. Demonstrating a combination of zeal and energy, he quickly restored order around the city. Impressed, the viceroy subsequently asked him to dislodge a bandit gang from an hacienda near Valladolid. The energetic Velázquez agreed, provided he could also apply immediate punishment. The Viceroy, Marqués Valero, granted the necessary power, and the bandits soon dangled from the nearest tree.

In order to regularize Velázquez's activities without damaging his freedom of action, the viceroy established a new agency—the Tribunal of the *Acordada*. It received that name because the viceroy made the new agency's sentences final and exempted it from the Audiencia's review procedures, with the agreement *(con acuerdo)* of that body. Unlike other judicial officials, the judge or captain of the Acordada could pursue criminals across the length and breadth of New Spain. Free of political responsibilities, he concentrated on enforcement. Headquartered in Mexico City, the Acordada's judge appointed volunteer agents to any part of the viceroyalty. The only considerations were need and the availability of volunteers—and where need existed, local interest could be counted on to supply personnel. Since the authorities placed no limitations on the number of Acordada agents, the judge could inundate troubled areas with appointees.

The judge in Mexico City sentenced the Tribunal's prisoners. Other competing institutions and local judicial officials, jealous of their own prerogatives, made sure that the agency's wide police powers did not become unacceptably oppressive. Viceroys usually backed the Acordada in its intrabureaucratic disputes, because it provided a reliable reserve system apparently able to deal with activities beyond the control of the traditional structure. Originally confined to rural areas, the Acordada soon extended its jurisdiction into urban centers. The Tribunal's effectiveness prompted the viceroy to use the organization to enforce liquor laws, and he expanded its paid staff. While the Acordada was never more than marginally successful in suppressing illegal intoxicants that competed with pulque and Spanish wines, the Crown credited the increased revenues from legal beverages to its efforts.

At the height of its activities, the Acordada numbered some 2,500 agents scattered unevenly throughout New Spain. As the century unfolded, the agency itself became somewhat outmoded. Increasingly complex social factors led to a desire for more formal methods and due process. As a result, the authorities introduced modifications that led to a much more restrained and bureaucratic administration of justice, complete with mounting paperwork. By the beginning of the nineteenth century, the Acordada had lost much of its effectiveness and needed reorganization.

The establishment of the Acordada in the early part of the century demonstrated the ability of the colonial bureaucracy to respond in a pragmatic, rational manner to New Spain's special needs. Breaking with the traditional system of geographically limited jurisdictions, confined within a mixture of political, administrative, and judicial responsibilities, the Tribunal concentrated on maintaining order. Moreover, it placed centralized police powers in the hands of the viceroy, who had direct control over the judge and his subordinates. The rationalization of law enforcement, and its subsequent approval by Felipe V, first monarch of the new Bourbon dynasty, indicated the importance of evolutionary factors in bringing about change. Innovative reforms, tailored to special needs, did not necessarily depend on Crown planners in Madrid. The Acordada's success, indeed, prompted plans to introduce the agency into other Spanish dependencies.

Another important adjustment occurred as a result of the monarchy's willingness to sell high positions in the bureaucracy. Although intended to raise money, the practice allowed the criollo elite to gain direct political representation, especially through purchase of Audiencia seats. Despite the protests of the Council of the Indies, Felipe IV (1621–1665) sold treasury offices, provincial governorships, and Audiencia positions to criollos. The systematic sale of Audiencia posts, however, began in 1687 and continued at a high rate until 1712, with only brief breaks caused by various reform decrees. Officials could also purchase exemptions from the prohibitions against marriage into local families, against landholding, and even against future reform decrees. Consequently, the Audiencia fell, at least partially, into the hands of the local elite, who exercised power through their judicial representatives and through their connection with the judges. They expected, and obtained, the oidores' cooperation. Illegal economic assistance, even joint ventures and other prohibited activities, occurred. The purchase of office permitted those who held economic power to exercise a degree of control over the political system.

Contraband, a natural if illegal rationalization of trade from New Spain's perspective, posed an entirely different problem for colonial authorities. It could not be eradicated, nor were colonial bureaucrats free to accommodate it legally. Overzealous efforts to suppress contraband inevitably failed, succeeding only in temporarily disrupting the local economy. Viceregal officials found it necessary to ignore all but the most blatant, or most politically embarrassing, violations. Without the freedom to respond rationally to the actual trade situation in a legal manner, officials had little choice but to ignore imperial restrictions. It is evident that some Crown officers themselves dealt, indirectly or directly, in the contraband trade. Under the circumstances, corruption may have been the most rational response. Bureaucratic planners in Madrid, however, viewed the existence of contraband, and the corruption that accompanied the illegal trade, as one of the major justifications for their sweeping reform measures.

JOSE DE GALVEZ IN NEW SPAIN

In spite of much discussion in imperial circles, little was accomplished, however, until the advent of the Seven Years War. Shocked by Britain's capture of Havana in 1762, and dismayed by the trading boom that resulted, Spain moved to initiate changes at the cessation of hostilities. Trade restrictions were gradually relaxed, allowing relatively free trade within the empire. A series of *visitas,* or inspections, were carried out, beginning in 1763 and 1764 with Cuba, where an intendancy was established in 1765. The implications of the new philosophical approach began to be evident in New Spain with the official visita (1765–1771) of José de Gálvez. Gálvez, accurately described as being as "prejudiced in favor of the rights of the metropolis as he was disposed to outrage those of the colonies," may have exaggerated the general feeling in Madrid, but his attitude was not unique. The visitador boldly assaulted the old structure, questioning the concept of the viceroyalty that formed the core of the Habsburg structure of empire.

José de Gálvez's aggressive approach, and his prompt decisive action to remedy perceived problems, offended Mexicans who viewed his acts as unrestrained use of authority. Accustomed to consensus politics, they found it difficult to accept his reforms. The visitador, however, reflected the new bureaucratic philosophy shared by Carlos III's enlightened ministers. While many imperial bureaucrats clung to the consensus corporativism of the Habsburgs, the king's ministers rejected such cautious and essentially passive governance. The new thought of the eighteenth century made it possible to elaborate a theoretical system that linked the empire's many problems together as part of a general pattern. The crisis-management techniques that characterized the old state could be laid aside in favor of long-range planning. It seemed possible to make coordinated decisions that affected diverse sectors previously viewed as unrelated to each other. An official philosophy based on the analytical tools of the Enlightenment had the advantage of both defining the problems and indicating their solution. The new bureaucratic ideology permitted the state to move away from consensus decision-making toward reliance on individuals who used the accepted philosophical guidelines for direction as well as support. Those who did not share the new ideology understandably, but incorrectly, viewed the actions of those who did as merely an arbitrary exercise of power.

José de Gálvez hoped to replace the viceroyalty with a system of commandants-generals and powerful secondary-level intendants, which he believed would increase disposable income by an estimated 3 million pesos. The Audiencia, as an important element of the traditional structure, also came under attack. In the eighteenth century, Madrid relied more on military men and fiscal officers than on judicial arbitrators. As a result, the high status of oidores diminished as the nature of the empire changed. Gálvez in fact reduced their functions by conceding to many agencies, such as the postal service, the gunpowder, tobacco, and playing-card monopoly, and fiscal bodies, the right to try their own dependents. Separate legal powers *(fueros)* existed even before the Habsburgs, but Gálvez now used them to weaken the Audiencia's dominant position in the judicial system.

Like other Spanish reformers, José de Gálvez failed to appreciate fully the political contribution of Mexicans, especially within the Audiencias. He distrusted them and rejected their claims to special consideration in their own region. He perceived the acquisition of Audiencia positions by native sons in their own areas *(patrias)* as a source of political turmoil and danger. José de Gálvez shared the views of Baylio Frey Julián de Arriaga, Secretary of Marine and the Indies (1754–1776), who favored the reduction of native-son officials as well as the indirect criollo influence acquired through marriage alliances. After 1750, the Crown refused to sell marriage dispensations, and granted few exemptions, usually with the proviso that the official accept an immediate transfer. Madrid's desire to hispanize the colonial bureaucracy deeply offended many criollos. The fact that colonists continued to be appointed outside of their region to other American Audiencias provided scant consolation; a judge born in New Spain, but employed in Peru, remained almost as much a foreigner as a Spaniard. Criollo nationalism, that transcended one particular region, developed later in the century, but never became sufficiently strong to overcome regionalism. What Madrid viewed as a necessary reform, the colonial elite saw as an arbitrary move to deprive them of bureaucratic representation within their own patria.

Not surprisingly, one of the first major structural changes directly affected the relationship between the viceroy and the Audiencia. In 1776 the Crown created the position of regent, ranked immediately below the viceroy with the power to assume that office in his absence or if it fell vacant. The regent presided over the Audiencia and resolved jurisdictional disputes, as well as monitored the general disposition of all cases. If necessary, he could create special civil or criminal committees for specific purposes. In the event of political turmoil resulting in the overthrow of the viceroy—as had occurred in the past—the regent would be the logical successor. The new post was consistent with the general belief that the colonial bureaucracy needed more connecting links between the different levels. Viceroy Revillagigedo, however, remained unconvinced, claiming that most of the regent's function already fell to the senior judge. To the viceroy, the new position, with a significantly larger salary than judges received, needlessly inflated the expense of government.

The key institution, however, was the intendancy system already operating in Spain itself, whose introduction brought colonial administration more in line with the mother country. Gálvez's *Plan de intendencias* (1768) compared New Spain's government to that of Spain during the worst days of Carlos II. He diagnosed Mexico's central problem as one arising from a combination of abuse and exploitation by the alcaldes mayores and structural weaknesses that failed to provide a middle bureaucratic level linking the top with local administrators. Moreover, Gálvez maintained that corruption among the alcaldes had become so ingrained that their suppression and replacement was absolutely mandatory. In their place he recommended the creation of *subdelegados* (subdelegates of the intendant) directly responsible to the intendant. He also urged that they be provided with an adequate salary to guarantee diligence and honesty. José de Gálvez believed that low tribute and tax revenues resulted from the corruption of local administrators, as well as from the widely accepted practice of controlling Indian production and consumption through the repartimiento de comercio. Merchants and administrators might profit, but not the Crown nor its Indian subjects.

Reformers like Gálvez viewed the repartimiento only as a system which exploited Indian society and deprived the Crown of needed revenue. The example of the alcalde mayor of Chalco provides an indication of what Gálvez believed was at stake. In the 1720s the town of Tlalmanalco supplied the alcalde with a cook and the services of three ranch hands without charge. The alcalde's main business, the compulsory sale of horses and cattle to the local inhabitants, provided a handsome profit. He merely drew up the necessary documents, set the price, and required an individual or group to accept the livestock. In case of resistance he relied on his official position to collect, occasionally holding an individual's wife as security. The alcalde's ability to control Indian production and consumption, through the repartimiento and other minor concessions, earned the official an amount 30 times his legal salary. While the authorities recognized that Chalco was especially lucrative, other alcaldes mayores also managed to extract a living from their political charges. Gálvez claimed that only the officials profited, noting that the alcalde mayor in Nejapa earned 10,000 to 15,000 pesos from the repartimiento, compared to the 500 pesos in sales taxes (alcabala) collected for the viceregal treasury. Moreover, royal interests were further damaged by failure of these officials to collect taxes on their own transactions. The removal of such parasitic officials, in Gálvez's opinion, would not only encourage production but also increase tax revenues.

The reformers, however, did not completely understand the economic system of New Spain. While it is true that many alcaldes mayores were corrupt and abused their authority, the repartimiento de comercio was much more than a simple mechanism for exploitation. It was the most important system of credit for Indian communities and small-scale agriculturalists. Alcaldes mayores profited because they provided needed services: they distributed seed, tools, and other agricultural necessities on credit; they facilitated the purchase or sale of livestock; and they often marketed products for groups who might not otherwise have found outlets for their commodities.

In his rush to introduce reforms, Gálvez tended to ignore Spain's weakness. Viceroy Antonio María de Bucareli (1771–1779) attempted to counter what he viewed as Gálvez's unrealistic position by urging moderation and caution. The viceroy's conservatism made him popular with the elite and the traditional bureaucracy. Bucareli had a more accurate perception of the colonial reality, as well as of Spain's financial, organizational, and political limitations. He suggested that ill-trained personnel and wanton disregard for laws and regulations, not the existing political structure, constituted the problem. The solution thus lay in strengthening the existing bureaucracy rather than embarking on costly reforms. Moreover, Bucareli indicated that it would be difficult to recruit well-trained subdelegates, and feared that if they did not receive adequate salaries they might be even more corrupt than the alcaldes mayores.

The viceroy was not alone in pointing out the problems and consequences of ill-conceived reforms. The Conde de Tepa, a judge of the Audiencia with wide administrative experience in the Philippines as well as within New Spain, also raised a cautious voice in protest. Significantly, he criticized the notion that the governments of Spain and Mexico should be uniformly structured. He noted that, after all, the inhabitants differed, and methods applicable in Spain might not succeed in Mexico. Like Bucareli, he advised strengthening the traditional system. The Conde de Tepa also defended the repartimiento as necessary to incorporate Indians into the economy. He did, however, recommend stricter regulations to assure a reasonable return for the natives, as well as the orderly collection of taxes. Both the viceroy and the judge had a vested interest in defending the traditional structure; nevertheless, their doubts and objections deserved closer attention. José de Gálvez, however, believed the situation was beyond mere adjustment; consequently, he brushed aside the cautious recommendations of colonial bureaucrats.

In 1776 José de Gálvez became Minister of the Indies, a position that gave him an opportunity to implement his ideas. That same year, the Crown appointed salaried directors to collect excise taxes in 24 of New Spain's urban centers under the supervision of a director-general in the viceregal capital. Veracruz, New Spain's principal port, had its own tax superintendent. Thereafter the tax system yielded a sizable revenue. Additionally, the royal tobacco monopoly, established by Gálvez during his stay in New Spain, returned a considerable profit. The Crown purchased tobacco from licensed growers, the only legal source of unprocessed tobacco, and manufactured cigars at royal factories situated in Puebla, Mexico City, Querétaro, Orizaba, and Guadalajara. The royal monopoly employed approximately 17,000 individuals who by 1801 produced a 4-million-peso profit which they remitted directly to Spain. Tobacco monopoly administrators, like other fiscal agents, were generally recruited from Spain.

The decade of the 1770s witnessed a gratifying surge in revenue from all sources, including the tribute, which went from 596,220 pesos in the 1760s to 955,813 pesos at the end of the 1770s. At the same time, the fiscal bureaucracy expanded almost beyond control. Although the viceroy retained ultimate fiscal responsibility, actual administrative supervision proved impossible. In an effort to rationalize the tax collection structure, Gálvez appointed a fiscal officer of the royal treasury in 1780 to oversee the various tax agents—a task which proved beyond that official's powers and limited staff. Subsequently the Crown named a special intendant, who attempted to supervise and coordinate the fiscal bureaucracy. Despite such difficulties, the new fiscal policy resulted in a substantial increase in revenue collection.

In keeping with the general policy of stimulating the colonial economy, and hence tax revenues, Gálvez recommended the establishment of a mining guild, the *Real Cuerpo de Minería,* which came into existence in 1777. A comprehensive mining code (*ordenanzas de minería*) governed the corporation as well as the activities of the miners. The Crown encouraged the introduction of modern technology through the appointment of the distinguished scientist, Fausto de Elhuyar, as director-general in 1786, and by establishing the School of Mines, the first technological institute, the following decade. Although it is difficult to specify the causes, eighteenth-century silver production consistently increased, except during the 1760s. Viceroy Revillagigedo believed that a combination of factors—among them the greater number of people employed in the industry, improved distribution of mercury, better technology, and the formation of companies to work older mines—caused the silver boom. Improved use of gunpowder and the general decrease in prices for powder, mercury, and other supplies also had an effect, as did better management and control of labor. For example, Guanajuato's Valenciana mine produced a steady profit, apparently because of its ability to manipulate labor, among other factors. In addition, trade reforms, tax incentives, and the new technology disseminated by the mining guild and its school also played a role in the expansion of silver production.

VIOLENT REACTION TO CHANGE: THE EXPULSION OF THE JESUITS

Royal actions based on a new eighteenth-century bureaucratic ideology were neither appreciated nor widely understood in Mexico. Reforms that overturned legal precedents and long-established customs, and which threatened existing accommodations, had a negative psychological and material effect on all groups. This was particularly true of the lower classes, who were now subject to military service, to new tax demands, and to more efficient collection of old levies, as well as to increasing stress from population growth and other adverse factors. In such circumstances, the uncertainty of rapid change combined with existing social pressures to make violence inevitable. The expulsion of the Society of Jesus provided the catalyst.

The government of Carlos III expelled the Jesuits from all Spanish territories in 1767, because it considered the order a threat to enlightened reforms and a dangerous competitor for the allegiance of the upper and middle classes. Mexicans, however, viewed the expulsion as an inexplicable act. In New Spain 700 members of the order were affected. Their arrest, pending deportation, occurred during the height of Jesuit influence in New Spain. The order had not only led the successful effort to secure papal recognition of the cult of Our Lady of Guadalupe, it had also blocked the efforts of the secular clergy in Mexico to obtain the beatification of Juan de Palafox, the Jesuits' sixteenth-century enemy, thereby retarding attempts to canonize the famous Bishop of Puebla. The Jesuits held unquestionable influence over the criollo elite, and their status among other elements of the population remained high. Nevertheless, secret instructions from Madrid abruptly destroyed the Society.

News of the expulsion decree shocked Mexicans. Such a violent governmental action, amid other upheavals, seemed unacceptable. Although the lower classes were the least affected by the expulsion, they expressed their discontent through riots and disorders; other social groups sympathized and, on occasion, supported the protesters. Racial and class conflicts, however, soon surfaced, thus reducing the danger of the incipient rebellion and facilitating its suppression.

Reaction to the expulsion decree varied throughout the viceroyalty. While Mexico City remained calm, a small group in Puebla plotted to overthrow the government and establish independence. Reaction in outlying areas, many of them familiar with urban disorders, proved more serious. Rioting in San Luis de la Paz prompted José de Gálvez to descend on the municipality with a force of regular troops and volunteers. Empowered by the viceroy to restore order through any means necessary, he was determined to enforce the expulsion decree and to make an example of troublemakers; therefore he executed four suspected ringleaders and exiled others. He assured the maintenance of order with a newly organized militia unit—financed, in part, through the new taxes levied on the lower classes. Meanwhile in Guanajuato, a rioting mob attempted to seize treasury funds before fleeing the city to escape punishment. With customary dispatch, Gálvez ordered 8,000 troops to establish a cordon around Guanajuato to isolate and capture the rioters, a process that lasted over three months.

The disorders in San Luis Potosí are indicative of the grievances underlying the opposition to expulsion of the Jesuits. Besides the new taxes and obligations imposed throughout the colony, the poor in San Luis Potosí were subjected to a series of bitterly resented restrictions, among them an order expelling vagabonds from the city. In addition, the authorities attempted to enforce laws against carrying small arms, an objective not readily accepted by the miners and workers in that frontier province. When authorities attempted to expel the few Jesuits in the area, widespread disorders erupted. Mobs attacked the jail, freeing prisoners and destroying municipal property; wild rumors abounded that the insurgents planned to create an independent republic and to reestablish the old Indian religion. The besieged authorities failed to carry out the Jesuit expulsion. But Gálvez arrived with troops, quickly restored order, and conducted summary trials. Eleven individuals died on the gallows and their heads were subsequently displayed on pikes; others received life sentences, exile, or whippings. Gálvez demolished the dwellings of the principal insurgents and scattered salt over the ruins. Forced labor and a maize tax were imposed to raise new public structures to replace those destroyed. The nearby village of San Nicolás witnessed the drawing and quartering of its leader, who had sworn to fight until all *gachupines* had been killed, and the execution of his aides—significantly, the authorities severed the hand of the scribe who had recorded the vow. San Nicolás lost all local autonomy as a result of the insurrection.

Pedro de Soria, the Indian governor of Pátzcuaro, led over 100 villages in revolt. After the rebellion was crushed, Valladolid authorities captured 460 Indians at Pátzcuaro and Uruapan, accusing them of serving with Soria. Gálvez arrived in Pátzcuaro to deliver the sentences. Soria and a mulato follower were executed and decapitated, while others received harsh punishments. In Uruapan, long a center of resistance to military recruitment, Gálvez ordered ten hanged and others suitably punished as a public lesson. In addition, he imposed a special tax to maintain the local militia.

José de Gálvez returned to Mexico City, well pleased with his labors, after four and a half months. Some 3,000 persons had faced trial: 85 had been executed, 674 sentenced to life imprisonment, 117 to exile, and 73 flogged. The number of executions stunned a public accustomed to relatively restrained use of capital punishment. The visitador's willingness to apply overwhelming force and inflict heavy punishment impressed all segments of the population. Although well aware that the root causes of the disturbances could be traced to socioeconomic factors, Gálvez nevertheless treated the disturbances as a question of treason. He believed that the alcaldes mayores shared the blame by aggravating, instead of resolving, long-standing problems. His harsh suppression of the insurrections was designed to guarantee political control until the benefits of the planned reforms alleviated the situation. The fact that the same type of disturbances did not recur until the independence period testified to his success, as well as to the lingering influence of his grim message.

ADMINISTRATIVE REFORMS

The long-debated intendant system went into effect in Mexico in 1786. The system divided New Spain into 12 *intendencias*, each administered by a *gobernador intendente* and further subdivided into districts *(partidos)* governed by subdelegados, nominated by the intendant and appointed for a five-year term by the viceroy. The *intendants*, who served an indeterminate term of office, received a salary of 6,000 pesos, a sum that exceeded the yearly wages of Audiencia judges and many other high functionaries. The new officials combined the political and judicial powers of the former governors and alcaldes, and also assumed important fiscal responsibilities. Instead of functioning as passive administrators, they were expected to stimulate economic activity and increase tax revenues, directly and indirectly, through public works, the revitalization of the municipal government, and the introduction of new methods to increase production. Their wide mandate, together with primary responsibility for military and Church affairs, made the 12 gobernadores intendentes a powerful political force only nominally under the supervision of the viceroy. Carefully chosen from a qualified pool of Spaniards, the intendants arrived in New Spain with a keen awareness of their responsibilities and Crown objectives. Consequently, they tended to view themselves as reformers sent to rescue an outmoded and corrupt colony. Concerned with fiscal efficiency, Madrid ordered taxes paid at the intendancy level rather than to the viceroyal treasury in Mexico City. Therefore the Crown opened new treasuries in Valladolid, Puebla, Oaxaca, and the mining centers of Guanajuato and Zacatecas.

The success of the new middle-range executives was impressive. Unfortunately, the Crown's unwillingness to pay an adequate salary to the subdelegados flawed the system. Instead of a fixed salary, those officials received 5 percent of the tribute revenue. Madrid's hopes that increased tribute payment would result from more efficient collection, providing not only support but also an incentive, were theoretically sound, but a failure in practice. The regulation led to an excessive subdivision of the old alcaldías mayores, reducing the number of tributaries in each new jurisdiction and thus increasing the burden on individuals. Moreover, administrative confusion over the actual jurisdiction of subdelegados hampered the new system. In Indian districts, a subdelegado supervised the municipal councils and the economy in general, as well as military affairs, justice, and tax collection. In non-Indian towns, the subdelegados assumed responsibility only for military and fiscal affairs; in contrast to the former alcaldes, they did not head the municipal council. The two-tier system was intended to avoid political conflict with the resurgent municipalities, while preserving their financial obligation. In practice it weakened the subdelegado, leaving him without much power or economic support.

A subsequent compromise arrangement, that gave the subdelegado full power in districts under municipal jurisdiction while restricting his power within the urban center, merely led to squabbles and maladministration. Ultimately recognizing the need for a strong royal official at the municipal level, the Crown ended distinctions between subdelegados by 1799. In the case of the important city of Querétaro, the Council of the Indies ordered the appointment of a trained legal officer *(corregidor de letras)* to represent Crown interests; elsewhere the standard system prevailed.

As some predicted, the recruitment of qualified individuals proved difficult. Many former alcaldes became subdelegados at the expiration of their terms. In less than desirable areas, however, merely finding an individual willing to serve proved difficult. Once the repartimiento ended, subdelegados were often unable to post a satisfactory bond. Previously merchants had guaranteed such bonds, but under the new system they had little incentive to aid the officials. Resentful over the new restrictions, newly appointed subdelegados often did their best to sabotage the system by engaging in thinly veiled illegal activities. As a result of such problems, demands for reinstatement of the repartimiento de comercio began almost immediately. The subdelegado system's obvious weaknesses made some compromise inevitable. Recognizing the interests of the merchant community, the viceroy, Marqués de Branciforte (1794–1798), consulted the Consulado. Not surprisingly, the merchants' guild advised a return to the old system and its guaranteed economic benefits. In November 1794 the viceregal *Junta superior de real hacienda* agreed to reinstate the repartimiento de comercio, but under the supervision of the intendants, who supposedly would closely monitor the subdelegados. On his return to Spain, Viceroy Branciforte testified before the Council of the Indies in favor of official reinstitution of the repartimiento de comercio. Nevertheless, the Council believed that its suppression was beneficial, and recommended that the issue be resolved by increasing the subdelegados' salary to a range from 1,500 to 2,200 pesos a year, based on a district's importance. A new revised ordinance drawn up in 1803, however, never went into effect.

Gálvez's reforms proved less successful in the ill-defined and underpopulated northern regions of the viceroyalty. Spanish sovereignty in that vast area was threatened by hostile nomadic Indians like the Apaches and by pressures from other European colonial powers. Therefore the Commandancy-General of the Provincias Internas was established in 1776 as a way of providing cohesion and protection for the settlers of the region. The new institution, which administered Northern Mexico—including California, New Mexico, and Texas—functioned poorly. The area's scattered population and limited resources were not sufficient to support the new government, and a serious lack of cooperation between viceregal authorities and northern officials frustrated efforts to improve the area. The Crown sought to ameliorate the administration of the Commandancy through further territorial divisions and modifications, but the region remained marginal and weak.

TRADE REFORMS

Although the Mexican economy was expanding, the restrictive and increasingly unworkable trade system prevented Spain from benefiting. Furthermore, the growth of illegal trade, following natural lines of commerce, undermined Spanish sovereignty by continually demonstrating its economic and institutional weakness. Spanish officials agreed that reforms were necessary, but well-entrenched interest groups opposed change. An inter-locking international network of merchants and financiers actively opposed imperial reforms that might disrupt the existing system and their illegal adaptation to it. Cádiz merchants, closely linked with foreign suppliers and New Spain's trading community, mustered international pressure and timely bribes to protect their interests. In normal circumstances, they could easily frustrate reforms. Ac-

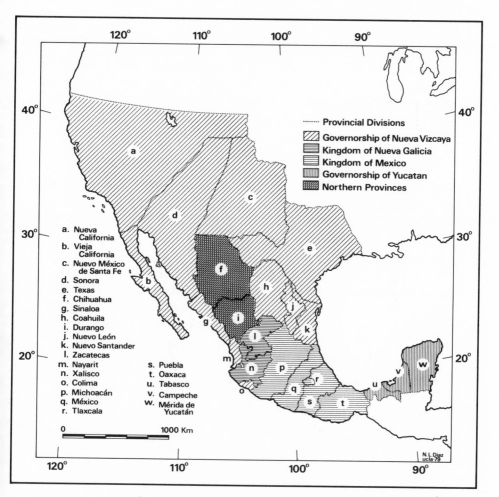

Map legend:

········ Provincial Divisions

▨ Governorship of Nueva Vizcaya

▥ Kingdom of Nueva Galicia

▤ Kingdom of Mexico

▥ Governorship of Yucatan

▨ Northern Provinces

a. Nueva California
b. Vieja California
c. Nuevo México de Santa Fe
d. Sonora
e. Texas
f. Chihuahua
g. Sinaloa
h. Coahuila
i. Durango
j. Nuevo León
k. Nuevo Santander
l. Zacatecas
m. Nayarit
n. Xalisco
o. Colima
p. Michoacán
q. México
r. Tlaxcala
s. Puebla
t. Oaxaca
u. Tabasco
v. Campeche
w. Mérida de Yucatán

0   1000 Km

N.L.Diaz
ucla-79

NEW SPAIN IN THE EIGHTEENTH CENTURY

tion became necessary, however, because the traditional system, increasingly dominated by British merchants, threatened to completely bypass Spain.

Resistance to trade reforms began to weaken by the 1700s. The convoy system no longer functioned; the fleet did not sail on a regular annual basis. When it sailed, merchants often found the Mexican market already glutted by contraband goods. Businessmen, who obtained a license to send an individual ship, found New Spain's market uncertain and profits slim.

Since Spanish merchants failed to develop modern commercial organization, they were at a disadvantage when trading with the great almaceneros of Mexico. Rather than distributing their own goods, the Spaniards wholesaled the merchandise at the trade fair which was held in Jalapa after 1729, to escape Veracruz's unhealthy climate. Wealthy Mexicans, who arrived at the fair with 200 to 400 thousand pesos in specie, were able to dictate prices because they could buy in bulk. The larger Mexican merchants subsequently held internal trade fairs in the northern centers of San Juan de los Lagos and Saltillo, where they resold small lots of goods to provincial traders, often on credit. Their warehouses in Mexico City supplied retailers. Almaceneros also operated retail outlets, both in the capital and in the provinces. Because of the interconnected and closed nature of the commercial structure, little money actually changed hands. Only at the trade fair in Jalapa were large amounts of specie exchanged. The use of bills of exchange *(libranzas)* rather than currency further protected the large merchants from competition. Although the Spanish merchants had no quarrel with the closed system, because they did not want competition, the decline in trade with Mexico seriously threatened their existence, particularly in the late seventeenth and early eighteenth century.

If Spanish authorities hoped to regain a share of the Mexican market, they would have to radically restructure the commercial system. The potential for increased trade was demonstrated dramatically during the Seven Years War. Before 1762, no more than 15 ships serviced the Cuban trade, yet during eleven months of British occupation some 700 merchant ships passed through Havana. Spain might not be able to capture the entire trade, yet even a modest percentage would stimulate commercial activity. Beginning in the early 1770s, a series of new regulations lowering duties on certain products, or abolishing them entirely, were implemented to stimulate production and consumption. For example, unprocessed cotton and Spanish wine enjoyed an exemption. The Crown legalized trade between Mexico and the Viceroyalty of Peru in 1774, although authorities still attempted to insure that intercolonial commerce did not compete with Spanish products. A decade earlier, the monarchy began to open more Spanish ports to the colonial trade. Finally, in 1789, it included New Spain in the so-called "free trade" system. The distinction between Spanish and colonial merchants virtually disappeared in 1796, when Spanish Americans obtained the privilege of legally owning and operating ships from a colonial homeport.

The trade reforms invigorated the Spanish economy. Stimulated by the 1771 exclusion of all cotton imports from the empire, Catalonia's cotton industry turned to the production of colorful cotton prints known as *indianas*. New Spain provided the raw materials—cotton and natural dyes— and consumed the finished product. Although other areas of the Iberian peninsula also experienced an economic revival, after 1778 Catalonia accounted for over half of the Spanish goods sold in the American trade. In Mexico the reforms lowered prices, cut inflated profit margins, and changed distribution patterns. A plentiful, generally uninterrupted, supply of goods at competitive prices attracted a new group of merchants into commerce. They traded directly with the provinces, and traveled widely in search of new markets. The new merchants received corporate recognition, and a degree of power, with the authorization in 1795 of two new consulados in Guadalajara and Veracruz. Quickly organized, the Veracruz merchants' guild proved both innovative and aggressive. The new Consulado collected and published trade information and otherwise attempted to expand commerce, and financed a new road from Veracruz through Jalapa to the capital. As a result, Mexico City's merchants' guild found itself pressed to adopt the more progressive attitude of the Veracruz organization. In an attempt to demonstrate its vitality, the Consulado of Mexico City constructed another road to Veracruz through Orizaba, and also opened a new link with Toluca.

The old merchants were loath to allow commercial initiative to pass to the new element. The liberalization of trade, and the uncertainties surrounding the repartimiento de comercio, greatly disturbed and disrupted the traditional merchant community. In his 1793 *Report on the State of Trade in New Spain*, Viceroy Revillagigedo declared that the old merchants felt threatened and that the subsequent creation of the Consulado of Veracruz only confirmed their fears. Many large trading houses withdrew from commerce and moved into banking or invested in mining or agriculture. They saw their old monopoly destroyed and remained apprehensive about further, as yet unknown, changes. Conversely, the new type of aggressive, even marginal, traders did not seem grateful for the reforms. Their modern pragmatic attitude made them impatient with any restriction on their activities. They did not hesitate to disregard imperial needs when they conflicted with their interests. The secretary of the Veracruz Consulado demonstrated this attitude in his 1798 *Discourse on the State of Commerce of Veracruz,* in which he complained of the detrimental effects of war on trade, commerce, and the general well-being of the merchant community. International politics, in his view, could not justify the suspension of trade nor the disruption of Mexico's economy. The new merchant community rejected the relevance of Spanish politics and diplomacy to New Spain.

In fact, the Crown had already conceded the point. In November 1797 Madrid permitted merchants to employ neutral ships and friendly ports to keep trade alive. As a result, North American ships carried illegal British goods to Mexican agents of foreign merchant houses. Neutral shipping in time of war, however, proved a mixed blessing threatening to drain the country of bullion. It was halted in April of 1799, only to be reinstated between 1805 and 1809.

CLERICAL REFORMS

Traditionally, Church–state relations rested on the idea of interdependence–the "twin swords," one spiritual, the other temporal, that served the Crown. While royal patronage of the Church in the New World clearly gave the state the upper hand, any serious philosophical or political divergence between them seemed impossible. In the eighteenth century, however, the relationship between Church and state turned to one of suspicion and even hostility. Rather than viewing the Church as contributing to the strength of the state, reformers considered the institution one of the obstacles that had to be overcome if Spain ever hoped to regain its former strength. They went beyond the issue of Church subordination to the Crown bureaucracy to examine the role of that body in a modern state. For example, Spanish reformers were concerned about clerical influence, control of economic assets, and education. They believed the clergy was too numerous, forming another unproductive element in an already burdened society. Church land, held in mortmain, appeared to them to be economically useless, depriving the state of revenues and removing productive wealth from secular society. The Conde de Campomanes, for example, suggested that expropriation might be required to remedy the imbalance. He also maintained that Church social services, such as public charities, had to be examined to assure that they actually reduced poverty rather than fruitlessly supporting beggars. Campomanes advocated direct state responsibility for investing the country's limited resources in the most productive manner.

To achieve their ends, the reformers sought to discredit the Church in order to diminish the general public esteem it enjoyed. In addition, they had to weaken or neutralize other groups and organizations allied with the Church. Reformers were particularly concerned about Church control of lay religious brotherhoods *(cofradías)* which formed a web of clerical influence and potential opposition. Therefore they encouraged competing, but enlightened, institutions such as the Masonic Order, while cautiously applying political pressure to achieve clerical reforms. By encouraging clerics to concentrate on strictly religious questions, competition and conflict with the state could be minimized.

Carlos III thus called New Spain's Church hierarchy together to consider a reform program. The fourth Mexican Provincial Council, convoked in 1771, was the first such meeting since 1585. The Crown anticipated the Council's reforms by conducting a series of inspections aimed at correcting administrative abuses within the regular clergy, with some limited success. The Council's resolutions, however, never received Crown nor papal approval. Steady, relentless ideological and political pressure weakened clerical status and modified the social role of the Church.

The redefinition of the state's legal jurisdiction over clerical affairs was the most important battlefield in the struggle between the reformers and the Church. Ecclesiastic fueros permitted diocesan courts to claim exclusive jurisdiction over certain offenses committed by the clergy. Through loose interpretation, however, churchmen had gone beyond the original intent of the Crown in extending such privileges; the Church thus came to occupy a privileged position. While the clergy enjoyed personal immunity from civil authorities, it claimed the right to interfere in secular society. In the case of asylum, the Church stood between the people and the king's justice. Even the Acordada could not ignore that privilege; the issue of asylum had long been a matter of political concern. The Crown attempted to exclude certain criminal categories and in 1737, as a result of a concordat with the papacy, declared certain churches *iglesias frías* (cold churches) that

276 Rationalization, Reform, and Reaction

could not offer asylum. Carlos III urged the pope to further restrict asylum, and in response Clement XIV directed that the number of churches offering protection be reduced to one or two where possible. In 1774, the Diocese of Mexico announced that within the city only the churches of San Miguel and Santa Catalina could offer asylum, while outside the capital the principal parish church, those of the regular orders, and churches more than four leagues from a sanctuary could grant refuge. The Church agreed to these changes because criminals seeking asylum often assaulted priests and worshippers and caused other disorders, not because of any willingness to abandon its privileges.

Crown bureaucratic-reformers attempted to establish a firm division between temporal and spiritual matters that would restrict the clergy to the latter while not diminishing the state's power to intervene in Church affairs. By declaring all property to be temporal, they transferred jurisdiction over land titles and other types of Church property to the secular courts. Thus in cases of "divorce" the diocesan court now handled only the issue of separation, while a secular court dealt with attendant property questions. The reformers also restricted personal immunity from prosecution or arrest by secular judicial officers. For example, in 1771 those in minor orders lost all such legal privileges. Critics of clerical courts observed that lax Church tribunals did not wield sufficient coercive power to be taken seriously by offenders; they were more interested in protecting the clergy than in administering justice. As a result, the clergy constituted a disorderly and privileged group that undermined public confidence in the state's ability to enforce its laws, and the traditional methods of dealing with clerical transgressions no longer sufficed. Widely circulated tales of immoral, and even criminal, behavior by churchmen confirmed the necessity for strong, direct state intervention. Archbishop Alonso Nuñez de Haro y Peralta found it necessary to establish a correctional institution *(Colegio de Instrucción y Corrección)* in Tepoztlán to deal with the large number of "unruly and vicious clerics." It is not clear whether clerical misconduct constituted more of a problem in the eighteenth century than previously. Those who favored stripping clerics of personal immunity, however, made a strong case for reform.

Dissension among the regular clergy, both male and female, often proved troublesome. The long-standing rivalry between Mexicans and Europeans degenerated into hostility and violence. All factions accused the others of wrongdoing, often resorting to slander. Indeed, charges and countercharges became so common that the viceroy was frequently forced to intervene in disputes and to supervise voting. In 1780 and 1787 the viceroy dispatched troops to calm armed clerics who had taken their dispute into the streets. The activities of the hospital order of the Bethlemites became notorious, and fruitlessly occupied the energies of a number of viceroys. Controversy among the nuns revolved around the question of lifestyles. The *vida comun*, or communal religious organization of nunneries, existed more in theory than in fact. Comfortably furnished cells, servants, adopted children, and even secular women companions made convent life quite pleasant. Inevitably a reformist group appealed to the Bishop of Puebla for strict enforcement of the vida comun. As a consequence, the bishop and archbishop moved to reform the nunneries, much to the dismay of many sisters. In response to their appeals, Carlos III ordered the issue referred to the Fourth Mexican Provincial Council for resolution. Continued pressure for reform, and the disorder it caused, prompted the monarch in 1774 to order application of the vida comun throughout New Spain for new entrants, while permitting a choice for those already professed. Thereafter the viceroy, the archbishop, and in particular the Bishop of Puebla struggled to restore a measure of peace, with mixed results.

Besides supporting internal reforms, the Crown hoped to establish the ascendancy of criminal procedures over Church regulations. Such a radical departure from past practices required a cautious approach. Consequently, the Crown waited until 1795 before decreeing the direct intervention of secular officials in criminal cases involving churchmen. Thereafter, the criminal court of the Audiencia began to process clerical offenders. In the four-year period between 1796 and 1800, royal officials moved against 15 ecclesiastical malefactors accused of such crimes as murder, theft, adultery, rape, and defying the royal jurisdiction. The law, however, provided for joint prosecution by clerical and secular authorities; as a result, not one of the accused received a sentence.

Church opposition and lack of cooperation doomed the new procedure to failure. The hierarchy supported reforms, but not the end of their legal rights. A steady stream of petitions to the monarch asked for full restoration of their fueros. The Church insisted that some of the king's ministers wanted to destroy religion—or, at the least, the priestly status and prestige which formed a large part of its power in society. Under pressure, the monarch ordered a reappraisal of official policy.

Before the Crown developed a new approach, however, New Spain plunged into the disorders of the independence period. As a result, many ecclesiastics believed that the Crown had turned against them. The real and threatened loss of status, while serious for all, particularly affected the lower clergy, for whom status and privilege constituted a significant reward.

ESTABLISHMENT OF THE ARMY

Colonial defense was not a major preoccupation for any European power, with the exception of Portugal, before the 1750s. While pirates threatened coastal settlements and the sea lanes, no one expected a foreign country to launch an invasion of a major colony. Local militias, although ill-trained and equipped, appeared sufficient. In 1758 New Spain employed only 3,000 regular troops, mainly for garrison duty in presidios on the northern Indian frontier. Distance from Europe and the absence of staging areas in the hemisphere lessened the threat of invasion. For example, English attempts to capture Spanish possessions under Oliver Cromwell, and again in the 1740s, were unsuccessful essentially because of the difficulty of mounting attacks from such great distances. After failing to take Santo Domingo, the English seized Jamaica in 1655 as a consolation prize. The loss of bits and pieces of Spain's island outposts, while annoying, did not alter the military situation. Militias remained the principal defenders of the colonies. Even the early eighteenth-century struggles beween the British and French (1713–1756) depended on colonial militias.

During the Seven Years War, however, significant changes occurred. After the conquest of Canada, the British stationed an army of 10,000 regular troops in North America, in spite of an estimated cost of 350,000 pounds a year. Shocked by the loss of

Canada as well as a number of island settlements, France also began stationing regular troops in the colonies. With the fall of the heavily fortified cities of Havana and Manila in 1762, Spain realized that Britain possessed the ability to invade New Spain. Distance and ill-trained militias were no longer adequate. In short, the British transformed the New World into a major sphere of military operations.

Madrid decided to defend New Spain with a colonial army built around a core of regular Spanish troops. In addition, an organized trained colonial militia would provide reserve strength, thereby minimizing the financial burden. Lieutenant General Juan de Villalba y Angulo arrived in Veracruz in November 1764 with a newly organized Regiment of Infantry of America and cadres of officers and men for the militias. By the middle of 1766 he had organized 6 regiments, 3 battalions of provincial infantry, and 2 mounted regiments. Old existing militia units continued, but on a reorganized basis. Consequently, by 1787 Spanish regiments were no longer necessary. A three-tier structure emerged, consisting of a modest number of well-trained regular units, a larger group of organized militia regiments, and an extensive network of reserve companies which could provide replacements as well as reinforcements for the organized levels. Military planners hoped to maintain a good percentage of trained Spanish officers and men distributed throughout the system.

Mexicans lacked enthusiasm for military service. Spanish officials could recruit officers with some success, but not common soldiers or militiamen. Frustrated recruiters blamed their failure on the absence of martial values among Mexicans, and despaired of instilling patriotic virtues in colonial troops. According to regulations, recruits had to be between 16 and 36 years of age, at least five feet in height, and in good health. Those of European and mestizo origin were liable for duty. Although blacks and Indians enjoyed exemption from military service, separate units of mixed-bloods were acceptable. In practice, it proved impossible to insist on physical or racial requirements. In order to keep the primary and secondary units up to strength, desperate military recruiters resorted to all sorts of socially and economically disruptive methods. The arrival of army recruiters usually resulted in the flight of eligible males into the hills rather than risk being forced into the king's service. If by some misfortune they found themselves inducted, the men seized the first opportunity to desert. Those with families found it impossible to support them or even feed themselves on their pay of 1½ reales a day. Impressment often meant that one's children had to be sent into the streets to beg, or turn to some form of criminal activity to survive.

The transfer of units to Veracruz, long recognized as a mortally unhealthy station, provided additional impetus to flee. With the outbreak of war with Britain in 1796, Viceroy Branciforte minimized losses from disease by holding the troops in the interior, but still within striking distance of the coast. Any viceroy who yielded to the pressure of Veracruz merchants to station troops in the port had to contend with mass desertion and epidemic disease. For example, in 1799 the Veracruz garrison, then approximately 4,000 strong, encamped in a swampy area near the city, and as a consequence 875 men died of yellow fever and another 358 deserted. Even harsh conscription tactics failed to keep the units at full strength. Out of 100 vagabonds rounded up in Puebla and delivered to the Veracruz garrison in 1801, 85 died within a month. Small wonder that Mexicans tended to equate mobilization with almost certain death.

The poor quality of recruits constantly caused the authorities concern. Often only vagabonds could be conscripted on any regular basis. Serious attempts to secure higher-quality individuals adversely effected the economy, political system, and society. Flight to avoid service could disrupt an entire region. Even in the capital, masters hesitated to send their servants on errands for fear that the night patrol, or the so-called *vampiros de día* (daytime vampires), would impress them. Although certain occupational groups enjoyed theoretical protection, in fact such exemptions meant little on an individual basis. The economic effects of military recruitment could be very direct. In mining regions, miners abandoned their jobs and fled, forcing the mines to close. In Pachuca, labor shortages, caused by the presence of military officials, threatened the vital drainage system that made mining operations possible. Taxco mine owners demanded that army recruiters stay out of the region entirely. Viceroy Branciforte responded, both to pressure from mining interests as well as to the obvious threat to the economy, by issuing a general order in 1798 exempting miners and related workers. Nevertheless, fear of impressment continued to disturb labor tranquility. Establishing regional quotas and making the municipal council responsible for recruitment almost guaranteed that the dregs of urban life would be swept up and delivered to the military authorities. Unable to meet its requirement at the end of the century, Mexico City inducted 220 artisan apprentices, causing howls of protest. Few of those drafted returned to productive occupations. In 1807 all racial categories became legally subject to military service because of a shortage of manpower. Almost inevitably, corruption accompanied the recruitment process. Local officials engaged in a widespread sale of exemptions from military service enabling the middle and upper classes to buy protection. It is evident that officials also used the threat of impressment to intimidate the local populations.

Recruitment of militia officers posed a somewhat different problem. Many criollos and mestizos were enticed by the prospect of officer status to the extent of contributing both money and their services toward the formation of a militia unit. Wealthy merchants, mine owners, and landholders were often quite generous. Many marginal merchants and shopkeepers, however, strained their slim resources to purchase military status. Alexander von Humboldt has left us a vivid picture of these individuals, "in full uniform, and decorated with the royal order of Carlos III, gravely sitting in their shops, and entering into the most trifling detail in the sale of their goods." Understandably, regular career officers, who trained these units, had little but contempt for militia officers. The desire for honors, however, did not make militia officers any more anxious for service than their troops. Mobilization, for any but the shortest period, tended to be economically disruptive and sometimes even disastrous for the marginal merchant or shopkeeper.

Corruption, draft evasion, and desertion undermined authority and pushed a large segment of the population into conflict with the state. The structure of viceregal justice had been weakened to encourage enlistments, thus aggravating a serious economic and political situation. In order to make service more attractive, the Crown extended military privileges *(fueros)* to members of militia units. Vaguely written statutes made the exact extent of such privileges difficult to determine. Members of the lower ranks often viewed the military fuero as license, relieving them of responsibil-

282 Rationalization, Reform, and Reaction

ity and of trial by civilian authorities. The Crown and military judges constantly emphasized that the military fuero did not grant immunity from punishment and that, in fact, those who held military privileges had an obligation both to uphold the law and to set a good example for the less-favored elements of the population.

Nevertheless, civilian magistrates resented any restrictions that limited their authority and lessened their prestige. Conflict between the military justice system and other officials became chronic. Long accustomed to an ad hoc administration, local officials now had to contend with an element which refused to acknowledge their authority within their own territorial jurisdiction. Army officers sometimes manipulated the fuero to cover their own private business pursuits, claiming that military courts had jurisdiction over contractual or other commercial disputes between military men and civilians. Since military courts were composed of fellow officers, it was easy to convince those courts not only to accept jurisdiction over such cases, but also to rule in favor of their comrades. Since the members of militia units were dispersed throughout entire regions, the potential for wide-spread conflict with all levels of civil justice was great. Moreover, military justice was often slow and cumbersome, since militiamen arrested in one location often had to be sent great distances to be tried by their commanding officer. Even the Acordada's agents found it difficult to control disorderly military offenders. The judge of the Acordada charged that, confident of military protection, soldiers brazenly violated the law, particularly liquor and gambling regulations. Soldiers or militiamen, tried by the military court of their own unit, could count on a sympathetic hearing and a lenient sentence, perhaps only a few days in the guardhouse. For example, militiamen in Tehuacán often idled drunkenly in the streets, insulting the genteel citizens and baiting judicial authorities. On one occasion, a group of militiamen brawled with customs guards, assaulted a police officer to free one of their companions, and ended the evening in church asylum. Their captain investigated, but declined to discipline the offenders.

The purpose of the military fuero became blurred. Viceroy Branciforte considered military privileges a "small but showy laurel" needed as a recruiting device. Indeed, disregarding complaints from law enforcement bodies, the viceroy professed to see no public harm in extending broad privileges to all segments of the armed forces. As a result of protests from various groups, however, the Crown eventually clarified the fuero of the regular units, but failed to define the militia's rights.

From an imperial standpoint, the organization of a military establishment in New Spain appeared at least marginally successful; in spite of many problems, an impressive number of men could be mustered. Viceroy José de Iturrigaray, for example, managed to mass some 15,000 men to deal with the English invasion threat of 1807. The major problem was financial rather than organizational. While the British ran a deficit in North America to meet their administrative and defense needs, Spain depended on its colonies to subsidize imperial operations. Between 1785 and 1789, defense expenditures in Mexico consumed 2 million pesos out of some 5.8 million raised locally. If Madrid had been willing to forego its subsidy, the viceregal budget would have been expanded, allowing the military a more realistic amount. Reasonable pay and provisions would have eliminated some of the negative impact of mobilizations and, perhaps, even stimulated the economy.

As it happened, the introduction of military obligations merely disrupted the country. To the lower classes, armed service hardly meant the defense of their homeland in the face of a foreign threat. Rather, it represented the destruction of their families, the abandonment of dependents, removal from their own region and, for the deserter, the uneasy life of a fugitive.

THE ECONOMY AT THE END
OF THE EIGHTEENTH CENTURY

The Mexican economy demonstrated remarkable strength at the end of the century. The leading entrepreneurs accumulated vast fortunes in mixed agriculture, mining, commerce, and manufacturing. New Spain's economy supported numerous millionaires: 18 Mexican families possessed more wealth than anyone else in the Western Hemisphere. The most impressive fortune belonged to Antonio de Obregón, a criollo who acquired the title of Conde de Valenciana in 1780. With capital borrowed from local merchants, Obregón reworked Guanajuato's old sixteenth-century diggings, spending over 2 million pesos to sink some of the deepest mine shafts in existence. His mines produced 30.9 million pesos in silver from 1788 to 1809, and in 1791 the amount of silver extracted equaled the production of the entire Viceroyalty of Peru. Obregón's impressive success depended entirely on local enterprise and management skills.

Livestock production was also very lucrative. The Marqués de Aguayo and his daughter-in-law, the Condesa de Alamo, owned 420,000 sheep occupying land from Monterrey to the viceregal capital. At the turn of the century, the Conde de Pérez Gálvez supplied over 96,000 head of sheep to fulfill meat contracts in Guanajuato and Puebla. Of course, not all entrepreneurs were equally successful. Spectacular failures occasionally reduced wealthy families to relative poverty; others redirected their economic activities to accommodate new conditions. For example, Antonio de Bassoco, a Basque who subsequently acquired the title of Conde de Bassoco, had interests in mining, mixed agricultural production, public finances, and even the China trade. He personified the large merchant-bankers who withdrew from the monopoly trade with Spain after 1789, leaving the field to the new merchant-speculator. Indeed, Bassoco lost part of a 500,000-peso deal before deciding to redirect his business interests.

Mining laid the basis for much of the late eighteenth-century economic expansion. Vast quantities of animals, foodstuff, wood, leather, and cotton products were required by the mining industry. The Mexican textile industry specialized in the manufacture of cheap durable woolens and cottons, while most of the finer material came from abroad. In the city of Puebla, the intendant estimated that fully half the population depended on textile production; some 28 merchant houses supplied as well as marketed the region's cotton products. In Querétaro, another important manufacturing center, large numbers also worked in the textile industry. Northern mining centers constituted a lucrative and expanding internal market for their products.

Urban markets also expanded; prices in the cities rose steadily as the population increased. Many entrepreneurs rushed to meet the demands of the growing urban populations, particularly for cheap intoxicants. The Conde de Tepa and the Marqués de Selvanevada, for example, built their fortunes on pulque. The demand for pulque stimulated the cultivation of maguey in areas too arid for other crops. The plant also generated industries based on its fibers, such as rope-making.

Large-scale agricultural production, however, was unstable in the eighteenth century. Competition from small farmers, especially in good years, made it difficult for large landowners to prosper through agriculture alone, because they could not normally sell their commodities beyond limited regional markets. Even though landowners varied their production to avoid reliance on one crop, agriculture was subject to repeated boom-or-bust cycles. Not surprisingly, large entrepreneurs attempted to buy out competing small farmers. The return on strictly agricultural investment was not great—those who profited most drew their wealth from mixed ventures, including commerce, mining, and manufacturing. The uncertain profitability of agriculture tended to discourage the introduction of new agricultural technology.

Family enterprises, many with impressive resources, continued to dominate the Mexican economy. Marriage alliances absorbed the riches of newly-established merchants and miners, helping to preserve large estates. The Sánchez Navarro family of Coahuila, for example, carefully husbanded a fortune in commerce and ranching. Family members retained individual land titles but managed them as one economic unit, placing relatives in administrative positions. By 1774, the extent of their activities required employing distant relatives to manage their assets. In 1821 the family controlled 800,000 acres, second only to the properties of the Marqués de Aguayo, who held 15 million acres in Coahuila. Remarkably, the Sánchez Navarros avoided encumbering their land titles with debts in the process.

The opulence of the Mexican elite challenged administrators to devise means of tapping those riches. Merely selling titles of nobility to socially pretentious families was not enough. Crown monopolies, such as the tobacco industry, provided direct access to New Spain's wealth, but state enterprises could only be developed to a limited degree. Madrid, likewise, succeeded in siphoning considerable wealth through fiscal reforms. However, imperial administrators failed in their grand scheme of joining New Spain's expanding economy with that of a resurgent, but still weak, Spain.

Frustration over the inability to share fully in Mexico's prosperity may have prompted the unreasonable, and economically irresponsible, demands later made by the monarchy during the Napoleonic crisis.

The great magnates, with their conspicuous wealth, were not the only ones who prospered in the late eighteenth century. Since most sectors of the economy—in particular, mining and commerce—remained strong, Mexicans as a group benefited. The secondary elite and the pequeña burguesía, whose interests were closely associated with the magnates, also enriched themselves. In addition, the Bourbon reforms opened new opportunities for enterprising individuals. The expanded bureaucracy provided new careers for educated Mexicans. Many entered commerce, which operated on a smaller scale after 1789, and others sought opportunities as small-scale financiers and distributors when the repartimiento de comercio was restricted by the Crown. Finally, many artisans and workers benefited from the expanding economy, although demographic pressures made life on the lower socio-economic levels increasingly insecure.

Since the eighteenth century was a period of rapid population growth, economic and political strains emerged despite the flourishing economy. Between 1742 and 1810, New Spain's population doubled, depressing wages and increasing the cost of living as more people competed for jobs and goods. The cities of New Spain, particularly Mexico City, were swollen with rural migrants in search of work. Social and economic mobility declined, affecting the lower classes most of all. The sharp increase in unemployed léperos, for example, aroused ethnic antagonisms, as Spanish officials and the lighter-skinned upper classes turned to negative racial stereotypes to explain the unfortunate situation of the lower classes. The purchase of *cédulas de gracias al sacar* by well-to-do mulatos, giving them the same legal privileges as those who claimed white blood, evoked bitter protest from criollos, many of whom were themselves of mixed blood. Even the small increase in the rate of Spanish immigration provoked anguished reaction by Mexicans, who viewed the newcomers as threats to their social and economic well-being. Thus the depressed condition of the working class adversely affected New Spain. It created a sense of insecurity and conflict in a society with a prosperous and expanding economy.

Tensions in eighteenth-century Mexico were exacerbated by a series of agricultural crises that led to temporary but severe food shortages and high prices. During these emergencies, the country endured famine and disease. Although authorities took steps to reduce suffering, their actions appeared ineffective to most Mexicans. Between 1720 and 1810, there were ten agricultural crises; the worst disaster struck in 1785, when an exceptionally severe August frost destroyed the maize crop in parts of central Mexico, particularly the Valley of Mexico. Grain prices soared as supplies dwindled. Large landowners aggravated the emergency by closing their granaries. As food shortages became acute, Mexico's economy virtually ground to a halt: mines and obrajes were closed, commerce nearly stopped, and thousands were unemployed. Although miners, manufacturers, and merchants denounced the hoarding of grain, the profit-minded hacendados refused to modify their policy. Even the threat of fines from the viceroy, and the damnations of the archbishop of Mexico and the bishop of Puebla, failed to move them. The authorities suspended tribute collection, distributed government grain supplies, and organized other relief measures. But despite their efforts, the disaster worsened, and epidemic disease spread as thousands of starving and sick unfortunates wandered across central Mexico seeking food and work. Over 300,000 lost their lives in the catastrophe. A good harvest improved conditions the following year; nevertheless, the effects of the 1785–86 crisis were felt for some time.

The agricultural crises and social tensions of late eighteenth-century Mexico impressed contemporary observers. Foreigners like Alexander von Humboldt, and some high officials attributed the region's ills to the huge gap between the rich and the poor. To these privileged social critics, there existed only two classes in Mexico: the extremely wealthy and the poverty-stricken. The majority of Mexicans, who were neither affluent nor impoverished, but relatively prosperous, escaped their vision altogether. Such observers failed to understand the complex nature of New Spain's economy and society as well as the stresses engendered by economic and demographic expansion.

THE INTELLECTUAL FRAMEWORK OF CHANGE

New Spain was not an intellectual backwater merely reacting to European ideas. Mexican intellectuals made important contributions to world knowledge; the country's centers of higher learning were outstanding, and a community of scientists worked in impressive research centers. As a result, the changes that occurred in eighteenth-century New Spain, including royal reforms that restructured Mexico's relationship with Spain, were observed and judged by persons who applied the critical methods of the age to those phenomena.

Internal adjustments, as well as external reforms, occurred within the context of a distinctive Mexican culture. New Spain's intellectuals, whose traditions reached back into the sixteenth century, responded to change and to new ideas in American ways. While Mexicans shared many of their philosophical roots with Spaniards, the unique experience of the New World set them apart. New Spain's thinkers did not react in a hostile fashion to the ideas of the Enlightenment, but neither did they accept them uncritically. In the exchange of ideas, however, enlightened Mexicans found themselves on the wrong side of the Atlantic. European authors, particularly French writers, believed that they alone possessed the new critical approach and could explain all phenomena, including the New World and its special characteristics.

To their dismay, enlightened Mexicans found themselves serving as specimens in the works of pompous and ill-informed Europeans, who often made wild and patently false statements about the Western Hemisphere in their efforts to draw instructive comparisons with their own world. The great French naturalist, the Comte de Buffon, concluded that American animals were weaker, less active, and not as varied as their European counterparts. He dismissed America by asserting that animal and vegetable life tended to degenerate in that environment. This meant, of course, that criollos were necessarily inferior to Europeans; such ignorance and bigotry naturally offended Mexicans. Cornelius de Paúw's *Recherches philosophiques sur les Americains* (1768) carried the notion of degeneracy to absurdity when he maintained that New World dogs could not bark, and the inhabitants of the American continent were impotent and cowardly. Even Abbé Raynal's *Histoire philosophique*, which appeared in over fifty editions between 1770 and the end of the century, contained errors unacceptable to Mexicans while presenting a favorable view of the New World.

Enlightened Mexicans defended themselves and their land by forming a critical framework based on their experience from which to examine European ideas. A modern climate of thought evolved in eighteenth-century New Spain in several stages. In a seminal essay, Roberto Moreno has suggested a four-step process: the antecedents (1735–1767), the criollo stage (1768–1788), the official or Spanish phase (1789–1803), and the period of synthesis (1803–1821). The vague and dispersed first stage evolved into a definable Mexican intellectual movement without any official effort to introduce or nourish it.

A number of impressive intellectuals stand out during the criollo phase. José Antonio Alzate (1737–1799), who was well acquainted with European writings, authored countless scientific works and published four periodicals, including the justly famous *Gazeta de literatura de México* (1788–1795). Another prolific scholar, Antonio de León y Gama (1737–1802), wrote a notable study, *Descripción de las dos piedras,* in which he applied the new scientific method to his country's Indian past, thereby integrating the Mexican environment into the universal strands of the Enlightenment. The physician José Ignacio Bartolache, also a distinguished scientist, edited the first American medical journal, the *Mercurio volante.* The mathematician, astronomer, and mining expert Joaquín Velázquez de León (1732–1786) wrote, among other studies, a major scientific survey of the Valley of Mexico. The list of enlightened Mexicans could be expanded with ease, and would include the readers of Manuel Antonio Valdés' *Gaceta de México,* which sprinkled scientific and philosophical articles among its materials, as well as the many university professors and secondary school teachers. Humboldt, for example, noted with approval the number of Mexicans engaged in scientific studies or otherwise participating in the modern penchant for new knowledge. In 1792, the Basque Society of Friends of the Country (Sociedad vascongada de los amigos del país), perhaps the most active organization dedicated to the dissemination of useful knowledge in the Spanish world, included 312 Mexicans out of a total membership of around 1,000 in the entire Hispanic world. Mexico City had 132 members, only five less than Madrid, while others were scattered throughout the viceroyalty.

The official or Spanish stage of the Mexican Enlightenment began in 1788 with the arrival of a distinguished group of Spanish scientists and scholars who came to direct and teach in three new Enlightenment institutions: the College of Mines, the Botanical Gardens, and the Academy of San Carlos. The Spaniards, many of whom had studied in Germany and had already established international reputations as scientists, arrived with a low opinion of colonial intellectual achievements. Martín de Sessé, for example, wrote to Madrid urging that a gardener be sent, because no one in Mexico knew how to cultivate lettuce. Others disparaged New Spain's past and disregarded the scientific contribution of Mexican scholars. Nevertheless, the cadre of Europeans, which included such distinguished Spanish scientists as Sessé, Vicente Cervantes, Andrés Manuel del Río, and Fausto de Elhuyar, made important contributions to knowledge and encouraged Mexicans to engage in scientific study and debate.

The regrettable alienation between criollo and Spanish scientists lessened the possibility of cooperation and prevented the development of new paradigms to accommodate the anomalies observed by New World scientists. For example, the Mexican scientist Alzate objected to Carolus von Linnaeus' botanical classification because of the many exceptions he noted in New Spain— but although Alzate's criticisms undermined the Linnaean system, the Mexican failed to suggest a new structure. Cooperation with the Spaniards might have led to a synthesis. In a similar fashion, the unwillingness of the Europeans to concede the importance of Mexico's Indian past retarded New Spain's contributions to archaeology, anthropology, and ancient history. Ironically, the exiled Mexican Jesuits became some of the most vigorous exponents of Mexico's ancient civilization. Francisco Javier Clavigero's *Historia antigua de México* expounded the value of Indian customs. His fellow Jesuit, Andrés Cavo, exalted Cuauhtémoc, the last of the Aztec rulers, in his efforts to give Mexico equal standing with Europeans in the development of civilization. Since the Jesuits wrote from exile, they were considered reactionary and anti-modern. Therefore the points they sought to make were often dismissed by the Europeans as an expression of homesick provincialism.

The visit of Alexander von Humboldt finally brought the criollo and the official stages of the Mexican Enlightenment together. The young German scholar had the good fortune to serve as a mediator between the two groups. They made their published and unpublished research available to Humboldt, discussed their views with him, and gave him access to the scholarly resources of the entire country. The viceroy and other officials also facilitated the German's travel and study. As a result, Humboldt wrote a masterful synthesis of eighteenth-century Mexico, *Ensayo político de la Nueva España*, in which he presented to the world the accomplishments of the Mexican Enlightenment. Although he indicated in his introduction that the scholars of New Spain assisted him, most readers—then and to this day—have given Humboldt sole credit for the work.

The generation that came of age at the end of the century consisted of many modern men steeped in the Mexican, as well as the European, Enlightenment. They were well prepared to cope with the crisis of the Western world that erupted in 1789 as a result of the French Revolution.

DIFFERING PERCEPTIONS OF CHANGE

The arrival of well-trained, single-minded European administrators, often drawn from a fiscal or military background, created resentment and bitterness instead of cooperation in Mexico. The Spaniards approached their task with grim efficiency, without sympathy for what they viewed as corrupt and backward methods. In the new scheme of things, competition for position seemed unfairly loaded in favor of the Spanish-born bureaucrat. Well-paid intendants, with rare exceptions Spaniards, contrasted sharply with the economically marginal Mexican subdelegados, desperately hanging on to the repartimiento de comercio. Increasingly, the top levels of public administration became closed to the colonial elite. In the Church the archbishop, and all but one bishop, were Spaniards, while the heavily Mexican lower clergy lost privilege and status as a result of imperial policy.

The colonial elite also found itself identified with corruption, inefficiency, and general backwardness. The new bureaucrats, allegedly representing rational progress, treated those who objected to change as mere reactionaries. Excluded from the process of reform, upper-class Mexicans viewed most changes, including many positive ones, as arbitrary. Imbued with European Enlightenment ideology, the Bourbon reformers failed to appreciate the growing economic, political, and intellectual maturity of Mexico. They expected the leaders of New Spain to accept an inferior role. Mexicans, however, believed that the ideas of the Enlightenment, and their command of modern methods, justified a more respectable role for them in their country's affairs. Indeed, many Mexicans considered themselves better educated than the narrow Spanish bureaucrats and believed that they, not the Europeans, represented the "true" new man. Increasingly, they called themselves *Americans* to emphasize their New World origins.

Spain's attempt to increase its share of colonial trade through restructuring of the commercial system also appeared to ignore reality. Free trade—in the restricted Spanish sense of the term—and a rational tax system could not alter the fact that Spain was not a major commercial power. Contraband trade, especially with the British, symbolized more than administrative or structural weakness. A worldwide trading network dominated by expanding industrial nations left little room for an economically weak Spain. The British undermined the Spanish economic resurgence, both with their goods and with their arms. The British merchant marine and the British navy controlled the Atlantic sea lanes, insuring that their commerce remained dominant.

Bourbon reformers alienated traditional groups by attacking corporate bodies, from the clergy to the Consulado. Yet the groups which benefited from imperial reforms felt little gratitude to the Crown, because the changes had been introduced only to further state objectives. The Habsburgs had bestowed privilege on corporate groups as a means of creating stable political support rather than pursuing a predetermined goal. The new bureaucrats, rational men rather than politicians, perferred to reach their objectives through reforms, not political accommodation. As a result the old consensus disappeared, not to be replaced.

Externally imposed change created an aura of uncertainty in

New Spain. What seemed reasonable in Madrid could be viewed quite differently in Mexico City. Mexicans were constantly forced to react to changes which often disrupted existing functional adaptations to colonial reality. Significantly, one of the major complaints of Mexico City's municipal council involved the constant need to initiate new officials fresh from Spain. Theoretically commendable attacks on corruption, such as ending the purchase of high office, deprived the Mexican elite of political representation.

The underlying assumption of Bourbon bureaucratic-reformers, that Spain deserved a greater material return from its empire, became increasingly unacceptable to New Spain's population. Mexico had outgrown its imperial guardian and developed its own distinct interests. Ironically, the traditional Habsburg concept of empire—kingdoms united only under the monarchy itself—might have provided a more expansive arena for Spain's maturing colonial possessions. The Bourbon planners, however, resisted movement toward a flexible structure that would have permitted internally rationalized reforms, rather than imperial modifications by distant bureaucrats. Nevertheless, war forced them to acknowledge the economic importance of New Spain; they allowed neutral shipping to carry goods to Mexico, and even ordered warships to transport the mercury vital to mining. Finally, the realization that Spanish interests were not synonymous with Mexico's aroused fears among high-level bureaucrats about New Spain's loyalty, particularly after the American Revolution.

In practice, Mexican resistance, coupled with limited resources, often transformed imperial reforms into simple adjustments, rather than the radical changes envisioned by Crown bureaucrats. Bold measures frequently failed to achieve even partial success after filtering through both the Spanish and Mexican institutional structures. As a result, the rhetoric of reform far outstripped actual accomplishments. Nevertheless, change, administratively initiated as well as natural and evolutionary, characterized the century.

Chapter 10

THE PROCESS OF INDEPENDENCE

INDEPENDENCE was the result of a long process which began in the second half of the eighteenth century and might have been checked or delayed by the Spanish government. Colonial Mexicans were slow to seek independence, even though many criollo and mestizo members of the secondary elite and the pequeña burguesia developed a strong sense of national awareness. Their patriotism was not anti-Spanish, nor was it directed toward separation from the mother country. Rather, it was an assertion of the values, the beauty, and the richness of Mexico, as well as a rejection of notions of European superiority that were widely accepted in the Old World.

Eighteenth-century Mexicans were proud of their land, but they did not question the Crown's authority. Although they had grievances against the colonial administration, they did not desire to abolish the system, but merely to participate more actively in it. The Bourbon reforms strained relations between Mexicans and the Crown, but those changes did not lead to a break with Spain. Mexicans remained loyal to the king, even though the French Revolution and the wars that followed forced the Spanish government to make extreme financial demands. Ultimately, the Spanish imperial crisis led the Mexican upper and middle classes to consider the value of home rule. Only when autonomy within a Spanish commonwealth proved unattainable did they opt for independence.

THE SPANISH IMPERIAL CRISIS

The French Revolution of 1789, which plunged Europe into twenty years of war, and the upheavals it unleashed precipitated the Spanish imperial crisis. The times required strong, far-sighted, and experienced rulers, but it was Spain's misfortune to lose the great reformer king, Carlos III, in December 1788. His son and successor, Carlos IV, was weak, vacillating, and ineffectual. Initially the new monarch continued his father's policies by retaining the Conde de Floridablanca as chief minister. But the radicalism of the French Revolution frightened Floridablanca, who imposed press censorship in an attempt to seal the Spanish world from French propaganda. When this tactic proved ineffective, he implemented other, more repressive measures, including the suspension of the press in 1791 and reactivation of the Inquisition to search out dangerous books and potential subversives.

These actions evoked strong opposition in Spain and threatened Carlos' cousin, Louis XVI of France, who had sworn to uphold the French Constitution and, if he were to remain on the throne, needed the understanding of his fellow monarchs. To calm the country and to reduce tensions between Spain and France, Carlos replaced Floridablanca, in February 1792, with the francophile Conde de Aranda. The change in ministry permitted news from France and revolutionary propaganda to pour into Spain, because Aranda relaxed censorship. He also continued Spanish reforms. Most traditionalists were horrified by the policy reversals. As French radicalism increased, palace intrigues against Spain's first minister gained support. The elderly Aranda was ousted and replaced by a favorite of the royal family, the 25-year-old guards officer Manuel Godoy.

Godoy governed Spain during most of 1793–1808, a period which would have taxed the talents of even an experienced and respected statesman. The new minister, unfortunately, possessed neither an extensive education nor political or administrative experience. He gained unprecedented power because he enjoyed the confidence and support of the king and queen, becoming a *valido* (crown favorite). While such situations had been prevalent during the seventeenth century, they were unknown in the eighteenth, when administration improved under a series of strong monarchs. Godoy, who considered himself a man of the Enlightenment, attempted to continue the reforms and policies of Carlos III. This tactic won him little support from the old bureaucrats and intellectuals, who still considered him a dictatorial upstart. At the same time, his policies alienated traditionalists. Since Godoy's administration was viewed as extremely corrupt, many of the officials appointed during his long tenure were discredited. The populace also resented Godoy's influence and his unmerited rise to power. When the king bestowed titles and favors upon his first minister, hostility toward Godoy increased. Godoy's lack of credentials and his relationship with the royal family made the minister a ready target for detractors. Rumors circulated that he was the queen's lover and that anyone could buy his favor. These stories tarnished the reputation of the royal family and the monarchy at a time when the grave international situation was creating discontent with the government.

War initiated a serious breach in the Spanish political system and caused severe economic dislocations. The Jacobin reign of terror and Louis XVI's execution shocked Spain. Carlos IV joined the other monarchs of Europe in war against the regicide French Republic, only to see his country defeated. When war began in 1793, royal finances were sound and the economy was in the midst of a boom. By the end of the year, however, the situation had changed drastically. The war forced the Crown to raise taxes, including the first direct levies on the nobility. To meet the emergency, the government also began to issue bonds *(vales reales)* and ordered the expropriation of Church property. These measures, which failed to halt the deterioration of the economy, eroded the government's popular support. The humiliating peace treaty which ended the conflict bound Spain to France, and made her an enemy of England.

The new international alignment forced Spain into a series of wars with England and her allies, placing new strains on the

Spanish economy. As mistress of the seas, Britain effectively cut Spain off from her overseas possessions and dominated Spanish American commerce. In a belated effort to retain some measure of control over American trade, Spain permitted neutral shipping to carry goods to the New World, particularly mercury and powder to Mexico's silver mines. This step was an admission that Spain could no longer maintain even the pretense of a monopoly with her American kingdoms. The Peace of Amiens (1802) ended hostilities between England and France, giving Spain a brief economic revival. Trade with America increased and national production recovered, reaching a peak in 1805–06—the government even began to withdraw vales reales from circulation. But by 1804 France and Spain were once again at war with England. The naval disaster at Trafalgar in 1805 destroyed the Spanish navy; the French blockade of 1806, Napoleon's "continental system," devastated Spain's economy. These disasters not only paralyzed commerce with Spanish America, they also resulted in massive unemployment and severe inflation in the Iberian peninsula and the virtual bankruptcy of the government. Spain's economic and political misfortunes were popularly attributed to Godoy's malign influence.

Many who despaired at Spain's decline and hoped to restore the nation to its former prosperity looked to Crown Prince Fernando as their champion, because he opposed Godoy and resented his parents' dependence upon the favorite. In March 1808 the prince's followers forced Carlos IV to abdicate in favor of his son, Fernando VII. The quarrel in the royal family coincided with the entry of French troops into the Iberian peninsula. In 1807 Napoleon had obtained permission to cross Spain and occupy Portugal. Once his troops entered the country, the Emperor of the French decided to replace the Spanish Bourbons. Using the dispute over the Spanish Crown as an excuse, Bonaparte lured the royal family and Godoy into France, where he compelled them to abdicate in his favor. Then he granted Spain to his brother Joseph.

Although all the Spanish authorities, the imperial bureaucracy, the nobility, the clergy, and the army, initially accepted Joseph Bonaparte as king of Spain, the people did not. On May 2, 1808, Madrid rose against the French, an example emulated throughout Spain. The Spanish Revolution had begun. The first impulse after May was centrifugal—that is, regional juntas were formed to govern individual provinces. In the absence of the king, political theorists argued, sovereignty reverted to the people, and each provincial junta acted as though it were an independent nation. Finally, the need for a unified defense led to the organization of a national governing committee, the Junta Suprema Central, which first met on September 25, 1808. Although some provincial bodies did not recognize the authority of the Central Junta, most agreed that it should be the government of national defense to wage a war of liberation.

THE EFFECTS OF THE
IMPERIAL CRISIS ON MEXICO

The imperial crisis profoundly affected New Spain, the most prosperous part of the Spanish empire. Mexico contributed two-thirds of the revenue from the empire; in 1799 this amounted to 14 million pesos: 4 million was spent for local administration and defense; 4 million subsidized other Spanish possessions in the Caribbean, North America, and the Philippines; and 6 million was remitted to the royal treasury in Madrid. But even this large sum proved inadequate to meet the mounting expenses generated by the European wars. Throughout the crisis, from 1789 forward, Spain demanded money at all costs. The people of Mexico were asked to put the needs of an imperiled Spain before their own economic interests, regardless of the cost—something that had never before been required in the nearly 300 years of colonial history.

The demands of the Crown hit the upper classes of New Spain hardest. Wealthy individuals, particularly Spaniards, had traditionally donated large sums to the king to meet an emergency, or simply to assist the monarch. The Mexican elite considered such donations acceptable so long as they were voluntary. But the European wars forced Spain to make extraordinary demands upon her subjects. The Crown introduced many new taxes and raised existing levies. Consequently the elite were alienated by taxes and policies which reduced or abolished their privileges.

The Crown's policy toward entail provides a good example of elite grievances. A *mayorazgo* (entail) was necessary to support a noble life and to maintain an estate intact. Although non-nobles could establish a mayorazgo, it was normally a step toward receiving or validating a title. But in 1789, the Crown raised taxes and fees so that only the very wealthiest could form a mayorazgo. In 1795 founding fees increased to 15 percent of the total value of the entail, and by 1818 they had risen to 25 percent. The Crown also levied a 3-percent war tax, and additional fees and charges were imposed to mortgage or alienate any part of an entail. The effect of such impositions was to end the formation of mayorazgos in New Spain. Recent nobles, many of them Spaniards, could not found entails. For example, in 1805 Diego de Rul paid 23,650 pesos in fees, taxes, and exemptions for his title. But when he attempted to found an entail worth 150,000 pesos, the authorities informed him that it would cost 50,000 pesos. The new Conde de Rul was outraged, and protested that the exorbitant charge was an affront to the Valenciana family which had rendered so many services to the Crown. The heirs of the Marqués de Inguanzo also abandoned their attempts to create a mayorazgo for financial reasons. In 1810 José Mariano Fagoaga and Gabriel de Yermo refused to accept noble titles because of the cost of founding an entail. For all intents and purposes, the formation of mayorazgos ended in 1800 as a result of Crown policy.

The greatest blow to Mexican interests was the systematic curtailment of the country's credit system. This had begun earlier with the attempt to abolish the *repartimiento de comercio,* the only credit system available to the natives and the rural poor. The situation was exacerbated by the periodic demands for loans to meet extraordinary expenses in the Iberian peninsula. Such requests had an adverse effect on credit by intensifying the shortage of specie in Mexico. When the European wars erupted, the Crown's exactions increased. In 1793 the mining guild, which had been established to provide credit to miners, was required to lend 2½ million pesos to Spain, while the craft guilds were forced to withdraw their funds from Church-affiliated sodalities and place them under government control. Merchant financiers and silver bankers were also directed to make their capital available to the state.

The Crown did not consider these and subsequent emergency actions a serious threat to the economic well-being of New Spain. But to Mexicans, and to Europeans resident in the colony, they posed a grave danger, because New Spain's economy operated on credit. Contemporaries estimated that two-thirds of all business transactions involved credit; only 10,000 of the approximately 200,000 entrepreneurs operated solely with their own money, and nearly nine-tenths of all *bienes raices* (real property) was encumbered in some way. Credit was the lifeblood of the Mexican economy; to restrict or interrupt it threatened the basis of New Spain's financial existence.

The major disruption in Mexico's credit system occurred when the king decreed the Royal Law of Consolidation. This law, first enacted in Spain in 1798 and extended to the empire in December 1804, ordered authorities in Mexico to seize and auction the real estate belonging to the Church's chantries and charitable foundations *(capellanías y obras pías)*. The government planned to use the proceeds of the sale, as well as any other wealth belonging to these institutions, to redeem the *vales reales* and liquidate other war debts. The Church institutions were to receive a 3-percent return on the funds they loaned the government. The Crown believed that the measure would be beneficial, because the auction would provide small farmers and other entrepreneurs an opportunity to acquire Church lands. But such an assumption did not apply in New Spain, where the chantries and pious works primarily held investments, not land. Since nearly all Mexican entrepreneurs, large and small, were indebted to the Church, enforcement of the measure would ruin the country. In normal times, such a miscalculation on the part of the government would have been corrected with the traditional formula, *"obedezco pero no cumplo."* Indeed, some officials in other parts of the empire did not enforce the law. But the pressure on Mexico was great, since it was Spain's most productive colony. Viceroy José de Iturrigaray promulgated the decree, insisting on its execution despite great opposition.

A storm of protest erupted in Mexico against the Law of Consolidation. Groups of landowners, merchants, miners, and municipal councils wrote petitions demanding that the viceroy cease enforcing the law. They argued that Spain misunderstood the situation in Mexico, that what was beneficial to the mother country would ruin the colony, and that Mexico did not contain enough money to redeem the outstanding debt. In the view of many, it was "the middle groups, the poorer farmers, miners, and merchants," the very people who contributed most to the economy, who would be hardest hit by the Consolidation. The rich had greater resources and were better able to survive the crisis—although, while some wealthy individuals profited from the mandatory sales of land, many plutocrats were also forced to repay large loans, some of which they had only guaranteed.

Despite the desperate and even threatening protests, Viceroy Iturrigaray recklessly proceeded to enforce the Consolidation decree. By 1808 the government had raised more than 12 million pesos, approximately one-fourth of the total debt owed to capellanías and obras pías. Of this amount, the viceroy received 72,000 pesos, Archbishop Lizana 22,000 pesos, and the royal collector 124,000 pesos in commissions for collecting the funds; the rest was remitted to the Spanish government, which delivered 5 million pesos to Napoleon. Such actions undermined the colonials' respect for royal authority. These policies not only threatened to destroy the entire credit system of Mexico, they also constituted a grave attack on the Church.

For the first time in nearly 300 years, Mexicans of all classes and castes, including European Spaniards resident in New Spain, had a common cause to unite them. This was surely an instance of the *bad government* which traditional political theorists taught should be opposed. Some malcontents talked openly of the need for insurrection. Before violence could break out, however, news arrived in New Spain that Madrid had been occupied by French troops. In an effort to rally Mexicans to the cause of Spain, the viceroy suspended the Law of Consolidation on July 22, 1808.

THE DRIVE FOR AUTONOMY

Many among the upper classes who led the opposition to the Law of Consolidation—the magnates, the secondary elite, and the pequeña burguesía—concluded that the best interests of Mexico would be served through autonomy. This was a traditional concept, not a revolutionary one. It mirrored the historic struggle in Spain between the provinces and the core—between regional autonomy and Castilian centralism. Like the Catalans, the Mexicans believed that their economic interests should come before those of Spain. Following the classic formula, the Mexican autonomists praised the king but decried bad government.

The drive for autonomy gained impetus from the political crisis in Spain. Events moved so swiftly that Mexicans were shocked, confused, and frightened by changes in the Iberian peninsula. In July 1808 they learned that Carlos IV had abdicated; Godoy had been jailed; the new king, Fernando VII, had renounced his crown; the capital had been occupied by French troops; and Spanish officials had recognized French authority. There was also the startling news that the Spanish people had rebelled, on *dos de mayo* (May 2), against the arrogant invaders. The Junta of Valencia and then the Junta of Seville asked for support in opposing the French. The situation mystified the authorities in Mexico. Who ruled Spain? Should anyone be obeyed? What should be done? Some, like the Marqués de Rayas, counseled caution. The Audiencia, then dominated by peninsulares, agreed; it advised that nothing be done until more news arrived from Spain.

The new situation shattered the recently-achieved unity of the upper classes in their opposition to the Law of Consolidation. Most European Spaniards wanted either to take no immediate action or to recognize an authority in Spain. Many criollos, on the other hand, favored some form of autonomy. Viceroy Iturrigaray, who wanted to remain in office to protect the fortune he had amassed through graft, was uncertain about the best course to follow.

The cabildo of Mexico City, which was dominated by American Spaniards, submitted a resolution to the viceroy on July 19, 1808, asking him to assume control of the government in Mexico during the crisis. Although this was to be done in the name of the king, it was nevertheless a proposal for autonomy. The municipal council justified its action on the basis of traditional Spanish political theory. It reminded Iturrigaray that "In the absence or during the impediment [of the king], sovereignty lies represented in all the kingdom and classes that form it; and more particularly in those superior tribunals that govern it and administer justice, and in those corporations that represent the public." Thus, in the view of the cabildo, the representatives of the *public* were the Audiencia and the cities, Mexico City being foremost among them. It proposed that a Mexican junta, composed of representatives from the cities, be convoked to govern New Spain. This too was in keeping with Spanish tradition. In the sixteenth century, Carlos V had recognized Mexico City's preeminent position in any possible assembly of cities in New Spain. In the seventeenth century, during the debate over the Union of Arms, Mexico City and Puebla had petitioned the viceroy to convene a congress of municipal delegates. Although the viceroy had rejected their proposal, neither he nor the Crown questioned the putative right of Mexican municipalities to have a regional cortes. The new criollo plan resembled those being carried out in Spain, where provincial juntas were also being formed in 1808.

The leading advocates of autonomy were criollos: Juan Francisco Azcárate, José Primo de Verdad, and the Marqués de Uluapa were regidores in the city council; Jacobo Villaurrutia, from Santo Domingo, was an alcalde de crimen in the Audiencia; other prominent supporters were the Conde de Medina, the Conde de Regla, and the Marqués de Rayas. The principal ideologue of autonomy, Fray Melchor de Talamantes, composed a series of political tracts for the Ayuntamiento. Talamantes proposed convoking a Mexican congress to govern and to reform the kingdom. The assembly would be empowered to appoint a viceroy, to fill civil and ecclesiastical positions, to manage the realm's finances, and to name ambassadors. Talamantes also proposed that this congress abolish the Inquisition, as well as ecclesiastical fueros; introduce free trade; and promote mining, agricultural, and industrial reforms. The proposals are strikingly similar to those subsequently implemented in Spain when a cortes met in Cádiz. The only difference is that Talamantes was proposing a regional congress for Mexico—something no Spaniard would accept.

To conservatives, and especially to peninsulares, any sort of action was dangerous, given the uncertain circumstances in Spain. But in their view, convoking a congress was treason. Some—like wealthy entrepreneur Gabriel de Yermo, oidor Ciriaco González Carvajal, and inquisitor Bernardo de Prado—maintained that the very idea of a Mexican congress was itself treasonable. Bishop Abad y Queipo, long considered a progressive reformer, declared that "a national junta violated the Constitution and was itself an act of rebellion." The conservative criollo regidor, Augustín del Rivero, took the most extreme position: in his view, "To call the cities is to initiate civil war."

In the face of such opposition, Viceroy Iturrigaray did not convoke an assembly of the cities. Instead, on August 9, he called a *cabildo abierto* to advise him. The corporations represented included the Audiencia, the Ayuntamiento, the Consulado, the mining guild, the military, the fuero courts of the royal treasury, the Cathedral chapter, the Inquisition, the University, the monasteries of Guadalupe, Santo Domingo, and Carmen, the nobility, and three Indian governors of the metropolitan barrios. Altogether, 86 representatives attended; according to Doris Ladd, 39 were criollos, 29 were peninsulares, and 18 could not be identified by place of birth.

The meeting was tempestuous. The representatives of the city council argued that sovereignty now resided in the people. When the Spanish-born oidor Guillermo de Aguirre inquired "Who are the people?," Primo de Verdad replied that the constituted authorities represented the people. But Aguirre maintained that they were not *the people*, that the views espoused by the Ayuntamiento were seditious—and that, in any case, the logic of Primo de Verdad's argument would return sovereignty to the Indians, who were the original Mexican people. The issue was not settled. On the important question of how to react to the situation in Spain, the delegates split into three factions: (1) recognize the Seville Junta, (2) wait until more information arrived from Spain, and (3) convoke a Mexican junta to act in the name of the king. Since the group was so divided, the only decision reached that day was to recognize Fernando VII as king.

Tensions mounted shortly thereafter when Juan Javat and Manuel Jáuregui, commissioners from the Seville Junta, arrived in Mexico City. The two commissioners maintained that Seville had been recognized by the rest of Spain and that Mexico had to acknowledge its authority. The claim was untrue; Seville was only one of many contending provincial juntas in Spain at that time. Iturrigaray correctly refused to recognize the Seville junta until he had more information. At issue was not only who should be obeyed, but who should receive the millions of pesos in Consolidation funds waiting to be shipped to Spain. The viceroy's actions, however, frightened the Spaniards, who feared he would betray them. Some even believed he wanted Mexican independence so that he could crown himself king. As a result, according to an eyewitness, "Europeans immediately bought all the arms and ammunition they could find in the capital." They also formed a militia corps, the Volunteers of Fernando VII. These acts only aggravated the situation; political disputes became more dangerous. Two people were shot to death in a political argument.

In an effort to reduce tensions, Viceroy Iturrigaray convoked a second cabildo abierto on August 31, to consider if Mexico should recognize the authority of the Junta of Seville. The pro-Seville group argued that, of all the areas of Spain, Seville's was the most logical junta to support, because of the port city's close ties with the New World. Javat and Jáuregui's arguments were convincing: when the vote was taken, the delegates favored Seville 49 to 26. Of those opposed, 12 favored waiting and 14 preferred a Mexican junta. But the entire situation changed later that day, when delegates from the Junta of Oviedo arrived.

Iturrigaray called an emergency meeting for the following day, September 1, 1808. The commissioners from Oviedo denied that the Seville Junta represented all Spain; instead, they claimed supreme authority, because they had received recognition and support from England. Viceroy Iturrigaray took a strong stand, declaring that "Spain is now in a state of anarchy, there are Supreme Juntas everywhere, and we should therefore not obey any of them." His arguments swayed the representatives, who voted 54 to 17 not to recognize the Seville Junta. While a few criollos still advocated forming a Mexican junta, most representatives preferred watchful waiting.

The cabildos abiertos exacerbated the differences among the upper class. The corporations were divided into three factions. Only a few, however, were steadfastly committed to any course; the majority altered their views as circumstances changed. The two most intransigent groups were the primarily Spanish minority who wanted to recognize Seville, and the primarily criollo minority who favored a Mexican junta. In a sense, the divisions were also generational; the elders sided with Spain, while the younger men sought autonomy. This cleavage was clearly demonstrated within the rich and politically active Fagoaga family: José Juan, José Mariano, and the old Marqués del Apartado supported Seville, but the young men—Francisco, the marqués' heir, and his cousin, José María—sided with their uncle Jacobo Villaurrutia in preferring autonomy. On this issue natal divisions were blurred, because there were criollos and Spaniards in both groups.

Iturrigaray's position became tenuous. His refusal to recognize Seville appeared treasonable to conservative Spaniards. In their view, he was pro-criollo and pro-independence. They misinterpreted his motives; the viceroy was merely trying to remain in office to protect his ill-gotten fortune, but he was also technically correct in waiting. To strengthen his position, Iturrigaray reinforced the city with loyal troops and convoked a fourth cabildo abierto on September 9, at which he threatened to resign. The representatives of the Ayuntamiento, who had been forewarned, asked him to reconsider; although it was the only body to do so, Iturrigaray agreed to continue in office.

The meetings resolved nothing. Governmental inactivity added to the fears of conservatives, who believed anarchy could only be averted by resolute action. News that mobs in Cádiz had removed Godoy's appointees, calling them French collaborators, only added to their apprehension. Conservatives were aware that in Mexico they ruled a nonwhite society and that a mass uprising would be disastrous. Men like Gabriel Yermo had a clear appreciation of the strength of the Mexican lower classes; the castas, he said were "men as brave as any European." If they took up arms, the authorities might not be able to control them. Therefore he and other conservatives decided to act.

With the connivance of conservative members of the Audiencia, the archbishop, prominent Spaniards and conservative criollos, Yermo organized a plot to overthrow the viceroy. He disliked Viceroy Iturrigaray for personal as well as political reasons. As an *abastecedor* (supplier) of the Mexico City markets, Yermo had been harassed and insulted by both the city council and Iturrigaray. The supply contract had cost him money; the new taxes on brandy, meat, and pulque had also affected him; and the Law of Consolidation had forced him to sell properties at a loss, to pay off debts to the Church. Yermo also despised Iturrigaray for his corruption, charging that any office or favor could be purchased from the viceroy, his wife, his children, or his servants. But Yermo's chief motivation was the fear of popular unrest among the castes. Shortly after midnight on September 16, 1808, Yermo led 300 men, including clerks from the Consulado and the Volunteers of Fernando VII, to the viceregal palace. They entered the building without opposition and arrested Iturrigaray and his family. The rebels found stored in the palace more than 2 million pesos in jewels and plate and more than 400,000 pesos from the mining tribunal, the graft that Iturrigaray had accumulated over the years.

Immediately after the coup, the archbishop and the Audiencia gathered in the palace at 2 in the morning to approve Iturrigaray's removal from office. They appointed the 80-year-old General Pedro Garibay acting viceroy. Afterwards the conspirators arrested the leaders of the autonomy movement—Talamantes, Azcárate, and Primo de Verdad; Francisco Beye Cisneros, abbot of the Convent of Guadalupe; José Beristáin de Sousa, canon of the Cathedral; and the auditor of war, José del Cristo y Conde. Primo de Verdad died in prison a few days later; Talamantes also died in jail, in Veracruz, of yellow fever, in April 1809; Azcárate remained imprisoned for three years. The other three were released shortly after their arrest.

Garibay rewarded Yermo and the Spaniards the same day. He abolished the new taxes, including the one on pulque, a "healthful regional drink" according to Yermo. The new Mexican regime recognized the Seville Junta and shipped 9 million pesos from the Consolidation fund to Spain. By the time it arrived, there was a true national government, the Junta Suprema Central formed on September 25, 1808, in Spain. The new Spanish authorities approved the actions taken in Mexico.

During the next two years, peninsulares dominated the government of Mexico. Garibay remained in office until July 19, 1809, when the "Spanish party" replaced him with Archbishop Francisco Javier Lizana y Beaumont. Lizana lasted only until May 8, 1810; the Audiencia seized the reins of government until September 12, 1810, when a new viceroy appointed in Spain arrived in Mexico. During those two years, the authorities in Spain had little control over their colony; the Spaniards in Mexico ran things to suit themselves. They had prevented autonomy by intimidating the criollos, but they found no means of restoring the earlier unity of the upper classes. Instead, they attempted to instill a sense of love for the mother country by exhorting the people of Mexico to support Spain's struggle against France. In this way they raised more than 3 million pesos to send to Spain—but the majority of the contributions came from those who had been responsible for Iturrigaray's overthrow. Most Mexicans believed that it was time New Spain protected its own interests.

The 1808 coup exacerbated the divisions in Mexico. Yermo and the Spanish leaders insisted that it had been a purely peninsular affair, even though some criollos participated in it. As a result, the differences between the Seville group and the autonomists came to be perceived as a conflict between criollos and peninsulares. The issue was particularly aggravating to the criollos because the Spaniards had broken the law and the new authorities in Spain sided with the men who had overthrown the king's viceroy. The deaths of Primo de Verdad and Talamantes fueled the discontent. The criollo autonomists never accepted the Spaniards' actions. Conspiracies and rumors of conspiracies became common.

The authorities discovered a serious criollo conspiracy in the fall of 1809. Lieutenant José Mariano Michelena of the Royal Infantry and Captain José García Obeso of the provincial militia had organized a movement in the city of Valladolid. The conspirators found supporters in other important provincial cities — Guanajuato, Querétaro, San Miguel el Grande, and Guadalajara. They had prepared an uprising on December 21, 1809, and expected support from the army and militia. In addition, they hoped to raise thousands of troops among the Indians and castes by promising to abolish tribute. Once they had gained control of Mexico, they planned to convoke a congress of the cities to govern in the name of Fernando VII. The plan differed from the earlier autonomy movement only in that the criollos had to rely on military force because the Spaniards had seized the government. Viceroy Lizana chose to exercise leniency when the movement was exposed, since he realized that many important persons openly declared that the conspirators were only seeking to redress rightful grievances the wrong way. When the leaders were tried, the prosecution was only able to prove that the conspirators planned to save New Spain from a possible French invasion. Lizana ordered them released. Their defense attorney, Carlos María Bustamante, convinced the viceroy that "the day the first insurgent is hanged, Spain must relinquish all hope of holding America."

The situation seemed to improve the following year. Although the French still occupied most of Spain, a national government continued to function with the aid of the English. The Spanish Regency, which had succeeded the Junta Central, convoked a national cortes to meet in September 1810. The Mexicans, like other Spanish Americans, were entitled to elect representatives to this new parliament. The newly-appointed viceroy to Mexico, Lieutenant General Francisco Javier Venegas, landed in Mexico on August 15, 1810 and entered Mexico City on September 12. He intended to restore confidence in the government, but he was not granted time. The Hidalgo Revolt erupted in the early hours of September 16, 1810.

THE HIDALGO REVOLT

Economic and social as well as political factors made the Bajío an ideal spawning ground for a great armed insurrection. This region, northwest of the capital in the valley of the Lerma River, between León and Querétaro, is one of the most prosperous agricultural and mining areas of Mexico. The city of Guanajuato, situated almost in the center of the region, was the site of the *Veta Madre* (mother lode), one of the richest silver mines in the world. The Bajío had a mobile and dynamic population, most of whom participated in the market economy. In 1806, for example, there were 285,154 persons subject to tribute in the province of Guanajuato: 28 percent were Indians living in communal villages, 58 percent were natives working in the cities and countryside as naboríos, and 16 percent were free blacks and mulatos. The cities of Guanajuato and Querétaro had a population of about 60,000 and 50,000, respectively; other smaller cities and towns dotted the Bajío.

Historically, the region had offered great opportunity and social mobility, but in the late eighteenth century conditions deteriorated. Population growth intensified the competition for jobs, and periodic agricultural crises caused rapid increases in food prices that outstripped the rise in wages. Banditry and unrest expanded in the countryside. Drought created unprecedented shortages and hunger in 1785. The lower clergy, who observed the situation firsthand, appealed to the authorities for relief. Bishop Antonio de San Miguel of Michoacán urged the Crown to abolish tribute, remove ethnic distinctions, open government jobs to all, and distribute land to the needy, in order to ameliorate conditions. But little was done. A severe drought in the summer of 1809 drastically reduced the harvest, and food prices quadrupled. The effects in the Bajío were devastating. Mines could not operate, because there was not enough grain to feed the draft animals or the workers. The obrajes of Querétaro were faced with similar shortages. Thousands were laid off and hunger was widespread. The masses, who remembered the disaster of 1785, were acutely aware of their marginality. Discontent was rife in 1810; all that was required was a leader to ignite an uprising.

The man who initiated the revolt, Miguel Hidalgo y Costilla, was a criollo priest, a member of the secondary elite who had had a successful academic career at the College of San Nicolás Obispo in Valladolid before becoming a parish priest in the prosperous town of Dolores in the Bajío. A man of the Enlightenment, Hidalgo made his parish a center of culture and a place where people met to discuss social and economic matters. He also stimulated local development by introducing pottery-manufacturing, silk-weaving, tanning, and wine-growing enterprises. His parishioners liked and trusted him, and Hidalgo had many important friends and acquaintances throughout the Bajío, among them Juan Antonio Riaño, the intendant of Guanajuato, whose home was a center of Enlightenment ideas and French culture; Manuel Abad y Queipo, the progressive bishop-elect of Valladolid; the corregidor of Querétaro, Miguel Domínguez, and his wife, María Josefa Ortíz; and militia captains Ignacio Allende, Juan Aldama, and Mariano Abasolo, all three landowning sons of Basque merchants.

With the exception of Riaño and Abad y Queipo, all these people were criollos of means who had grievances against the Spanish regime. Many had suffered financial reverses during the Consolidation; Hidalgo, for example, had lost an hacienda because he could not redeem his debts. But it was Iturrigaray's overthrow and the subsequent actions of the Spaniards which induced the criollos to act. Many Mexican officers respected Iturrigaray, who had assembled the militia for maneuvers in 1806. For the first time since the conquest, a large army had gathered in New Spain; the sight awed the Mexicans and gave them a sense of their potential power. Iturrigaray's overthrow was an affront not only because it removed an official who had honored Mexicans, but also because a small group of Spaniards had contemptuously dismissed the importance as well as the rights of Mexicans.

The Valladolid conspiracy of 1809 encouraged a similar movement in Querétaro, where Allende, Aldama, and Domínguez began informal talks. By March 1810 the plotters had recruited

Hidalgo and other disaffected criollos. Their goals, like those of Michelena, were to depose the Spaniards with the aid of the workers of the Bajío—so-called "Indians"—and establish a criollo junta to govern Mexico in the name of Fernando VII. The conspirators planned the uprising for October 1810, but they were discovered by the Spanish authorities on September 13, and the Querétaro group was arrested. However, Doña María Josefa Ortíz de Domínguez, who had been an extremely active participant, managed to get word to Hidalgo that the Querétaro conspiracy had been exposed. The Spanish authorities were not initially frightened by news of another intrigue. Quite the contrary—they were inclined to be lenient. Intendant Riaño had known about the plotting for some time, but had been reluctant to arrest his friends. Had events gone no further, most of the participants might have remained free like the Valladolid group.

Aldama arrived in Dolores at about 2 in the morning of September 16 with the news that the scheme had been discovered. Allende was visiting Hidalgo at the time. The three men discussed their situation and, after some deliberation, Hidalgo convinced the other two to initiate the revolt in Dolores. The priest had a cache of weapons and his factory workers were ready to participate in the movement, as were the soldiers of Abasolo's company stationed in Dolores. The group was convinced that their cause would be enthusiastically received by most Mexicans and that their movement would triumph easily. September 16 was a Sunday, a market day, and many people began gathering in Dolores early that morning. Father Hidalgo rang the church bells to attract a crowd. The priest exhorted the people to join his rebellion, an event known in Mexican history as the *grito de Dolores*. According to Aldama, about 8 o'clock in the morning

> there were gathered more than 600 men on foot and on horseback, for it was Sunday and they had come to Mass from the nearby ranches, and the cura [Hidalgo] exhorted them to join him and help him defend the Kingdom because they [the Spanish usurpers] wanted to turn it over to the French; that now oppression had reached an end; that there was no longer any tribute; that those who enlisted with horses and arms would be paid a peso daily, and those on foot four reales.

Thus Hidalgo appealed to the traditional view that bad governments ought to be removed, while the monarchy remained inviolate. He undoubtedly concluded his exhortation with the cry: *Death to bad government, long live the king.*

The insurrection spread rapidly. The rebels arrested authorities in Dolores who resisted. Then the crowd of about 700 marched to San Miguel el Grande, where the rebel leaders expected to win the support of militia units. Along the way, the insurgents took the standard of the Indian Virgin of Guadalupe from the church of Atotonilco and adopted it as their banner. San Miguel was occupied without difficulty, and there the movement attracted new adherents. Many joined, lured by the opportunity to loot rich haciendas. At first the properties of Americans were spared, but given the scarcity of food and the widespread unemployment in the region, it was difficult to control the masses. In an attempt to maintain order in the insurrectionary forces, the leaders introduced a chain of command. Hidalgo, who was the most popular among the masses, assumed the post of Captain General of America, while Allende became his lieutenant; other militia officers assumed command of the newly-formed regiments of untrained men. Within a week the rebel army had swollen to more than 25,000. Militia leaders were unable to discipline these untrained volunteers armed with primitive weapons, the overwhelming majority of whom belonged to the working and the lépero classes. They were, as Francisco Bulnes declared, a horde rather than an army.

The Hidalgo Revolt began as a criollo movement for autonomy, and as such it was favorably perceived by the Mexican upper classes. Indeed, many magnates and other large property owners contributed food and supplies to the rebel cause. The Marqués de Rayas, for example, wrote that Hidalgo was a man of integrity and his followers were distinguished for their bravery. The initial support by the upper class faded when it became apparent that the rebel leaders could not or would not control their followers. Within a short time the hungry rebels began to plunder indiscriminately, making no distinction between the property of bad and good Spaniards or even between that of peninsulares and criollos.

The sack of Guanajuato marked the turning point in the revolt; thereafter enthusiasm for the movement declined. Guanajuato was the capital of a rich agricultural and mining intendancy; with a population of about 60,000, it was the third-largest city in the Spanish empire after Mexico City and Havana. The city had a reputation for beauty and progress which was enhanced by the enlightened administration of the Intendant Riaño. But when the rebels approached the city, Riaño made a fatal miscalculation: he decided to retreat into the *Alhondiga de Granaditas,* a large granary, to await reinforcements. He moved government records, the treasury, the most valuable belongings of the leading citizens, and enough supplies to feed 500 people for two months, and the royalists and the royalist garrison withdrew into the massive stone walls of the alhondiga on the night of September 24. These actions caused great distress among the rest of the population, who felt abandoned. The lower classes, initially on the side of the royalists, turned against them. On September 26 Riaño tried to regain their support by abolishing the tribute, but the measure backfired because most urban Indians and castas regarded this move as an act of hypocrisy that would be rescinded if Hidalgo were defeated. When the insurgents attacked Guanajuato on September 28, Riaño refused to surrender, believing that he could hold out until reinforcements arrived from Mexico City. The city's lower classes joined the thousands of irregular rebels in an attack on the granary. Although defenders inflicted terrible losses on the insurgents, the building fell after five hours. The mob then butchered the royalists, making no distinction between Spaniards and criollos; sacked the granary; and then destroyed mining equipment in the city. The insurgent leaders managed to end the carnage only with great difficulty.

News of the fall of Guanajuato alienated the Mexican upper and middle classes, as well as many in the lower classes. The magnates, the secondary elite, and the pequeña burguesía could no longer interpret the Hidalgo revolt as a criollo autonomist movement. The looting, carnage, and destruction of Guanajuato clearly indicated that the insurrection promoted class conflict which the leaders could not control. The upper classes feared that such confrontations would spark a race war. Royalist propaganda took advantage of this theme. Bishop Abad y Queipo, once so favorable to criollo interests, argued that the Haitian upper class had been the most prosperous and peaceful in the world until race conflict destroyed them. The same fate awaited their Mexican counterparts if the impious Hidalgo were not stopped. To make his point, Abad y Queipo excommunicated the four principal leaders of the insurgent movement.

Royalist propaganda proved successful. The army and most of the militia, which were 95 percent Mexican, remained loyal. Although a few members of the upper class favored the rebels, most sided with the government—but they did so reluctantly. Most Mexicans, even the magnates, maintained an uneasy neutrality. While remaining loyal to the government, they did not actively oppose the insurgents. The autonomist movement had not died, it was merely postponed. Because of the danger of class and race war, the Mexican elite believed the time was not ripe for home rule. No one, however, doubted that the day would come when the issue of autonomy would be raised again. In the meantime, everyone tried to survive the Hidalgo Revolt. For landowners in rebel areas, this meant cooperation with the insurgents. If they did not meet the demands for food and supplies, they and their properties might be destroyed.

After Guanajuato, Hidalgo turned south to Valladolid, where he had been a student and later a professor. The city surrendered without resistance on October 16. This established a pattern: cities threatened by the rebels surrendered, to escape violence; when the royal forces returned, the same cities proclaimed their loyalty to the government. In Valladolid, Hidalgo asked the Conde de Sierra Gorda—now a canon in charge of the bishopric, since Abad y Queipo had fled to Mexico City—to lift the excommunication. Sierra Gorda, who sympathized with the rebels, agreed immediately. Later the titled cleric encouraged Father José María Morelos to join the insurgency, an event that would have far-reaching consequences.

From Valladolid, Hidalgo led the rebel horde, now swollen to 80,000, toward Mexico City. When it reached Toluca on October 29, only a low range of mountains stood between the insurgents and the greatest metropolis in the New World. There at the Monte de las Cruces, an elevation overlooking the passes to the Valley of Mexico, the royalist Colonel Torcuato Trujillo, in command of an army of 2,500 troops, chose to defend the capital. The well-disciplined, better-armed royalists controlled the heights. Their modern artillery proved a deadly and terrible surprise to the rebels. On October 30, the two armies engaged in a day-long bloody struggle. Allende and the other rebel commanders could not control their brave but chaotic troops. Although the rebels encircled Trujillo's army, the well-disciplined royalists fought their way out of the encirclement and retreated into the Valley of Mexico toward nightfall. While Trujillo's decimated army could no longer defend the capital, the rebels had suffered heavily: more than 2,000 insurgents died, thousands were wounded, and thousands more deserted. Half the rebel forces disappeared overnight. The long string of easy victories and triumphal marches had come to an end. The royalist force had shown what even a small well-trained and disciplined army could do.

The remaining insurgents paused to regroup before advancing on Mexico City. Hidalgo sent emissaries to the Indian villages of the valley in hope of recruiting new men. Unlike the workers of the Bajío, the native communities in central Mexico did not rally to Hidalgo's cause. Most Indian pueblos hastened to express their support for the royalists. Some were disturbed that "among the traitors there are individuals of Indian origin." The cabildo of Santiago assured the viceroy "that none of its sons" would march with the rebels. Tlaxcala rejected the "scandalous and detestable" acts of the insurgents, and assured the viceroy that it would oppose the rebellion in that area. Thus within six weeks of the "grito," most criollos, mestizos, Indians, and castas repudiated the Hidalgo Revolt. The danger of civil war frightened all classes, castes, and ethnic groups, who perceived the insurrection as a potential threat to their interests. The corporate Indian villages were particularly afraid that their communal lands might be occupied by the landless gañanes and naboríos in Hidalgo's forces.

Unwilling to acknowledge that his movement had lost momentum, Hidalgo demanded that Viceroy Venegas surrender the capital and avoid a pitched battle. The viceroy refused. Reinforcements were on their way from San Luis Potosí under the command of General Félix Calleja; Venegas only needed to hold out for a few days. Allende and Hidalgo both understood that they could not control their forces once they entered the city. Indiscriminate

(overleaf) NEW SPAIN'S MAXIMUM CLAIMS IN NORTH AMERICA, 1802 ▶

INDIOS LIEBRE
INDIOS NATHANAS

INDIOS DE LA MONTAÑA

R. del Oro grande
L. del Oro grande

Indios del interior

INDIOS CASTOR

Montes corn.res

Chesterfield

L. Theye Checho
L. Theye Kye-lynel

Theye-heye-Kied L.
L. Chifadaud
Muchas alturas
L. Anawab

Muchas alturas

Paso de...

Rio. de los Canales...

Whitduschuck L.
Alturas
Ft. Chepewyan
R. de la Paz

Tierras altas cuyas aguas unas van
à la Bahia de Hudson y otras al Oceano. Artico

Fto de la Herca
L. Buffalo
L. y L.
à la Crosse
Port. del Central
L. del Pelicano

Habitacion de
los Guadianos
Casa Buckingham
Lo mas alto
del Pais

Casa Manchester
Casa de Hudson
Casa del brazo del Sur

INDIOS NANSCUD

Cascada
INDIOS NAGAILERS

Rio Taconteha-tessi

Braz del Sur

Cattanahowes

Rio Missouri
en 1786 per M.Tanda

Grandes llanos

Punto mas N del Missouri
segun M.r Tompson en 1798.

Entr.a de Juan de Fuca

Tierra despoblada

Laguna en la qual terminaron sus reconocim.to
los PP.es Velez y Escalante.

Mendocino

R. Salado
R. del Norte

PROVINCIAS INTERNAS
N.o de MEXICO

R. Gila
Colorado de Nachitos

California ó de Cortès

I. de Guadalupe

Tropico de Cancer

I. de los Pajaros?

GRANDE OCEANO EQUINOCCIAL

MEXICO

MEDITERRANEO

E DAVIS

DE

AMERICA

Mte. Raleigh
C.º Divers
C.º Walsingham de Davis

Estrecho de Cumberland

Estrecho de Probisher ó Paso de Lumley

Estrecho de Anian hoy de Hudson

Iª Salisburi
Iª Nothingham

Iª Mansfield

C.º Smith
Bª Musquitto

Pta. Thompson
Pta. Portland
I. Solstun

BAHIA DE

HUDSON

Severn

GRAN TIERRA DEL ESTE

TIERRA DE LABRADOR

Bahia
James

Nain
establecimiento de
los Moravos

Entrª de Davis

Ogbuckluck
Bª de Byron

Entrª de Yvuckioke

I. Huntingdon

Bª de S. Miguel

C.º Carls

Isla de
Terranova

Golfo de
S. Lorenzo

Gran Banco de Terranova

Banco Jaquet

NUEVA FRANCIA

L. Superior

Quebec

ESTADOS UNIDOS

FILADELFIA

Delaware
Hudson
Chesapeak

Richmond
Hamburg
Halifax

C.º Albemarle
C.º Hatteras
C.º Lookout

Charlestown
Savannah
Darien
Bª Santa Maria

FLORIDA OCCIDENTAL

FLORIDA ORIENTAL

Cayo Anclote
C.º de Tampa
C.º S. Carlos

de Mexico

Islas Lucayas

Tortugas
S. Salvador ó Guanahani

P. Bermudas

Iª de Cuba ó de Juana

Islas Antillas

OCEANO ATLANTICO

I. Española

MAR DE COLON

Golfo de Honduras

looting would occur, and Calleja's forces would catch the rebel army at a vulnerable moment. The punishment inflicted by Trujillo at Monte Cruces had also weakened the resolve of many officers and men, and a larger army under Calleja would surely be harder to defeat. Hidalgo ordered his men to turn back on November 3, leaving Mexico City frightened but intact.

From the capital, the insurgents turned northward in the direction of Querétaro. Hidalgo's army was still imposing—perhaps 40,000 men followed him—but it was not a well-organized fighting force. On November 7, General Calleja intercepted the insurgents at Aculco with a well-disciplined army of 7,000 troops. Allende and Hidalgo had planned to meet the enemy and then rapidly disengage to avoid serious losses, but instead of an orderly retreat the withdrawal turned into a rout. The rebels abandoned most of their artillery and supplies in their desperation to flee from the royalists. The lack of discipline, confusion, and apparent cowardice of the rebels disgusted the loyal criollo and mestizo troops. Thereafter, the militia was the most relentless enemy of the insurgents.

Following the battle, the disorganized rebels split into two groups; Hidalgo marched to Valladolid, while Allende returned to Guanajuato. Hidalgo had done little to restrain the fury of his men, but in Valladolid he initiated a deliberate campaign of terror against the peninsulares. He ordered the execution of 60 European Spaniards to please his followers and to make up for the loss of confidence resulting from the two defeats. Later, in Guadalajara, he ordered 350 Spaniards killed. These political acts pleased his proletarian followers, but alienated most sectors of Mexican society.

Hidalgo transferred his headquarters to Guadalajara at the end of November, and during the next month and a half, he attempted to revive his movement. A rebel newspaper, *El Despertador americano*, sought to counter royalist propaganda; it published Hidalgo's program, which included the abolition of tribute, of slavery, and of taxes on liquor and tobacco—and, in an attempt to win the support of native communities, laws to protect Indian lands.

Meanwhile the royalists gained strength. Viceroy Venegas coordinated the offense, but it was General Calleja who played the main role in defeating the rebels. On November 24 he drove Allende from Guanajuato. Before departing, the mob massacred 138 gachupín prisoners; after retaking the city, Calleja ordered 69 citizens of Guanajuato, believed to have cooperated with the rebels, executed in retaliation. Thereafter anyone harboring insurgents risked execution. The terror and counter-terror forced people to choose sides, and most opted for the better-organized and more socially acceptable royalist cause.

Allende and his battered forces retreated to Guadalajara, where Hidalgo had established control over a wide region in the west. The insurgents concentrated on recruiting and training a new army and reorganizing their government. By mid-January, the rebel army again numbered more than 40,000. Against the advice of his military commanders, especially Allende, Hidalgo decided to intercept the royalist forces which were advancing on Guadalajara. They met Calleja's 6,000-man army on January 17, 1811, at the Bridge of Calderón, eleven leagues east of Guadalajara. After six hours of bitter fighting, Calleja's army swept the field.

The insurgent leaders fled north in disarray. Two days later they rendezvoused at Pabellón, an hacienda northwest of Aguascalientes, where Allende and his officers stripped Hidalgo of command. Ignacio Allende assumed the title of generalisimo, but retained Hidalgo as a puppet chieftain to placate the masses. Despite the reorganization the rebels were unable to regain the initiative. Most criollos, mestizos, and community Indians now opposed the movement, while news of the defeat at Calderón alienated potential supporters. For several weeks the rebels attempted to rally support in the north. Finally, on March 21, 1811, royalist forces captured the insurgent leaders near a town ironically called Nuestra Señora de Guadalupe de Baján. The leaders were brought to Chihuahua in chains, tried, found guilty, and executed. The royalists placed the heads of Hidalgo, Allende, Aldama, and Jimenez in cages on the four corners of the granary of Guanajuato, where they remained until independence, as a grim reminder of the consequences of treason. In a last effort to discredit the revolt, the authorities claimed that Hidalgo had recanted, begging God's forgiveness for the crimes he had committed.

In the final analysis, the Hidalgo Revolt failed because it alienated nearly all classes of Mexicans with its violence and anarchy.

The rebels' bitterest enemy, General Calleja, understood this clearly when he declared: "The natives and even the Europeans themselves are convinced of the advantages that would result from an independent government [home rule]; and if the absurd insurrection of Hidalgo had been built upon this base, it seems to me, as I now look at it, that it would have met little opposition."

THE SPANISH CORTES

The movement for home rule, which had to be abandoned during the Hidalgo Revolt, found new life in events taking place in Spain. The Central Junta had been waging a losing battle against the French since 1808. Because it desperately needed the support of the American kingdoms, the Spanish national government decided to strengthen the bonds of unity with the New World by inviting the kingdoms of America, as well as the provinces of Spain, to elect representatives to the Junta. The decree of January 22, 1809, emphasized the equality of Spain and America and instructed local authorities to elect representatives to the Central Junta. The provisional government also decided to convoke a cortes to deal with the crisis, a Spanish tradition that antedated the monarchy's unification under Carlos V.

Initially the Junta had intended to call a traditional parliament consisting of representatives of the three estates: the clergy, the nobility, and the cities. New French victories, however, forced action. On January 1, 1810, the Central Junta decreed that elections be held. In Spain each provincial junta and each city entitled to representation in earlier cortes was to elect a deputy. Also, a deputy was to be elected for every 50,000 inhabitants. In America a deputy was to be elected for each province, a vague and undefined term. Since the Junta had no idea how large Spanish America was, it inadvertently provided the New World with great power by allowing each American province individual representation. Apparently the Central Junta also intended to summon the clergy and the nobility—but this was never done, because the Junta could not compile a membership roll for these two groups and because the supine attitude of the first two estates toward the invader had gained them the antipathy of the people. Therefore the Spanish Cortes met as one body and became a national assembly.

The Mexicans received the invitation to elect representatives to the Spanish Cortes with enthusiasm. This was their opportunity to obtain a measure of home rule, which Yermo and his faction had denied them in 1808. Elections were held throughout the viceroyalty from Yucatán to New Mexico during the months of June, July, and August 1810. In many cases they were occasions for celebrations, including *Te Deums* and popular festivities. In Puebla, for example, the regidores carried their elected deputy, Canon Antonio J. Pérez, through the streets on their shoulders, accompanied by bands and the firing of artillery. Although twenty Mexican deputies were elected, only fifteen actually attended the Cortes.

Spain's first modern Cortes, which met in Cádiz, remained in session from September 24, 1810, until September 20, 1813. During that time it attempted to transform the Spanish world. It abolished archaic institutions, ended the Inquisition, and established firmer control over the Church. Freedom of the press, already a fact in Spain, was formally extended to the commonwealth. The Cortes also realized that the provinces of Spain and America resented the earlier Bourbon efforts toward centralization. Therefore, it recognized the diversity of the Spanish commonwealth by creating two new home-rule institutions: the provincial deputation and the constitutional city council. The provincial deputation was an administrative body consisting of locally-elected members and an executive appointed by the national government. Thus, Spanish provinces already governed by local juntas and rebellious American provinces could retain local administration while maintaining strong ties with the central government. With the provincial deputation, the Cortes abolished the viceroyalty, reduced the Audiencia from quasi-administrative body to a high court, and divided the commonwealth into provinces that dealt directly with the central government. The second local body, the constitutional city council, replaced the hereditary elites, who had hitherto controlled city government, with popularly elected officials.

These and other reforms were embodied in the Constitution of the Spanish Monarchy, promulgated in March 1812. The new charter created a unitary state with equal laws for all parts of the commonwealth. A unicameral legislature, the Cortes, would meet yearly in the capital; the king was substantially restricted, and the

Cortes was entrusted with decisive power. The new government thus encouraged some decentralization, but it also continued and, in some ways, strengthened the resented Bourbon policies of integration.

The Mexican deputies to the Cortes were among the leading champions of American interests. José Miguel Ramos Arizpe from Coahuila was the chief architect of the provincial deputation. His compatriots José Miguel Guridi y Alcocer and José María Coutó, representing Tlaxcala and Mexico respectively, distinguished themselves as parliamentarians; Guridi served as president of the Cortes in 1812, and Coutó as vice-president in 1813. Two Mexican clergymen who subsequently became conservative bishops, Antonio Joaquín Pérez of Puebla and José Miguel Gordóa of Zacatecas, often sided with the liberals; as a member of the constitutional commission, Pérez supported the liberals against the traditional faction. The Mexican deputies also joined other American representatives in arguing for autonomy for their areas. On August 1, 1811, all of the American deputies presented a statement in which they declared that while only a tiny minority wanted independence, many overseas residents were dissatisfied with the government, particularly the illegitimate actions of the conservative European Spaniards. Dr. José Beye Cisneros, professor emeritus of law at the University of Mexico and a deputy for Mexico, argued forcefully in a separate representation that the New World needed home rule. He declared that "under the best laws, the inhabitants of America suffer a weightier yoke than that of any other nation." And he went on to state that the Hidalgo insurrection had resulted from the high-handed and illegal overthrow of Iturrigaray by the Europeans. He accused the new officials, including Viceroy Venegas, of anti-American bias, and urged that provincial juntas be established to govern the American kingdoms. This was much more autonomy than even the Spanish liberals were willing to grant. Ultimately, the Cortes reached a compromise through the skillful negotiations of Ramos Arizpe in introducing the provincial deputation, which partially satisfied the desire for home rule while maintaining strong ties with the mother country.

The royal authorities in Mexico and the conservative European Spaniards viewed the actions of the Spanish Cortes with alarm. Venegas, now reduced to political chief of the Province of Mexico—an area that included most of central Mexico—refused to implement all the new reforms. He suspended freedom of the press in his area, fearing that it would serve the interests of the insurgents. But when the Constitution was promulgated, the authorities in Mexico had no alternative but to institute it. The charter was formally proclaimed in Mexico City on September 30, 1812, and the week that followed was one of celebration. Thereafter the contending factions—European Spaniards and conservatives versus the criollos and liberals—openly campaigned for the parish elections of November 19, 1812. A European–conservative faction victory would have vindicated Venegas and his supporters. But the liberals and American Spaniards won an overwhelming victory throughout New Spain.

In Mexico City all of the successful electors were criollos associated with the autonomy movement. Fearful that the electors would choose men of their own persuasion for office, Venegas once again suspended freedom of the press and ordered the election annulled on the grounds that irregularities had occurred in the voting. He also moved against suspected insurgent-sympathizers: he ordered Judge Villaurrutia to Spain; indicted the elector Juan Martínez on charges of corresponding with the rebels; jailed the writer José Joaquín Fernández de Lizardi; and put a price on the head of Carlos María Bustamante, who fled to join the insurgents. Thus by the middle of December 1812, the authorities of Mexico City had once again broken the law and thwarted the efforts of the autonomists. But this time, unlike 1808, other provinces of New Spain were being governed by the Constitution. Venegas' coup d'etat kept him in office for only a few months. On March 1, 1813, he was replaced as superior political chief by General Calleja, who ordered the suspended elections completed. To the consternation of the Audiencia, not a single European was elected to the cabildo, the provincial deputation, or the Cortes.

Calleja continued to pacify New Spain. He disobeyed the Constitution whenever it impeded his efforts to end insurgency in Mexico. The traditional formula, *obedezco pero no cumplo,* served the imperial bureaucracy as well as local interests. But Calleja no longer possessed the authority of a viceroy. The Cortes had divided the former viceroyalty into 7 smaller districts, commanded for military purposes by captains-general: New Spain, Nueva Galicia, San Luis Potosí, the Eastern Interior Provinces, the Western Interior Provinces, Yucatán, and Guatemala. For administrative purposes, each of these districts was, in turn, divided into provinces with their own provincial deputations and political chiefs. For example, New Spain, the most populous region of the country, consisted of 9 provinces: Mexico, Puebla, Michoacán, Guanajuato, Oaxaca, Veracruz, San Luis Potosí, Tlaxcala, and Querétaro. Central authority was further weakened because the new constitutional cabildos and the provincial deputations asserted their rights to home rule. Dominated by Mexicans, these bodies insisted that the imperial bureaucracy obey the Constitution. In addition, Mexicans were allotted more than 60 seats in the Cortes, giving them not only an important voice in commonwealth-wide affairs but also another mechanism for restricting central authority and insisting on home rule for New Spain. Thus the once-powerful office of viceroy was reduced to captain-general of the Kingdom of New Spain and political chief of the Province of Mexico.

THE MORELOS REVOLT

The political transformations wrought by the Spanish Cortes since 1810 affected Mexican politics in a variety of ways. They restricted the ability of the royalist forces to deal with the continuing insurgency, thus indirectly aiding the rebels. But they also forced the insurgents to take Spanish liberalism into account, if they were to win the support of most Mexicans. As a result, the autonomists were able to play off the royalists against the rebels in an effort to win concessions from the Spanish government.

Ignacio Rayón, a lawyer who served as the rebel secretary of state, assumed leadership of the movement after Hidalgo's death in 1811. Initially, Rayón attempted to effect a reconciliation with General Calleja. He wrote on April 22, 1811, that the insurrection's principal concern had been preventing a French occupation of Mexico, and he invited the general's cooperation in the formation of a national junta to govern the kingdom in the name of Fernando VII. When Calleja rejected this new attempt to obtain Mexican autonomy, Rayón and other insurgent leaders organized a Supreme National Junta and established themselves in the mountain retreat of Zitácuaro, about midway between Valladolid and the capital. The Junta worked to win support for its programs until January 1, 1812, when Calleja captured Zitácuaro. Rayón escaped, but lost his position as leader of the rebels. Father José María Morelos, who had been waging a guerrilla campaign in the south since 1810, emerged as the most important insurgent chieftain. Thereafter the Supreme National Junta existed with Morelos' sufferance, because it provided the movement with the appearance of continuity and the semblance of national representation.

The rebel priest had a better understanding of the socio-economic conditions of Mexico than his predecessor. A member of the *pequeña burguesía*, Morelos was the son of a mestizo artisan and a criolla; he knew southern Mexico well, since he had spent his youth working in his uncle's hacienda near Apatzingán and as a muleteer. He had studied with Hidalgo at the College of San Nicolás in the wealthy city of Valladolid—now called Morelia. Although Father Morelos did not rise rapidly in the Church—he spent 11 years in the small parish of Caracuaro, in the *tierra caliente* (tropical lowlands)—he managed to accumulate some property, a small farm and a substantial house in Valladolid. Morelos was a strict but kindly priest who earned the respect of his parishioners and Church authorities. He was also an ardent nationalist. Thus when the Conde de Sierra Gorda and Hidalgo convinced him of the justice of the rebel cause and asked him to organize a rebellion in the south, Morelos was ready. Unlike his former teacher, however, Morelos rejected senseless violence and anarchy as instruments of war. Instead, he insisted on strict discipline and forbade indiscriminate brutality and plunder which would, in his view, "be the cause of our total ruin, spiritual and temporal." He concentrated on building a small, well-trained army which could challenge the royalist forces. At the same time, he sought support among the Mexican upper and middle classes by promising to respect property. He exhorted his men to put aside race and class antagonisms:

> The whites are the principal representatives of the kingdom, and were the first to take up arms in defense of the Indians and other castes, allying with them; therefore the whites ought to be the subject of our gratitude and not the hatred which some people are stirring up against them. . . . It is not our system to proceed against the rich simply because they are rich, much less against rich criollos. Let no one dare to attack their property, no matter how rich they are.

The Morelos Revolt flourished not only because of its skillful leader, but also because he found capable commanders. Leonardo and Miguel Bravo, Hermenegildo Galeana, Manuel Félix Fernández (better known as Guadalupe Victoria), and Vincente Guerrero, for example, knew the land and its people as well as he. The Bravo brothers, Galeana, and Victoria were the sons of landowning secondary-elite families, while Guerrero belonged to a marginal pequeña burguesía family. Although none of them were professional soldiers, they soon learned how to command disciplined irregular forces; thus Morelos could rely on an effective fighting force. He intended to encircle Mexico City and compel its surrender. During 1811 and 1812 he and his commanders concentrated on cutting the capital's lines of communications. They achieved control of the south, occupying Taxco and other centers along the road to Acapulco. Although they failed to take Puebla in the east, the rebels temporarily severed communications between the capital and Veracruz. By the end of 1812, the insurgents were gaining strength in central Mexico.

Politically active Mexicans used the revolt to gain concessions from the Spanish government. In the Cortes, the Mexican deputies argued vehemently that bad administration *(mal gobierno)* had caused the insurrection, and demanded reforms. In Mexico, prominent individuals maintained ties with the rebels. Landowners provided supplies, rich entrepreneurs financed some of their operations, and other influential Mexicans kept them informed of royalist policies. For example, a secret society known as the "Guadalupes" operated in Mexico City, providing the insurgents with crucial information. Its membership included distinguished lawyers, merchants, and members of the Mexico City cabildo. Some wives were also active participants; they smuggled supplies and even a printing press out of the capital to the rebels. The outstanding female conspirator was Leona Vicario, a wealthy heiress who contributed funds, equipment, and military information to the insurgents; ultimately she fled the city and joined the rebels to avoid arrest. The Guadalupes even attempted to suborn Mexico's leading royalist general at the beginning of 1813, when Venegas and Calleja were divided over military policy. Councilman Francisco Sánchez de Tagle and José del Cristo y Conde met with Calleja in an effort to win his support. The general, who had just received his appointment to replace Venegas, rejected their entreaty. But he took no action against these prominent Mexicans, because he could not hope to retain control of the country if he alienated the upper class at a time when the insurgents were gaining influence.

Morelos achieved his greatest success in 1813. He captured Oaxaca and, in the spring, began a seven-month siege of Acapulco. Despite his success, however, he could not claim authority merely by force of arms, particularly since the Spanish Cortes had ratified the notion of popular sovereignty. Therefore he decided to call a congress to legitimize his claim to supreme authority. Although Carlos María Bustamante urged him to hold the assembly in Oaxaca, Morelos convoked it in September 1813 at Chilpancingo, a small, easily defended, and friendly town. The first national assembly held in Mexico was not a popularly-elected congress. It was, instead, a hand-picked body of 8 men instructed by Morelos to prepare a constitution granting him vast power as Generalisimo of the Army and chief executive of the new government. Unlike Hidalgo and other insurgents, Morelos openly advocated independence. Before the congress had accomplished its task, however, Morelos suffered a series of reverses that radically altered the situation.

After capturing Acapulco, Morelos marched upon Valladolid. There the 5,000-man rebel force was routed by an able young criollo officer, Agustín de Iturbide. Calleja, who as captain-general of New Spain assumed command of the royalist army, broke the encirclement of Mexico City. In a series of well-executed campaigns he began to recover insurgent-held territory—Oaxaca, Cuernavaca, Taxco, and finally Chilpancingo. The handful of rebel congressional delegates fled to Apatzingán to escape the royalist army. Although he still commanded the rebel forces, Morelos had lost most of his prestige by 1814. The tiny rebel congress sought to assert itself and give new direction to the movement.

Events in Spain, however, radically altered the situation in Mexico. Fernando VII returned from captivity in France and abolished the Cortes and all its acts on May 4, 1814. The constitutional structure fell like a house of cards. In Spain the regular army pursued the liberals. Some escaped to France or Italy; countless others, including José Miguel Ramos Arizpe, were imprisoned.

The number of liberals imprisoned or exiled had been estimated at between 4,000 snd 12,000, among them the country's most important men of letters, professionals, and scientists. In Mexico, Calleja received the news of the king's return and acted energetically to reassert viceregal authority. Within a short time, he ordered the abolition of all the constitutional bodies and the restoration of the older institutions. Thereafter he imprisoned and tried the principal leaders of the movement for autonomy, among them many high-ranking criollos.

Restored to full viceregal power, and no longer hampered by the Constitution, Calleja was free to destroy the insurgents. The rebel congress, now reduced to 6 men, made a desperate effort to win support for its cause by offering home rule as alternative to absolutism. On October 22, 1814, it promulgated the Constitution of Apatzingán which created a republic with a plural executive and a powerful legislature. The rebel congress clearly rejected Morelos' pretensions and attempted to win pro-Cortes supporters, since the new Mexican charter was modeled on that body's procedures and on the Spanish Constitution of 1812. The maneuver failed; the Constitution of Apatzingán was never put into effect and had little influence on subsequent Mexican constitutional development.

Royalist forces relentlessly pursued the rebels throughout 1815. Calleja's superbly disciplined troops regained most of the country. Finally, Morelos was captured, tried, found guilty of heresy and treason, and executed on December 11, 1815. Only a few rebels continued the struggle. Vincente Guerrero led guerilla forces in the south, and Guadalupe Victoria went into hiding. Once again, all hope for home rule seemed lost.

PACIFICATION AND THE
LOSS OF CONSENSUS

Viceroy Calleja had pacified New Spain by 1816. A ruthless and dedicated soldier, he had disobeyed many laws to achieve victory. As Lucas Alamán wrote: "If Spain had not lost its dominion over these countries by later events, Calleja would have been recognized as the reconqueror of New Spain and the second Hernán Cortés." However, Calleja achieved victory at a high price. Some of the wealthiest parts of the country were devastated by the fighting.

More important, the old political consensus was eroded by his tactics. In 1815 and 1816 Calleja arrested not only suspected rebels, but also four former regidores, an oidor, a fiscal of the Audiencia, a marqués, and a canon who was a deputy-elect to the Cortes. These high officials had been among the leading partisans of the Constitution. Their imprisonment and harsh treatment demonstrated the defeat of constitutional rule, but it also violated the traditional rights and privileges of their rank. Even the restored cabildo protested such utter disregard for protocol. One former councilman, Francisco Galicia, died in prison, thus adding to Mexican grievances against the government of Fernando VII.

Political unity had already been weakened by earlier shocks: the Bourbon centralization, the imperial crisis, the illegal actions of conservative Spaniards, and the Hidalgo and Morelos revolts. The actions of Calleja as well as those of Fernando VII only confirmed Mexicans in their view that New Spain was living under mal gobierno. The consent of the governed, that had sustained Spanish rule for nearly 300 years, had almost ceased to exist. Mexicans obeyed the government principally because it possessed the monopoly of force.

In September 1816, Juan Ruíz de Apodaca replaced Calleja as viceroy of Mexico. Apodaca introduced a policy of reconciliation in an effort to heal the wounds caused by the conflict. In contrast to his predecessor's policy of fire and sword, he offered amnesty to the rebels. During his tenure, Apodaca pardoned more than 17,000 insurgents. His policies might have been successful if Fernando VII had not repudiated reform and introduced a rigid absolutism that was previously unknown in the Spanish world. Most Mexicans realized that Apodaca's actions were at odds with Fernando's government and they were certain that his program of conciliation would be overturned at any moment. Consequently, Apodaca was able to achieve only a fragile peace.

THE CONSUMMATION OF INDEPENDENCE

Spanish liberals rejected Fernando VII's policies by rebelling and restoring the Constitution in January 1820. As a result, the political structure of Mexico changed once again. The constitutional cabildos and the provincial deputations were restored, and elections were held in May. The new Cortes in Spain proved more radical than its predecessor: it extended suffrage to all men, except the castas; passed anti-clerical decrees; abolished the military fuero; and introduced other social reforms. Some of these actions alienated the upper and middle classes in Mexico, but what was most disturbing was the political turmoil in Spain and the Cortes' unwillingness to resolve American problems.

The Mexican deputies, led by Ramos Arizpe, Michelena, and Alamán, once again argued for autonomy. They proposed that America be divided into three kingdoms: New Spain and Guatemala; New Granada and Tierra Firme; and Peru, Chile, and Buenos Aires. Each of the three kingdoms would have its own cortes and govern itself according to the Constitution of 1812. A Spanish prince, or a person appointed by the king, would preside in each kingdom. Spain and the American kingdoms would have special relationships in the areas of trade, diplomacy, and defense, and the new kingdoms would pay portions of Spain's foreign debt. This proposal would have granted Mexicans the autonomy they had been seeking since 1808, but the Spanish majority in the Cortes ultimately rejected the plan.

While Mexicans in New Spain strongly favored the Constitution of 1812 because it granted them considerable autonomy, they feared that any viceroy or high official could abrogate it, as Venegas and Calleja had done. In these circumstances, Colonel Agustín Iturbide—the criollo son of a secondary-elite Spanish family, who had joined the army quite early to oppose the insurgents—published the *Plan of Iguala* on February 24, 1821, which provided Mexicans with an alternative method of achieving home rule.

The Plan of Iguala offered something to all groups. It fulfilled the Mexican desire for autonomy by establishing a separate limited monarchy. Liberals were attracted because it proclaimed the Constitution of 1812 and the statutes passed by the Cortes as the laws of the land. Traditionalists could support the plan because it invited Fernando VII or, if he did not accept, a Spanish prince to come to New Spain to head the government. The plan guaranteed that the country would remain Catholic, thus appealing to a majority of the nation as well as to the Church. The clergy and the army were also sympathetic to the plan, because it preserved their fueros. Government officials, particularly Europeans, could support the plan because it guaranteed their jobs and rank. The Spaniards were also reassured, because the Plan of Iguala removed ethnic distinctions, declaring all Mexicans, whether American- or European-born, equal. Not only would Europeans have an equal opportunity with criollos in independent Mexico, but nonwhites, the castas, and the Indians would also receive equality under the law, something the Spanish Cortes had failed to grant. Finally, the plan invited the rebels who were still in the field to join a new national army. These provisions came to be known as the three guarantees of *Religion, Independence, and Union.* The plan also proposed to call a Mexican congress. Until elections were held, the country would be governed by the Regency, a plural executive, and a Sovereign Junta composed of 12 members, equally divided between liberals and conservatives; these bodies were modeled on the institutions that functioned in Spain between 1808 and 1814.

Iturbide's Plan of Iguala satisfied Mexican aspirations, providing the only alternative to the Spanish Cortes acceptable to Mexicans of all classes. Insurgent leaders like Vicente Guerrero and Guadalupe Victoria joined prominent autonomists like José María Fagoaga and conservative Spaniards like oidor Miguel Bataller in endorsing the compromise proposal. Iturbide, a relatively unknown officer, was suddenly catapulted into prominence because his plan was supported by all groups, including the army. This was crucial. During earlier autonomist movements, the army of New Spain remained loyal to the Crown and destroyed the insurgency. But the actions of the king and politicians in Spain had undermined that loyalty.

The royal government in Mexico collapsed seven months after Iturbide published the Plan of Iguala. Initially, the new insurgent leader invited Apodaca, now political chief of Mexico, to accept independence as inevitable and to become president of the Sovereign Junta. Surprised by the unexpected rebellion, Apodaca temporized. He tried to convince Iturbide that his actions would harm constitutional government in Mexico, and he urged him to return to royal service. But as the movement gained support, Apodaca tried to end the insurrection with force. This time, however, the royal government could not depend on Mexican troops. Apodaca had to rely on newly-arrived Spanish units to maintain order. Large parts of the country were in insurgent hands by May, and royalist troops, former rebels, and many civilians joined Iturbide's Army of the Three Guarantees. On May 29, a desperate Apodaca wrote Spain that "the majority of the troops in the kingdom, with many of their officers, . . . have been seduced and, passing to the rebels, have left me in the greatest agony, and the kingdom is on the verge of being lost."

Unlike Venegas and Calleja, Apodaca was unable to cope with the new situation. The Constitution and the constitutional bodies limited his ability to respond. Finally in June, he declared a state of emergency and reintroduced Calleja's wartime practices of 1813. He began to draft men between 16 and 40, restored war taxes, and suspended parts of the Constitution. These actions confirmed Mexican fears that they would be subject to arbitrary government. At the same time, conservative Spanish officials judged his response as weak and inadequate. On July 4, 1821, Spanish troops mutinied, removed Apodaca, and installed General Francisco Novella as captain-general in a desperate effort to retain control of New Spain.

Shortly thereafter, Juan O'Donojú, the newly-appointed political chief, arrived in Mexico. To his dismay, most of the country was in the hands of the new insurgents. Only two cities, Veracruz and Mexico City, remained under royalist control. Iturbide offered to negotiate and after much consideration, on August 24 O'Donojú signed the Treaty of Córdoba, which recognized Mexican independence and accepted the Plan of Iguala. Until the Spanish Cortes approved the treaty, a junta, which included O'Donojú, was to govern Mexico. O'Donojú could do little else. As a Spaniard, he strove to retain whatever ties were possible with the mother country. As a liberal, he attempted to insure that constitutional rule was firmly implanted in Mexico. O'Donojú also entered into negotiations with Novella and the Spanish troops in Mexico City. After extensive talks, Novella recognized O'Donojú's credentials and on September 13 placed the royal garrison under his command. Five days later, O'Donojú announced that a government would be formed under the provisions of the Treaty of Córdoba. The Sovereign Junta was established on September 24, 1821, and Iturbide made his triumphal entrance into the capital three days later. A few days later, O'Donojú died of pleurisy. The Spanish government repudiated his actions, but it was too late. Mexico was independent.

Mexico's independence was received joyously throughout the country. Iturbide was widely acclaimed as a great hero, a far-sighted statesman, and the liberator of Mexico. However, his universal popularity was as short-lived as the temporary consensus based on the Plan of Iguala; it evaporated after he made himself emperor, and as the new nation grappled with difficult economic and political questions.

The independence of Mexico was not inevitable. For nearly twelve years, from 1808 to 1821, the upper and middle classes favored autonomy. The Spaniards, however, were unwilling to accept such a demand. Neither the liberal Cortes nor the absolutist government of Fernando VII ever seriously considered such a possibility. In the end, Mexicans simply agreed to be independent. The Spanish regime ended not because it was defeated, but because Mexicans abandoned it. Yet the leaders of the new nation did not agree on Mexico's future. The Plan of Iguala was a massive compromise that could not long survive. It would take many years before a new national consensus emerged.

Chapter 11

A REJECTED
LEGACY

N EW SPAIN, the Western Hemisphere's most successful
colony, was a dynamic society enjoying both a stable government and a prosperous economy. By incorporating Indians, Europeans, Africans, and Asians into a unique cultural mix,
colonial Mexico formed a society that differed substantially from
its contemporaries. A true mestizo society emerged only in New
Spain. The creation of a class structure from various castes produced remarkable cultural, social, and economic mobility.
Mexico's institutional structures, which functioned effectively and
responded to changing circumstances, facilitated that process. Indeed, a notable feature of the colony's government was the confidence it engendered in all classes and ethnic groups. All disputes
were not settled peacefully; violence occasionally erupted. Yet
such outbursts generally sought to redress limited and specific
grievances, not to challenge the colony's political, social, or
economic order. Mexico's great wealth contributed to the stability
as well as to the dynamism of the new society. New Spain's healthy
and balanced economy, for the most part, functioned indepen-

dently of the mother country. The rich silver mines served as an engine of economic growth that stimulated agricultural expansion, pastoral activities, commerce, and manufacturing. In many respects, Mexico's economy appeared stronger, better balanced, and more complex than that of Spain.

Internal stresses and externally imposed reforms, in the second half of the eighteenth century, shook the relatively autonomous development of New Spain. The country's growing prosperity coincided with increasing demographic pressures, so that the fantastic wealth of a few contrasted sharply with the expanding ranks of the poor. The resulting social crisis exacerbated race and class conflicts, as the rich defended their possessions and status against the dispossessed. Changes introduced by eighteenth-century Spanish reformers further disrupted the delicate balance of groups and economic interests which had formed over the years.

These problems, however, did not seem insoluble. Colonial Mexico turned to its domestic elite, who participated in the Enlightenment and were themselves able to apply the new knowledge to local conditions, for solutions. New Spain's leaders responded to their country's crisis with moderate, rational, and practical solutions. Social critics urged decisive action, including the abolition of tribute, elimination of all ethnic barriers, equal access to government office, and the distribution of public lands to the impoverished. Mexicans did not readily embrace extreme measures to solve critical problems, as is evident in their response to the large number of unemployed and underemployed léperos who threatened public security and political stability. While the authorities sought to control these unfortunates, they did not employ harsh and arbitrary measures. Indeed, at a time when crime increased in response to deteriorating social conditions, Mexico's officials ended the semi-vigilante nature of the Acordada, and introduced a greater measure of due process in that institution.

The Spanish imperial crisis aggravated tensions in New Spain, straining relations between the colony and the mother country. Nevertheless, Mexicans responded in a characteristic manner by proposing compromises to accommodate the interests of both countries. Mexican deputies to the Spanish Cortes proposed autonomy for their nation within a Spanish commonwealth. Although colonial Mexico's institutions and its leaders were capable of formulating solutions to the early nineteenth-century crises, authorities in Spain proved unable to adapt to the new circumstances. Ultimately, Mexicans chose independence as the only solution to their conflicts.

European events and Spanish vacillation disrupted the relatively smooth maturation of the Mexican state. As a result, New Spain plunged into a violent and traumatic conflict which destroyed the legitimacy of its institutions, ruined the economy, and provoked class as well as race warfare. The consensus that had endured for 300 years ended with independence.

In their efforts to restore legitimacy and political agreement, post-independence Mexicans experimented with various forms of government. All were found wanting until Juárez, Lerdo, and Díaz restored stability in the 1860s and 1870s. A profound economic depression intensified the political upheavals of the years 1821–1867. The destruction of the silver mines during the wars of independence was perhaps the most important factor in Mexico's prolonged economic decline. Without the great wealth from mining, economic recovery proved extremely difficult. As the nation stagnated, cities declined, fields lay abandoned, unemployment increased, and race and class conflict intensified.

Revolutionary violence and post-independence failures led to a rejection of New Spain's mestizo culture. The national loss of confidence that accompanied Mexico's political, economic, and social calamities prompted a reevaluation of national reality. The country's leaders engaged in wide-ranging debate to determine the unique character of Mexico and its citizens. Liberals of various stripes blamed the "negative weight of the colonial past" for the nation's ills and urged the extirpation of its malign influence. Lucas Alamán and other conservatives maintained that the true national character was to be found within a traditional Spanish heritage, now buried in the ruins of the colony. A few nationalists, like Carlos María Bustamante, attempted to circumvent the colonial experience by identifying Mexican nationality with the preconquest Aztec state. Others, such as José María Luis Mora, asserted that the nation's character must be sought in the "white" race. Although their views differed, the critics agreed in negating 300 years of colonial reality by rejecting Mexico's mestizo culture. While conservatives longed for an imaginary Spanish past, liberals pinned their hopes on alien cultural models and the importation of European immigrants, capital, and technology. The triumph of the liberals culminated in the Porfiriato (1876–1911), with its denigration of mestizo culture and its rush to place Mexico's development in the hands of foreigners.

The assumption that many negative aspects of the nineteenth century were rooted more in the past than in a different economic and social reality distorted nineteenth-century Mexicans' approach to their very real problems. The pragmatism necessary to deal with North American expansionism, economic dependency, and other challenges was blunted and diverted by the country's view of its history. Failure that could be rationalized as the inevitable consequence of the colonial past provided politicians with the means for avoiding their responsibilities to solve the nation's problems, and instead to rely on foreign panaceas. Only with the violent Revolution of 1910, which resulted in the social and political acceptance of the nation's mestizo culture, was a more positive balance restored. Now the time has come to convert the "burden of the colonial past" into a useful cultural legacy through a realistic examination of New Spain's history.

Bibliographical Essay

This study is based on our own archival research; the voluminous published literature; unpublished theses and dissertations written since World War II; and collections of printed documents, particularly those of an economic and social nature that have appeared in the last decade. Original investigation proved necessary for some economic and social topics as well as for interpreting aspects of social conflict and stress.

The amazingly rich resources of the Archivo General de la Nación in Mexico City provided material from the following ramos:

Bandos y Ordenanzas	Matrimonios
Criminal	Reales Cédulas
Inquisición *é*	Tierras
Justicia	

Sources for pre-Columbian and colonial Mexico are so extensive that any comprehensive bibliography would itself constitute a separate volume. Therefore we have noted only those works we found particularly useful or which have influenced our interpretation. The interested reader will find additional material in several fine bibliographical guides, among them the *Handbook of Latin American Studies* and *Bibliografía histórica mexicana.*

Scholarly articles provided much valuable information. However, their number precludes listing each individual article. Studies appearing in the following journals were most important for this work: *Estudios de cultura náhuatl, Estudios de historia novohispaña, Humanidades, Historia mexicana, Hispanic American Historical Review, The Americas, Revista de historia de América,* and the *Journal of Latin American Studies.* The *Handbook of Latin American Studies* and *Bibliografía histórica mexicana* provide a useful annotated bibliography of these and other journals.

Spanish history has an extensive bibliography. The studies that most influenced our interpretation are: Jaime Vicens Vives' (ed.) pioneering *Historia social y económica de España y América* (5 vols.; Barcelona, 1957–1959); John Lynch's excellent *Spain Under the Habsburgs* (2 vols.;

London, 1964–1969); John Elliott's enlightening analysis of Spain's rise to power, *Imperial Spain, 1469–1716* (New York, 1963); and Antonio Domínguez Ortiz' synthesis, *The Golden Age of Spain, 1516–1659* (New York, 1971). Richard Herr, *The Eighteenth-Century Revolution in Spain* (Princeton, 1958) discusses the rise of the Enlightened reformers. For the best synthesis of Spanish history, see Stanley G. Payne, *A History of Spain and Portugal* (2 vols.; Madison, 1973); and for the recent period, Richard Herr, *A Historical Essay on Modern Spain* (Berkeley, 1971).

The literature on ancient Mexico consists of archaeological site reports and scholarly articles. Much of the material utilized in this volume appears in the journals *American Anthropologist* and *American Antiquity*. Other important sources were the publications of the Instituto Nacional de Historia y Antropología, the Carnegie Institution, the Smithsonian Institution, Tulane University's Middle American series, and the archaeological series of the University of California, the University of Utah, and the Peabody Museum. A recent scholarly synthesis is Robert Wauchope (ed.), *Handbook of Middle American Indians* (16 vols.; Austin, 1964–1976). William Sanders and Barbara Price present a theoretical framework for interpretation in *Mesoamerica: the Evolution of a Civilization* (New York, 1968). The most useful one-volume surveys of pre-Columbian Mexico are: Muriel Porter Weaver, *The Aztecs, Maya, and Their Predecessors* (New York, 1972); Román Piña Chan, *Una visión del México prehispánico* (Mexico, 1967); Michael Coe, *Mexico* (New York, 1967); and Walter Krickeberg, *Las antiguas culturas mexicanas* (Mexico, 1961).

Helmut de Terra analyzes the significance of Tepexpán Man—actually a female—in *Man and Mammoth in Mexico* (London, 1952). Marvin Harris discusses various aspects of ancient life in his controversial *Cannibals and Kings* (New York, 1977). The findings of the Tehuacán Botanical-Archaeological Project are ably reported in Douglas Byers and Richard S. MacNeish (eds.), *The Prehistory of the Tehuacán Valley* (5 vols.; Austin, 1967–1972). Robert M. Adams considers the rise of civilization in his comparative analysis, *The Evolution of Urban Society* (Chicago, 1966); and Angel Palerm examines Mexican agriculture in *Agricultura y sociedad en Mesoamérica* (Mexico, 1972) and *Obras hidráulicas prehispánicas* (Mexico, 1973).

The importance of the Olmecs is a widely debated topic. Ignacio Bernal provides a brilliant portrayal of *The Olmec World* (Berkeley, 1969); and the *Dumbarton Oaks Conference on the Olmec* (Washington, 1968) brought together many experts to assess the importance of Olmec culture. Michael Coe briefly discusses his research at San Lorenzo in *America's First Civilization* (New York, 1968) and *The Jaguar's Children:*

Pre-Classic Central Mexico (New York, 1965). Charles Wicke gives an excellent analysis in *Olmec: An Early Art Style of Pre-Columbian Mexico* (Tucson, 1971). There are many works on other ancient cultures; among the most useful are: John Paddock, *Ancient Oaxaca* (Stanford, 1966); Joseph Whitecotton, *The Zapotecs* (Norman, 1977); and Ronald Spores, *The Mixtec Kings and Their People* (Norman, 1967).

The Valley of Mexico has been extensively studied. Ignacio Bernal's *Mexico Before Cortés* (New York, 1975) is an excellent brief synthesis. The School of American Research sponsored a seminar to evaluate recent work on the Valley; the results, edited by Eric C. Wolf, are in *The Valley of Mexico: Studies in Pre-Hispanic Ecology and Society* (Albuquerque, 1976). Several teams of scholars are engaged in studies of Teotihuacán. Aside from learned articles, the most important publication to appear thus far is Rene Millon's magnificent map study, *Urbanization at Teotihuacán*, vol. I (2 parts; Austin, 1973). Tula, in contrast, has not been investigated as extensively. Richard Diehl's *Preliminary Report, University of Missouri Archaeological Project at Tula* (Columbia, 1971) and another volume which he edited, *Studies in Ancient Tollán* (Columbia, 1974) are very useful. Nigel Davies has attempted to resolve the historiographic problems of Tula in his outstanding *The Toltecs Until the Fall of Tula* (Norman, 1977).

The Aztecs have attracted many talented scholars. Alfoso Caso's *The Aztecs: People of the Sun* (Norman, 1958) is an excellent interpretive synthesis, although now somewhat dated. Burr C. Brundage has attempted to write a political history of the Aztecs in *A Rain of Darts* (Austin, 1972); while Jacques Soustelle's *The Daily Life of the Aztecs on the Eve of the Spanish Conquest* (Stanford, 1970) is a very helpful, if somewhat romantic, version of Aztec society. Nigel Davies has written an outstanding political synthesis, *The Aztecs* (London, 1973), and two monographic analyses of the evolution of the Aztec empire, *Los mexicas: primeros pasos hacia el imperio* (Mexico, 1973) and *Los señoríos independientes del imperio azteca* (Mexico, 1968). Robert H. Barlow's imperial study, *The Extent of the Empire of Culhua Mexica* (Berkeley, 1949), is still valuable, although difficult reading. Alfredo López Austin analyzes the relationships between religion and sovereignty among the Nahuas in his masterful *Hombre-dios: religión y política en el mundo náhuatl* (Mexico, 1973). There are several works on Aztec society; among the best are: Carlos Bosch García, *La esclavitud prehispánica entre los aztecas* (Mexico, 1944); Victor M. Castillo F., *Estructura económica de la sociedad mexica* (Mexico, 1972); Friedrich Katz, *Situación social y económica de los aztecas durante los siglos XV y XVI* (Mexico, 1966); Frances M. Berdan, "Trade, Tribute, and Market in the Aztec Empire" (Ph.D. thesis, University of

Texas, 1975); and Jesús Monjarás-Ruíz' thesis, "Nacimiento y consolidación de la nobleza mexica" (National Autonomous University of Mexico, 1977). Miguel León-Portilla examines Aztec thought in his now-classic *La filosofía náhuatl*, 3rd ed. (Mexico, 1966).

The conquest, which traditionally has been the subject of much scholarship, receives new emphasis in two works: Miguel León-Portilla (ed.), *Broken Spears: The Aztec Account of the Conquest* (Boston, 1962), provides the native view; while Robert C. Padden's beautifully written and controversial *The Hummingbird and the Hawk: Conquest and Sovereignty in the Valley of Mexico, 1503–1541* (Columbus, 1967) examines the interaction between religion and sovereignty in the conquest.

Colonial institutions have received extensive treatment. Peter Gerhard, in *A Guide to the Historical Geography of New Spain* (Cambridge, 1972), offers a detailed desription of the political divisions of colonial Mexico. Peggy K. Liss' *Mexico Under Spain, 1521–1556: Society and the Origins of Nationality* (Chicago, 1975) explains the evolution of New Spain as the result of Spanish theories; while Jacques Lafaye, in *Quetzalcóatl and Guadalupe* (Chicago, 1976), presents a controversial interpretation of the formation of Mexican national consciousness. The Indian response to Spanish institutions is discussed in a number of works: José Miranda, *El tributo indígena en la Nueva España durante el siglo XVI* (Mexico, 1952); Charles Gibson, *Tlaxcala in the Sixteenth Century* (New Haven, 1952), and his masterful *The Aztecs Under Spanish Rule* (Stanford, 1964); Delfina López Sarrelangue, *La nobleza indígena de Pátzcuaro en la epoca virreynal* (Mexico, 1965); Gonzalo Aguirre Beltrán, *Regiones de refugio* (Mexico, 1967); and Silvio Zavala, *Los esclavos indios en la Nueva España* (Mexico, 1968).

The two classic studies of the encomienda are: Silvio Zavala, *La encomienda indiana*, 2nd ed. (Mexico, 1973); and Lesley B. Simpson, *The Encomienda in New Spain*, 2nd ed. (Berkeley, 1950). Bernardo García Martínez, in *El marquesado del Valle* (Mexico, 1969), discusses the development of the semi-autonomous estates granted the Cortés family. Philip W. Powell studied the northward expansion in *Soldiers, Indians, and Silver: the Northward Advance of New Spain, 1550–1600* (Berkeley, 1952); while David Adams examines "The Tlaxcalan Colonies of Spanish Coahuila and Nuevo Leon" (Ph.D. thesis, University of Texas, 1970).

The standard work on the Church and its activities is Robert Ricard, *The Spiritual Conquest of Mexico* (Berkeley, 1966). The distinguished Inquisition scholar Richard E. Greenleaf has contributed two illuminating studies, *Zumárraga and the Mexican Inquisition, 1536–1543* (Washington, 1961) and *The Mexican Inquisition in the Sixteenth Century* (Albuquerque, 1969). John L. Phelan, in *The Millenarian Kingdom of the*

Franciscans in the New World (Berkeley, 1956), and Fintan B. Warren in *Vasco de Quiroga and his Pueblo Hospitals of Santa Fe* (Washington, 1963), offer insights into the nature of utopian thought in Mexico.

Irving Leonard provides a fascinating glimpse into the cultural life of seventeenth-century Mexico City in *Baroque Times in Old Mexico* (Ann Arbor, 1959); while George Kubler, in *Mexican Architecture in the Sixteenth Century* (2 vols.; New Haven, 1948), examines the early construction boom, particularly church-building, and the socioeconomic conditions that made it possible. José Miranda has analyzed the political and institutional framework in *Las ideas y las institutiones políticas mexicanas* (Mexico, 1952); and Jonathan I. Israel examines the socioeconomic basis of seventeenth-century Mexican politics in *Race, Class, and Politics in Colonial Mexico, 1610–1670* (Oxford, 1975).

Lillian E. Fisher's pioneering *Viceregal Administration in the Spanish American Colonies* (Berkeley, 1929) is still a useful institutional study; the most important more recent contribution to viceregal scholarship is J. Ignacio Rubio Mañé, *Introducción al estudio de los virreyes de Nueva España 1535–1746* (4 vols.; Mexico, 1955). Several viceroys have received individual attention: for example, Arthur Aiton, *Antonio de Mendoza, First Viceroy of New Spain* (Durham, 1927); and Bernard E. Bobb, *The Viceregency of Antonio María Bucareli in New Spain, 1771–1779* (Austin, 1962). Mexico's two high courts are examined by Constance A. Carter, "Law and Society in Colonial Mexico" (Ph.D. thesis, Columbia University, 1971), and John H. Parry, *The Audiencia of New Galicia in the Sixteenth Century: A Study of Spanish Colonial Government* (Cambridge, 1948). Mark A. Burkholder and D. S. Chandler, *From Impotence to Authority: The Spanish Crown and the American Audiencias, 1687–1808* (Columbia, 1977), is an important study of royal officials and bureaucratic behavior. An interesting study of the early ayuntamientos is Dominic A. Nwasike's "Mexico City Town Government, 1540–1650" (Ph.D. thesis, University of Wisconsin, 1972); and for a later period, Reinhard Liehr's *Ayuntamiento y oligarquía en Puebla, 1787–1810* (2 vols.; Mexico, 1976). The classic account of the Council of the Indies is Ernst Schäfer, *El Consejo real y supremo de las Indias* (2 vols.; Seville, 1935–1947). The effectiveness of the colonial government under stress is ably presented in several works: Louisa Hoberman, "City Planning in Spanish Colonial Government" (Ph.D. thesis, Columbia University, 1972); Richard E. Boyer, *La gran inundación: Vida y sociedad en la ciudad de México* (Mexico, 1975); and Donald B. Cooper, *Epidemic Disease in Mexico City, 1761–1813* (Austin, 1965).

Tomás Zepeda Rincón's *La instrucción pública en la Nueva España* (Mexico, 1933) remains useful, while Dorothy Tank Estrada provides an excellent description of primary education at the end of the colonial period in *La educación ilustrada, 1786–1836* (Mexico, 1977). Elisa Luque Alcaide's *La educación en Nueva España en el siglo XVIII* (Seville, 1970) is useful for earlier developments as well as for the eighteenth century. Alberto María Carreño examines the National University of México in *La real y pontificia Universidad de Mexico, 1536–1865* (Mexico, 1961).

Recent investigations have modified our view of New Spain's economy. Woodrow W. Borah suggested in his influential *New Spain's Century of Depression* (Berkeley, 1951) that Mexico sank into a long depression owing to the decline in Indian population. At the same time François Chevalier, in his classic *La Formation des grands domains au Mexique: Terre et société aux XVIᵉ–XVIIᵉ siécles* (Paris, 1952), contended that Mexico withdrew into a form of feudalism in the seventeenth century as the great estates emerged. Lesley B. Simpson's *Exploitation of Land in Central Mexico in the Sixteenth Century* (Berkeley, 1952) and two works by William H. Dusenberry, "The Mexican Wool Industry in the Sixteenth Century" (Ph.D. thesis, University of Michigan, 1941) and *The Mexican Mesta: The Administration of Ranching in Colonial Mexico* (Urbana, 1963), noted the expansion of European livestock-raising and seemed to support Borah's and Chevalier's views.

Although this interpretation was widely accepted, it has had its critics. In 1947 José Miranda demonstrated in *La función económica del Encomendero en los orígenes del régimen colonial, 1525–1531*, 2nd ed. (Mexico, 1965) that the earliest settlers were concerned with profits and not simply status. Nevertheless, it was not until the second edition of Miranda's work was published in 1965 that the standard interpretation was challenged by several other scholars who maintained that there was a seventeenth-century readjustment rather than a depression. The decline in silver exports to Spain can be accounted for by three factors: the retention of bullion in Mexico for internal uses; export to Asia, both to support the Philippines and to increase trade with the East: and changes in the sale and distribution of mercury. These views are supported by several studies of mining, among them: Robert C. West, *The Mining Community in Northern New Spain: The Parral Mining District* (Berkeley, 1949); Peter J. Bakewell, *Silver Mining and Society in Colonial Mexico: Zacatecas, 1546–1700* (Cambridge, 1971); Miguel León-Portilla, Jorge Gurría Lacroix, Roberto Moreno, and Enrique Madero, *La minería en México* (Mexico, 1978); and Mervyn F. Lang, *El monopolio estatal del mercurio en el México colonial, 1550–1710* (Mexico, 1977), as well as by John TePaske's path-breaking quantititaive analysis, *La Real Hacienda de Nueva España* (Mexico, 1976).

Recent hacienda studies have also undermined the notion that estates were semi-feudal. Instead, they have been shown as profit-oriented enterprises. In addition, the new research indicates that the rural sector was diverse and that the Indians retained most of their lands, particularly in the south. Among the best hacienda studies are: William Taylor, *Landlord and Peasant in Colonial Oaxaca* (Stanford, 1972); Jan Bazant, *Cinco haciendas mexicanas: tres siglos de vida rural en San Luis Potosí, 1600–1910* (Mexico, 1975); Enrique Semo et al., *Siete ensayos sobre la hacienda mexicana* (Mexico, 1976); James D. Riley, *Haciendas jesuíticas en México: El Colegio Máximo de San Pedro y San Pablo, 1685–1767* (Mexico, 1976); and Edith B. Couturier, *La Hacienda de Hueyapán, 1555–1936* (Mexico, 1976). Enrique Florescano has an important and stimulating analysis of rural conditions, *Estructuras y problemas agrarios de México, 1500–1821* (Mexico, 1971).

In recent years, research on the socioeconomic history of Mexico has uncovered relationships among the family, credit, and enterprise. Richard Lindley examines these connections in "Kinship and Credit in the Structure of Guadalajara's Oligarchy, 1800–1830" (Ph.D. thesis, University of Texas, 1975); while Charles H. Harris' outstanding *A Mexican Family Empire: The Latifundio of the Sanchez Navarros, 1765–1867* (Austin, 1975) traces the evolution of an important family enterprise. Ida Altman's "The Marqueses de Aguayo: A Family and Estate History" (M.A. thesis, University of Texas, 1972) looks at that important noble family, while Patricia Seed has studied "A Mexican Noble Family: The Counts of the Orizaba Valley, 1560–1867" (M.A. thesis, University of Texas, 1975). Among the best regional studies are: Marta Espejo Ponce de Hunt, "Colonial Yucatán: Town and Region in the Seventeenth Century" (Ph.D. thesis, University of California, Los Angeles, 1973); John C. Super, "Querétaro: Society and Economy in Early Provincial Mexico, 1590–1630" (Ph.D. thesis, University of California, Los Angeles, 1973); John M. Tutino, "Creole Mexico: Spanish Elites, Haciendas, and Indian Towns" (Ph.D. thesis, University of Texas, 1976); David A. Brading, *Haciendas and Ranchos in the Mexican Bajío: León, 1700–1860* (Cambridge, 1978); and the useful but uneven essays in Ida Altman and James Lockhart (eds.), *Provinces of Early Mexico: Variants of Spanish American Regional Evolution* (Los Angeles, 1976).

There are several excellent studies of other areas of the colonial economy. Woodrow W. Borah's *Silk-Raising in Colonial Mexico* (Berkeley, 1943) is the authoritative work on that short-lived but important industry. Sugar production is examined by Fernando Sandoval in *La industria de azúcar en Nueva España* (Mexico, 1951), and by the distinguished historical geographer Ward Barrett in *The Sugar Hacienda of the Marqueses del Valle* (Minneapolis, 1970). Michael G. Riley, in *Fernando*

Cortés and the Marquesado in Morelos, 1522–1547 (Albuquerque, 1973), adds significantly to the view of Cortés as an entrepreneur. On artisans, see: Manuel Romero de Terreros, *Las artes industriales en la Nueva España* (Mexico, 1932); Manuel Carrera Estampa, *Los gremios mexicanos, 1521–1861* (Mexico, 1954); and George Martin Vegue, "The Silversmiths in Mexico: A Study in Colonial Trade Guilds" (Ph.D. thesis, University of Texas, 1951). Sam Kagan has studied the nature of penal labor and its negative impact on the obrajes in "Penal Servitude in New Spain; the Colonial Textile Industry" (Ph.D. thesis, City University of New York, 1976).

Voluminous trade data may be extracted from Pierre and Huguette Chaunu, *Seville et l'Atlantique* (8 vols.; Paris, 1955–1959), especially volume 8. Trade between New Spain and other parts of the New World is discussed in Woodrow W. Borah, *Early Colonial Trade and Navigation Between Mexico and Peru* (Berkeley, 1954), and Eduardo Arcila Farías' *Comercio entre Venezuela y Mexico en los siglos XVII y XVIII* (Mexico, 1950). William L. Schurz's *The Manila Galleon* (New York, 1939) is still a useful study of that exotic trade. Antonio García Baquero analyzes eighteenth-century monopoly trade in *Cádiz y el Atlantico, 1717–1778* (Seville, 1976). The changes in the late eighteenth century are examined in Humberto Tandrón, *El comercio de Nueva España y la controversia sobre la libertad de comercio, 1796–1821* (Mexico, 1976). Some of the difficulties of internal transportation are discussed by Peter Rees, *Transportes y comercio entre México y Veracruz, 1519–1910* (Mexico, 1976); while Salvador Ortíz Vidales discusses mule transport in *La arriería en Mexico* (Mexico, 1929).

The reconstruction of colonial society relies on our own unpublished archival research, on the valuable material scattered in the socioeconomic studies previously noted, and on the following works. The demographic history of colonial Mexico has been examined by Woodrow W. Borah and Sherburne Cook in a variety of works, most notably *The Aboriginal Population of Central Mexico on the Eve of the Spanish Conquest* (Berkeley, 1963); *The Indian Population of Central Mexico, 1531–1610* (Berkeley, 1960); *The Population of Central Mexico in 1548* (Berkeley, 1960); and *Essays in Population History* (2 vols.; Berkeley, 1973–1974). The social adjustment of the Indians to Spanish values and institutions is shown in Arthur J. O. Anderson et al., *Beyond the Codices: The Nahua View of Colonial Mexico* (Los Angeles, 1976); Alfonso Caso, *Métodos y resultados de la política indigenista en México* (Mexico, 1954); and, for an extended period, Wayne S. Osborn, "A Community Study of Metztitlán, New Spain, 1520–1810" (Ph.D. thesis, University of Iowa, 1970). Various social groups have received attention, particularly in recent years. Nicolás

León discusses the social role of mestizos in *Las Castas del México colonial* (Mexico, 1924). Seymour B. Liebman has contributed to our knowledge of the Jewish community in *The Enlightened: the Writings of Luis de Carvajal, el Mozo* (Miami, 1967) and *The Jews in New Spain* (Miami, 1970). Francisco Morales examines the social composition of the regular clergy in *Ethnic and Social Background of the Franciscan Friars in Seventeenth-Century Mexico* (Washington, 1973). The African presence in Mexico is discussed in the excellent and now standard work by Gonzalo Aguirre Beltrán, *La población negra en México*, 2nd ed. (Mexico, 1972). Colin A. Palmer reexamines the early history of slavery in *Slaves of the White God: Blacks in Mexico* (Cambridge, 1976); and Patrick J. Carroll studies the role of blacks in late colonial society in "Mexican Society in Transition: The Blacks of Veracruz, 1750–1830" (Ph.D. thesis, University of Texas, 1975).

Magnus Mörner analyzes the interplay between race and social change in *Estado, razas y cambio social en la Hispanoamérica colonial* (Mexico, 1974); while John K. Chance combines anthropological techniques with detailed archival research in his study of *Race and Class in Colonial Oaxaca* (Stanford, 1978). José Durand charts the pace of social change in *La transformación social del conquistador* (2 vols.; Mexico, 1953). The stresses of a formative society are well portrayed in Norman F. Martin, *Los vagabundos en la Nueva España, siglo XVI* (Mexico, 1957); Luis González Obregón, *Rebeliones indígenas y precursoras de la independencia mexicana en los siglos XVI, XVII, y XVIII*, 2nd ed. (Mexico, 1952); and María Teresa Huerta Preciado, *Rebeliones indígenas en el noroeste de México en la época colonial* (Mexico, 1966).

Material on the role of women in colonial society may be found in several of the new socioeconomic studies already noted, particularly Marta Espejo Ponce de Hunt and John C. Super. Only a few works deal principally with women; among the best are Asunción Lavrin's "Religious Life of Mexican Women in the Eighteenth Century" (Ph.D. thesis, Harvard University, 1961), and a volume she edited, *Latin American Women* (Westport, 1978), which has several excellent essays on Mexico; Daisy Rípodas Ardanaz, *El Matrimonio en Indias: Realidad y Regulación jurídica* (Buenos Aires, 1977); and Silvia M. Arrom's two studies, *La mujer mexicana ante el divorcio eclesiastio, 1800–1857* (Mexico, 1976) and "Women and the Family in Mexico City, 1800–1857" (Ph.D. thesis, Stanford University, 1978). Some of the essays in *Condición jurídica de la mujer en México* (Mexico, 1975), commemorating International Women's Year, provide an analysis of the legal condition of women in colonial Mexico. Josefina Muriel de la Torre has written two informative accounts, *Conventos de monjas en la Nueva Espāna* (Mexico, 1946) and *Los recogimientos de mujeres* (Mexico, 1974). Although somewhat dated and mainly literary, James Fitzmaurice-Kelly's *The Nun Ensign* (London, 1908) is a useful biography of Catalina de Erauzú. Sor Juana Inés de la Cruz has been the subject of numerous scholarly works: see, for example, Ludwig Pfandl, *Sor Juana Inés de la Cruz, la décima musa de México* (Mexico, 1963); Gerald C. Flynn, *Sor Juana Inés de la Cruz* (New York, 1971); and the excellent edition of her own *Obras completas* (4 vols.; Mexico, 1951) edited by Alfonso Méndez Plancarte.

Germán Somolinos D'Ardois in *Historia de la psiquiatría en México* (Mexico, 1976) provides a unique view of coping with social reality. The expression of that reality in art, the integration of Indian and European values, is skillfully presented in Donald Robertson, *Mexican Manuscript Painting of the early Colonial Period* (New Haven, 1959).

Mexican scholars have studied their country's intellectual history in detail. José M. Gallegos Rocafull's outstanding synthesis of Mexican thought, *El pensamiento mexicano en los siglos XVI y XVII* (Mexico, 1951), underscores its rational nature. Although dated, the standard work is Irving Leonard's *Don Carlos de Sigüenza y Góngora: A Mexican Savant of the Seventeenth Century* (Berkeley, 1929). More recently, Elías Trabulse has attempted to place Sigüenza within the context of his time in *Ciencia y religión en el siglo XVII* (Mexico, 1973).

The development of modern thought has been of great interest to Mexicans. Monelisa Pérez-Marchant measured the nature of intellectual change in *Dos etapas ideológicas del siglo XVIII en México a traves de los papeles de la Inquisición* (Mexico, 1945). Bernabé Navarro probed the dissemination of modern ideas in *La introducción de la filosofía moderna en México* (Mexico, 1948), and the character of the Mexican Enlightenment in *Cultura mexicana moderna en el siglo XVIII* (Mexico, 1964). More recently, Roberto Moreno has reinterpreted the Mexican Enlightenment and demonstrated its remarkable intellectual depth in a series of erudite monographs, among them *Ensayo biobibliográfico de Antonio de León y Gama* (Mexico, 1969) and *Joaquín Velázquez de León y sus trabajos científicos sobre el Valle de México* (Mexico, 1977). Charles E. Ronan, *Francisco Javier Clavigero, S. J. (1731–1787); Figure of the Mexican Enlightenment: His Life and Works* (Rome, 1977) is an excellent study of that enlightened scholar. José Miranda's *Humbolt y México* (Mexico, 1962) is a masterful analysis of the German savant's role in New Spain. Germán Cardozo examined Enlightenment activities at one provincial center, Valladolid, in *Michoacán en el siglo de luces* (Mexico, 1973). There are several excellent works on the new Enlightened institutions. Joaquín J. Izquierdo's *La primera casa de ciencias en México: el Real Seminario de minería, 1792–1811* (Mexico, 1958) is a model study.

Clement G. Motten's brief *Mexican Silver and the Enlightenment* (Philadelphia, 1950) examines the relationship between science and mining; while Thomas A. Brown studies *La Academia de San Carlos de la Nueva España* (2 vols.; Mexico, 1976) at length. Although not a monograph on the University of Mexico, John Tate Lanning's prize-winning *The Eighteenth-Century Enlightenment in the University of San Carlos de Guatemala* (Ithaca, 1956) provides an indication of the intellectual activities that probably existed in Mexico.

A number of skillful monographs discuss the eighteenth-century reforms. Walter Howe's *The Mining Guild and Its Tribunal General, 1770–1821* (Cambridge, 1949) is a detailed examination of that institution. The commercial reforms are studied in E. Arcila Farías' pioneering *El siglo ilustrado en América: Reformas economicas del siglo XVIII en Nueva España* (Caracas, 1955). Brian R. Hamnett's *Politics and Trade in Southern Mexico, 1750–1821* (Cambridge, 1971) clarifies some previously confused issues; while David A. Brading places the reforms in perspective in *Miners and Merchants in Bourbon Mexico, 1763–1810* (Cambridge, 1971). Horst Pietschmann's *Die Einführung des Intendantensystem in Neu-Spanien* (Cologne, 1972) reinterprets the nature of the intendancy system. A still-useful study of the great imperial reformer is Herbert I. Priestley, *José de Gálvez, Visitor-General of New Spain* (Berkeley, 1916). Luis Navarro García examined his efforts to stabilize the frontier in *Don José de Gálvez y la comandancia general de las provincias internas del norte de Nueva España* (Seville, 1964). María del Carmen Velázquez studied the question in a broader perspective in *Establecimiento y pérdida del septentrión de Nueva España* (Mexico, 1974).

The army has received the attention of several scholars. María del Carmen Velázquez' *El estado de guerra de Nueva España, 1760–1808* (Mexico, 1950) and Lyle N. McAlister's *The Fuero Militar in New Spain, 1754–1800* (Gainesville, 1957) broke new ground and paved the way for the impressive study by Christon I. Archer, *The Army in Bourbon Mexico, 1760–1810* (Albuquerque, 1977). Nancy M. Farriss' outstanding analysis of clerical reforms, *Crown and Clergy in Colonial Mexico, 1759–1821: The Crisis of Ecclesiastical Privilege* (London, 1968), helps explain clerical dissatisfaction in the late eighteenth century. For changes in the administration of justice, see Colin M. MacLachlan, *Criminal Justice in Eighteenth-Century Mexico: A Study of the Tribunal of the Acordada* (Berkeley, 1974). José Antonio Calderón Quijano (ed.), *Los virreyes de Nueva España en el reinado de Carlos III* (2 vols.; Seville, 1967–1968), discusses the viceroys appointed by one of Spain's most enlightened monarchs.

The eighteenth-century socioeconomic changes have been examined in some of the works already mentioned, but in addition several new studies influenced our views. Enrique Florescano links population pressure with food prices and suggests their negative impact on social order in his *Precios de maíz y crisis agrícolas en México, 1708–1810* (Mexico, 1969). William B. Taylor attempts to understand the villagers through an analysis of *Drinking, Homicide, and Rebellion in Colonial Mexican Villages* (Stanford, 1979). Richard L. Garner examines the resurgence of the north in "Zacatecas: The Study of a Late Colonial Mexican City, 1750–1821" (Ph.D. thesis, University of Michigan, 1970); and R. M. Serrero provides a view of the west in "La región de Guadalajara en el Virreinato de Nueva España" (Ph.D. thesis, University of Seville, 1975). James Lewis makes an interesting assessment of Mexico during an early period of crisis in "New Spain During the American Revolution, 1779–1783" (Ph.D. thesis, Duke University, 1975).

The literature on the Mexican independence is so large that any listing must be highly selective. The following works were especially valuable to us: Lillian E. Fisher, *The Background to the Revolution for Mexican Independence* (Boston, 1934) and *Champion of Reform: Manuel Abad y Queipo* (New York, 1955); Nicolás Rangel, *Los Precursores ideológicos de la guerra de la independencia, 1784–1794* (Mexico, 1929); and Luis González Obregón, *La vida de México en 1810* (Mexico, 1943), are dated but helpful. Doris M. Ladd's prize-winning *The Mexican Nobility at Independence, 1780–1826* (Austin, 1976) provides important social and economic data as well as a reinterpretation of the process of independence. Soviet historian M. S. Alperovich has written an interesting Marxist analysis, *Historia de la independencia de México, 1810–1824* (Mexico, 1967), which remains curiously traditional in its interpretation.

The violent revolt led by Father Hidalgo is interestingly and authoritatively presented by Hugh M. Hamill, Jr., in *The Hidalgo Revolt* (Gainesville, 1966). Peggy A. Korn (Liss) skillfully analyzes Hidalgo's thought in "Miguel Hidalgo y Costilla and the Ideology of Mexican Nationalism" (Ph.D. thesis, University of Pennsylvania, 1964). The standard biography of Hidalgo is Luis Ledon Castillo, *Hidalgo, la vida del héroe* (2 vols.; Mexico, 1948–1949). Alfonso Teja Zabre, *Vida de Morelos*, 3rd ed. (Mexico, 1959), and Wilbert H. Timmons, *Morelos of Mexico, Priest, Soldier, Statesman* (El Paso, 1963), are good modern studies of that important leader. The controversial liberator of Mexico is ably presented in William S. Robertson's *Inturbide of Mexico* (Durham, 1952). The secret conspirators have been studied by Ernesto de la Torre Villar in *Los Guadalupes y la independencia* (Mexico, 1966). The great heroine of independence is the subject of a biography by Genaro García, *Leona Vicaro: heroína insurgente* (Mexico, 1910).

On the opposite side, two viceroys have received consideration. Enrique Lafuente Ferrari's *El virrey Iturrigaray y los orígenes de la independencia de México* (Madrid, 1941) blames that hapless official for events beyond his control; while Carol Ferguson places the great war viceroy in perspective in "The Spanish Tamerlaine? Félix María Calleja, Viceroy of New Spain, 1813–1816" (Ph.D. thesis, Texas Christian University, 1973). The collapse of the royal regime is clearly analyzed in the excellent revisionary study by Timothy E. Anna, *The Fall of Royal Government in Mexico City* (Lincoln, 1978).

Romeo Flores Caballero presents a penetrating analysis of the socioeconomic conflicts at independence in *La contrarrevolución en la independencia* (Mexico, 1969). The development of constitutional government is examined in Nettie Lee Benson's classic study of the origins of Mexican federalism, *La diputación provincial y el federalismo mexicano* (Mexico, 1955); and a volume she edited, *Mexico and the Spanish Cortes, 1810–1812* (Austin, 1966), analyzes the impact of that Spanish parliament on Mexico. Brian R. Hamnett also examines the impact of Spanish constitutional liberalism in *Revolución y contrarrevolución en México y el Perú* (Mexico, 1978). The short-lived Congress of 1813 is discussed in three excellent studies: Luis González, *El Congreso de Anahuac de 1813* (Mexico, 1963); Ernesto de la Torre Villar, *La Constitución de Apatzingán y los creadores del estado mexicano* (Mexico, 1964); and the revisionary interpretation by Anna Macías, *Génesis del gobierno constitucional en México, 1808–1820* (Mexico, 1973). Luis Villoro probes the ideas of independence in his penetrating *El proceso ideológico de la revolución de la independencia* (Mexico, 1967); while Javier Ocampo chronicles the enthusiasm with which Mexicans received independence in his excellent *Las ideas de un día: El pueblo mexicano ante la consumación de la independencia* (Mexico, 1969). Jaime E. Rodríguez O. analyzes the relationship between Spanish and Mexican liberalism in *The Emergence of Spanish America: Vicente Rocafuerte and Spanish Americanism, 1808–1832* (Berkeley, 1975).

Sources for Illustrations

Lienzo de Tlaxcala (Mexico, 1964); *Códice Osuna* (Madrid, 1973); Carl Nebel, *Voyage pittoresque et archéologique dans la partie plus intéressante du Mexique* (Paris, 1836); Claudio Linati, *Costumes et moeurs de Mexique* (London, 1830); Pedro O'Crouley, *A Description of the Kingdom of New Spain in 1774* (San Francisco, 1972); Museo de América, Madrid; Museo Nacional de Antropología, Mexico; Museo Nacional de Historia, Mexico; Archivo General de la Nación, Mexico; José de Alzate, *Gazeta de literatura de México*, 1788.

Index

Abad y Queipo, Manuel: and Hidalgo, 310; opposes autonomy, 303; reaction to rebels, 313–314.
Abasolo, Mariano, 310, 311
Acamapichtli, 37
Acculturation: of Asians, 222; and European women, 198; effects of, 198; process of, 208–209; tribute as a factor in, 204
Acordada, Tribunal of: described, 256–258; and the army, 282; and the Church, 275–276
adit: defined, 170
Adrian IV, 97
Adrian VI, 123
Africans. See blacks
Agricola, Georgius, 170
Agriculture: Aztec, 41; colonial Indian, 165–168; crises, 287; early development of, 16–17; and elites, 21; in eighteenth century, 285, 287; Mexican, 150–165; prices of, 154–155; mentioned, 145
Aguayo, Marquéz de: daughter of, 136; estates of, 157, 158, 284; wealth of, 285
Aguirre, Guillermo de, 304
Ahuítzolt, 39, 64
Alamán, Lucas: argues for autonomy, 330; opinion of Calleja, 328–329
Alamo, Condesa de, 284
Albornoz, Rodrigo de, 89
Alcaldes: defined, 78; of the Mesta, 161
Alcaldes mayores: defined, 103; 107, 111
Alcaldes ordinarios: defined, 108

Aldama, Juan: and Hidalgo Revolt, 310–319; executed, 319
Alexander VI, 97
alhóndiga: defined, 155
allegado: defined, 148
Allende, Ignacio: and Hidalgo Revolt, 310–319; executed, 319
almacenero: defined, 185, 187; control trade, 272
alternativa: defined, 118–119
Alvarado, Pedro de: advises Cortés, 69; death of, 98; and massacre at temple, 73; mentioned, 239
Alzate, José Antonio: activities of, 289, 290
Apartado, Marqués del, 305
Apodaca, Juan Ruíz de: seeks reconciliation, 329; unable to control Mexico, 331–332
Aragón, José, 244
Aranda, Conde de, 295
Arias, Rodrigo, 244
army: and the acordada, 282; establishment of, 278–283
Arriaga, Baylio Frey Julián de, 260
arriero: defined, 193
artisans: Aztec, 56, 57; and army, 280–281; ethnic origin of, 226; income of, 226; as manufacturers, 187–188; restrict competition, 188; as a social group, 226–227; slaves as, 226–227; Teotihuacán, 29; Toltec, 32, 56
Asians, 3, 4, 174; population size of, 196; role of, 222
Audiencia: deposes viceroy, 121–122; introduction of, 89; and local

Indians *(continued)*
    forced labor by, 204–206;
    importance of community to,
    206; legal status of, 197–198;
    numbers of, 196, 201–202; as
    officials, 202–203; rebellions by,
    206–207; tribute by, 203–204;
    wage labor by, 206
Inquisition, 212–214
intendencias: establishment of,
    268–296; support for, 261–262
investment: nature of, 146–147; in
    silver mines, 173; in sugar
    plantations, 159–160
Iturbide, Agustín de: defeats rebels,
    327; enters Mexico city, 332;
    elected emperor, 333; proposes
    Plan of Iguala, 330, 331
Iturrigaray, José: and the army, 283;
    criollo reaction to overthrow of,
    310; enforces Law of
    Consolidation, 300–301;
    overthrow of, 307
Isabel I, 95
Ixtilxóchitl, Fernando de Alva, 111

Jáuregui, Manuel, 304, 305
Javat, Juan, 304, 305
Jesuits. *See* Society of Jesus
Jews: immigration of, 212; persecution
    of, 212–214; social status of, 214;
    women as, 212
Juzgado de Indios, 103
*Juzgado de Testamentos, Capelliás y
    Obras Pías:* defined, 149

labor: in agriculture, 159–160, 164;
    and the army, 280–281; forced by
    Indians, 204–206; in mines,
    173–174; in obrajes, 191–192; use
    by Olmec, 24; problems
    following conquest, 82, 83; as
    tribute, 79; for wages by Indians,
    202, 206
labores: mentioned, 160, 162, 165
Ladd, Doris, 304
ladinos: defined, 218; Asians as, 222
land: distribution of following
    conquest, 80, 81, 108; impact of
    Indian population size on tenure
    of, 203; Indian, 49, 165–168;

types of holdings, 150–151,
    155–165
Las Casas, Bartolomé de, 84
Law of Consolidation, 300–301
legitimacy: loss of, 329
léperos, 227–228
León de Gama, Antonio de, 289
Linnaeus, Carolus von, 290
Lira, Manuel de, 253
Lizana y Beaumont, Javier: mentioned
    301, 307, 308
López de Mendizabal, Bernardo, 214
López Portillo y Weber, José, 99
Louis XIV, 253
Louis XVI, 295, 296
lugares: defined, 78

macehualli (macehualtin pl.): defined,
    57; pressures on, 65
macho: defined, 235
MacNeish, Richard S., 16
Malinche, 71
Manila: galleon, 184–185; mentioned,
    102, 105; trade, 184–185
manufacturing, 187–192
manumission, 221
market: Mexican, 272–273; role of,
    144–146, 168, 179
marquesado, 90
marriage: alliances, 147, 285; Aztec,
    49; consensual unions as form of,
    233–234; and the casa chica, 234;
    as form of social mobility, 162,
    186, 221–222; prohibitions
    against, 115, 258; role of in
    colony, 230–232; role of dowry
    in, 242–243; role of elopement in,
    234–235
Martínez, Juan, 323
mathematics, 27, 44
Maya: and Aztecs, 40; contact with,
    68; and mathematics, 27; and
    Olmecs, 22–23, 28; as slaves, 58;
    and Teotihuacán, 30, 32; Toltec
    influence on, 33, 34
mayeque, 59
mayorazgo: Cortés receives right to,
    90; destruction of, 298–299
mayordomo: mentioned, 147, 157, 162
media anata: defined, 111
Medina, Conde de, 303

Designer: Eric Jungerman
Compositor: Viking Typographics
Printer: Vail-Ballou Press
Binder: Vail-Ballou Press
Text: VIP Stempel Garamond
Display: Typositor Bernhard Modern Bold
Cloth: Holliston Roxite B 53538
Paper: 50 lb. P&S Offset